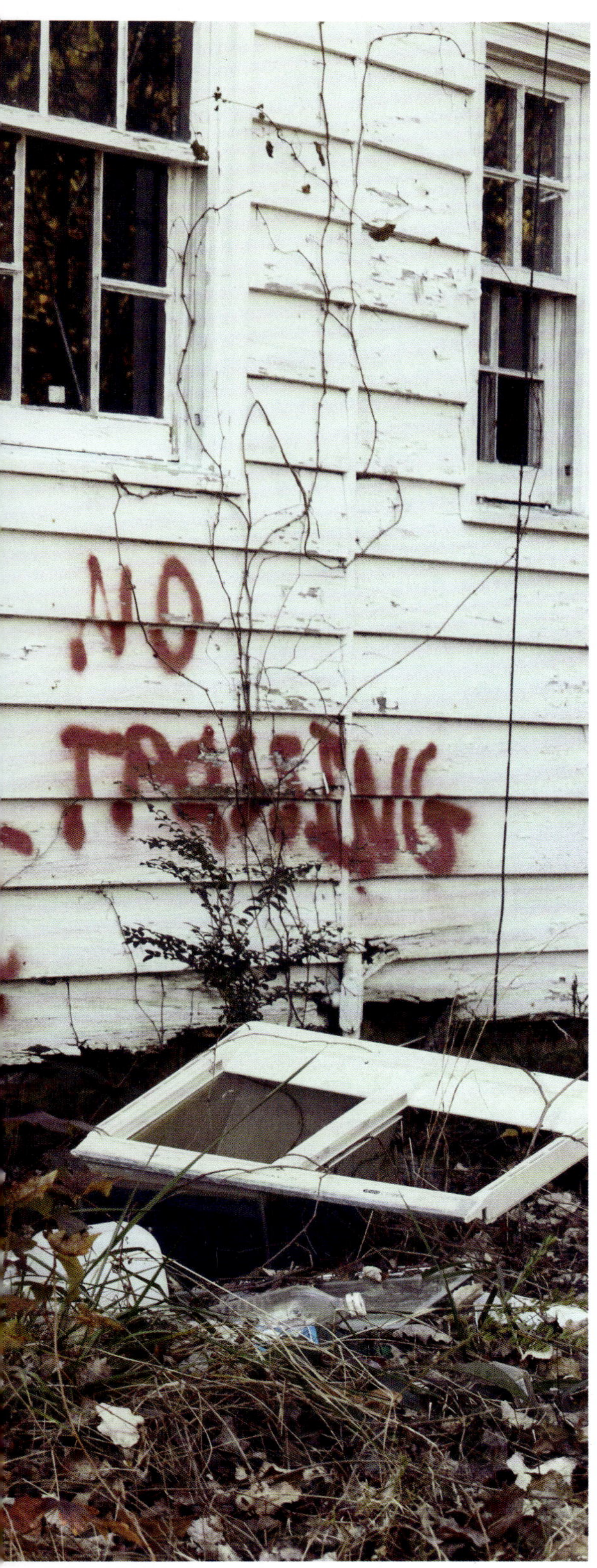
NO

AF479056

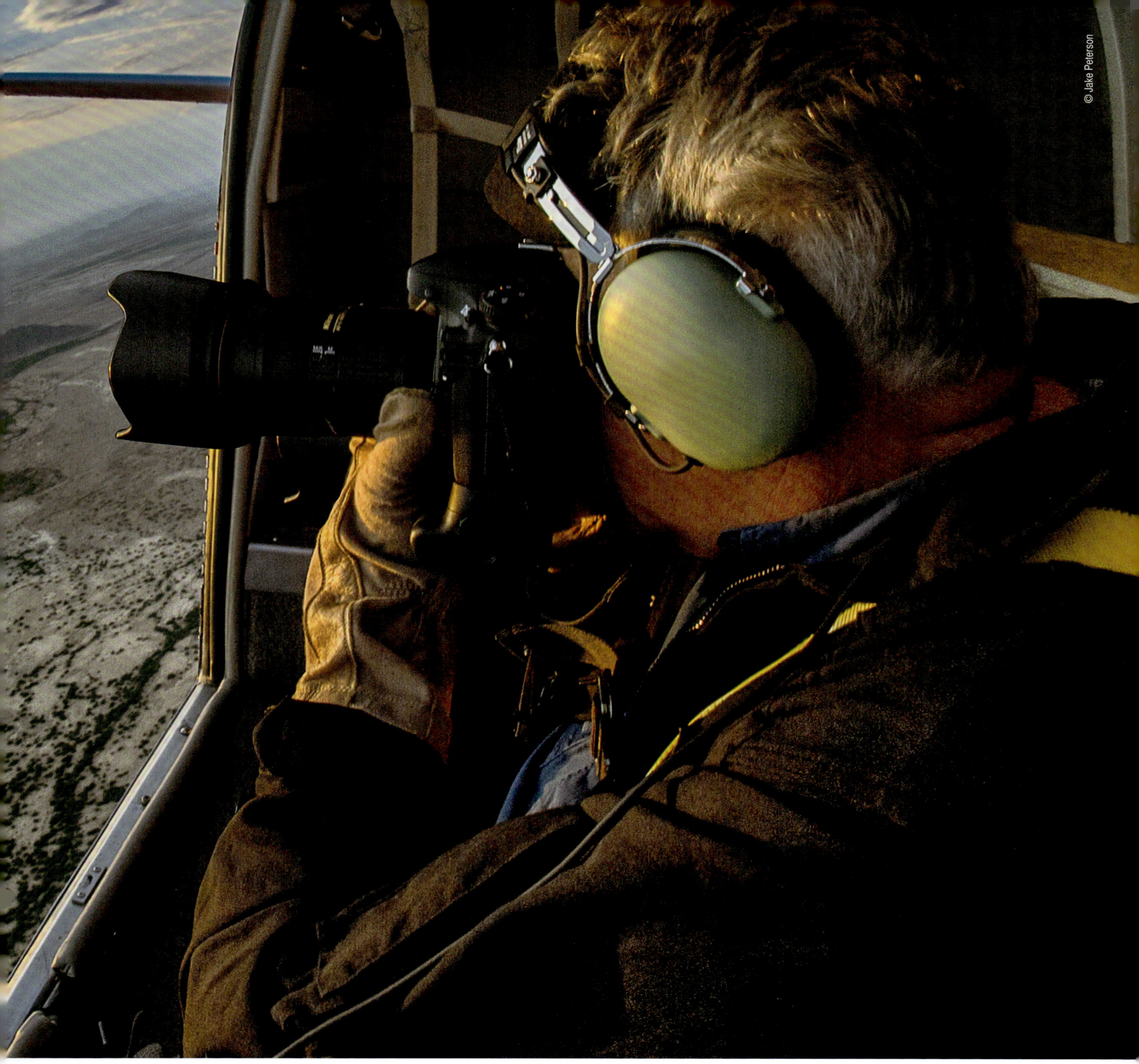

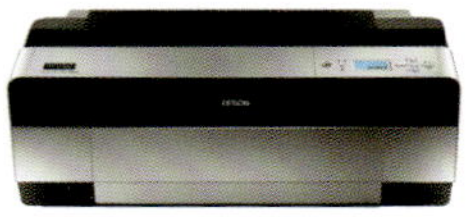

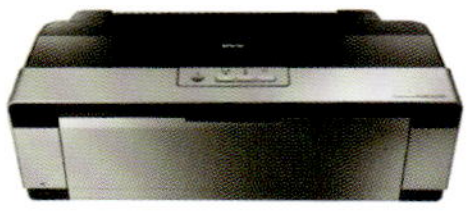

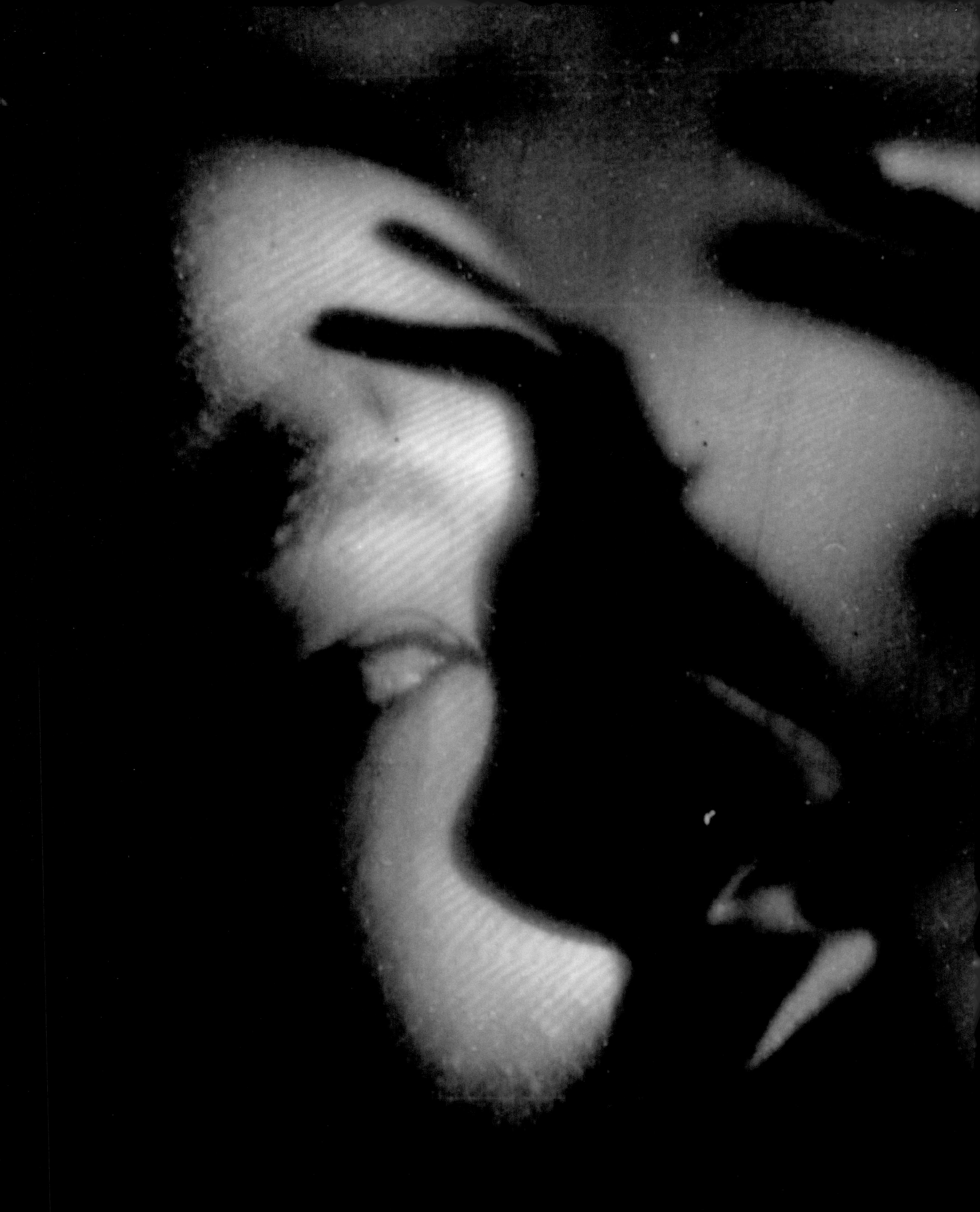

Image: *SC 13* | 2012 | Handmade photograph on 3/8" glass plate | Unique print | 48"x 72"

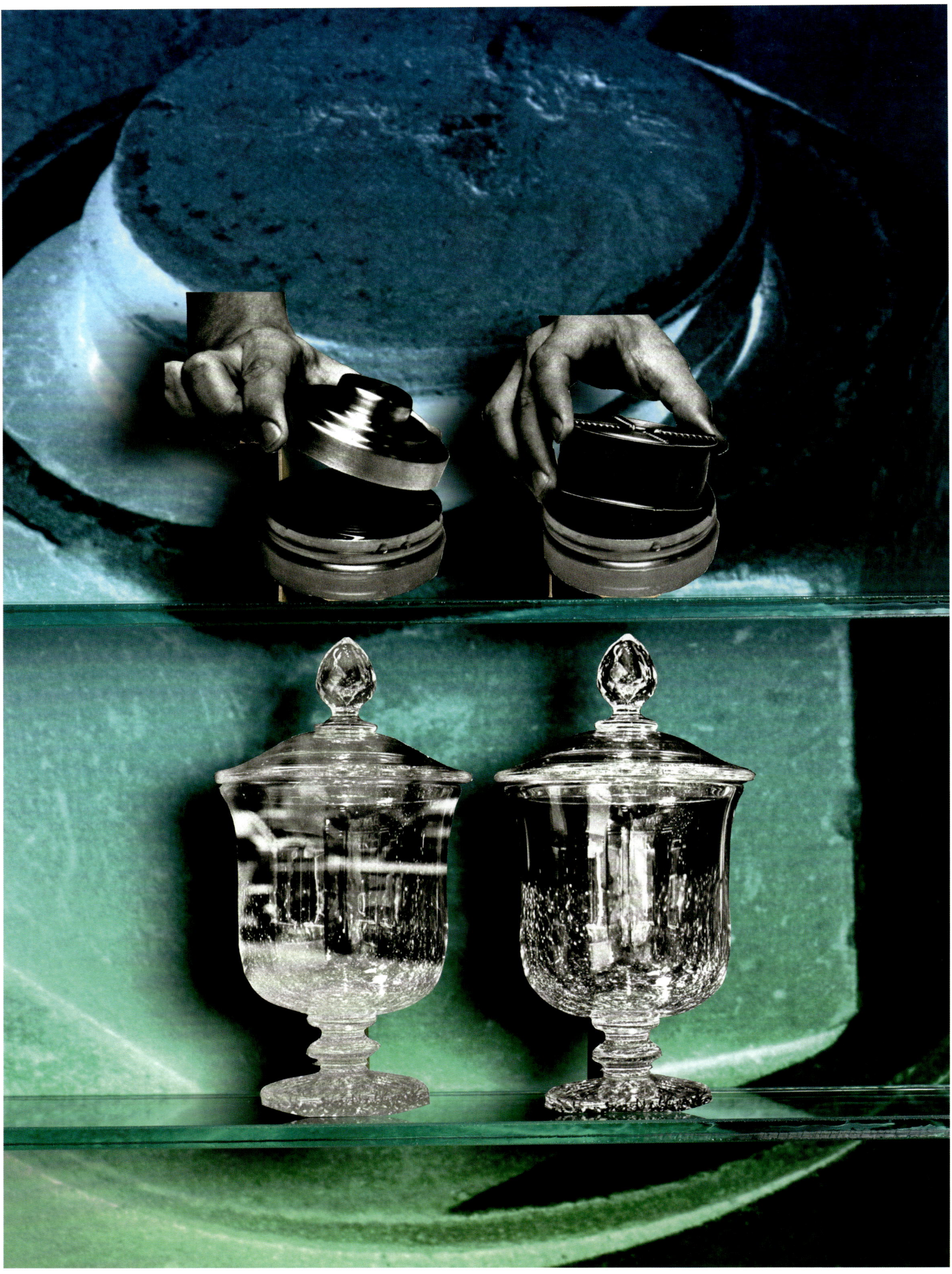

Spring 2013

Words

Pictures

Front

Back

Opposite:
Matt Lipps, *Untitled (Bolt)*, 2012 Courtesy the artist and Marc Selwyn Fine Art, Los Angeles

Front cover:
Christopher Williams, photograph of an Exakta camera, part of a new series made in 2012 (image detail) Courtesy Galerie Gisela Capitain, Cologne, and David Zwirner Gallery, New York/London

Aperture, a not-for-profit foundation, connects the photo community and its audiences with the most inspiring work, the sharpest ideas, and with each other —in print, in person, and online.

Help maintain Aperture's publishing, education, and community activities by becoming one of our Philanthropists ($5,000), Benefactors ($2,500), Patrons ($1,000), or New Collectors ($500). Donors are acknowledged in *Aperture* magazine and invited to private salon events with artists, receive complimentary publications and special discounts, and enjoy many other benefits. Aperture Foundation welcomes support at all levels of giving, and all gifts are tax-deductible to the fullest extent of the law. For more information about supporting Aperture please visit www.aperture.org/donate or contact the Development department at 212-946-7108.

Aperture (ISSN 0003-6420) is published quarterly, in spring, summer, fall, and winter, at 547 West 27th Street, 4th Floor, New York, N.Y. 10001. In the United States, a one-year subscription (four issues) is $75; a two-year subscription (eight issues) is $124. In Canada, a one-year subscription is $95. All other international subscriptions are $105 per year. Visit www.aperture.org to subscribe. Single copies may be purchased at $24.95 for most issues. Periodicals postage paid at New York and additional offices. Postmaster: Send address changes to *Aperture*, P.O. Box 3000, Denville, N.J. 07834. Address queries regarding subscriptions, renewals, or gifts to: *Aperture* Subscription Service, 866-457-4603 (U.S. and Canada) or email custsvc_aperture@fulcoinc.com.

Newsstand distribution in the U.S. is handled by Curtis Circulation Company, 201-634-7400. For international distribution, contact Central Books, www.centralbooks.com.

Library of Congress Catalog Card No: 58-30845.

Printed in Germany by optimal media.

Additional support for this issue was provided by RGM Advisors, LLC.

Editor
Michael Famighetti
Senior Editor
Diana C. Stoll
Assistant Editor
Paula Kupfer
Production Editor
Brian Sholis
Production
A2/SW/HK and Matthew Harvey
Work Scholars
Martina Caruso, Francisco Correa-Cordero, Maeve Gately

Art Direction, Design & Typefaces
A2/SW/HK, London

Editor-at-Large
Melissa Harris

Publisher
Dana Triwush
magazine@aperture.org
Advertising Representative
Bill Besch
631-665-0467
bbesch1@verizon.net
Executive Director, Aperture Foundation
Chris Boot

Minor White, Editor (1952–1971)

Michael E. Hoffman, Publisher and Executive Director (1964–2001)

www.aperture.org

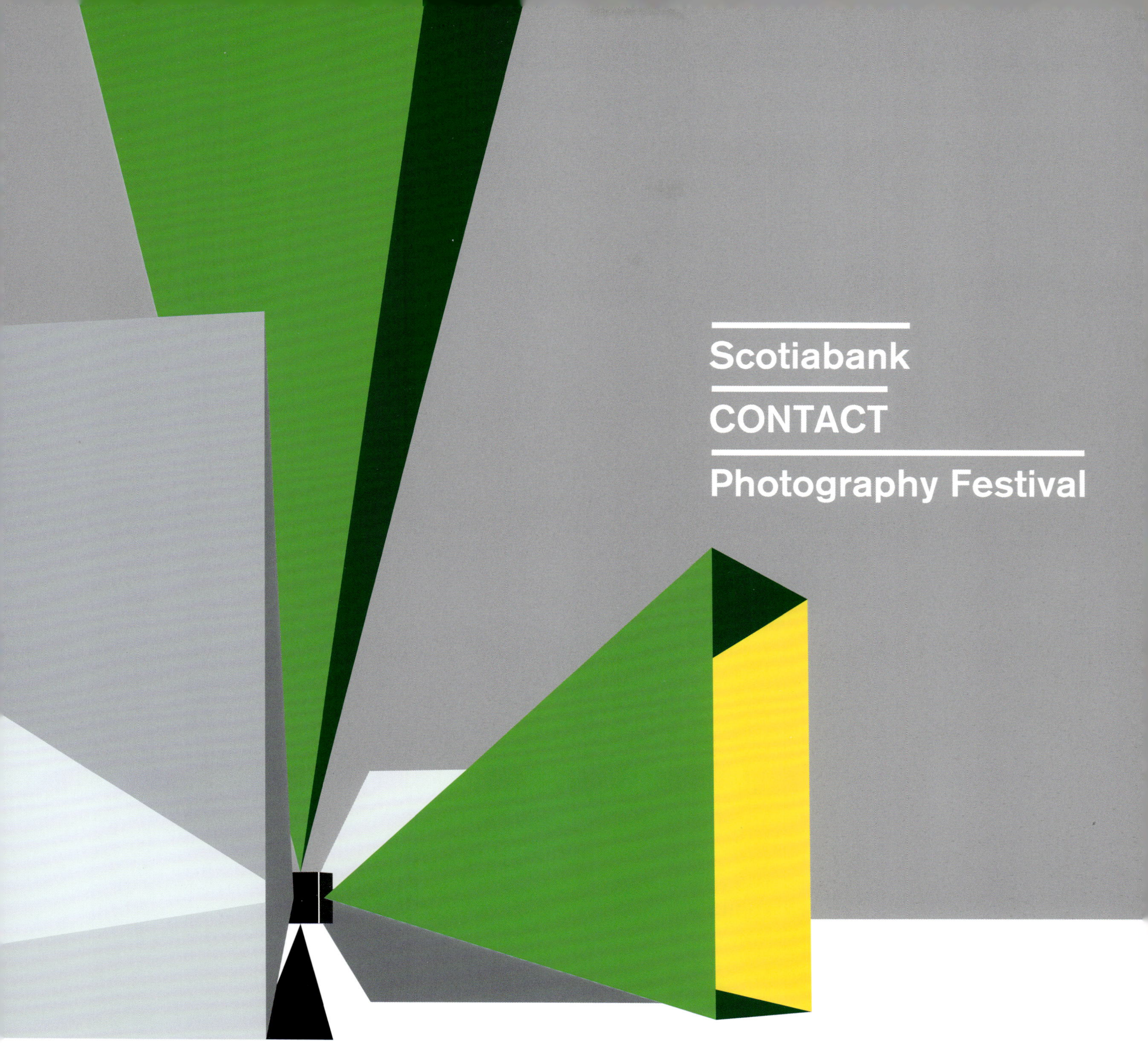

Scotiabank

CONTACT

Photography Festival

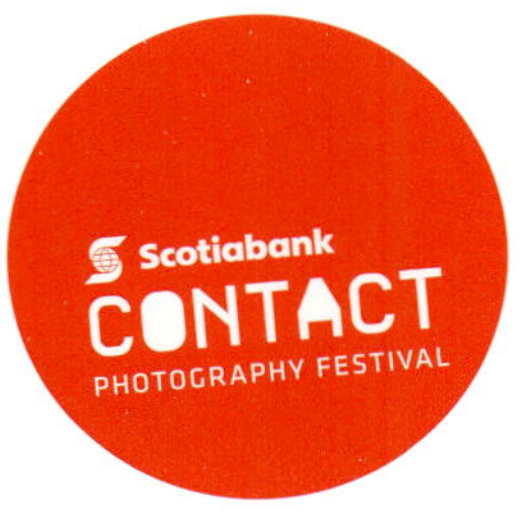

Field of Vision

May 2013 Toronto

scotiabankcontactphoto.com

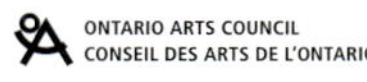

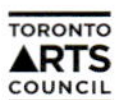

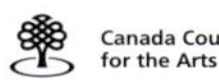

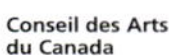

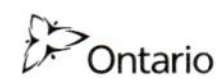

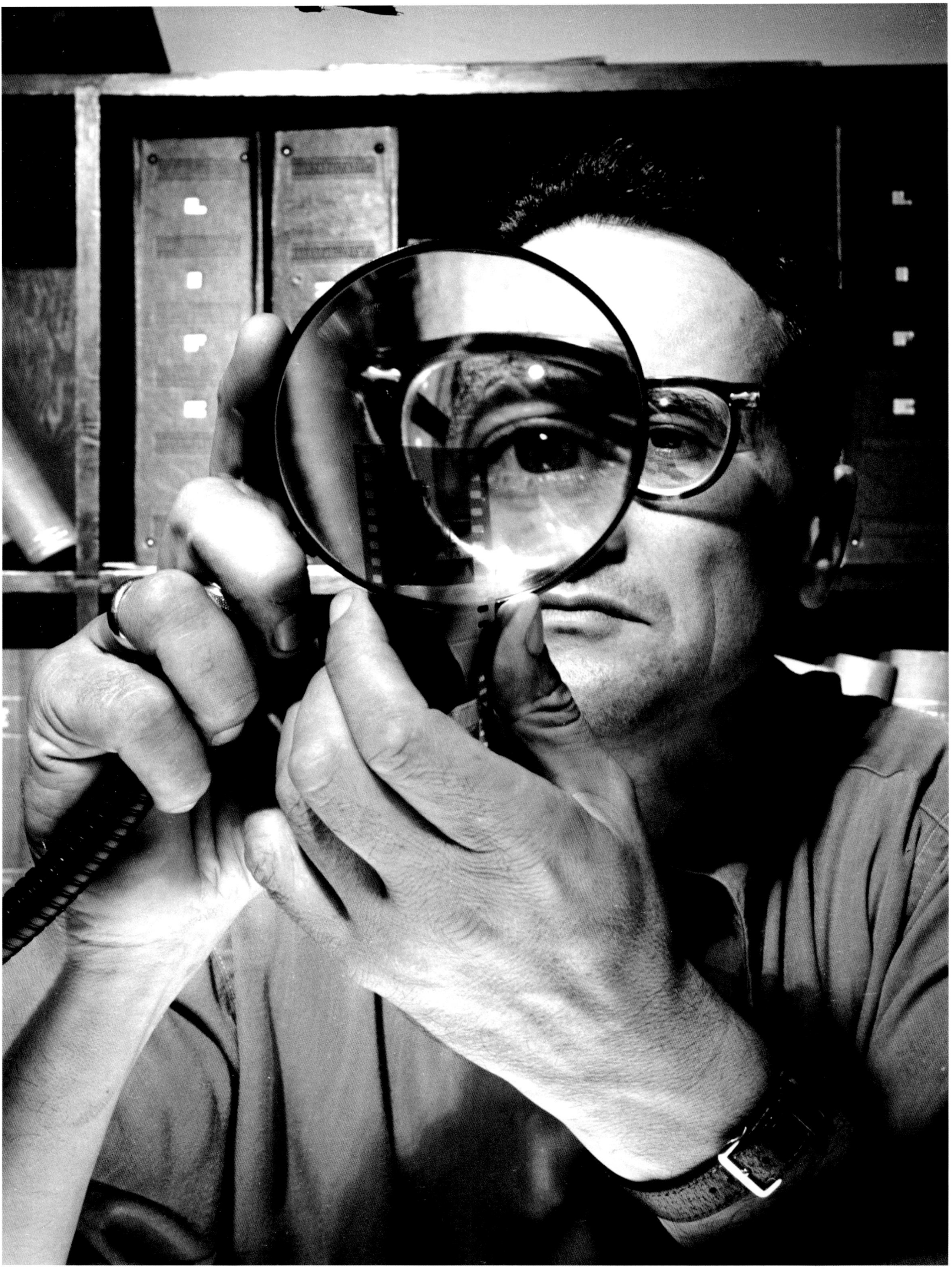

Opposite:
Andreas Feininger, Self-portrait at the Time & Life Picture Collection Library, New York, 1951
Andreas Feininger/ Time & Life Pictures/ Getty Images

Hello, Photography

What should a photography magazine be? This question propelled a long conversation at Aperture Foundation about how we can navigate the next chapter of photography's evolution and make a vital contribution as a print publication. The new *Aperture* was created with two steady assumptions in mind: First, that in a time when photography is abundant on digital platforms, images in print—ink on paper—continue to offer a uniquely *actual* experience. Second, that a magazine can engage photography's changing narrative—while remaining attentive to the medium's history—through thoughtful, accessible writing.

For these reasons, the main section of the magazine is now divided into two parts, "Words" and "Pictures." In each issue, these two will cohere around an inquiry into a field or topic: the "Words" section will feature the longer, more substantial textual contributions, as well as interviews; in "Pictures" the emphasis will be on individual artists' projects and photo series, generally introduced by short statements. A2/SW/HK, our new art directors, have re-envisioned the magazine to capitalize on how this print publication can continue to assert itself as an object, through its tactile presence, dynamic typography, and high-quality reproductions—all housed in an elegant design geared toward both reading and viewing.

We thought it fitting to organize our relaunch issue around a broad set of concerns for photography today. To get started, we called upon a group of thinkers, curators, and photographers to consider language from *Aperture*'s original 1952 mission statement proposing that the magazine should serve as a platform to "comment on what goes on" and to "descry the new potentials" of the medium. Our title, *Hello, Photography*, is a reversal of Daido Moriyama's 1972 title *Bye Bye Photography*, his book of blown-out, fractured photographs that seemed designed to thwart easy comprehension—an acknowledgment that the medium was shedding its skin, becoming something else. Today, it's a truism to talk of photography being in flux. The definition of photography, always multivalent, charting a promiscuous course across disciplines and contexts, feels especially slippery now, and this has caused much recent consternation and reevaluation. This installment of the magazine does not seek to replicate such inquiries, but rather to begin with the premise that all bets are on for the medium.

In his essay on contemporary scholarship, photography historian Robin Kelsey notes that the central concern for the medium today may be the fact that it occupies two homes: a tangible, material world of objects and prints, and a digital world of files and servers. The conflicting characteristics between the two can be felt across the photographic contexts represented here, as contributors to the "Words" section grapple with a host of ideas: the mandates and expectations for institutions dedicated to photography; how we might rethink photography education to better reflect our image culture (and how this image culture, which fluidly flattens and divorces images from context, potentially alters their evidentiary capacity); the interplay, as well as the familiar conflicts, of digital and analog; how to establish a taxonomy of vernacular photography when image output has grown too voluminous to parse; and how it might be productive, from our current vantage shaped by technological innovation and antic image traffic, to revisit older ideas—like that of artistic freedom—which take on new shadings in the current terrain.

In "Pictures," opening with a selection from Christopher Williams's new series based on a manual for an East German camera (also featured on this issue's cover), it is primarily the photographers who, through their own work, make the arguments. Williams's images of hands manipulating an analog apparatus lead into a series of portfolios that address a diversity of topics, such as our media-saturated society, the medium's history and mechanics, photography's indexical relationship to the world, as well as new modes for producing documentary work.

Like *Hello, Photography*, future issues of *Aperture* will be organized around specific inquiries: we will engage with photography as an art form, as a social phenomenon, and as an elastic lexicon for creating and shaping ideas. Hence our new tagline: "Speaking the language of photography." Some issues will be guest-edited; others will be produced offsite, through the prism of a specific city or institution. The two main sections will carry the principal investigation, whereas the front and back will feature a series of rotating columns, including "Studio Visit," "Collectors," "Redux," "Dispatches," "What Matters Now?" and our new closing page, "Object Lessons." While we are required, for the first time in a decade, to raise the subscription and newsstand prices of the print edition, all of *Aperture*'s content is now accessible in the digital version of the magazine at a new, lower price. Print subscriptions will include access to the digital edition as well as our semiannual publication, *The PhotoBook Review*. The magazine will also be more closely integrated with Aperture Foundation's live and online programming: the debates, ideas, and work published in print will be explored through events at the Aperture Gallery and other venues, as well as on our website.

For sixty years now, *Aperture* has charted the concepts and changes shaping photography's evolving narrative. Minor White, the magazine's founding editor, noted in an editorial of 1953, a moment when the photography world was much smaller: "Photography seems to be reevaluating itself these days—probably preparatory to taking off in a new direction." The magazine has always had as its mandate a goal of serious disquisition on the state of the medium. The following pages introduce a range of vital questions with a view to animating—and reanimating—key ideas on photography. This lies at the heart of *Aperture*'s purpose as it moves in a new direction, the better to respond to the medium's many new directions. — The Editors

We called upon a group of thinkers, curators, and photographers to consider language from *Aperture*'s original 1952 mission statement proposing that the magazine should serve as a platform to "comment on what goes on" and to "descry the new potentials" of the medium.

What Matters Now?
Photography, Technology, and the World

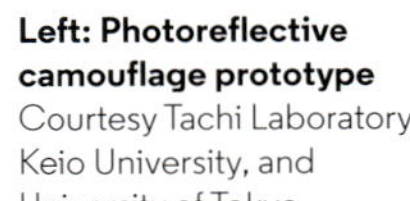

Left: Photoreflective camouflage prototype
Courtesy Tachi Laboratory, Keio University, and University of Tokyo

Center: Still from *Libya: Bloody Vengeance in Sirte*, a 2012 video report prepared by Human Rights Watch, released on October 17, 2012
Courtesy Human Rights Watch

Right: Jonas Bendiksen, *Klo, Norway*, 2012
Courtesy Jonas Bendiksen

Smartphone Evidence

A mobile-phone video clip provides the most powerful new evidence of war crimes taking place in Libya following the capture and killing of Muammar el-Qaddafi. The rudimentary video clip filmed by opposition militia members shows a large group of men, captured with Qaddafi's convoy, held in detention and being cursed at and abused by anti-Qaddafi rebels. Human Rights Watch used this video to identify at least seventeen bodies found near the city of Sirte, victims of an apparent execution.

"In case after case we investigated, the individuals had been videotaped alive by the opposition fighters who held them, and then found dead hours later," said Peter Bouckaert, emergencies director at Human Rights Watch. "Our strongest evidence for these executions comes from the footage filmed by the opposition forces, and the physical evidence at the Mahari Hotel, where the sixty-six bodies were found." The video footage thus became the strongest piece of evidence framing the killings as war crimes.

—Veronica Matushaj, director of photography and video at Human Rights Watch, New York

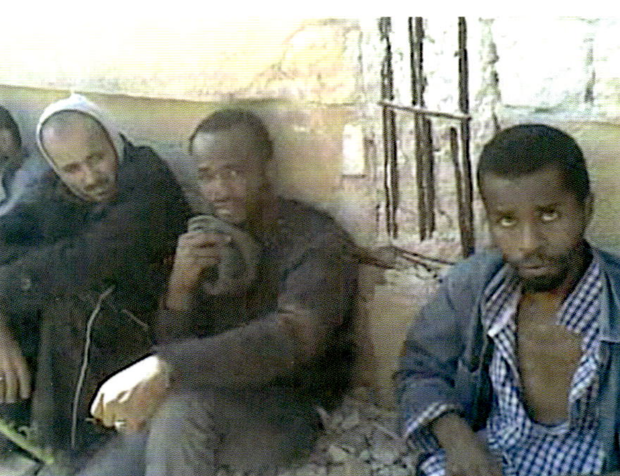

Invisibility

This is an image of a state-of-the-art camouflage technology. The cloak has embedded in it a tiny imaging system that projects onto its outer surface a photographic picture of that which lies beyond the wearer. The effect is to render the wearer nearly invisible, although in this phase of development it works only from certain vantage points.

Since its invention, photography has been used to make the world visible; camouflage during World War I was a set of practices organized around hiding from photographic detection. Now we find ourselves at an exciting crossroads: new developments in imaging technology are being used for the inverse purpose, making us invisible.

—Hanna Rose Shell, professor at MIT and the author of *Hide and Seek: Camouflage, Photography, and the Media of Reconnaissance* (Zone Books, 2012)

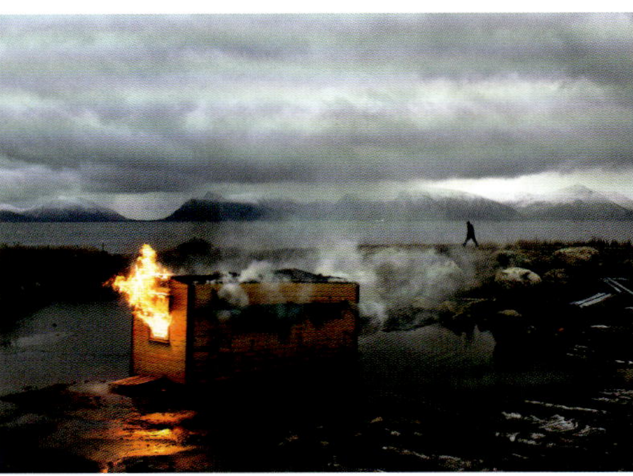

Varieties of Apocalypse

Long before the words "climate change" were part of daily discourse and our understanding of our destiny, Robert Frost wrote a short poem that told us what to expect: "Some say the world will end in fire, / Some say in ice." Those lines leapt to mind when I saw this fantastic picture—at once operatic and existential—and got to thinking about how Jonas Bendiksen harnesses Instagram, the most to-the-minute smartphone technology, to depict indelibly the primal line humankind is walking (individually and as a species) between varieties of apocalypse. He reminds us beautifully, too, that "man-made" is also natural, and he makes us ask if perhaps that means it is natural for us to be destroying nature.

—Philip Gourevitch, longtime staff writer at the *New Yorker* and the author most recently of *The Ballad of Abu Ghraib* (originally published as *Standard Operating Procedure*, Penguin, 2008)

Top: 360-degree view of the Badlands, South Dakota, 2012 Photograph by Paula Kupfer

Bottom: Instagram photograph by Kathy Ryan, New York, November 2012
Courtesy Kathy Ryan

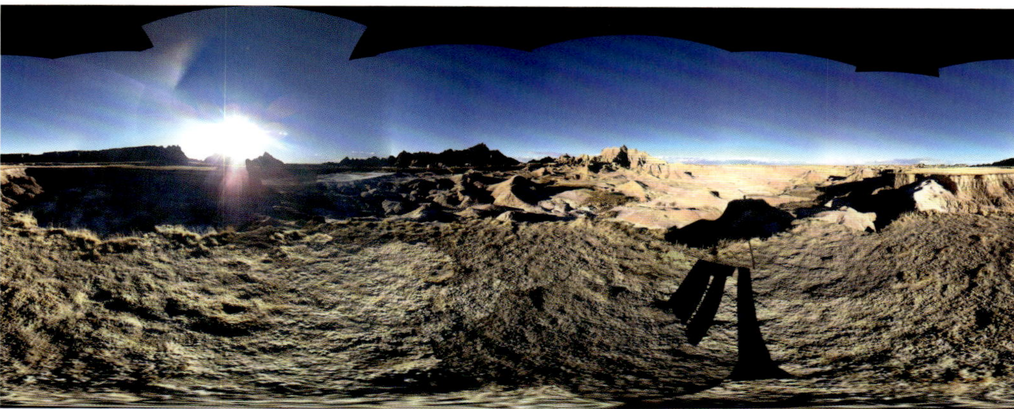

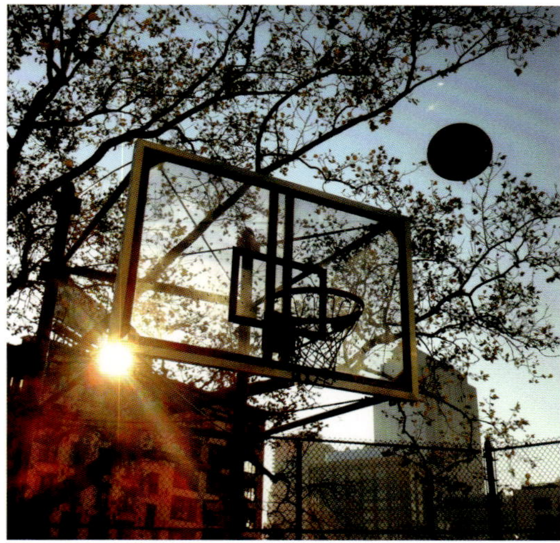

Instagram

What matters now is Instagram. It's intoxicating. I've recently become hooked. It's nectar for visual people, like having a poem in your pocket. Just the act of looking for Instagrammable pictures has opened my eyes more widely. I see all kinds of things I didn't see before: from the big landscape to the tiny, intimate moment, it encourages a closer engagement with the world—tiny visual meditations throughout the day. It's the perfect medium for ridiculously busy people who feel the urge to create and communicate, but need to do it on the run. For visualists, it is also the perfect way to check in on friends and keep up on them—no need to write the umpteenth email of the day!

It also raises the bar on what makes a good photograph, because there are so *many* good photographs on Instagram. It's a reminder that photography is a weirdly democratic medium and that a photographer has to be incredibly disciplined about his craft. On the flipside, Instagram is so friendly and forgiving that anyone can post images without having to worry about whether they are great. This kind of loosening of restraints is surely good for the creative process, as can be seen in all those good Instagram photographs.

—Kathy Ryan, director of photography at the *New York Times Magazine.* Ryan is the editor of *The New York Times Magazine Photographs* (Aperture, 2011)

The World as Image

The great drive and desire fueling a vast range of photography has always been the belief that the entire world, in all its glory, misery, and complexity, could be captured in images if only enough cameras were snapping all the time. The belief in a one-to-one correspondence between the Earth, our world, and its photographic model found its first expression in panorama picture modes that emerged alongside the earliest cameras. The nineteenth-century development of vistas that exceeded the range of human vision has come full circle today. Photosynth, an application for your smartphone, creates panoramic views and changes not only how we take images but also how we pose for them and how we view them. As profound as this reorientation of our photographic practice will be (just try it on your phone), these changes anchor photography more deeply in the age-old dream of beholding the entire world as an image.

Panorama mode captures a series of images in a 360-degree circle and then stitches these parcels of visual data into a seamless vista. Gone is the frame; gone is the need to position subjects in clusters that fit into that frame; gone is the need for the photographer to step back in order to capture everything. Gone is our habit, ingrained through a century-and-a-half's worth of photographic practice (and a much longer history of painting and other visual media), to relate to the world as if viewed through a window. Diminished, if not fully gone, is the intuition that images conceal as much as they reveal through the aesthetics of framing, as well as photography's erstwhile magical disclosure of the world as being continually born, rather than found, before our eyes. In panorama mode we return to the Platonic idea that the world is nothing but images on a cave wall.

We can now look forward to a new generation of photographers who will turn this technology against itself by showing us that the world is not an image and that images make and unmake many worlds.

—Ulrich Baer, vice provost for Arts and Humanities at New York University, and author of, among other books, *Spectral Evidence: The Photography of Trauma* (MIT Press, 2002) and *Beggar's Chicken: Stories from Shanghai* (Earnshaw Books, 2012)

IMOGEN CUNNINGHAM

Published by TF Editores/D.A.P.
Text by Celina Lunsford, Jamie M. Allen, Marisa C. Sánchez.

Published to accompany a major European traveling exhibition, this volume celebrates the pioneering American Modernist's seven-decade career—from her abstract shots of plants and nudes to optical illusions created with inverted positive/negative images and double exposures, to her iconic portraits for *Vanity Fair* of creative figures such as Man Ray, Alfred Stieglitz, Martha Graham, Frida Kahlo, Gertrude Stein and Merce Cunningham. Includes many rarely reproduced works, scholarly essays, an illustrated chronology and selected bibliography.

Clothbound, 9.5 x 11.75 inches, 262 pages, 220 duotone, $65

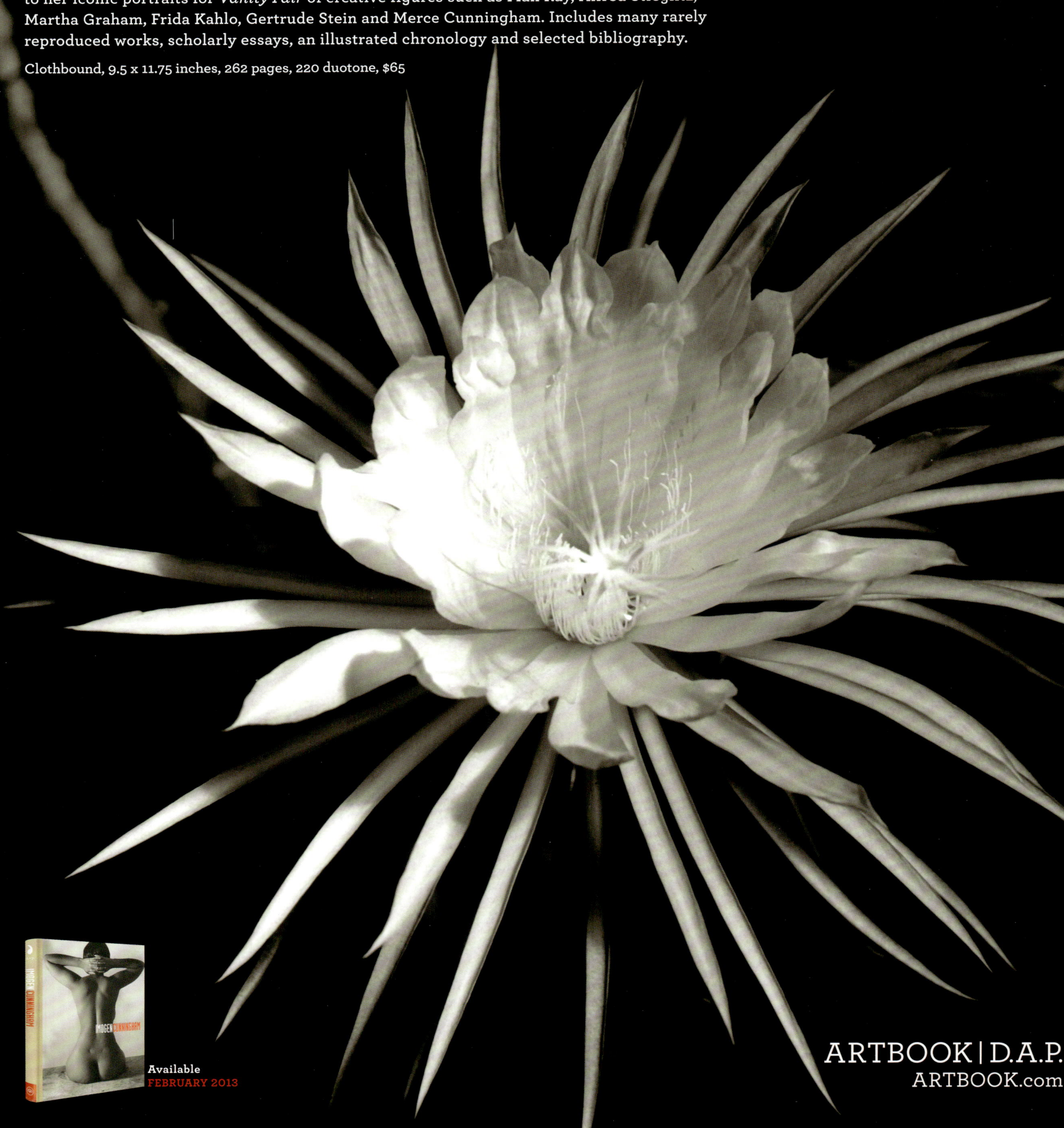

Available
FEBRUARY 2013

ARTBOOK | D.A.P.
ARTBOOK.com

Redux
Rediscovered Books and Writings

Victor Burgin's *Between* (1986)
David Campany

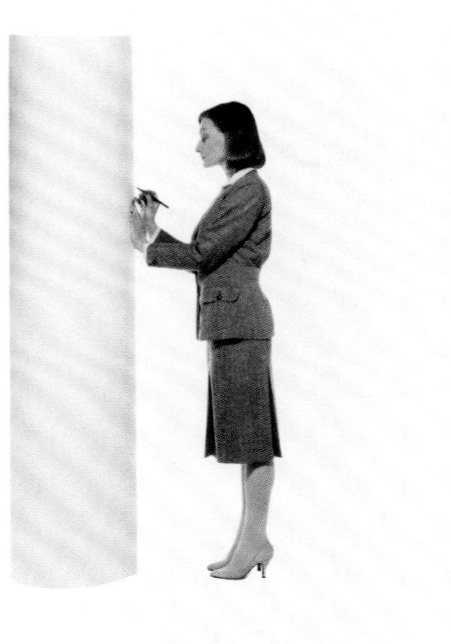

Above and page 18: Pages from Victor Burgin's *Between* (Blackwell, 1986).

"Literature," Susan Sontag once said, "is writing one wishes to reread." Works of art, one might extend, are images or objects or performances one wishes to re-view. Early in his long career, in 1973 to be exact, the artist-writer Victor Burgin offered a slightly different definition: "A job the artist does which no-one else does is to dismantle existing communication codes and to recombine some of their elements into structures which can be used to generate new pictures of the world."

Here an artist isn't simply someone who works within the institutions of art; it is someone who works at odds with and in relation to the structures of culture at large. An artist may well exhibit in galleries but may also be a writer, architect, filmmaker, designer, musician, or speaker. Burgin himself has made visual work and written essays for over forty years. His photography and video pieces are visual and textual, and so is his writing.

My first encounter with his work came in the form of the book *Between*, published by Blackwell in 1986. Elegantly designed, it contains sequences of black-and-white photographs with overlaid texts. The photographs are quite like many things: film stills, classic street photography, fashion, advertising, and reportage. The texts seem "theoretical" but are also poetic, aphoristic, polemical, and sometimes fragmentary. *Between* also contains short, freestanding paragraphs full of insight into the presumptions of the mass media, the clichés of artspeak, the role of the unconscious in looking, and the shaping of class, gender, and sexuality. The contents are ordered in rough chronology although it's not necessary to read it that way. But this is how Burgin begins:

> ***My decision to base my work in cultural theory, rather than traditional aesthetics, has resulted in work whose precise "location" is uncertain, "between": between gallery and book; between "visual art" and "theory"; between image and narrative—"work" providing* work *between reader and text.***

Books of photographs and words may construct a space set apart, a world in which the oppressive conventions of daily life may be suspended and rethought. *Between* is as rich as the best movies by Jean-Luc Godard: fiercely critical, joyously playful, wildly idiosyncratic yet always interested in telling us about the culture in which we live and the alternatives. And like Godard, Burgin opened more doors than I have been able to explore in the years since. From this one book I found my way to writers such as Roland Barthes, Sigmund Freud, Jacques Lacan, Viktor Shklovsky, Louis Althusser, Julia Kristeva, and Karl Marx. It also led me to Lee Friedlander, Garry Winogrand, Aleksandr Rodchenko, Henri Cartier-Bresson, Alfred Hitchcock, and John Cage. Sure, all these figures came before Burgin but none of us discovers things chronologically. We are always going backwards and forwards.

US 77

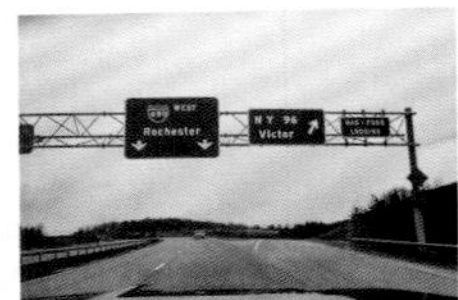

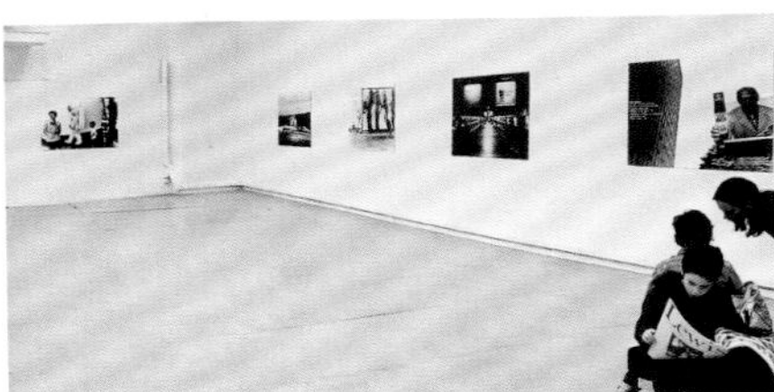

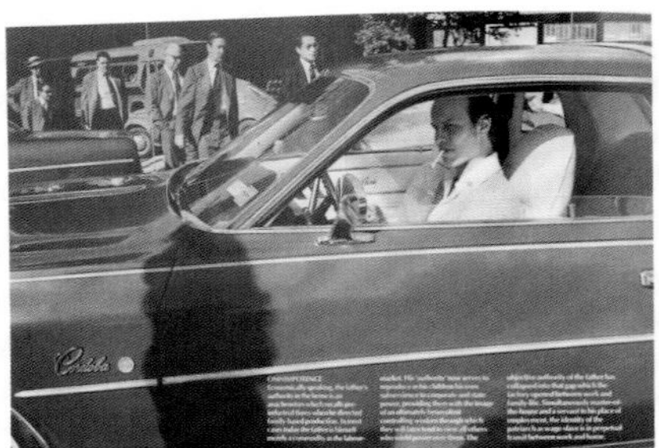

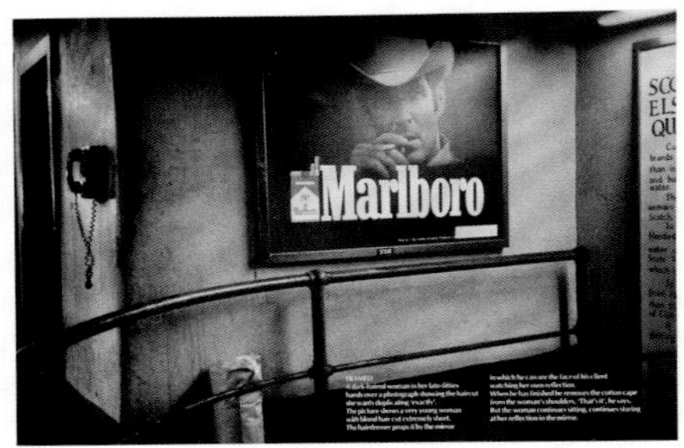

Between charts Burgin's passage from early conceptual art, via appropriations and critiques of mass-media imagery, to a series of photo-texts informed by psychoanalysis, semiotics, and cinema studies. During this period, the art markets came to dominate and dictate as never before. Art was no longer that stubborn space of resistance and reflection. It was to be part of the spectacle of neoliberal capitalism in which image is all—self-congratulatory art fairs, artists as media celebrities, bloated auction prices, and the reduction of criticality to recognizable and increasingly empty gestures. Burgin includes an extract of a letter to a collector:

We are a consumer-society, and it seems to me that art has become a passive "spectator sport" to an extent unprecedented in history. I have always tried to work against this tendency by producing "occasions for interpretation" rather than "objects for consumption." I believe that the ability to produce rather than consume meanings, the ability to think otherwise—ways of thinking not encouraged by the imperative to commodity production, ways condemned as "a waste of time"—is fundamental to the goal of a truly, rather than nominally, democratic society. I believe art is one of the few remaining areas of social activity where the attitude of critical engagement may still be encouraged—all the more reason for art to engage with those issues that are critical.

Burgin makes photographic work like no other artist, but his themes and motifs are drawn from experiences common to us all—the modern city, the structures of family, language as something that forms and reforms us, the power of images, principles of government, memory, and history. And yet, encouraged by the media to look to art for quick messages, some audiences and critics have found the work "inaccessible." Actually Burgin's work is among the most accessible I know, if by that we mean "easy to get into"; it's the *getting out* that's tricky. To be truly challenged and changed is to find yourself unsure, slightly lost, forgetting where you came in but pleased you did. As Roland Barthes once put it: "To get out, go in deeper."

You won't see this publication in the canon of photobooks, nor on lists of recommended theory books. It's not a catalog, or a monograph, or an "artist's book." It is between.

David Campany's latest book is *Walker Evans: The Magazine Work* (Steidl, 2013). He is curating a major show of Victor Burgin's work to be presented this year at P3 in London.

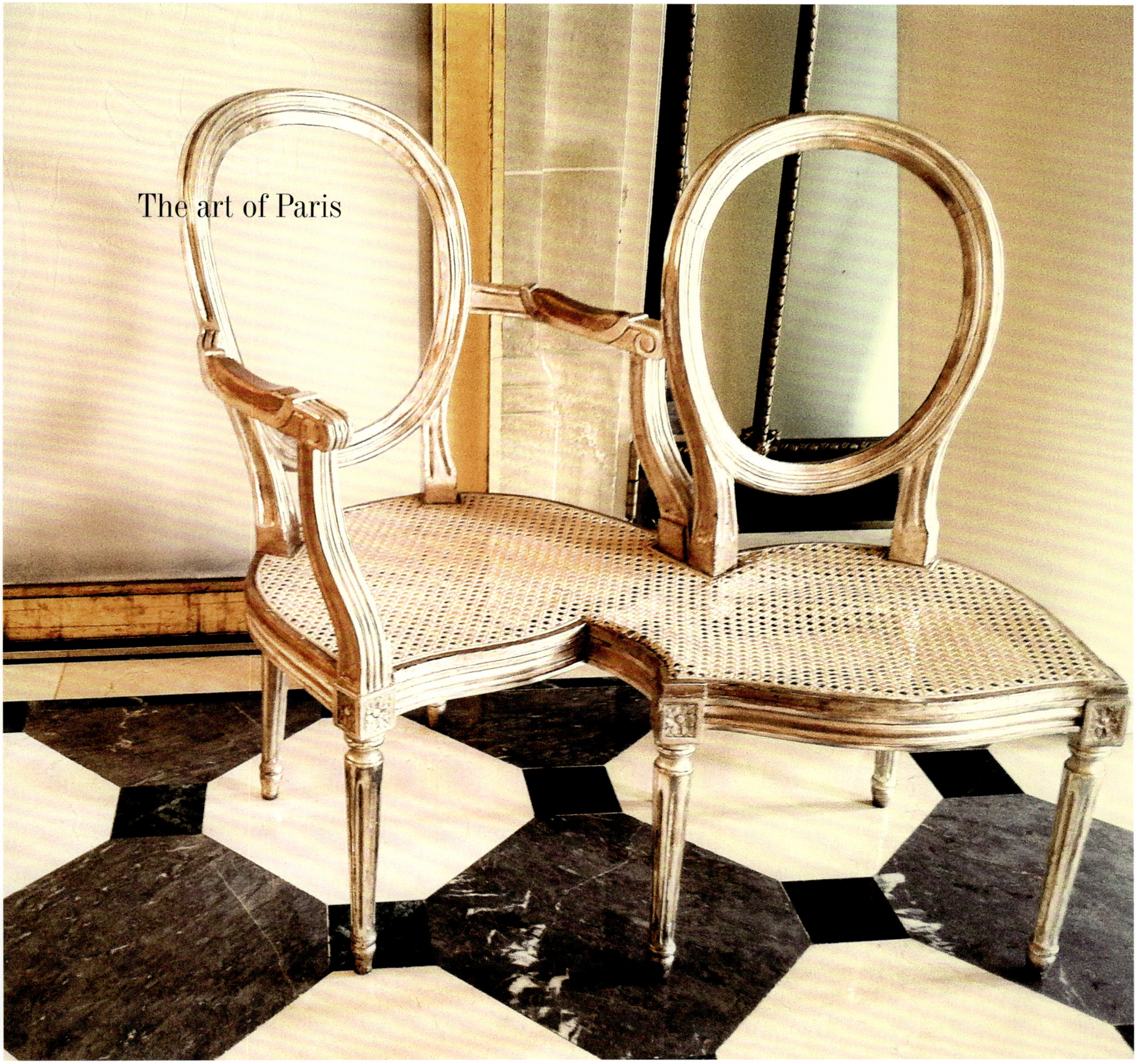

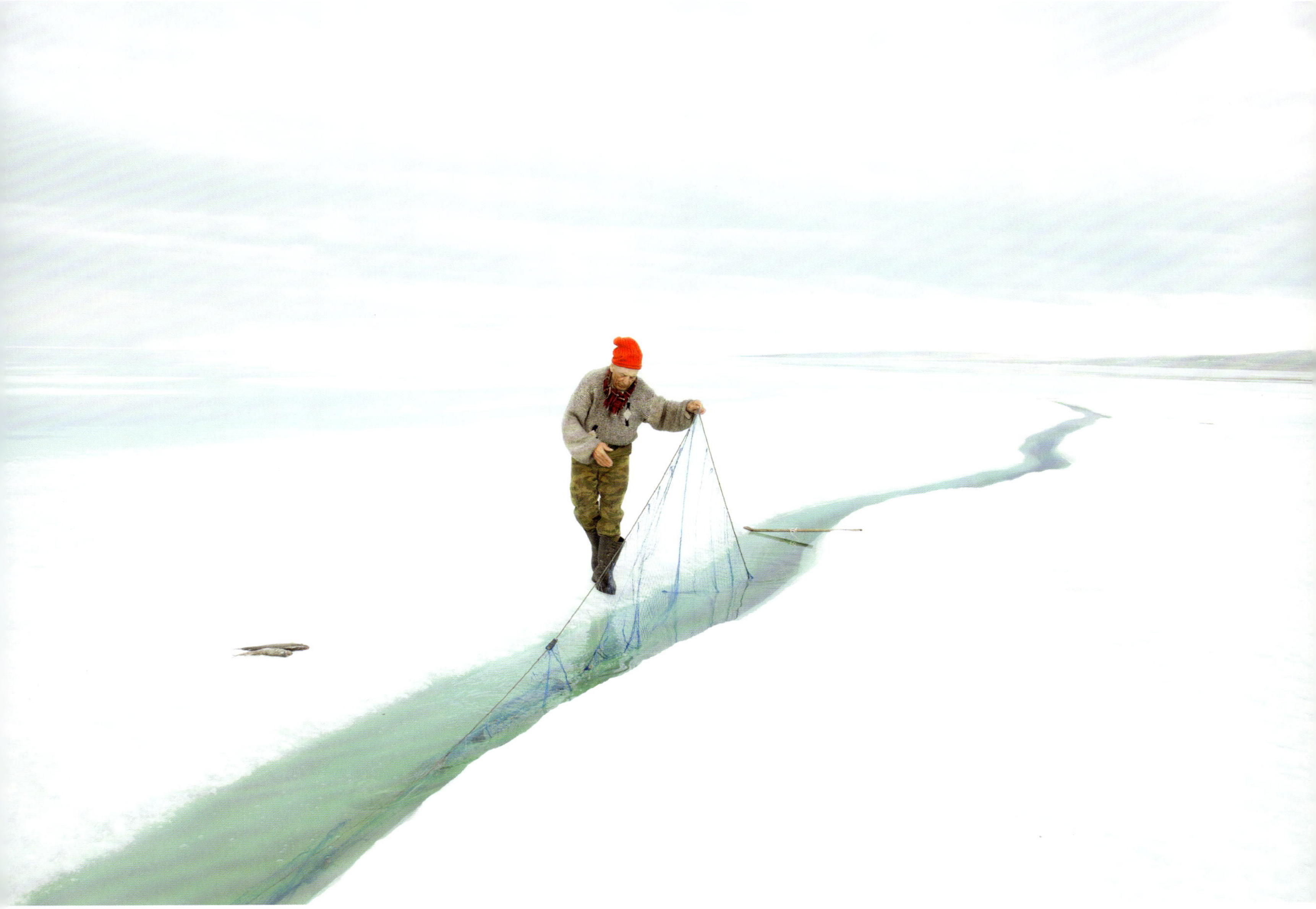

Collectors The Novelists On Recent Acquisitions

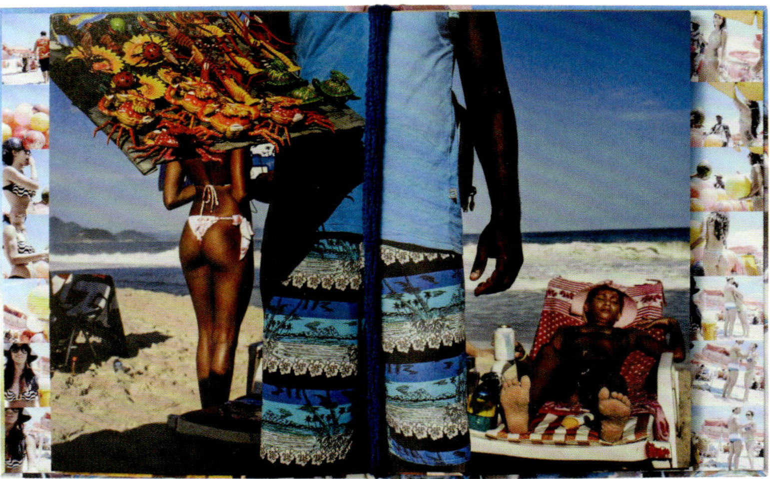

Spread from David Alan Harvey's *based on a true story* (Burn, 2012)

Teju Cole

There's a pleasure proper to the almost antique technology of the photobook. There are things possible in a photobook that digital dissemination cannot hope to emulate. That was certainly how I felt when I received my copy of *based on a true story*, published this year by Magnum photographer David Alan Harvey. The book is a visual record of Rio de Janeiro but it is also a bold experiment in book making.

Though full of Harvey's justly celebrated street photography, what makes this different from his earlier books, like *Divided Soul*, is not the fractured and emotional approach to color shooting, which is unchanged, but rather the way we are compelled to encounter images side by side with each other. Flipping through the large matte pages, we encounter half of each photograph, and understand it first of all in relation to half of another photograph. In almost all cases, the pairings are breathtakingly apt. We can temporarily detach each print from the loose binding and see it as a whole. And then we reassemble the startling halves again.

The book makes the viewer feel the multiple fragments of life in Rio: the pleasure, the violence, the sun, the doubts, the darkness. It plunges the viewer into the markets, beaches, parties, favelas, homes, and streets of one of the most interesting cities in the world. The book is an instant classic, and already a favorite in my growing collection of photobooks.

Teju Cole is the author of *Open City* (Random House, 2011).

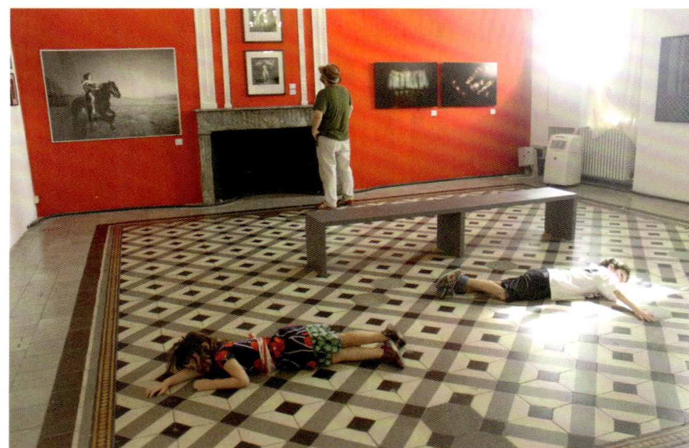

View at Rencontres d'Arles, 2012. Photograph by Ceridwen Morris

Sam Lipsyte

I acquired this photo from my wife, who took it at the famous photography festival in Arles, France. That's me with my back turned, and those are my children on the floor. It wasn't posed, though it kind of looks like maybe Jeff Wall was involved. I'm not sure if the kids were overwhelmed by the art or just tired, but it does seem they've achieved a certain dreamy peace on the well-trafficked gallery floor.

Sam Lipsyte's most recent novel is *The Ask* (Farrar, Straus & Giroux, 2010).

Sheila Heti

I keep these postcards, which I bought at an artists' multiples shop in Toronto, on the tall bookshelves near my desk. One is on one shelf, leaning against a row of books; the other on another shelf, leaning against some more books. These vintage postcards were found by the artist Sandy Plotnikoff, then foil-stamped with *Toronto*. I bought them in 2007, when I was really dissatisfied about living here, in Toronto, my hometown, where I have been almost my entire life. Toronto seemed to me to be just one thing, a thing I knew well, a thing I no longer wanted to engage with. I wanted to be on the sea. I wanted to be on a double-decker bus! I wanted to be in the desert. When I saw these postcards, I knew that they would make me feel better about being in Toronto. They did. They remind me, whenever I look at them, that the imagination is the best place to travel; that your city is not one thing—a thing you know well—but as mysterious as any other place; it's an illusion to think we know what a place is. Why isn't Toronto a barge on the sea, or the Bahnhof Zoo? Every place is every place else.

Sheila Heti's most recent novel is *How Should a Person Be?* (Henry Holt, 2012).

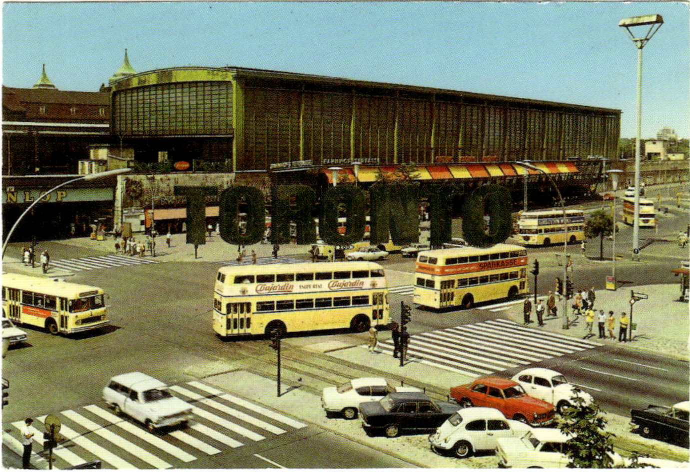

Vintage postcards foil-stamped with the word *Toronto*, by artist Sandy Plotnikoff

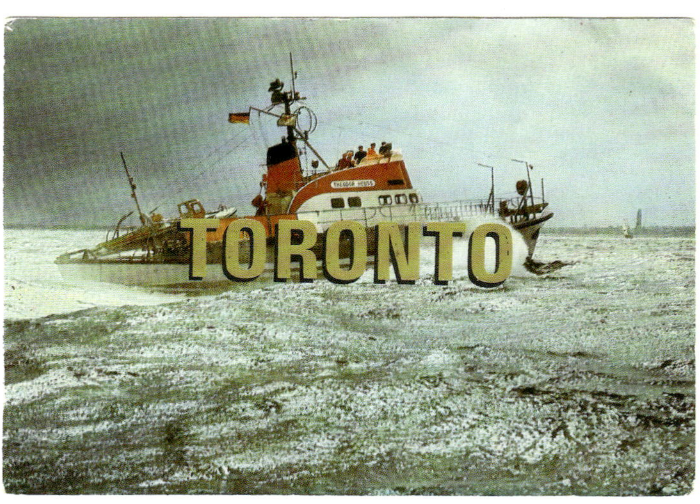

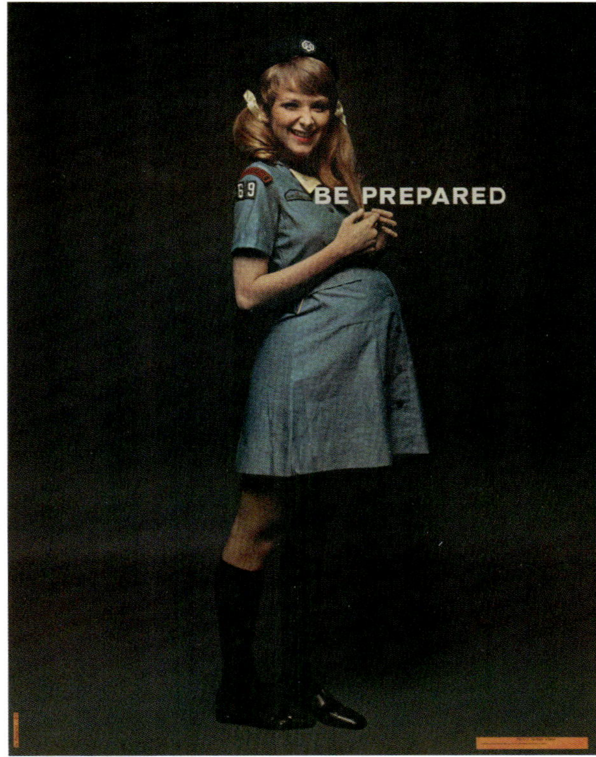

George Adams, Be Prepared poster, ca. 1969. Yanker Poster Collection, Library of Congress

Heidi Julavits

I found this poster at an antiques shop in Maine. I'd invited my daughter and her friend along as my shopping enablers. They did not fulfill their mandate. They counseled me not to buy the poster. I tried to sell them on selling me on buying it. "Why do you like it?" they asked. "Because it's so funny!" I said. They scrutinized the poster. "Why is it funny?" they asked. I didn't know why it was funny. Because teenage pregnancy is hilarious? I bought it because I didn't fully get the joke, and because I wasn't certain there was meant to be a joke at all. But I liked the Girl Scout's coffee-colored patent-leather shoes and her knee socks, I liked that she has no idea she's pregnant, I liked that "Be Prepared" might simply refer to her stylishness and her psychotic smiling gameness, both of which, it seemed to me, were classic Girl Scout traits. And isn't being prepared to be unprepared the best form of preparedness? If you think you're ready for anything, you're really not ready at all.

Heidi Julavits's most recent novel is *The Vanishers* (Doubleday, 2012).

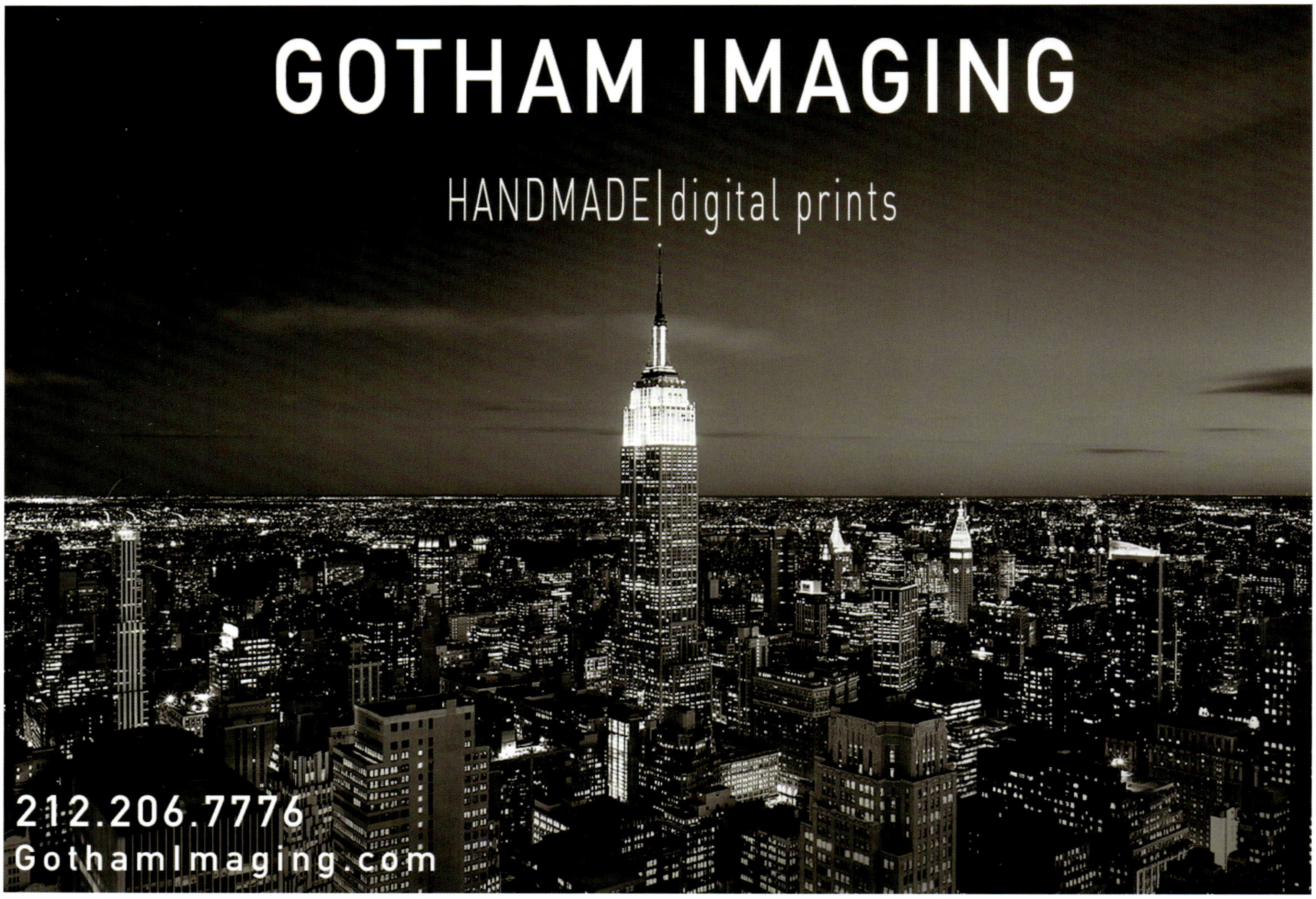

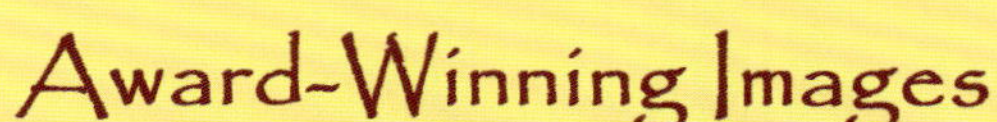

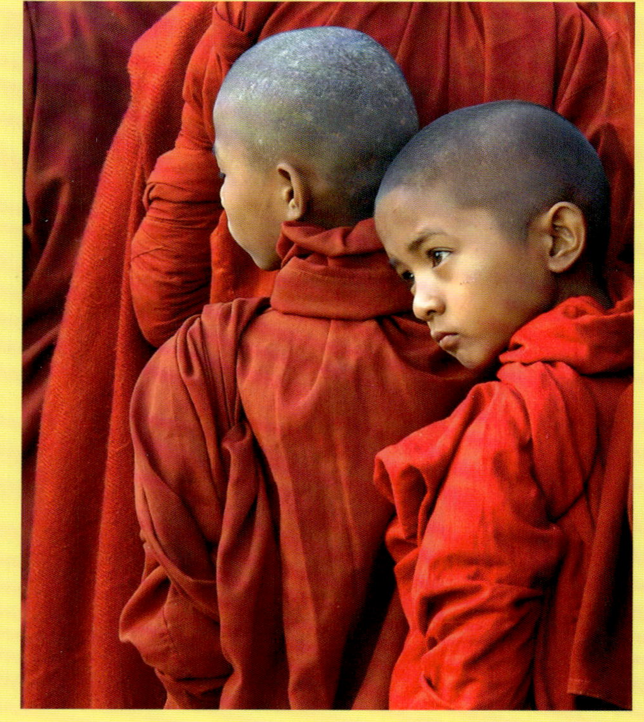

Statement of Ownership, Management, and Circulation (Required by 39 U.S.C. 3685). 1. Publication Title: Aperture; 2. Publication no.: 0003-6420; 3. Filing Date: October 1, 2012 4. Issue Frequency: Quarterly; 5. No. of Issues Published Annually: 4; 6. Annual Subscription Price: $40.00; 7. Complete Mailing Address of Known Office of Publication: 547 West 27th Street, 4th Floor, New York, NY 10001-5511; Contact Person: Dana Triwush; Telephone: 212-946-7116; 8. Complete Mailing Address of Headquarters or General Business Office of Publisher: 547 West 27th Street, 4th Floor, New York, NY 10001-5511; 9. Full Names and Complete Mailing Addresses of Publisher, Editor, and Managing Editor: Publisher: Dana Triwush, 547 West 27th Street, 4th Floor, New York, NY 10001-5511; Editor: Melissa Harris, 547 West 27th Street, 4th Floor, New York, NY 10001-5511; Managing Editor: Michael Famighetti, 547 West 27th Street, 4th Floor, New York, NY 10001-5511; 10. Owner: Aperture Foundation, Inc., 547 West 27th Street, 4th Floor, New York, NY 10001-5511; 11. Known Bondholders, Mortgagees, and Other Security Holders Owning or Holding 1 Percent or More of Total Amount of Bonds, Mortgages, or Other Securities: None; 12. Tax Status: The purpose, function, and nonprofit status of this organization and the exempt status for federal income tax purposes: Has Not Changed During Preceding 12 Months; 13. Publication Title: Aperture; 14. Issue Date for Circulation Data Below: Fall 2012 #208; 15. Extent and Nature of Circulation (Average No. Copies Each Issue During Preceding 12 Months; No. Copies of Single Issue Published Nearest to Filing Date): a. Total Number of Copies (Net press run): 22,291; 21,428; b. Paid Circulation; 1. Mailed Outside-County Paid Subscriptions Stated on PS Form 3541: 14,724; 13,858; 2. Mailed In-County Paid Subscriptions Stated on PS Form 3541: 0; 0; 3. Paid Distribution Outside the Mails Including Sales Through Dealers and Carriers, Street Vendors, Counter Sales, and Other Paid Distribution Outside USPS: 2,144; 2,278; 4. Paid Distribution by Other Classes of Mail Through the USPS: 20; 20; c. Total Paid Distribution: 16,887; 16,156; d. Free or Nominal Rate Distribution: 1. Free or Nominal Rate Outside-County Copies included on PS Form 3541: 558; 542; 2. Free or Nominal Rate In-County Copies Included on PS Form 3541: 0; 0; 3. Free or Nominal Rate Copies Mailed at Other Classes Through the USPS: 400; 400; 4. Free or Nominal Rate Distribution Outside the Mail: 549; 569; e. Total Free or Nominal Rate Distribution: 1,507; 1,511; f. Total Distribution: 18,394; 17,667; g. Copies not Distributed: 3,897; 3,761; h. Total: 22,291; 21,428; i. Percent Paid: 91.81%; 91.45%; 16. Publication of Statement of Ownership: Will be printed in the Spring 2013 issue of this publication.; 17. I certify that all information furnished on this form is true and complete. I understand that anyone who furnishes false or misleading information on this form or who omits material or information requested on the form may be subject to criminal sanctions (including fines and imprisonment) and/or civil sanctions (including civil penalties). Signature and Title of Editor, Publisher, Business Manager, or Owner: Dana Triwush, Publisher, October 1, 2012

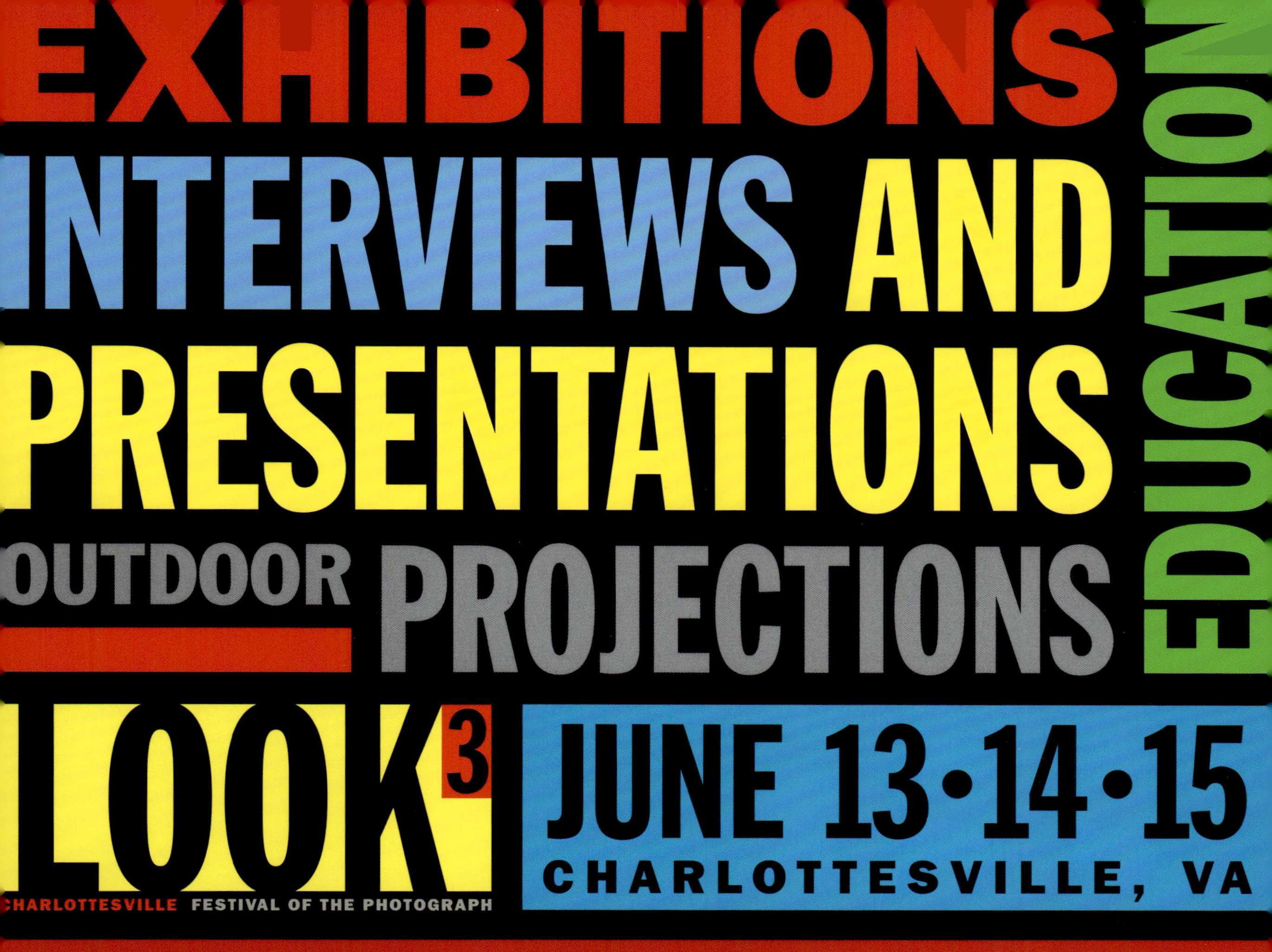
EXHIBITIONS
INTERVIEWS AND
PRESENTATIONS
OUTDOOR PROJECTIONS
EDUCATION
LOOK3
CHARLOTTESVILLE FESTIVAL OF THE PHOTOGRAPH
JUNE 13•14•15
CHARLOTTESVILLE, VA
FESTIVAL PASSES ON SALE AT www.look3.org

advertisement

New Aperture Books Spring 2013

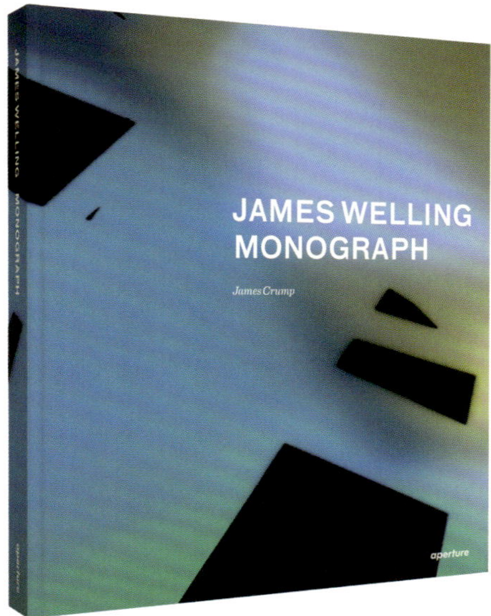

James Welling: Monograph
The first major overview of a leading figure of contemporary art photography
Clothbound, $80.00

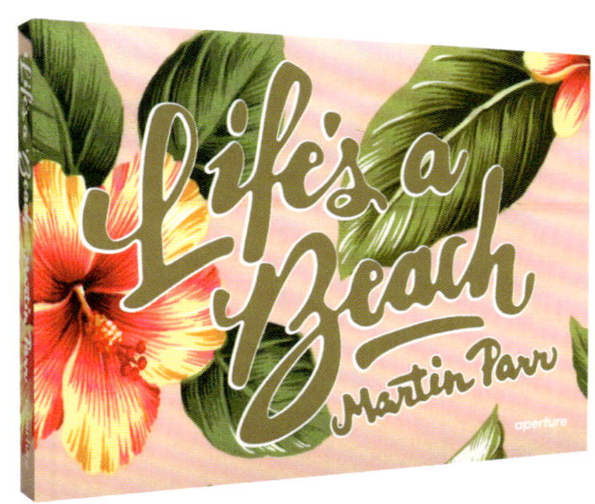

Life's a Beach (mini edition)
Photographs by Martin Parr
From the U.S. to China, the local quirks of life on the beach
Hardcover, $25.00

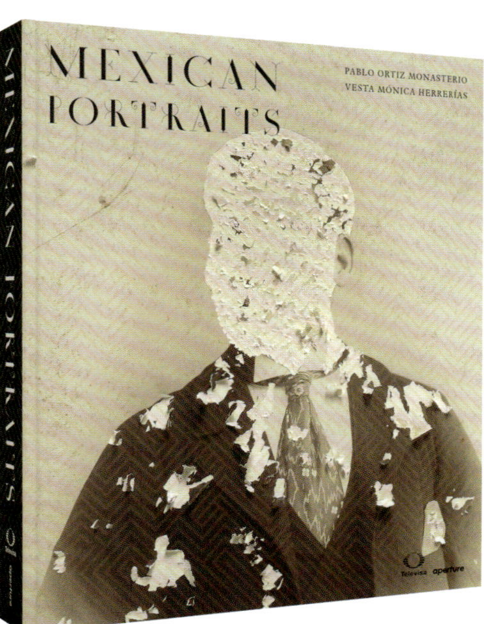

Mexican Portraits
By Pablo Ortiz Monasterio and Vesta Mónica Herrerías
Includes over 350 portraits from over eighty well-known Mexican photographers
Hardcover, $85.00

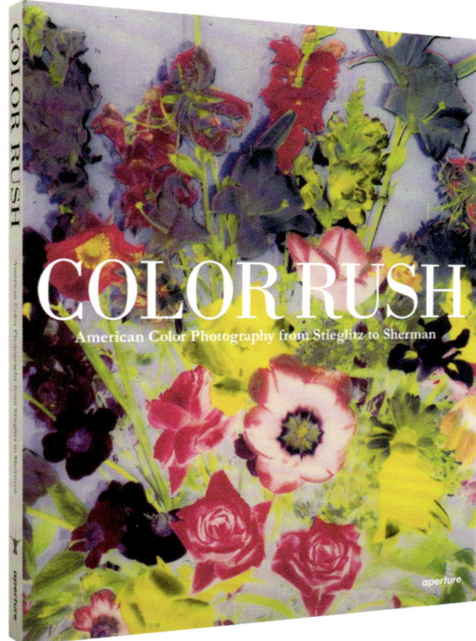

Color Rush: American Color Photography from Stieglitz to Sherman
By Lisa Hostetler and Katherine A. Bussard
Traces a new history that fully accounts for color's pervasive presence today
Hardcover, $60.00

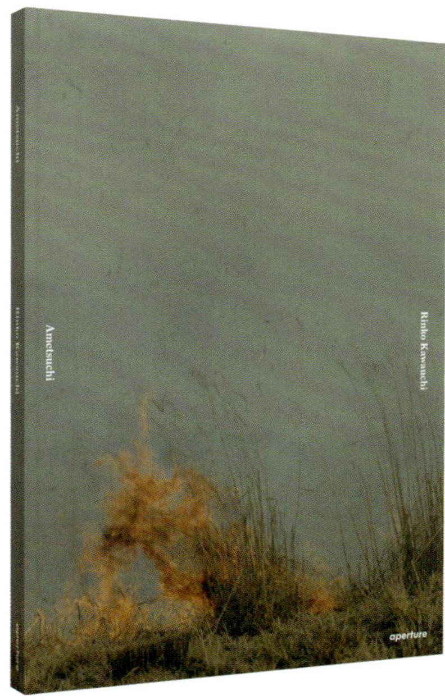

Ametsuchi
Photographs by Rinko Kawauchi
A luxurious and unique edition presenting Kawauchi's latest body of work
Hardcover, $80.00

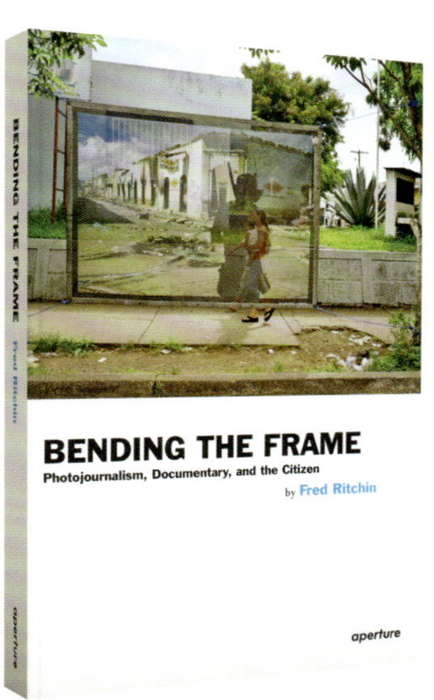

Bending the Frame: Photojournalism, Documentary, and the Citizen
By Fred Ritchin
Author and critic Fred Ritchin addresses new and emerging potentials for visual media to impact society today
Paperback, $24.95

aperture 547 West 27th Street, 4th Floor, New York, N.Y. 10001 www.aperture.org @aperturefnd facebook.com/aperturefoundation

Inside Takashi Homma's Studio

Ivan Vartanian

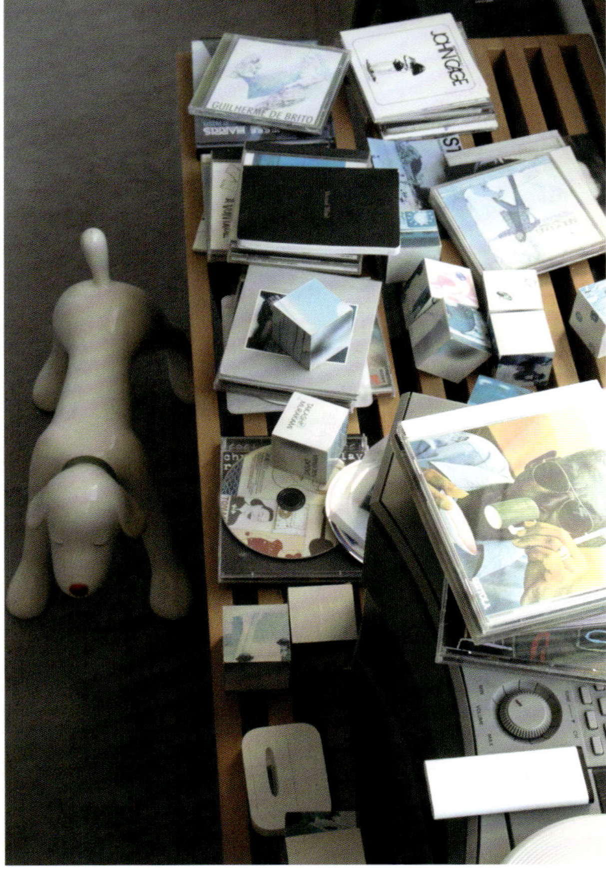

Left: Homma's studio. On the desk are the photographer's CDs and on the floor is an object by Yoshitomo Nara.

Above: Storage cabinet of negatives and prints

Environment is a reflection of one's identity, and vice versa, and this is nowhere made clearer than in Takashi Homma's 1999 series and book *Tokyo Suburbia*. Homma's project asked what it means to be Japanese to a generation entrenched in an alien fast-food culture and living in apartment blocks in the city's outskirts—housing for Tokyo's large commuter workforce. His portraits of young people and children in these vast complexes are deadpan and flat, and their environments are pristine, isolated, and isolating.

The context from which Homma's images derive is worth outlining. The 1990s was a time of reflection and probing self-interrogation for many in Japan, who were reevaluating their relation to society, work, family, and the self in the doldrums of the country's post-bubble economy. A number of independent creators took advantage of this time of transition to make a name for themselves in fields that had previously been closed to radical change. In the mid-1990s artist Takashi Murakami started his art "factory" Hiropon (later renamed Kaikai Kiki); fashion brands like A Bathing Ape became part of the definitive look of street and youth culture; and experimental pop musicians were creating new, unstructured sounds and lyrics. The entrepreneurial spirit provoked by the country's limping economy was infectious and seeped into all aspects of life and activity in Tokyo.

It is no coincidence that this period also engendered a vibrant new wave of photographers, many of whom turned their attention and lenses to questions of identity and self. It was a moment of heightened importance for the photobook and photography-magazine culture in Japan as well; these elements played an important role in the country's acute yearning to make sense of things in a confusing era.

•

Since the appearance of *Tokyo Suburbia*, Homma and his photography have been prominent presences in Japan. Through workshops and lectures, he has influenced a great number of younger photographers; it would, in fact, be difficult to consider contemporary Japanese photography without taking into account Homma's work.

I became aware of Homma's activities with the publication of *Tokyo Suburbia*; at the time I was working for Korinsha Press, the publisher of that monograph. As I recall, the book's production was a logistics nightmare, but the seriousness and respect with which Homma's work was treated made it clear that this project would garner a lot of acclaim. That experience stayed with me, so a couple of years ago I signed up for one of the photography workshops Homma offered after the publication of his book *Tanoshii Shashin* (*Fun Photography*, Heibonsha, 2009). The workshop also provided an opportunity to get better acquainted with his work and ideas about photography.

As an artist, Homma is clearly very aware of his process of observation: his intellect is constantly engaged. Even when operating with large-format film and a tripod, he works as speedily and nimbly, it seems, as if he were using a compact camera. He chooses his subjects carefully, and tends to frame what he is shooting with a pulled-back and balanced approach: composition, he believes, plays an important role in the photograph's meaning.

In May of last year, I produced a performance event titled *rrreecconns-sstrucctt* in Tokyo that involved Homma cutting up his prints and having participants reconstruct the images. It was interesting to ask a photographer who is so keenly attuned to composition to break down his images and see what would come of the mix. We were all fascinated by the creative results of the recomposed photographs, and Homma in particular was elated to see his work take on a new form through the hands of participants.

Left: Takashi Homma

Top: Studio veranda

Bottom: The darkroom

All photographs by Takashi Homma

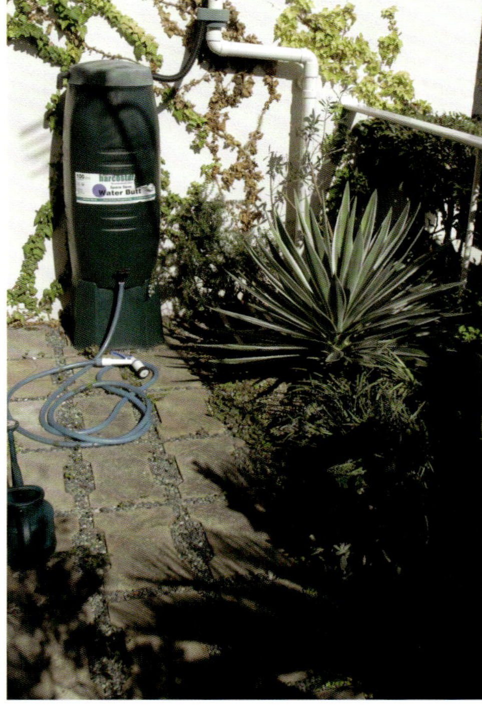

Homma's studio is near Tokyo's Ebisu train station, which is within walking distance of the Tokyo Metropolitan Museum of Photography (one of the city's many bubble-era construction projects). This part of town was once mostly residential, but a number of independent retailers have moved in and appropriated spaces for commercial purposes: the LimArt bookstore/gallery, a fashion showroom for Maison Martin Margiela, and several furniture and clothing boutiques. Architectural conversion and multi-purposing are leitmotifs in the neighbor-hood, as is the creative overlap of start-ups and established businesses. There is a homey sense of community in the area: Homma's work, for example, has been shown at both LimArt and the Maison Martin Margiela as special projects.

The photographer's studio is on the second floor of a residential building—a living space converted to a workspace. Like a lot of photographers, Homma takes on commission projects, which requires a balancing act of speed and creativity; the pace at the studio is often hectic. Nonetheless, in spare moments he can frequently be found reading—usually rather heady subject matter: a history of Jean-Luc Godard's films, books on cognition, perception, the mind's eye. Also in his studio is the inevitable trove of photobooks—the staple of any photographer's visual diet—which he consumes with an insatiable appetite. The studio—indeed, Homma's entire operation—is remarkably tidy and surprisingly modest, and it seems to suit him. "My studio in Tokyo is small," he says. "I wish I had a bigger space. But I like it here." Several of his cameras are out in one corner. I'm not sure if they are all fully operational, but he clearly has a love of the equipment. (His father was a camera retailer.)

In his interactions with people, Homma tends toward a dry and very rational affect. He is no different as a teacher; I can attest that his frankness is never sacrificed to compassion. At the same time, he's quite upfront about himself and his photography, and I would say that he doesn't appreciate people pulling punches when talking about his work.

Through his teachings and his contributions to contemporary photography discourse, Homma has a secure spot in the cosmos of photog-raphy in Japan. Unfettered by excess, the economy of Homma's working environment seems a reflection of both his photography and his approach.

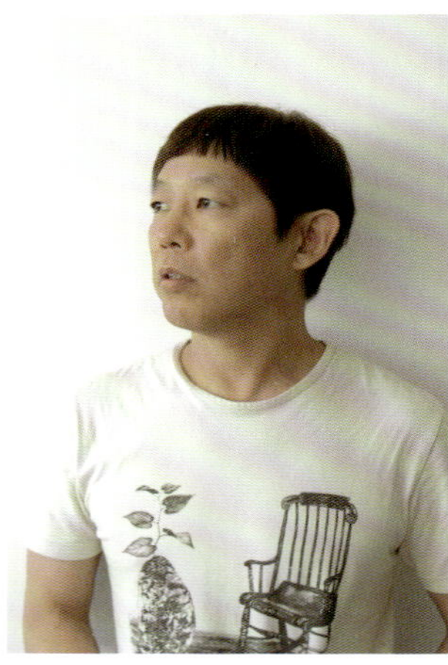

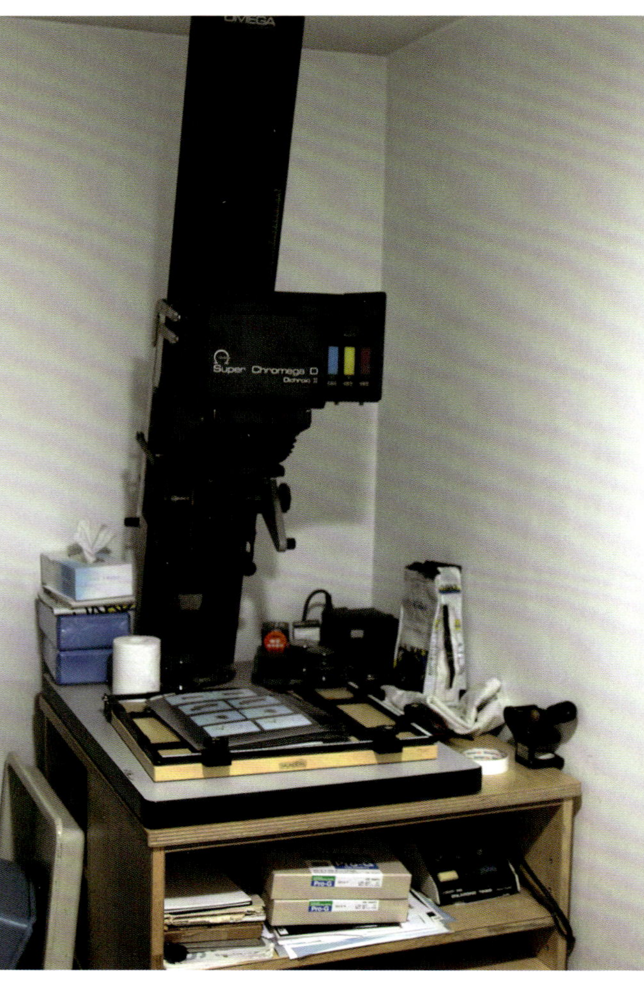

Ivan Vartanian is a writer, curator, and publisher based in Tokyo. Under the imprint Goliga, he has collaborated on and produced many projects—books, exhibitions, installations, performances, events, and limited editions—with Japanese photographers.

Vartanian is the coauthor of *Japanese Photobooks of the 1960s & '70s* (Aperture, 2009) and *Setting Sun: Writings by Japanese Photographers* (Aperture, 2006).

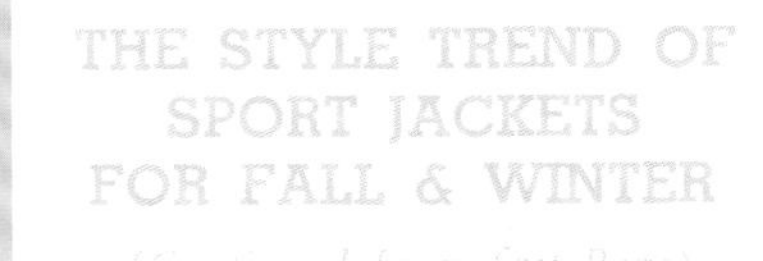

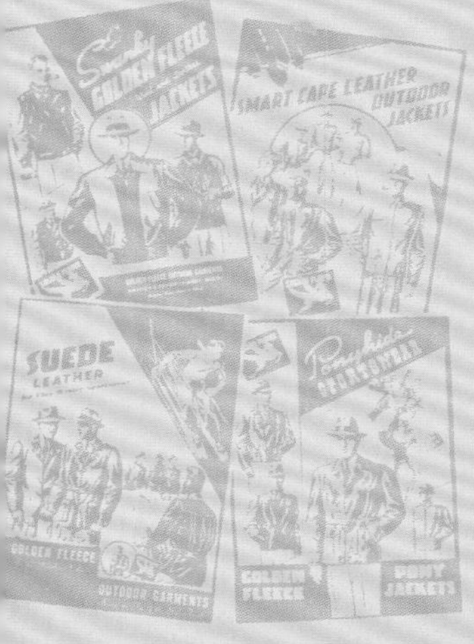

Akram Zaatari,
***Personal Audiotapes from 1981–1982*, 2007.**
C-print
Courtesy the artist and Sfeir Semler Gallery, Hamburg/Beirut
(See page 60)

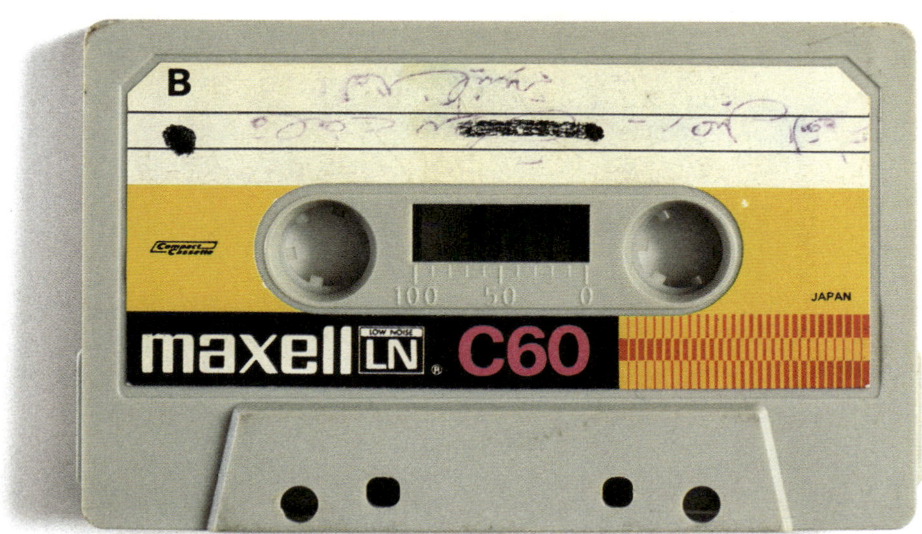

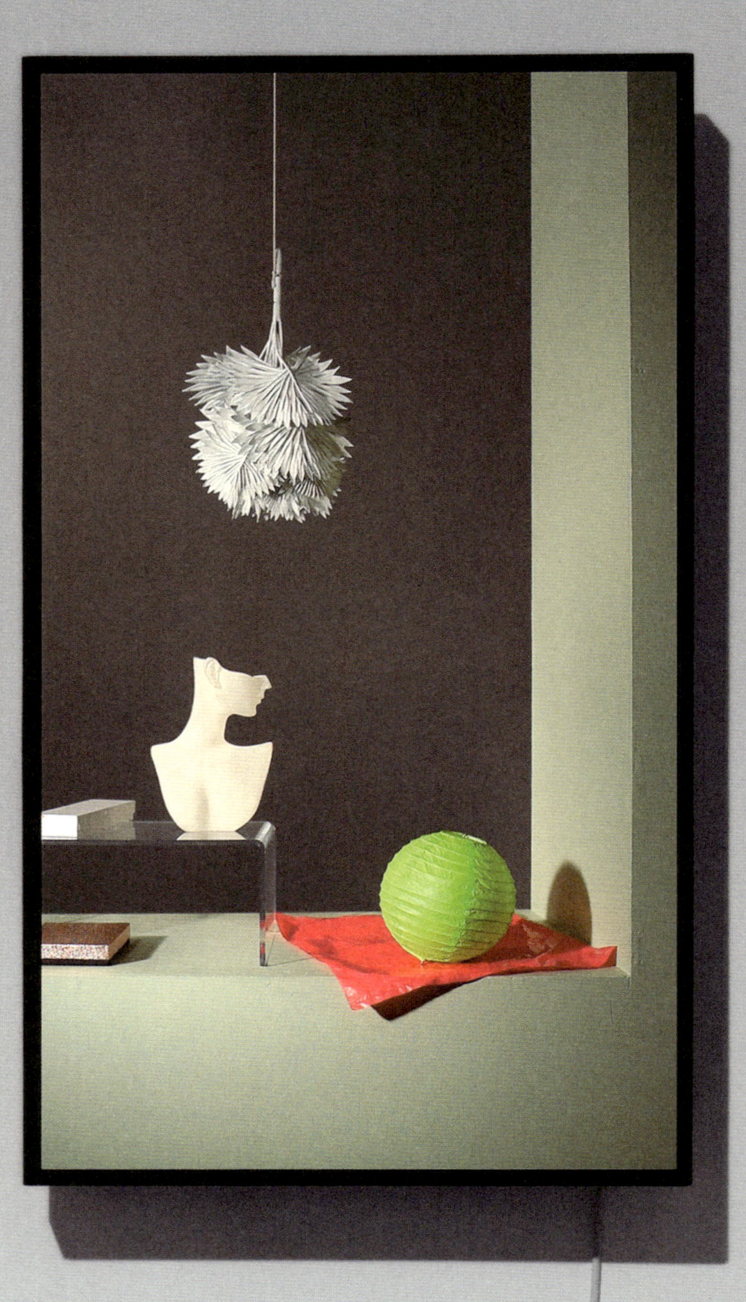

Contemporary art photographers are opening up new ways of thinking about the medium. Are institutions ready for this wave of photographic innovation?

Nine Years, A Million Conceptual Miles

Charlotte Cotton

Opposite:
Owen Kydd, *Canvas Leaves, Torso, and Lantern, August 2011*, 2011
Installation photograph by Michael Underwood
Courtesy Nicelle Beauchene Gallery, New York

It has been nine years since I wrote *The Photograph as Contemporary Art* (Thames & Hudson, 2004), my survey of photographic practice over the previous five years. The slow and cumulative battle to validate photography as contemporary art had long been won by the time we went to print. The market for photography as art—at the time this almost invariably meant Lightjet color prints laminated behind sheets of Plexiglas, at least 30 by 40 inches in size—was buoyant. With the final death throes of traditional editorial photography as a means to earn a living, there was a shift of emphasis in the realms of documentary photography and photojournalism, away from the pages of magazines and newspapers and into museums and galleries and the pages of photobooks. Few knew how digital capture or postproduction would impact independent and artistic photography. And I suspect that no one anticipated the extent to which digital dissemination would increase the number of independent photographers and the potential to self-publish. If anything, the schools of and growing market for contemporary art photography seemed content with digital photography mimicking its analog predecessors' conventions and not particularly interested in deciphering what might be uniquely digital characteristics, in either its aesthetics or its channels of dissemination.

Watching these developments, I've oscillated between feeling we are on the cusp of seeing unimaginably brilliant, liberated, and different iterations of photographic ideas in a wholesale digital world and being worried that we may be marking the cynical end of a once-central visual medium that is now being put out to a niche pasture.

My own drama over this problematic cultural paradigm doesn't stem from a sense of photographic practice per se becoming redundant in its capability for social and cultural awakening. Far from it. Instead, it comes from a genuine concern that the very mechanisms of the medium's dissemination—publishing houses, museums, commercial galleries, and art schools—that could be seen as having won the good fight to legitimize photography as a contemporary art form with its own medium-specific history are becoming part of the problem. These structures, with their gamut of agendas, unwittingly risk placing a stranglehold upon the evolution of the medium.

Below:
Kate Steciw,
***Don't worry, we will all be dead soon 1*, 2012**
Courtesy toomer labzda, New York

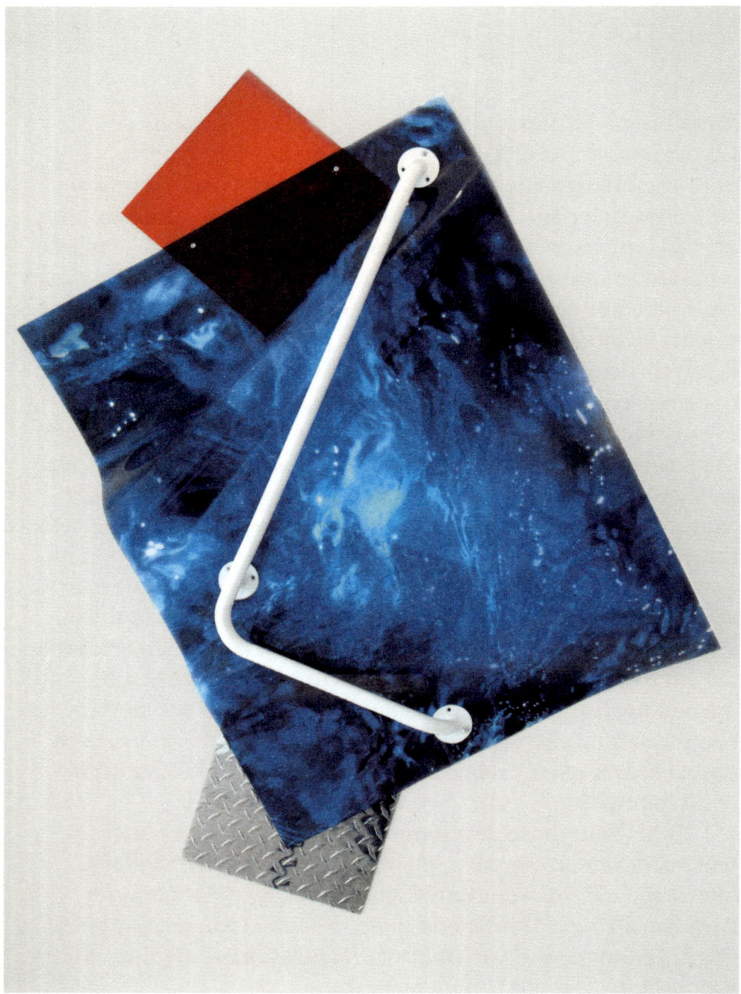

It may be stating the obvious to say that no one person—indeed, no institutional matrix—is powerful enough to hold back the momentum of creative change or its full cluster of mitigating factors. The ecosystem of image making continues to evolve, and does not require the validation of art galleries and museums. What is at stake is how the mainstream instruments of "photography as culture" can deal with the arrival of the first wave of independent photographic practice that does not look like or model itself upon the separatist story of photography that institutions have already told.

I have worked as a curator of photography in museums for most of my professional life; perhaps I should be more generous than I feel toward the cultural organizations that have attempted to engage with the newly dominant forms of photography—such as citizen journalism, visual social media, photography as activism and social practice, and collective creativity. Perhaps there is a way to blend some contemporary photography into a seamless continuum of the museological story of the medium, a story that began in the 1840s. But in my own experience, museums' engagement with contemporary photography—outside the increasingly narrow band of consciously, conventionally, unwaveringly "high art" photography—is littered with misunderstandings and meanings lost in translation, and has accomplished little to expand a cultural understanding of this beautifully complex medium.

Photography is, and has been since its conception, a fabulously broad church. Contemporary practice demonstrates that the medium can be a prompt, a process, a vehicle, a collective pursuit, and not just the physical end product of solitary artists' endeavors. Addressing that multifarious terrain is a hefty challenge for most museums and galleries, and a genuinely impossible task for those who continue to believe photography is best sliced into monographic exhibitions and sometimes into classic genres and themes. (What other medium is still exhibited so regularly in those dreadfully tired categories "landscape," "portraiture," and "still life," as per forty years ago?)

Of course it's a tough economic moment for museums and nonprofit spaces to rethink both their remit and their mode of operation. It is chancy to change rather than to go into a holding pattern, doing what you have always done for whom you have always done it, but with much less money. It is no wonder that in recessionary times such as these, galleries and museums cling hard to the work and narratives of photographers with watertight authorship, blue-chip track records of collectability, and blatant signature styles, even though the glory days of such an approach seem to be over. This would be sad but fine if it weren't for the fact that practically everything that surrounds mainstream cultural organizations engaged with photography *has* changed, and this, by extension, changes the meaning of even an unchanging enterprise.

Our attitudes to authorship, shifted massively by our common use of the Internet, confuse our understanding of where photography will fit in the cultural landscape of the future. Anyone invested in high-art photography (where authorship is king, where influences are conventionally hidden, and where reusing existing imagery is consciously acknowledged as appropriation) sees this intellectual-property amnesia of the age of the "digital native" as a problem, at least on the level of terminology. All photographic imagery circulating on the Internet is the raw material for millions of "unique" stories of (educators, hold your breath) "self-expression": found illustrations that quasi-communicate millions of people's homogenized experiences and emotions. The Internet does not adhere to the inherent, necessary asymmetry of high-versus-low-art categorizations that we use in the cultural sector: in a

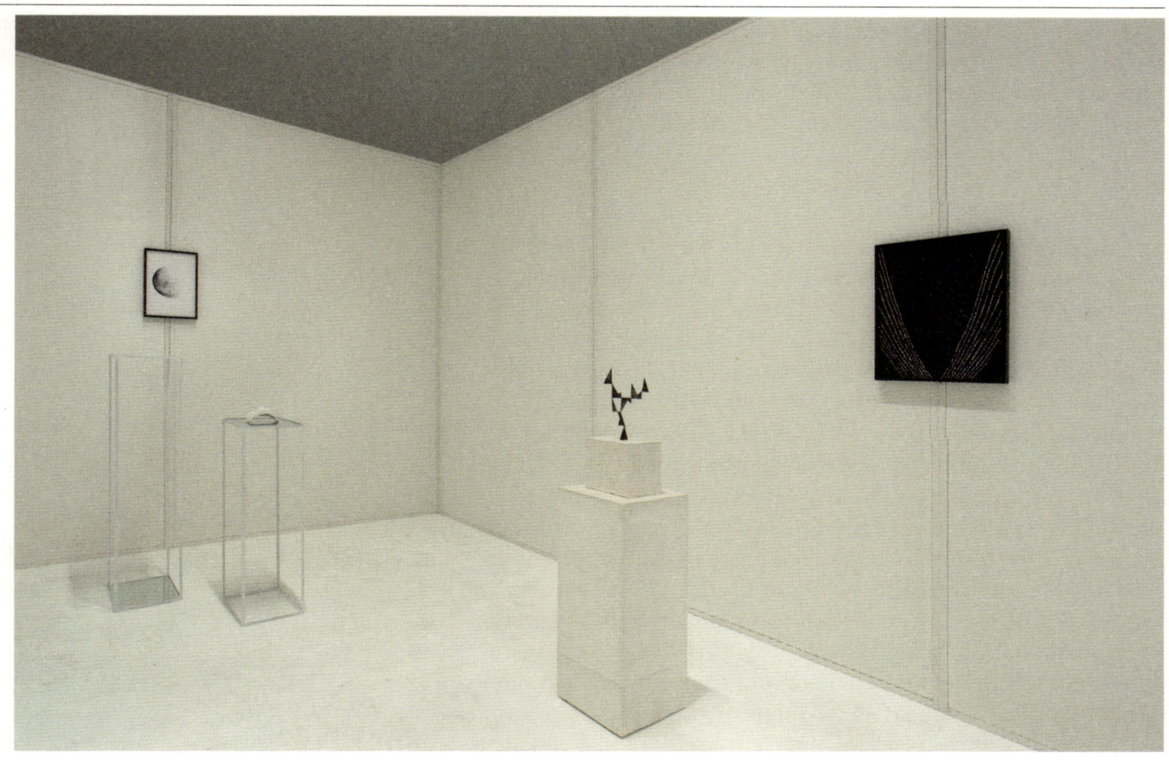

***Hammer Projects: Sara VanDerBeek.* Installation view of the Hammer Museum, Los Angeles, 2011–12.**
Photograph by Brian Forrest
Courtesy Hammer Museum, Los Angeles

Photography is, and has been since its conception, a fabulously broad church. Contemporary practice demonstrates that the medium can be a prompt, a process, a vehicle, a collective pursuit, and not just the physical end product of solitary artists' endeavors.

banal sense, all photographs on the Web are orphans ready to be claimed.

We are not only a civilization of amateur photographers; we are amateur curators, editors, and publishers. Some of the new amateurs are pretty noble—like the citizen journalists who put in serious hours of work and comprehend so thoroughly the intelligent capacities of our pervasive image-led technologies. And just as this pro/am (professional/amateur) school of journalism seems to be a counterpoint to the ever-decreasing realm of independent news media, we at least have to think through the groundswell of pro/am photographic artists who self-publish, collectivize, and find their audiences themselves, knowing full well that the professional infrastructure for art photography is never going to accommodate them during their productive lifetimes.

And what really is the difference between a serious amateur who is disciplined enough to use his or her nonprofessional hours to create independent photography (subsidized by first and second jobs) and the economic reality for most artists who are not among the handful of well-known names whose practice is underwritten by sales? On an individual level, I'd guess the main difference is a debt of somewhere in the region of sixty to eighty thousand dollars, built up during the span of an MFA program. Of course there is a handsome number of MFA photography graduates who have made good use of their education to store up a degree of criticality and experience that will nourish them throughout their creative lives. But there is an underlying conservatism that graduates have to wrestle with when considering how such an expensive education will literally pay off. It's a risk to propose new forms of photographic art to a market that took almost ten years to feel comfortable with the idea of pigment prints. And it is the same pressure for postgraduates entering curatorial work—except they have to deal with curating being a newly fashionable lifestyle choice (see J.Crew's "curator pants" for starters).

I don't think it's good for anyone if the new professionals of curating distinguish themselves from pro/am lifestylers, stylists, picture editors, artist-curators, and even their more enlightened professional predecessors by aligning themselves with photographers who produce splendid, unmistakably "high-art" spectacles. It's like a generation of photography curators not being allowed to wage their battle to expand the notion of photography as a subject and potentially to win new terrain within cultural discourses for the medium.

•

Still, within this mercurial climate, I see something magical beginning to happen: a critical mass of contemporary art photographers whose clarity and sentience to the image-making epoch in which we live transcend all the blockages I've outlined. It's a critical mass rather than a grouping because, mercifully, the ways in which they open up the *subject* of photography are diverse. Some of these image creators have found their footing in the haptic and social era of photography; they make works that think through how new technologies feed into the analog-framed discourses of photography as contemporary art. Invariably these digital-native photographers experiment across platforms: the gallery context is one of several; there are also online formats, and traditional and e-publishing. This latest generation of practitioners is distinctly high-versus-low agnostic while being meticulous about the meaning and values of photographic language in its different contexts, and cognizant of the variance in the types of engagement that these different sites create with an audience.

Other contemporary art photographers that are giving cause for robust hope began their relationship with photography through analog thinking and processes, marveling at the prospect of photography as an expanding field while perhaps more acutely treasuring the sensory pleasure of traditional photographic prints for their pronounced craftsmanship and authorship. Contemporary art photographers are the only full-time creators of photography who labor over the production of photographic prints destined only for the spaces of art galleries and museums. Photography's materials (straddling analog and digital technologies) have never been more readily understood by artists or audiences as a series of conscious choices.

At its most literal, contemporary art photography is beautifully dialogical. Photography is the central subject within photography as an artistic medium, an entity best understood *in relation* to a host of mitigating factors, from its quotidian cousins in social image-making to the elder statesmen of highbrow art—especially painting and sculpture but also installation arts, including video.

For instance, Carter Mull's floor-based installation of scattered prints *Connection* (2011–12) offers a deeply visceral experience of photography that combines a heritage of conceptual-art references with a very contemporary meditation upon the state of the mediated photographic image. *Connection* places us in a space that fuses the dissemination and production methods of photographic imagery. The installation takes into account the permeation of imagery on the pages of the declining empires of print media, and our promiscuous capturing of transitory visual experience via mobile devices—specifically the iPhone. *Connection* encourages us to take stock of both the plethora of contemporary imagery and its impact on our consciousness, while showing our disregard as we tread on its physical detritus. It is an experience that could only be so abstracted and pinpointed in the rarefied context of a contemporary art gallery and through the authorial voice of the artist.

The relationship between photography and sculpture has perhaps been the most imposing signature of contemporary photography of the twenty-first century so far. About a decade ago, Sara VanDerBeek made a significant contribution to the art-world celebration of photography's materiality with gorgeous

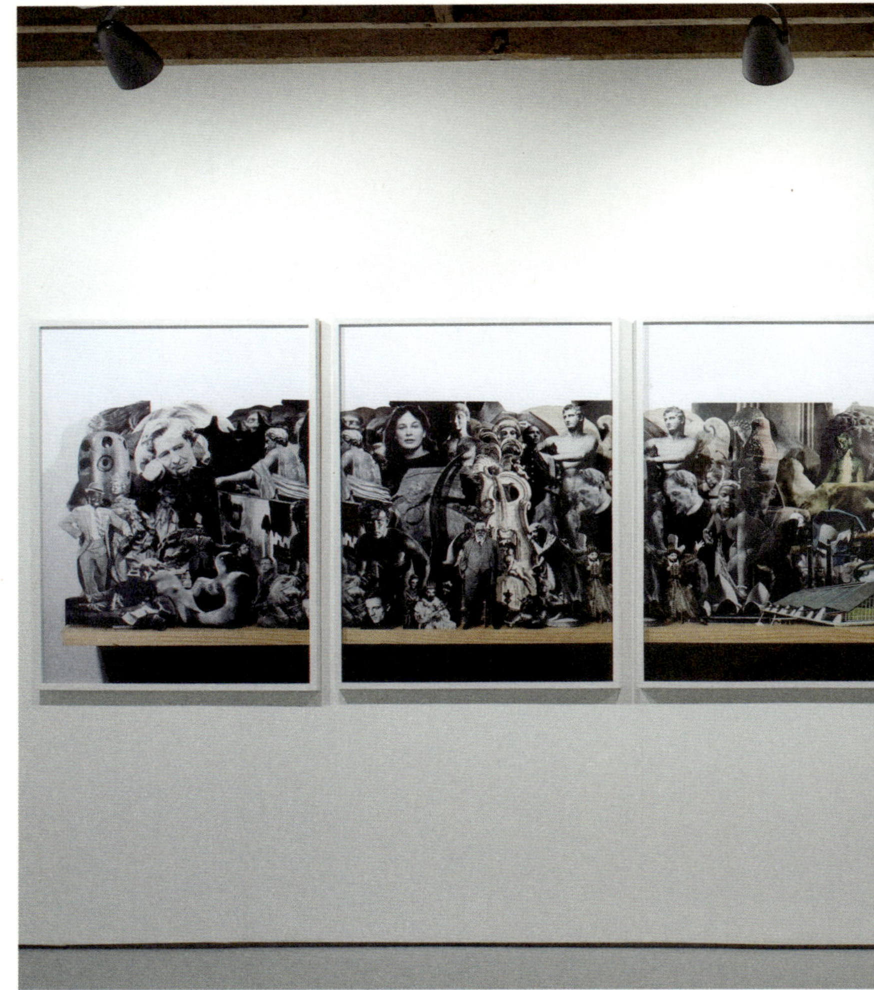

Matt Lipps, *Untitled (Horizon Archive)*, 2010
Courtesy the artist and Josh Lilley Gallery, London

The Internet does not adhere to the inherent, necessary asymmetry of high-versus-low-art categorizations that we use in the cultural sector: in a banal sense, all photographs on the Web are orphans ready to be claimed.

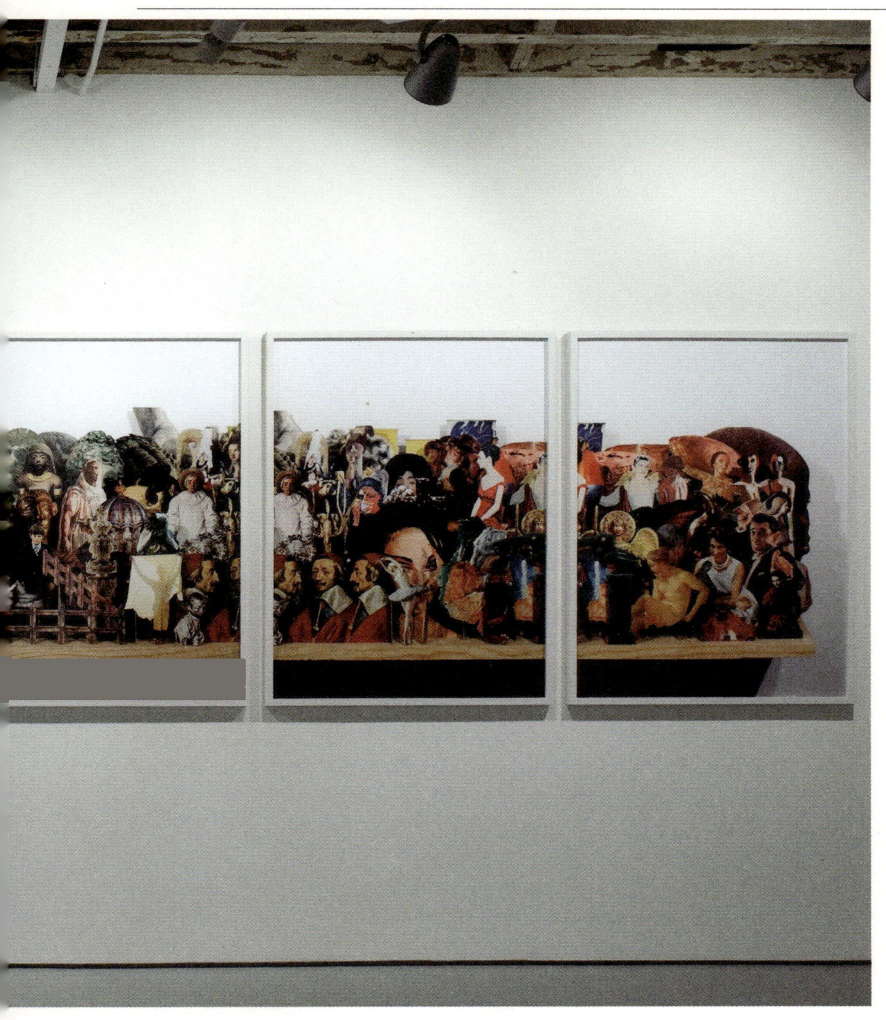

It is so *unreconstructed* of him! His most ambitious work so far is the six-panel *Untitled (Horizon Archive)* (2010), in which a huge cast of real-life and art-historical characters are lined up for an imaginary photo-call. With the theatrical use of lighting, Lipps re-animates these orphaned images into his own story construction—in a way that brings to mind the compiling and connecting of the best Tumblr "curators," but with more gorgeous photographic drama.

Lipps's work is not unconnected to the mesmerizing strangeness in the composite work of Daniel Gordon and also the videos of Brian Bress. The three share a knowing originality in the ways they physically rework the mass of image production, mediation, and crass default settings to create works that function in high-art settings. For me, this mode of taking the essence, rather than the aesthetic, of default lowbrow photographic imagery into the art world feels like the planting of intellectual incendiary devices that at some point are going to explode the conventional ideas of where photography can be positioned in contemporary art.

The manner in which future generations of image makers will configure the idea of photography as contemporary art can be as seemingly effortless and open to the happenstance of photographic observation as ever. Jason Evans's recent installations, including the one at the 2012 Krakow Photomonth, set up a joyous binary dance between photography and sculpture by coupling sculptural arrangements of objects on plinths with photographic posters of still-life arrangements pinned to gallery walls. Evans's photographs of lyrical still lifes are titled *Pictures for Looking At* (2007–11) and his plinth-based sculptural arrangements of mass-produced, handmade, and found objects are titled *Sculptures for Photography* (2012), delightfully inviting us to perceive these constructions as photographs just waiting to happen.

photographs of her handmade sculptures. With her recent installations (including her 2011–12 commission for the Hammer Museum in Los Angeles) she breaks important new ground. Every element of VanDerBeek's Hammer installation was clearly an intricate web of finely crafted acts and artistic decisions that rendered a tangible sense of the photographic. Small, framed black-and-white photographs (a portrait, a still life, a lunar image) seemed pronounced in their material perfection; sculptural pieces incorporated found objects, including bird feathers and a beaded curtain. The elements on display prompted the curiosity of looking that has driven the history of observational photography. Each framing device, from the exterior walls of the installation to the sculptural frames and supports within the space, reiterated the construction of classical photographic vantage points.

Much of the production of digital video art by photographers in the past five years does not go beyond an explorative sketching out of ideas, but in some cases we are starting to see important artistic proposals for how the "photographic" can credibly be explored through video. Owen Kydd creates short, fixed-shot video works that are also meditations upon the notion of the photographic. In what he calls "durational photographs," Kydd sets up a dynamic for the viewer to search in his thirty- or forty-second videos for the photographic moment, anticipating the single, decisive observation. We forget the distinction between our own looking (for a determined length of time, given the seamless looping of the video imagery) and the durational and endlessly repeating video recording of a now-past moment.

We also see a confident use of the photographic frame, holding and condensing an impossibly large amount of visual information. I enjoy the way Matt Lipps literally cuts and pastes imagery, principally from mid-twentieth-century magazines and books, and carefully creates sculptural photomontages.

•

It is clear that we are a million conceptual miles from where we were even nine years ago—when there was a pernicious idea that photography had to adopt the values, traditions, and rhetoric of other art forms and simultaneously deny its own broad lexicon of dynamic and quotidian meaning in order to have credibility. I look at the work of photographers such as Artie Vierkant and Kate Steciw, as well as that of Asha Schechter and Lucas Blalock, for instance, and get a mighty rush of excitement about photography's bright new future. I find myself struggling to find the words to discuss their work—though I am neither short of opinions nor inexperienced at looking at new photography. My stumbling block is this: for the first time in my professional life, I am seeing independent photography that doesn't operate in a conventional art-photography way… and I don't know how to position *myself*. It is beyond the discourse that I know, and I experience this as a really positive expectation for the field of photography as art. This is why I think that those of us who have a genuine vested interest in the future of photography as contemporary art should open our doors and just let this new life come in.

Charlotte Cotton is a curator and writer. Among the positions she has held are director of the Wallis Annenberg Department of Photographs at the Los Angeles County Museum of Art and curator of photographs at the Victoria and Albert Museum in London. Cotton is the author of *The Photograph as Contemporary Art* (2004) and founder of Words Without Pictures (2008–9) and Eitherand.org (2012).

↞ *Words Without Pictures* was published as a print and ebook by Aperture in 2010.

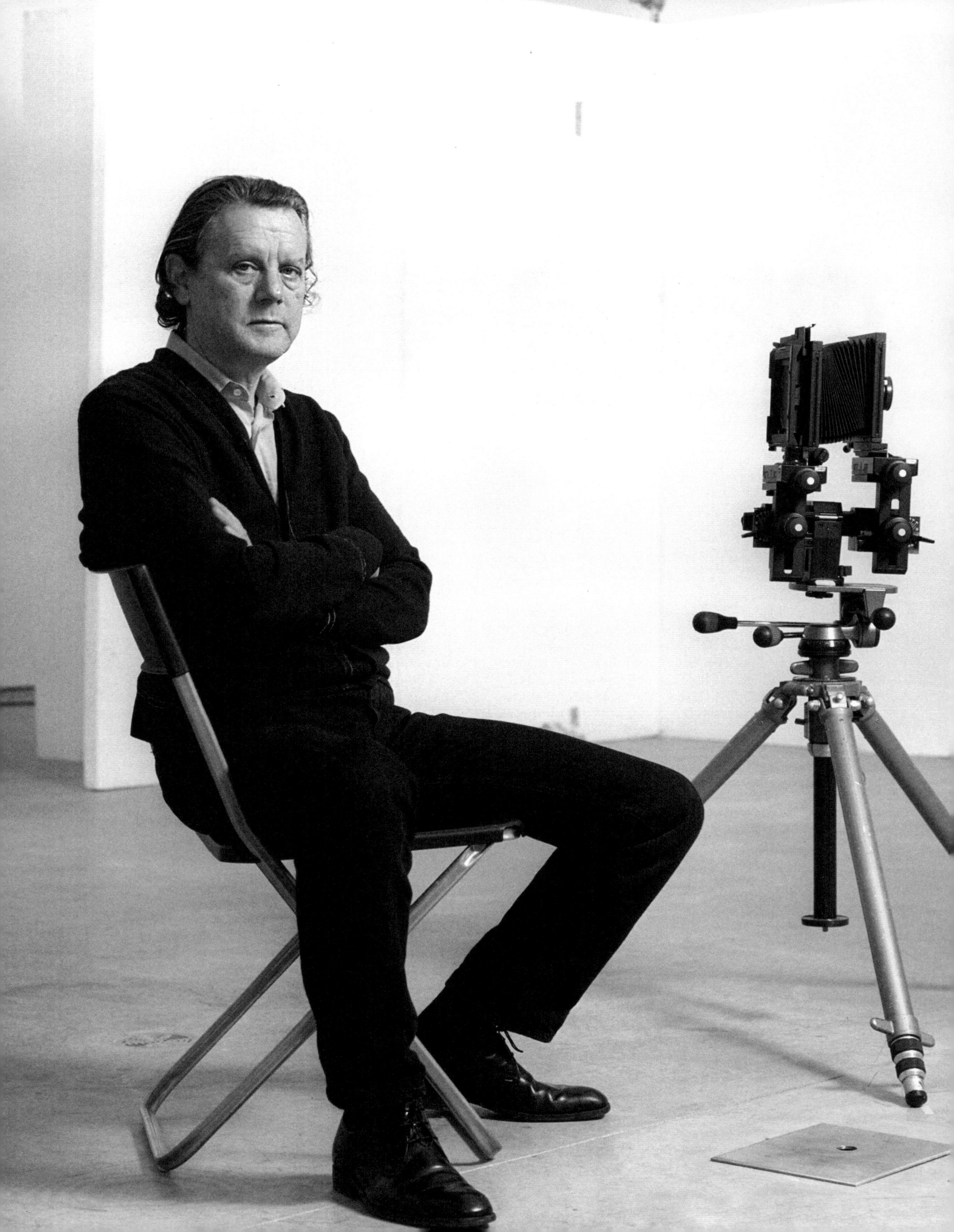

Jeff Wall's photographic work made over four decades has opened up the parameters of the medium to issues long understood to be outside its provenance. At the same time, his prolific writing has been an important factor in the development of a much-needed critical vocabulary. Wall's contributions in both arenas provide conceptual underpinnings for contemporary artists. He requires photography to do the work of reflecting not only the world, but also the terms of that engagement. And his explicit relationships to both painting and film have opened new paths of understanding photography's possibilities and place in the world. Wall makes use of a form of "cinematography" to pry photography from the narrow confines of technique and definition. His coinage *phantom studio* proposes that any given location can be imbued with the intentionality of the studio. These concepts and others have shaped the way we think about photography. In the conversation below, Wall speaks with Lucas Blalock about the current state of the medium, his recent work, and the freedom of the artist.

Jeff Wall: On Pictures
Conversation with Lucas Blalock

Lucas Blalock: **Considering the changes that photography has undergone in the past decade, how might we consider it as a "medium" in its current situation? I mean here not the physical support, but the set of conventions or historical uses that act as a ground, making the decisions of the photographer legible.**

Jeff Wall: I cling to the notion of photography as a medium insofar as it is an authentic way to achieve what we can call "the picture." The physical nature of any medium has never been free from the conventional—and therefore historical—manners in which the physical elements have been handled. So I don't feel there is anything particularly new happening in photography in that regard.

LB: **You have written about the idea of "emphatic picture making," which I think provides a compelling structure for thinking about photography. Could you talk about what you mean by this idea of the "emphatic"?**

JW: "Emphatic picture making" is a phrase that I think expresses how photography can be free just to be an art form. Sculpture, painting, drawing, and the other older visual arts freed themselves this way a long time ago, but photography is still tied up with the practicalities of image production, and it's hard for a lot of people working with it to achieve some sort of distance from that almost overpowering identity.

Opposite:
Photograph of Jeff Wall by Greg Girard, October 2012

Still from Rainer Werner Fassbinder's 1981 film *Lola*. Shown: Armin Mueller-Stahl, Barbara Sukowa
United Artists/Photofest

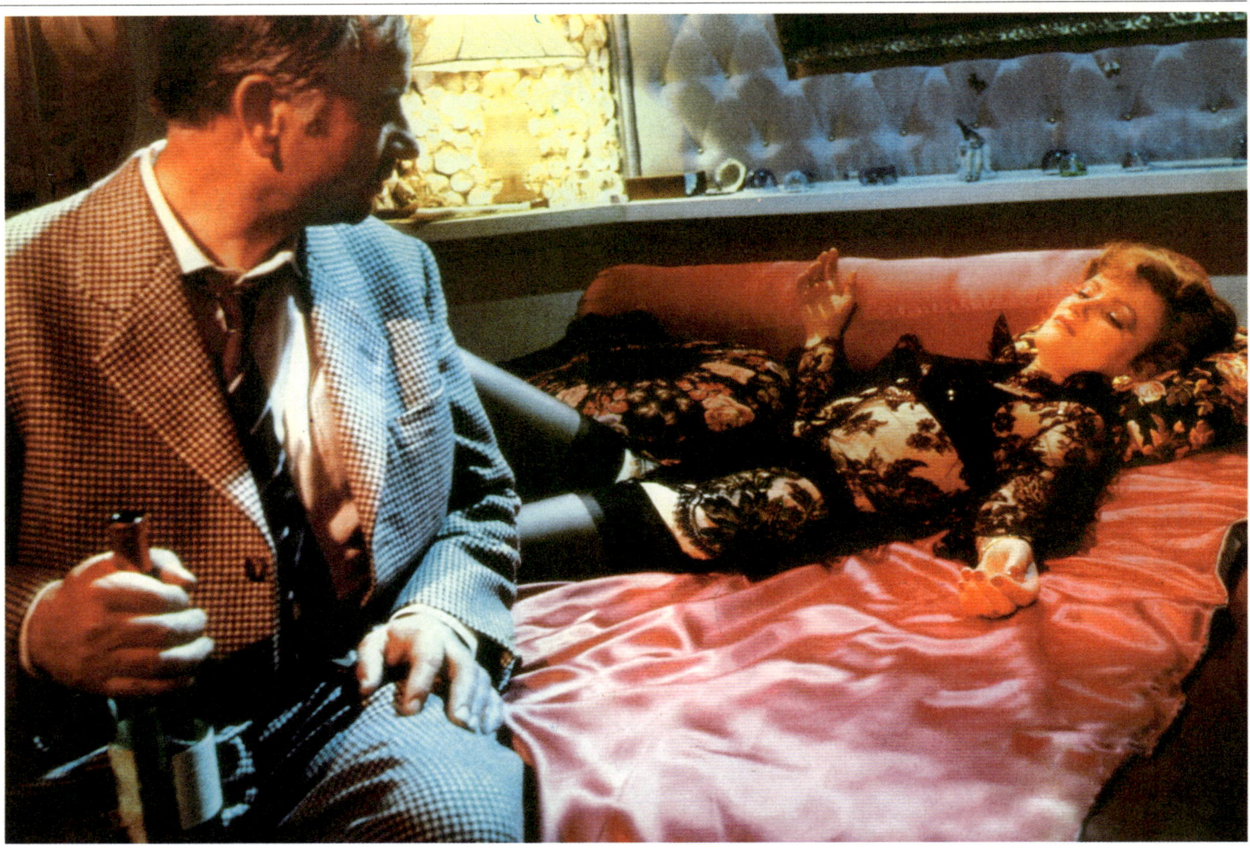

I've been criticized over the years for the perceived artificiality of some (or even most) of my pictures, for their apparently unwarranted, overcooked, and roundabout relation to the actualities of life—things that can be addressed much more immediately by remaining "true to the nature of photography." But I like photographs that don't look altogether the way photographs are supposed to look. We don't really know how photographs are "supposed to look." The existing conventions make it seem that we do, because they are authentic and central to photography, but they cannot predict what the next interesting photograph is going to look like. Nobody claims to be able to predict what the next good painting will look like.

I like photographs that don't look altogether the way photographs are supposed to look. We don't really know how photographs are "supposed to look."

LB: **Lately we have seen the reemergence of a more literal "studio picture," and the photographer's studio itself as the site of looking and picturing. The studio is being used by some artists for its particular conventional attributes: as a site with a specific history and the possibility of a kind of play on genre images (still lifes, commercial pictures, and so on). Do you find the work of artists like Christopher Williams, Roe Ethridge, or Michele Abeles to be in dialogue with your own thoughts on making studio pictures in the 1970s, or related to your "phantom studio" work of the past few years?**

JW: A studio is a set of relationships, not so much a specific kind of interior—it doesn't have to be an interior at all. But it can manifest in the kind of workspace that's traditionally been used as a studio by photographers, or painters, or sculptors. There is no reason to view that kind of workroom as obsolete, as it seemed to be a few years ago, when everyone was excited about "post-studio art."

Today the studio is not thought of in the binary, polarized sense that tended to prevail in the period when documentary-type photography was the norm, when the studio was defined as an artificial environment somehow not part of the real life that real photographers hunted and captured. That polarity was affected by the cinema of the 1960s, '70s, '80s—filmmakers such as Rainer Werner Fassbinder, Jean-Luc Godard, Pier Paolo Pasolini, and Ingmar Bergman could move from extreme artifice to moments of apparent documentary immediacy within a few seconds. Now we recognize the studio as a site of actuality no different in principle from any other site.

LB: **In your 1993 essay on the Japanese artist On Kawara, you talk about how, in painting, the attraction to "lower"-genre pictures in the early modern era was understood as a movement toward the freest space, that these kinds of pictures are particularly good at "permitting a picture to be seen as a picture." Can we look at contemporary photographic practice through a parallel lens? Do you think that there is a certain kind of work that these minor-genre pictures are particularly suited for?**

JW: As photography becomes more and more familiar with itself as high art, and in some sense begins to be absorbed into the whole idea—the institution—of high art, photographers seem to be able to go through the same sorts of dialectics that painters and sculptors went through in the past century. In the nineteenth and twentieth centuries, "lower"-genre pictures were less constrained by the social and cultural ambitions that were woven into the structure of the higher types, so they became a less-delineated space in which a process of experimentation took place. Photographers were aware of this, and to some extent responded to it. But since there were no real "high" genres of photography back then, there wasn't the intensity of engagement that there was in painting. Maybe now that there are apparently high genres in photography, the situation has evolved to the point at which it is possible to respond to their presence by moving away from them and, to an interesting degree, repeating aspects of what happened in painting a hundred or more years ago.

But it looks like people are trying to extend the sense of what permits a *something* to be seen as a picture—that is, with an ambition to matter in terms of proposing what a picture is at its most significant level. Younger artists (and some older ones, too) seem to be testing out this dialectic of higher and lower genres. The engagement with what have often been seen as trivial and compromised studio types—like the still life that started out as a commercial product photograph—seem to have to do with finding those little voids in the canon that can still disturb the consensus of what is worth bothering to photograph in the first place. This whole direction is really complex and sophisticated, and has been an undercurrent throughout the history of modernism. It became "problematic" when product photography had evolved to the point where, vampirically, it almost destroyed the genre of still life, in the 1920s.

LB: **Interestingly, the same period saw the rise of commodity culture, which was arguably made possible by the cheap circulation of photographic images. I wonder if this is in part because objects again have a central role in this stage of capitalism, a role that will eventually be subsumed by the abstract strategies of brands and identity marketing. And, in an increasingly digital environment, commodity objecthood—once seen as a tremendous abstraction and mode of distancing from the world—can now be seen instead as a *connective* possibility.**

In the digital age, images are infinitely transferable, editable, and contiguous with their surroundings. They relate as much to the bodiless virtual archive as to the "having-been-seen" of the camera's subject. To me, this is a new problem for a picture.

Top:
Jeff Wall, *Passerby*, 1996
Courtesy the artist

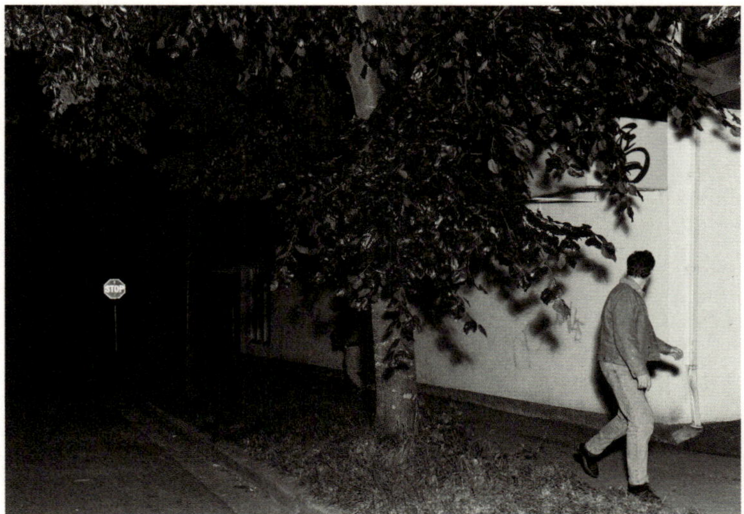

Bottom:
Roe Ethridge, *Pigeon*, 2001
Courtesy the artist and Andrew Kreps Gallery, New York

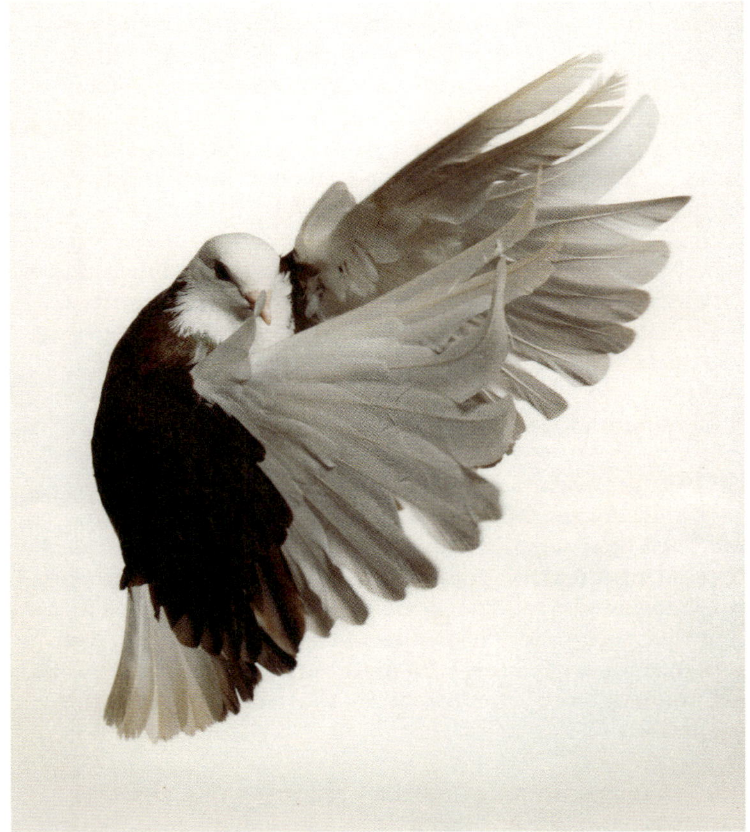

JW: That's interesting—the idea that the network of electronic image traffic has become present in the relation between the photographer and the picture he or she sees in a viewfinder. But I think that that is true if you want it to be, not in itself. Because image traffic has become so heavy and so continuous, it now seems as if these millions of images came into being by themselves, without the agency of a person. And in a certain percentage of them, it's true, because a lot of images are now made robotically and circulated automatically.

But that is more about the experience of seeing images than of making them. Artists have been fascinated by the notion of imitating a robot since the emergence of machines. But it is a willful imitation, an individual decision, not caused by the nature of the economy or technology. This is a good moment to look once again at the old idea of artistic freedom. In this context, artistic freedom means the awareness that as an artist you can choose your relation to the technologies; none is imposed on you the way it would be if you were an operative in an automated image-generating system of some kind. You cannot point to any institution that requires this or that behavior from you—art can be anything now.

Your own pictures, Lucas, show a sort of angst about this disembodiment—there's an almost expressionistic aspect to the rough handling of the digital information. That does make them resemble paintings or prints ... and you're aware of this and very into it. You could say that your angst is your take on a social condition, and you'd be right about that. But there's no social necessity to respond to social conditions artistically this way or that. There are no rules for this, so another artist could just as legitimately respond in a very different manner. All we have to compare between them are the results. And your results can be art of the highest quality, and mine, which could come from a completely different and even dissenting take on the same social material, could also and simultaneously be art of the highest quality, and both could be in touch with some true state of that same social material at the same time, but other to each other. So, to answer your question "Is this disembodiment a new problem for the picture?"—yes, it is a new problem if you need it to be one. If you need to ignore it and pretend it isn't happening, you might get laughed at socially, but there's no way to claim that that, probably childish and neurotic, act cannot lead to something artistically significant and first-rate.

LB: **I want to ask about a shift I have felt more generally in the last decade from a discussion about photography modeled on cinematic tropes to one that is ostensibly based in painting. I feel like your work has long been a bridge across these two models and am curious to know if you have felt that this realignment has impacted your practice. You have said that some of your recent pictures were made in a "more pronounced" way, and I wonder if that might relate to this discussion.**

JW: The relationship of photography to cinema and painting has always been the important thing for me. If it is just painting, then you fall into the situation that's been so constantly criticized over the decades—that you are betraying this medium in the name of another one. If it's cinema, you're relegated to being commentary on the more complex results of another medium that therefore seems more powerful, and predominant, than it really is. It could be that at the moment artists are drifting further in the direction of the painter's studio and métier, away from either cinematography or the documentary style. But there is a wide band where you're in touch with all three elements even if you're tending toward one or another pole.

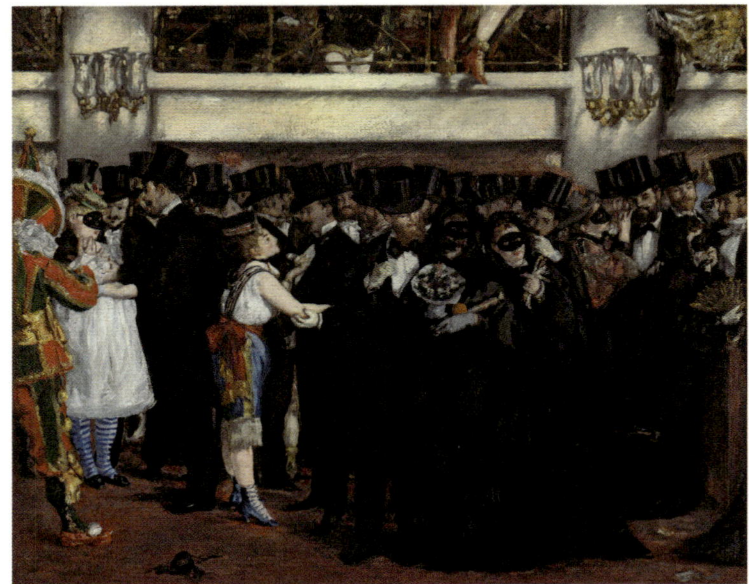

Édouard Manet, *Masked Ball at the Opera*, 1873
Oil on canvas
Courtesy National Gallery of Art, Washington, D.C.

It looks like people are trying to extend the sense of what permits a *something* to be seen as a picture—that is, with an ambition to matter in terms of proposing what a picture is, at its most significant level.

My take on it has been that photography as art is constituted by this complex interrelationship between the documentary root, the cinematographic, and the kinship with the other, manual, depictive arts. This is a very large and high-energy entity; it's not swamped by the vast "social" identity of photography—I mean, the aspects that aren't art. It is almost magnetically attracted to them, because they aren't art. As we know, art needs non-art in order to recognize itself. So I'm not aware of realignment because I feel that the domain is so large and internally various that one can shift this way and that and not really go anywhere radically different. I spent quite a bit of time over the past ten years or so exploring a kind of "near-documentary" picture, one that resembled snapshots or documentary photos. That was something I really wanted to do consistently, for a lot of reasons—the main one being to find out what that kind of picture actually looked like. And now more recently I've felt the need to diverge from that and try to make pictures that are more emphatically pictorial. I'm tired of struggling with a certain kind of problem, but the result of that struggle is that I find myself in a different spot, with a different relation to "near documentary."

LB: **That reminds me of Garry Winogrand's remark that he made photographs "to see what things looked like photographed." Although I think that the character of Winogrand's statement actually has a very different inflection. To make pictures that make a *something*—the thing pictured—be seen not only as itself but as a picture of itself sets up a certain kind of problem.**

JW: A few years ago I wrote a short essay on Édouard Manet's 1873 painting *Masked Ball at the Opera*. I noticed it seemed that Manet created a particular amount of space between his own position and the large group of people at the masked ball. That gap could easily have occurred in real life—anything can occur—but, still, what he did was interesting. I thought he insinuated into the social event he was depicting the kind of space that would almost naturally exist between a painter and a model in a studio situation. He created a subtle bracketing of the immediacy of what he was depicting by stepping back ever so slightly. He could not deny himself the excitement of making the most complex event hover with a very slight sense of suspension, in the form of the tableau—that form that can absorb and arrest any and every event once it becomes a picture.

I find this pictorial structure itself so suggestive and rich because it transforms the thing it depicts in the process of depicting it, of recording it. The "motif," the thing depicted, comes to life not because of its own liveliness—even though it has that, too—but because of the way it almost vanishes into the tableau. The tableau-form, like a magic substance, both records with great fidelity and transforms the thing to which it is being true into another thing: a picture.

LB: **You have used the term *occultation* in connection to similar ideas, and I'd like to get at the relationship between the "occulted" picture and the notion of immediacy. Please correct me if I'm wrong, but the immediate here is a presentation of the world that tries to suppress its qualities as a *picture*. The advertising image or the swimsuit photo might be good examples; an image depicting the seamlessness of technology might be another. I want to press this question of immediacy because it is potentially a defining characteristic of our time. I feel like, from this vantage, the dull, the boring, and the unspectacular have in turn been imbued with a lot of promise.**

JW: *Occultation* was a term used by André Breton, I think in the *Second Manifesto of Surrealism* in 1929. He meant it partly in the sense of getting serious about the turn to myth and esotericism. But there was also a side of it that had to do with moving artistic work away from direct engagement with public matters and with "the public" as such in favor of a radical idea of artistic experiment, but also of artistic seriousness. Art that took into account the expectations of the public and of the existing domain of convention and taste was seen as compromised and kitsch. This attitude originated before Breton, with the Romantic and Symbolist poets, and it carried over into the New York School and the attitude toward seriousness and "high art." It's part of a long, and I hope still meaningful, tradition or lineage that expects art to dissent from conventional artistic taste at any given time, for all the well-known reasons, and to dispense with the idea that it is necessary to be popular in any way to be significant and even to be successful.

I have tried to practice photography in intense empathy with that, though not always in the same way. There is no one kind of "serious" art. Fassbinder's work is "occultish" to me even though he parodied and pastiched popular genres and styles. It's the way he did his pastiche that gives his films their occulted feeling. It might not be something you can point to precisely and identify but it is there. On the other hand, Mark Rothko's paintings are examples of the grand style of occultation. They are "classic," where Fassbinder is "mannerist," but both are great—and they are akin somehow because they are great. In both you are looking at something that never occurred, did not exist, but has been made visible nevertheless. There is therefore a feeling of emanation, of something surfacing; the surface is coming into being, into visibility, not as a response to an existing surface, a social surface. And when a *something* surfaces as a picture, it can't be dull or boring—no matter the subject.

Jeff Wall's photographs have been exhibited internationally, and his critical writings have been widely published. The most recent of Wall's retrospective exhibitions was presented at the Museum of Modern Art, New York, in 2007. He has received many prizes, including the Hasselblad Award for photography in 2002. He is based in Vancouver.

Lucas Blalock is a photographer and writer who lives and works in Los Angeles.

With billions of networked images flowing through social media, how can we understand what photography looks like today?

Observing by Watching: Joachim Schmid and the Art of Exchange

Geoffrey Batchen

It is surely telling that in the same month—January 2012—Eastman Kodak declared bankruptcy and Facebook, the world's largest online social-network site, moved toward becoming a publicly traded company valued at $100 billion. The following April, Facebook spent one of those billions acquiring Instagram, a startup offering mobile apps that let people add quirky effects to their smartphone snapshots and share them with friends.

The inference could not be clearer: social media has triumphed over mere media, or at least over the photographic medium as we once knew it. But what is the nature of the social in digital image-sharing sites? And what about the nature of photography itself? Has it too become bankrupt, reduced to no more than a vehicle for conveying sentimental platitudes? Or does it continue more or less as it always has, banal or fascinating according to the prejudices or interests of each viewer, avoiding its own obsolescence through yet another one of its strategic technical transformations?

Everyone concedes that photography is now a medium of exchange as much as a mode of documentation. Able to be instantly disseminated around the globe, a digital snapshot initially functions as a message in the present ("Hey, I'm here *right now*, looking at this") rather than only as a record of some past moment. This kind of photograph is meant primarily as a means of communication, and the images being sent are almost as ephemeral as speech, so rarely are they printed and made physical. As Michael Kimmelman once put it in the *New York Times*, photographing has become "the visual equivalent of cellphone chatter." That chatter demands a different kind of body language than in the past, with arm outstretched and photographer looking *at*, rather than through, the camera. Contemporary photographers gaze at a little video screen and decide when to still (or not) the moving flow of potential images seen there. In operating that camera, they enact a sort of cultural convergence, in which the distinction between production and reception, and between moving and still images, has clouded. Danish scholar Mette Sandbye has proposed we consider this convergence a "signaletic" one, such that the "that-has-been" temporality of photography once described by Roland Barthes has been replaced with a "what-is-going-on," a sharing of an immediacy of presence.

That said, the sheer number of photographic images being loaded onto social-media sites makes any analysis of the phenomenon difficult. Facebook has reported that more than three hundred million photographs are uploaded onto its site every day, meaning that the site currently hosts more than 140 billion images. That makes Facebook about forty-six times more photographic than Flickr, the next largest depository. Established in February 2004 by a Vancouver-based company, Flickr reportedly gains about 4,500 new photographs every minute (so nearly 6.5 million a day), mostly gathered into the electronic equivalent of personal photo-albums. Nevertheless, even the White House releases its official photographs there. And it's just one of a number of such sites (the oldest, South Korea's Cyworld, has boasted that at one stage 37 percent of the South Korean population had an account). How can anyone examine a representative sample of contemporary photographic practice in the face of such overwhelming statistics?

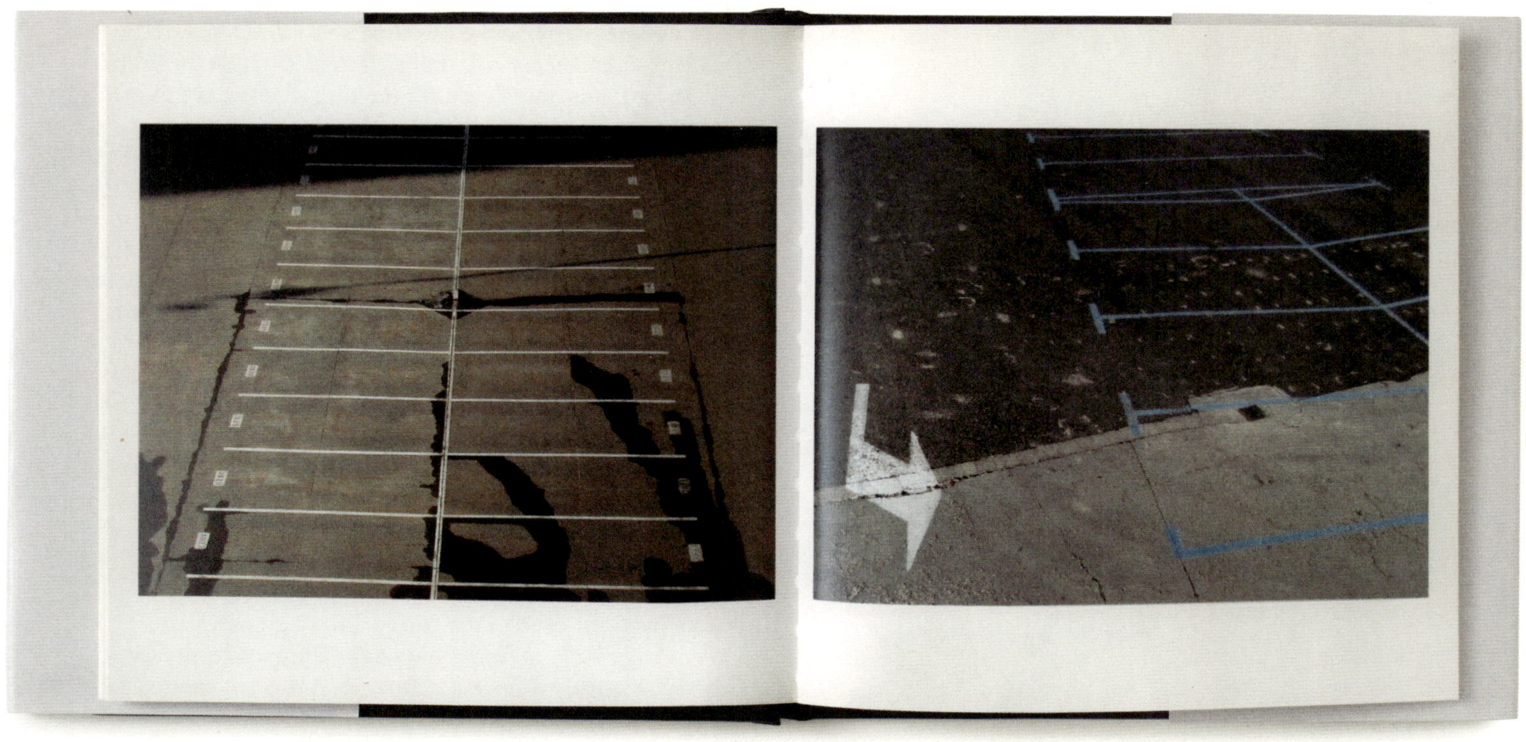

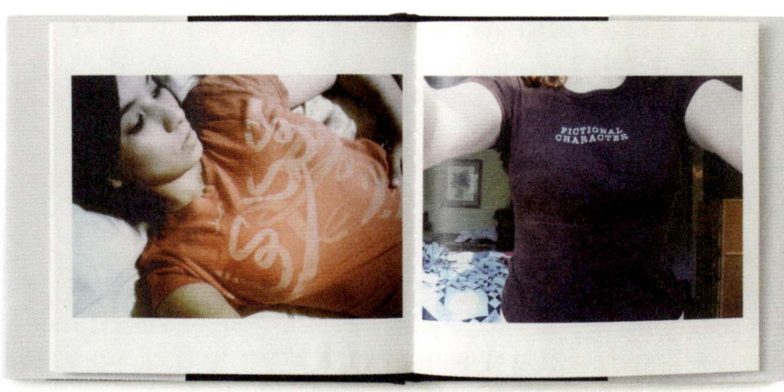

As it happens, a German artist named Joachim Schmid spends six hours a day perusing and grabbing images from Flickr, using them to illustrate his own artist books under the title *Other People's Photographs*. When I asked him why, he told me: "I do it so that you don't have to." In the process of saving me the trouble, he also provides a kind of anecdotal, surrealist ethnography of global photography today. Again, it has become a truism to remark on the refashioning of privacy in our digital age, with social media stretching the word "friend" to include a vast array of relative strangers. Schmid's unauthorized publication of Flickr photographs merely extends this array to comprise discriminating denizens of the art and book-collecting world. His website discusses *Other People's Photographs*:

Everyone concedes that photography is now a medium of exchange as much as a mode of documentation. A digital snapshot is meant primarily as a means of communication, and the images being sent are as ephemeral as speech.

> *Assembled between 2008 and 2011, this series of ninety-six books explores the themes presented by modern everyday, amateur photographers. Images found on photo sharing sites such as Flickr have been gathered and ordered in a way to form a library of contemporary vernacular photography in the age of digital technology and online photo hosting. Each book is comprised of images that focus on a specific photographic event or idea, the grouping of photographs revealing recurring patterns in modern popular photography. The approach is encyclopedic, and the number of volumes is virtually endless but arbitrarily limited. The selection of themes is neither systematic nor does it follow any established criteria—the project's structure mirrors the multifaceted, contradictory and chaotic practice of modern photography itself, based exclusively on the motto "You can observe a lot by watching."*

For one such book, Schmid first gathered some ten thousand images of "currywurst," the local fast food of his hometown of Berlin, lovingly photographed by those unlucky souls about to consume it (he tells me that, over his many earlier years spent gathering discarded analog photos, he found only a handful of such images). People visiting Berlin apparently want to remember the food they are about to eat, or at least to share the experience

Top:
From *Other People's Photographs: Parking Lots*

Bottom:
From *Other People's Photographs: Self*

This page, top:
From Other People's Photographs: Cleavage

This page, bottom:
From Other People's Photographs: Currywurst

Opposite:
From Other People's Photographs: Self

All images from Joachim Schmid's series of ninety-six publications *Other People's Photographs*, 2008–11. Courtesy the artist

of that want with others. Even within the apparent global homogeneity of Flickr we can thus find viral traces of the local asserting themselves—if, that is, we care to look for them.

In fact, it is only Schmid's looking that turns this otherwise international genre of food photography into a regional, even an autobiographical, focal point. Indeed, it might be said that a collapsing of the global into the personal is at the heart of his practice, making it true to the character of social media itself. Sitting at his computer screen, he downloads certain subjects and motifs that seem to recur in the constant stream of photographs he sees on Flickr's "Most Recent Uploads" page, which he refreshes constantly. Of course, there are now sites that set out to facilitate this same sort of distillation process, such as Pinterest, a social-media website launched in 2010, on which its twelve million users compile collections of pictures they find on the Internet. But Schmid brings both a distinctively ironic eye and the play of chance to this process (he finds his images rather than searching for them), thus allowing us to take note of exhibitionist desires that might otherwise remain scattered and lost in the infinity of digital space. In short, each of the thirty-two-page samplers in *Other People's Photographs* imposes a thematic unity on an otherwise unruly universe of images. A diverse group, these samplers include the titillating flash of *Cleavage*, the deadpan documentation of *Mugshots*, the concrete poetry of *Fridge Doors*, and the more literally concrete jungle of *Parking Lots* (surely a choice of category inspired by Ed Ruscha), to name only a few of his titles.

Among other things, Schmid has recognized the sudden popularity of previously unknown genres of image, such as the proliferation on Flickr of photographs of camera boxes, apparently now the first thing everyone takes with their new camera: takes, and then shares online. In a similar vein, one of his recent books comprises nothing but photographs of the photographer's shadow. Some things, it seems, never change. Or maybe they do: what's interesting about this digital genre is that all these shadow-pictures seem to have been deliberately made, a significant shift in an amateur practice in which clumsy accident once ruled the pictorial roost.

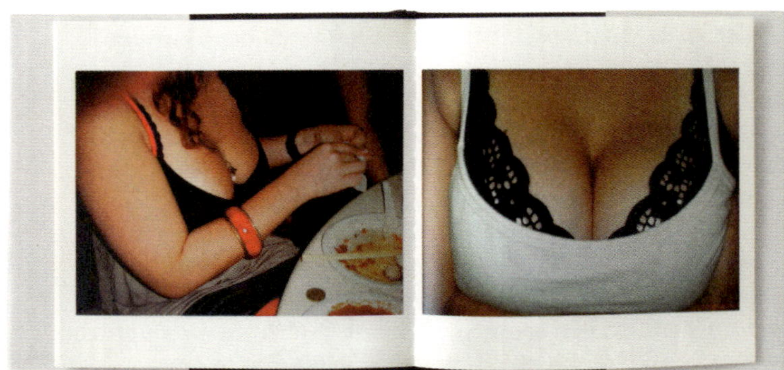

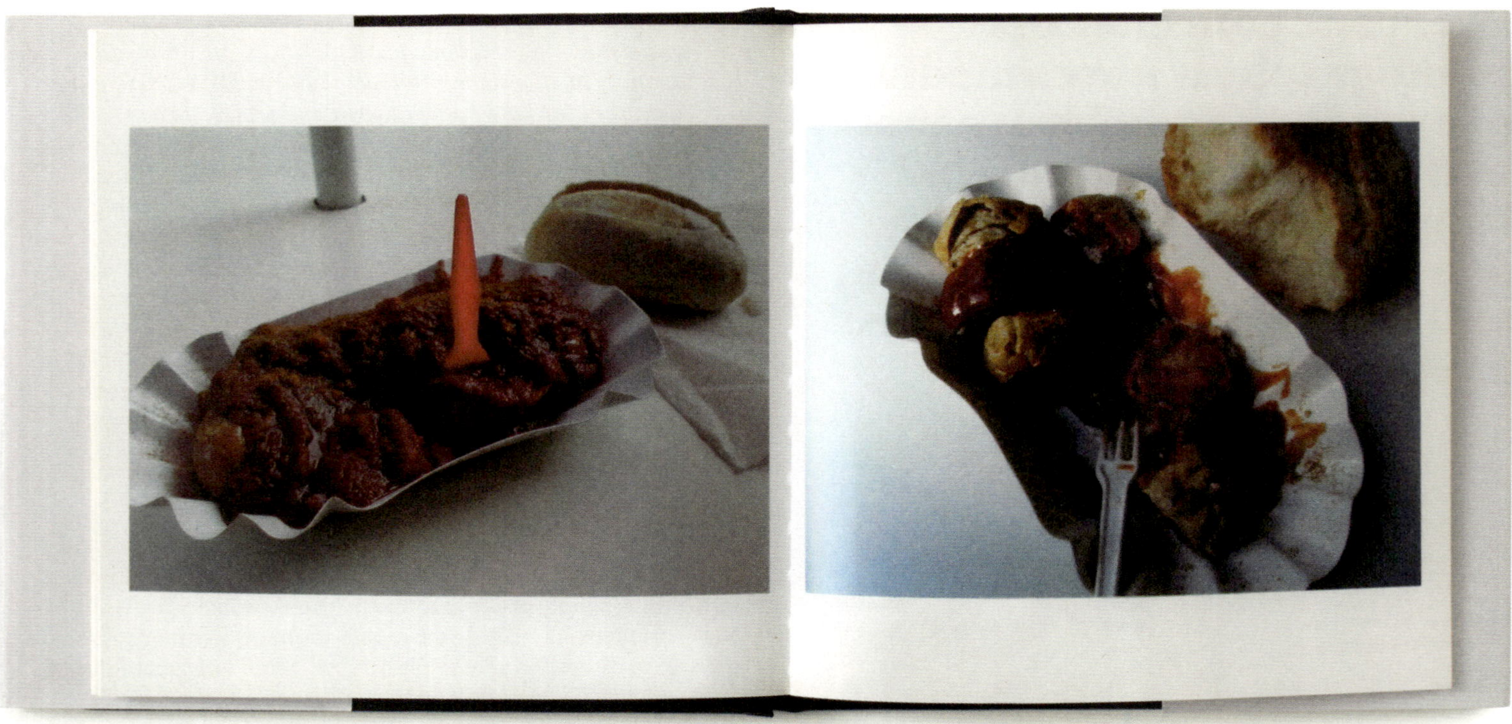

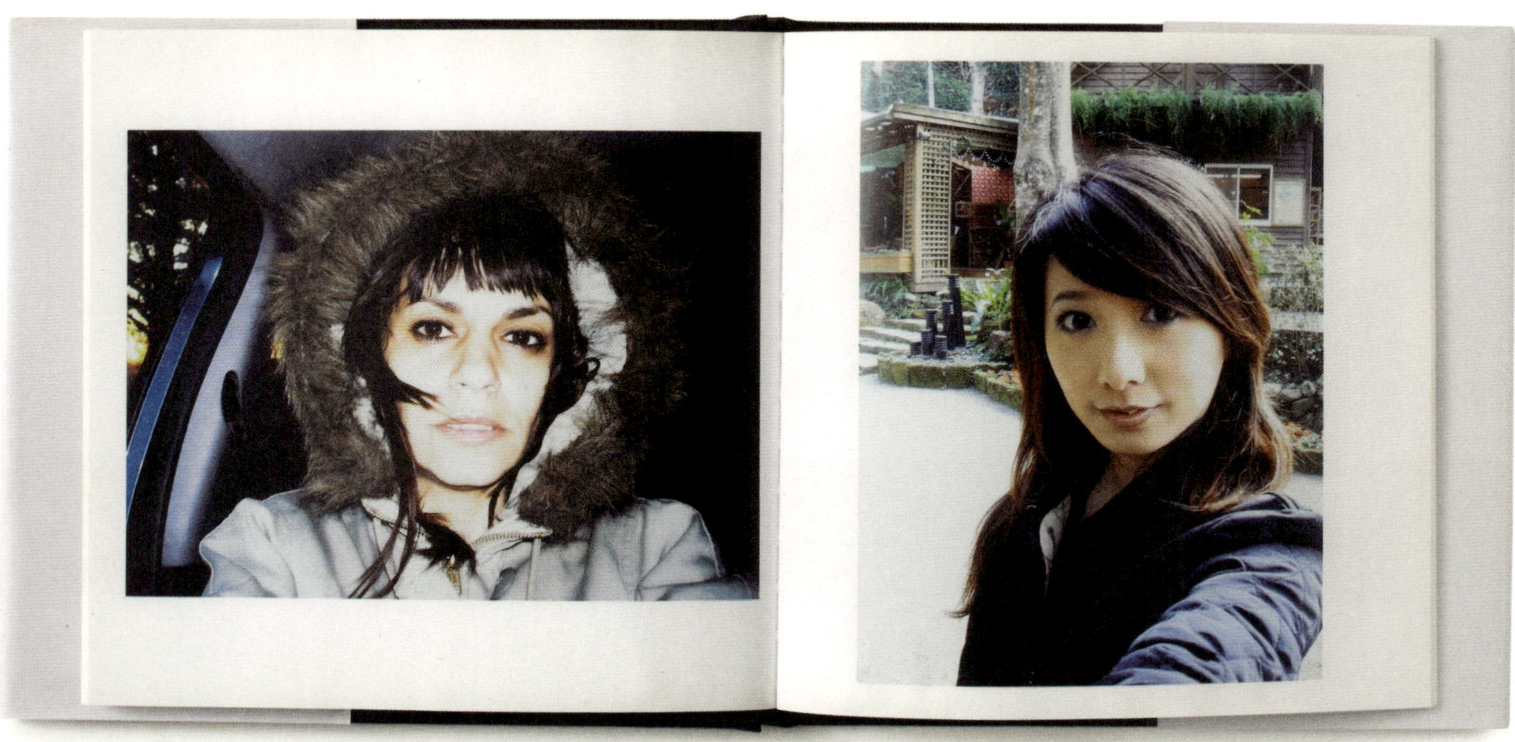

Here on Flickr, through the mediating agency of Schmid's hunting and gathering, we get to see the art world, which once upon a time mimicked this aspect of the so-called snapshot aesthetic, now having that mimicry copied and reabsorbed back into vernacular practice. It seems the analog snapshot is indeed remembered in digital form, but only via a historic artistic mediator.

Another frequent image appearing on Flickr is the self-portrait made with camera in hand, arm outstretched, a type of photograph made possible only with the advent of lightweight digital cameras. Schmid's book on this genre implies that there are many more young photographers doing this than those over thirty, and more women than men. His selection also leaves the impression that this practice is more popular in Japan than in other countries (although, as he admits, this could be because Japanese teenagers upload their files onto Flickr as he starts work in Germany, whereas American members upload while he is asleep). In Korea, this kind of photograph has its own name: *selca* (self-camera). Korean scholar Jung Joon Lee reports that many young women who practice selca adopt specific angles and facial expressions that are designed to give them bigger eyes, a higher nose bridge, and a smaller face. But this kind of specificity, and a critical engagement with the Orientalism it internalizes, is subsumed in Schmid's book to the startling conformity of the genre, to a blithe repetition of form that appears to obey no identifiable cultural imperative beyond narcissism. Here, then, is the challenge his project lays before us—not just to make sense of contemporary photography, but to find ways to creatively intervene within it; not just to wonder at its numbing sameness, but also to exacerbate into visibility the abrasive political economy of difference.

Schmid brings both a distinctively ironic eye and the play of chance to this process (he finds his images rather than searching for them), thus allowing us to take note of exhibitionist desires that might otherwise remain scattered and lost in the infinity of digital space.

Geoffrey Batchen teaches the history of photography at Victoria University of Wellington in New Zealand.

S. Billie Mandle,
Our Lady of Perpetual Help*, 2008. From the series *Reconciliation

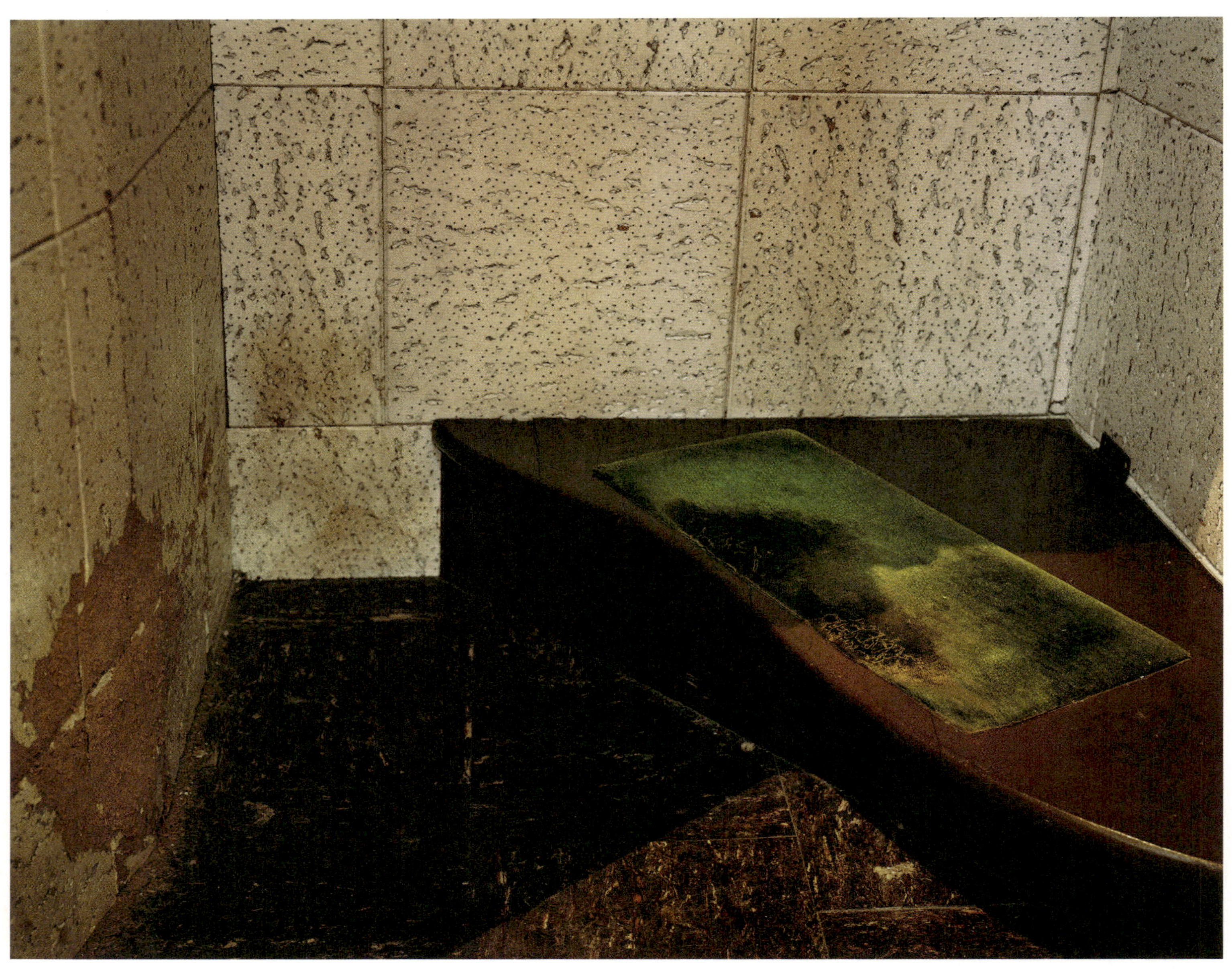

What new debates and ideas are occupying scholars of the medium? Photography historian Robin Kelsey outlines the key ideas animating research today.

Our Lady of Perpetual Help: Thoughts on Recent Scholarship on Photography

Robin Kelsey

Scholarship on photography is so abundant and varied today that discerning trends is no easy task. But perhaps photography itself can assist us. In particular, *Our Lady of Perpetual Help* (2008), one of a series of photographs by S. Billie Mandle of compartments for penitents in confessionals, may serve as a helpful touchstone. It has in common with much recent scholarship a set of paired concerns: structural division and exchange, materiality and trace, community and ritual, revelation and absence, sin and history. Reflection on these concerns in the light of *Our Lady of Perpetual Help* may stimulate new thoughts about the current state of photography scholarship.

Structural Division and Exchange

Part of the power of Mandle's photograph is that the space it shows us is inseparable from another we cannot see; the compartment of the penitent is bound to the unseen compartment of the priest. The concourse between these spaces is restricted by tradition: individuals enter each space bodily but interact as disembodied voices passing through a screen. The two spaces are asymmetrical. We see the space of the sinner who seeks forgiveness, while the space of authority, the space from which absolution can issue, remains hidden.

Perhaps the primary challenge to scholarship on photography today is the division of the subject into two distinct but connected spaces. One is the space of things, where photographs are made of paper, glass, silver, dyes, and other materials, and where we handle them, hang them on walls, move them about, and put them in boxes. The other is the virtual space of our digital network of server farms and hard drives, where photographs have no substance or size and arrive suddenly when we beckon them to our glowing screens. Photographs pass from one space to the other through the prescribed channels of digitization or printing, or meet in hybrid contraptions, such as the digital picture frame.

Curiosity about the division between these spaces has displaced concern for older divisions, such as that between photography and painting. Questions about medium have mostly given way to questions about *pictures* or *images*. The rise of *picture* as a category is revealing. In 1977 curator and art historian Douglas Crimp's *Pictures* exhibition used the word's nonspecific quality to set a postmodern interest in photography, video, and film against a modernist exaltation of painting. By 1994 scholar and theorist W.J.T. Mitchell, in his book *Picture Theory*, was using the category to open up a new discussion of visual culture. Following precedent, he distinguished between picture ("a constructed concrete object or ensemble") and image ("the virtual, phenomenal appearance that it provides a beholder"). Although he introduced his book with a discussion of television, Mitchell wrote on the cusp of a digital revolution that would make television seem feeble as a purveyor of visual representations and threaten to wash away the significance of older pictorial forms.

In recent years, reference to visual representations on computer screens and to the phenomenal experiences they engender has collapsed into the term *images*, obscuring the distinction between electronic representations and mental experiences. We tend to reserve the term *picture* for representations of an older and more concrete kind. As Diarmuid Costello and Margaret Iversen noted in the summer 2012 issue of *Critical Inquiry*, for Crimp, the turn to *picture* was a way of opposing the modernism of critic and art historian Michael Fried, but by 2008 Fried himself had taken up the notion of the picture to shore up the aesthetic promise of pictorial art in his book *Why Photography Matters as Art as Never Before*. For modernist aesthetes such as Fried, Jeff Wall, and others, the category of *picture* became the route by which photography could come to be taken seriously as art and thus brought into alliance with painting. The new culture industry of the Internet has made the old high-low rivalry between painting and photography beside the point; they have a shared fate now. Meanwhile, the surge of photography into contemporary art has raised a host of issues, from philosophical questions about the role of agency in art production to historical questions about how this surge came to pass.

The recent negotiation of the divide between modernism and postmodernism can be traced within a narrower body of scholarship on photography proper. Between the 1930s and the 1970s, writing on photography was dominated by a modernist emphasis on formal experiment and medium autonomy. The Museum of Modern Art in New York was the principal American organ for this scholarly strain, with works such as Beaumont Newhall's *History of Photography* and John Szarkowki's *The Photographer's Eye* becoming canonical in the field. Between the mid-1970s and early 1980s, writers such as Rosalind Krauss and Allan Sekula led a rebellion against such modernist narratives and the historical amnesia that the assimilation of photography into the modernist art museum had entailed. They focused instead on the production of photographic meaning by *discourse*—a term that cultural critic Michel Foucault had momentously used to refer to systems of communicated knowledge. In the wake of this rebellion, writers on photography tended either to attend to the specific formal qualities of pictures in a modernist mode or to draw away from pictures and unmask the mystification of photographic discourse through postmodern critique. In recent years, scholars have begun working across this modernist/postmodernist divide by attending to photographic form as a historically positioned and politically saturated intervention in its own right. Art historian Jae Emerling's 2012 book *Photography: History and Theory* offers a splendid account of this new scholarly turn.

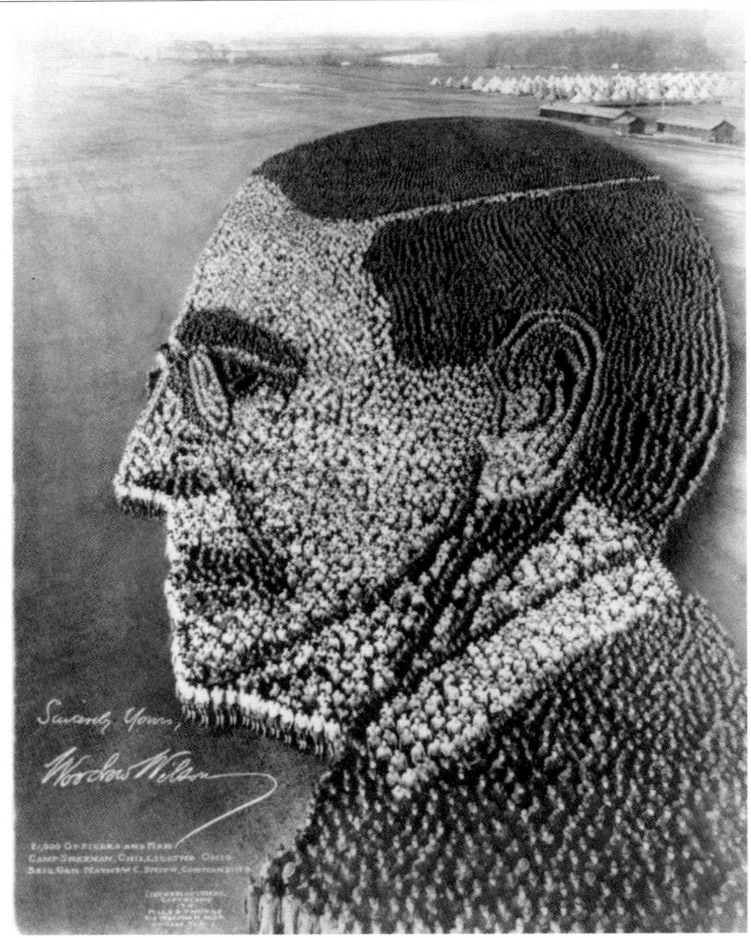

Arthur Mole and John Thomas, *Sincerely Yours, Woodrow Wilson, 21,000 officers and men, Camp Sherman, Ohio*, ca. 1918
Library of Congress, Prints and Photographs Division, Washington, D.C.

Louise Lawler,
War Is Terror,
2001/2003
Courtesy the artist and
Metro Pictures, New York

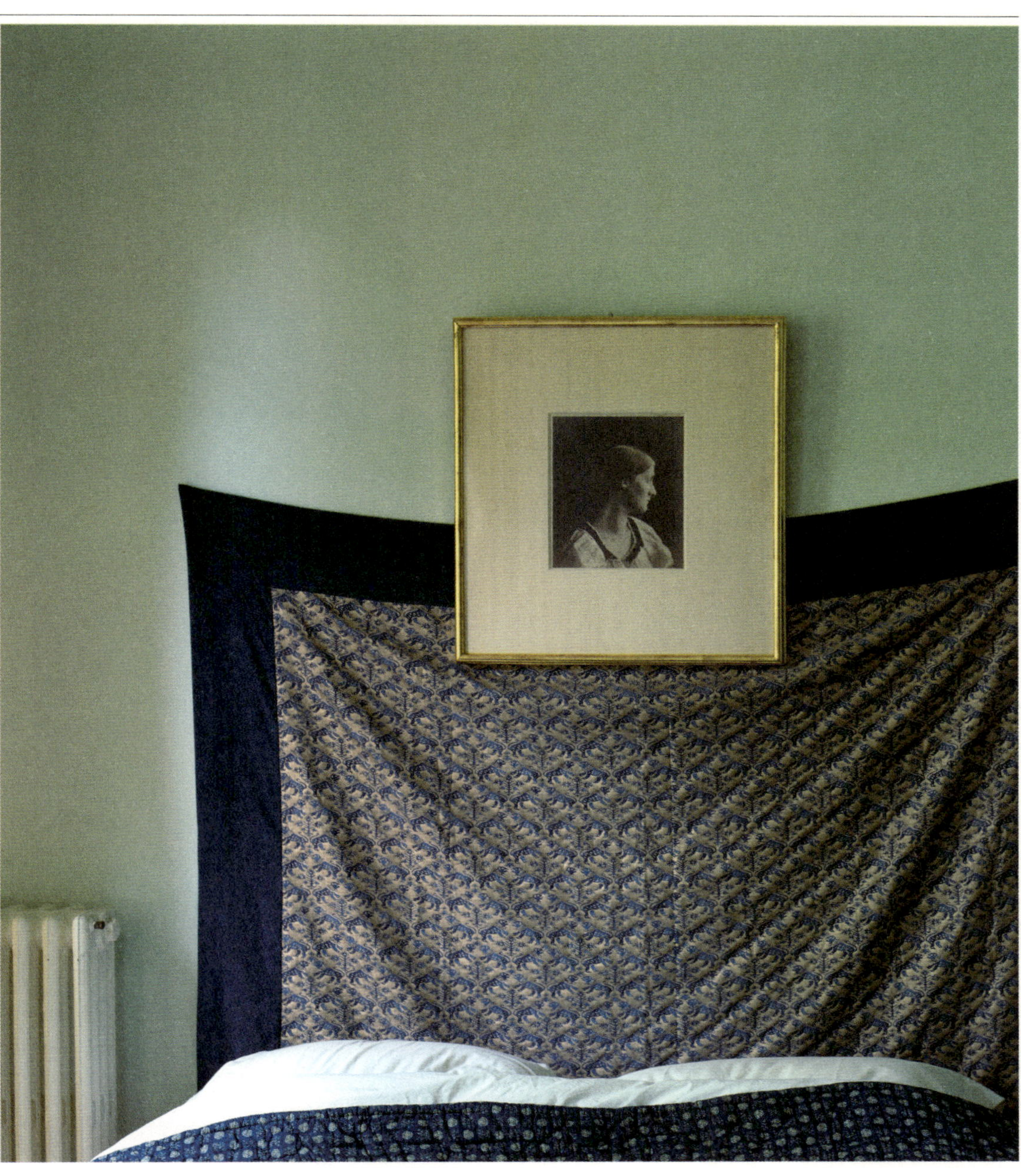

Scholars have taken a keen interest in how photographs and their circulation establish social ties, negotiate commonalities and differences of identity, confirm cultural assumptions, and generate moral obligations.

Materiality and Bodily Trace

Another strength of Mandle's photograph is its concern for bodily traces. The cumulative kneeling of penitents has left a worn and darkened patch on the rectangle of green felt, and their shoes have scraped the surface of the acoustic tiles. These traces remind us of the anatomical effort of kneeling in this cramped space, and of the repetition of this action over time. These corporeal imaginings mingle evocatively with thoughts of the disembodied interlocution for which the penitents kneel and the forgiveness it purports to deliver.

One effect of the emergence of the virtual space of the Internet is a new fascination with the material tactility and obduracy of photographs as things. Prior to the Internet, scholars tended to regard photography as a dematerializing medium. Now interest has surged in the material substrate of photography, from the accidents of its liquid chemistry to the creases and stains of its paper supports. The turn toward the tactile is exemplified by the title of Margaret Olin's book *Touching Photographs*, published last year. The motivation behind this turn is less nostalgia than a desire to understand the history of photography anew in light of our digital moment. Indeed, even as scholars investigate the materiality of old photographs, their specific inquiries pursue contemporary concerns. For example, in these days of digital cutting and pasting, scholarship on composite printing and

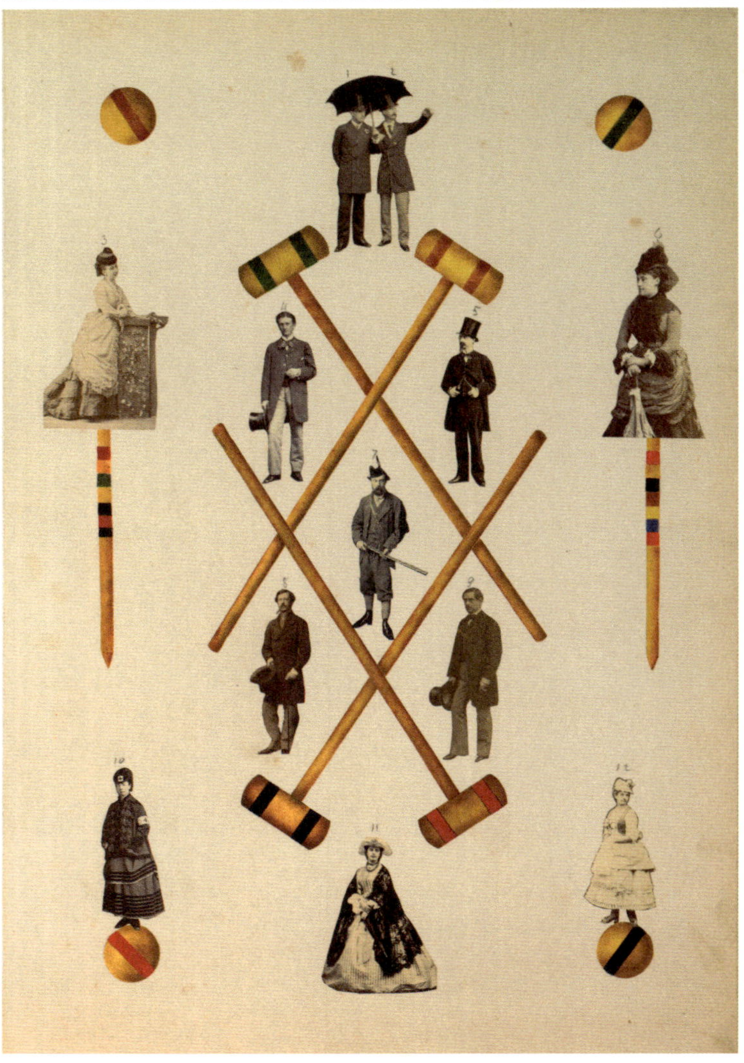

Sir Edward Charles Blount, from the *Blount Album*, 1860s/1880s, a sixty-page collection of collages made from watercolors and albumen prints. Featured in Elizabeth Siegel's *Playing with Pictures: The Art of Victorian Photocollage* (Art Institute of Chicago/Yale University Press, 2009)
Gernsheim Collection, Harry Ransom Center, University of Texas, Austin

photocollage has been burgeoning. From Jordan Bear's work on the composite photographs of Oscar Rejlander to Elizabeth Siegel's exhibition and catalog on Victorian photocollage, *Playing with Pictures* (2009), to Andrés Zervigón and Sabine Kriebel's recent studies on John Heartfield and photomontage in Weimar Berlin, we know far more about the history of these practices today than we did several years ago. This incisive scholarship has attuned us to signs of process and labor, and to the issues of economy, identity, and culture in which they are enmeshed.

Community and Ritual

The interior of the penitent's compartment in Mandle's photograph has a specificity that raises questions about the church that houses it and the community to which it belongs. Confession is an intimate exchange between penitent and priest, but that exchange is sanctioned by an institution that binds a community in ritual. The ritual in question is predicated on a sense of obligation, an act of conscience, and the disclosure of truth. The community it affirms has left the cumulative marks of its membership in the worn patches of felt and wall, making the space we see at once both intensely private and profoundly shared.

There has been much interesting recent scholarship on photography and community. Scholars have taken a keen interest in how photographs and their circulation establish social ties, negotiate commonalities and differences of identity, confirm cultural assumptions, and generate moral obligations. Ariella Azoulay's 2008 *The Civil Contract of Photography*, Blake Stimson's 2006 *The Pivot of the World: Photography and Its Nation*, and Louis Kaplan's 2005 *American Exposures: Photography and Community in the Twentieth Century* are three notable examples of recent literature in this area. The growing interest in photography and community follows the postmodernist preference for the study of photographic practices rather than individual photographs. But relative to the path-breaking postmodernism of Sekula and Krauss this new scholarship is less in the sway of Foucault and his notion of discourse, more interested in practices outside the control of large institutions, and less certain of its disillusionment. By pursuing the nexus of photography and community, this recent scholarship takes a fresh look at photography's promise as a democratic instrument and its claims to universality. Azoulay writes of "the citizenry of photography," while Stimson considers "photography and its nation." Both of these scholars take seriously the possibility of photography having a politics that counters the volatile and often oppressive divisions of social identity. The role of ritual in the affirmation of photography's social value as a token of the moral claims that reality makes on us has led Stimson and this author to redefine the photographic index as "a secular ritual form, as a post-postmodern Salah or Shabbat or wafer and wine." *Our Lady of Perpetual Help* can remind us of photography's own operations of truthful disclosure and moral obligation, and of the community that its rituals reinforce.

The new culture industry of the Internet has made the old high-low rivalry between painting and photography beside the point; they have a shared fate now.

Some scholars who are drawing attention to social practices of photography have taken heed of the field's poor record of prognostication in the early digital era. Many predictions of the end of photography, or at least of its reliability in the wake of the digital turn, exaggerated the import of mechanical process and ontology and slighted the determining effects of social practice. As several scholars have observed, personal and family photography and the assumptions undergirding them have changed remarkably little in recent years. The means of production, storage, and dissemination have changed, but many of the rituals endure.

Revelation and Absence

For a contemporary picture, *Our Lady of Perpetual Help* traffics in many of photography's hoarier qualities. It portrays a camera of sorts: a box infused with light. By bringing illumination to a social space ordinarily darkened and unseen, Mandle follows in the footsteps of many celebrated practitioners, such as the Progressive Era reformer Jacob Riis, who aimed his flash into tenement airshafts and bunk-filled flophouses. Mandle's long exposure allows the dim light in the confessional compartment to accrete, supplying a degree of visibility unavailable to the ordinary eye at the site itself. Photography is here living up to its Enlightenment promise to penetrate the veils of our ignorance and offer us a clearer vision of reality. But this clarity has its conditions: the long exposure precludes any direct registration of the fidgety bodies that regularly occupy this space. We are left instead with evidence of past action—the stains, the wear, the soiling—that calls to mind the absent life. In this respect, the photograph takes us back to the early history of the medium, when sensitized plates reacted too slowly to capture action, and photographers of the Civil War (to take a prime example) had to content themselves with posed camp scenes and battlefield remains. An article in the *London Times* from 1862 asserted: "The photographer who follows in the wake of modern armies must be content with conditions of repose, and with the still life which remains when the fighting is over."

Coming in the wake of a long succession of confessional encounters, Mandle offers us conditions of repose. But what is most affecting about these conditions is less their stillness than their degraded banality. The floor and the acoustic tiles are of a very common kind, and the disrepair of the compartment adds to the disparity between the base conditions of this space and the lofty aspirations of the sanctified practice that takes place within it. This disparity brings home the fallen state of the penitent, while also invoking the transubstantiations associated with photography as art. Since the days of the Victorian photographer Julia Margaret Cameron, who welcomed conspicuously clumsy props and weary sitters into her allegorical scenes, photographers have sought to alchemically transmute unpromising everyday matter into something divine.

In recent years, scholars have continued to bring forgotten and neglected practices and histories to light. These efforts have often revealed photography's grubby underside, which in the heyday of Newhall and Szarkowski lay largely hidden beneath canonical exemplars, whitewashed accounts, or honorific tales of technological advance. This critical strain in recent scholarship includes Steve Edwards's 2006 book analyzing photographic discourse in nineteenth-century England (*The Making of English Photography: Allegories*); André Gunthert's trenchant critical reappraisals of key photographic myths in the journal *Études photographiques*; Clément Chéroux's 2003 book on photographic errors (*Fautographie*); and Tanya Sheehan's recent work on race in early American photography. From these authors, we now have a clearer and more capacious understanding of many matters, including photographers as a class in Victorian England (Edwards), the emergence of the instantaneous photograph (Gunthert), the history of aesthetic delight in photographic distortion (Chéroux), and the role of race and humor in the shaping of photographic conventions (Sheehan). The desire to understand specific photographic practices across a broad range of social and geographical domains has driven new publishing schemes. Such initiatives as the journal *Photography and Culture*, launched in 2008, and Reaktion Books' *Exposures* series, which now has over a dozen books, with titles such as *Photography and China*, *Photography and Science*, and *Photography and Literature*, exemplify the broad scope of current scholarship.

Sin and History

The scrapes and stains in *Our Lady of Perpetual Help* linger like the material residues of castoff sins. They are traces of the many stories that penitents have told about wayward steps and failed struggles with temptation. They are thus doubly removed from the sinful actions that confession is designed to address, and these actions are themselves only echoes of original sin. The photograph is the polar opposite of the decisive moment of street photography, which once promised to catch modernity instantaneously and on the fly. Mandle's camera comes after the many transgressions, and after their many histories, to slowly produce a picture suffused with scrutiny, meditation, and belatedness. The act of recording this room carries with it a sense of unveiling the past, and even of disinfecting its soiled spaces with light. The picture recalls not only the sins of petitioners but also those of the church and its representatives. This community bound in ritual has been riddled with segregations, intolerance, and sexual scandal.

Contemporary scholarship on photography often seems similarly removed from immediacy and concerned with reflective matters of conscience. Scholars have been writing histories of photography theory, such as Bernd Stiegler's 2006 *Theoriegeschichte der Photographie* (History of the theory of photography) and Hilde Van Gelder and Helen Westgeest's 2011 *Photography Theory in Historical Perspective: Case Studies from Contemporary Art*. We also have many histories of histories, accounts of how the archives and canonical stories of photography were formed. These accounts frequently wrap themselves around the moral missteps of prior generations, noting their egregious exclusions, hidden biases, and self-serving assumptions. The tone is often more prosecutorial than confessional. But these critical appraisals of past sins serve a shedding and lightening function of their own. A desire to rectify past wrongs has driven the expanded reach of scholarship and brought oppressed subjects into a more sympathetic visibility. Shawn Michelle Smith's 2004 *Photography on the Color Line: W.E.B. Du Bois, Race, and Visual Culture*, an investigation into archives and photographs of African-Americans, is a case in point.

The tiles lining the confessional compartment depicted in *Our Lady of Perpetual Help* signify a mid-twentieth-century interior. Repositioned in the space of art, they recall that period's modernism and its decline. The shabby, mass-produced echoes they provide of the monochromes and field paintings of high modernism allow the photograph to speak to a larger history, and to the sins for which it must account. Eugène Atget's photographs of Paris have been famously likened to those of a crime scene, and part of the productive friction of *Our Lady of Perpetual Help* is that it bears the same affinity. But here we cannot think of crime without thinking of punishment and forgiveness—and of a paradigmatic modernist aim: grace.

Robin Kelsey is the Shirley Carter Burden Professor of Photography and Chair of the Department of History of Art and Architecture at Harvard University.

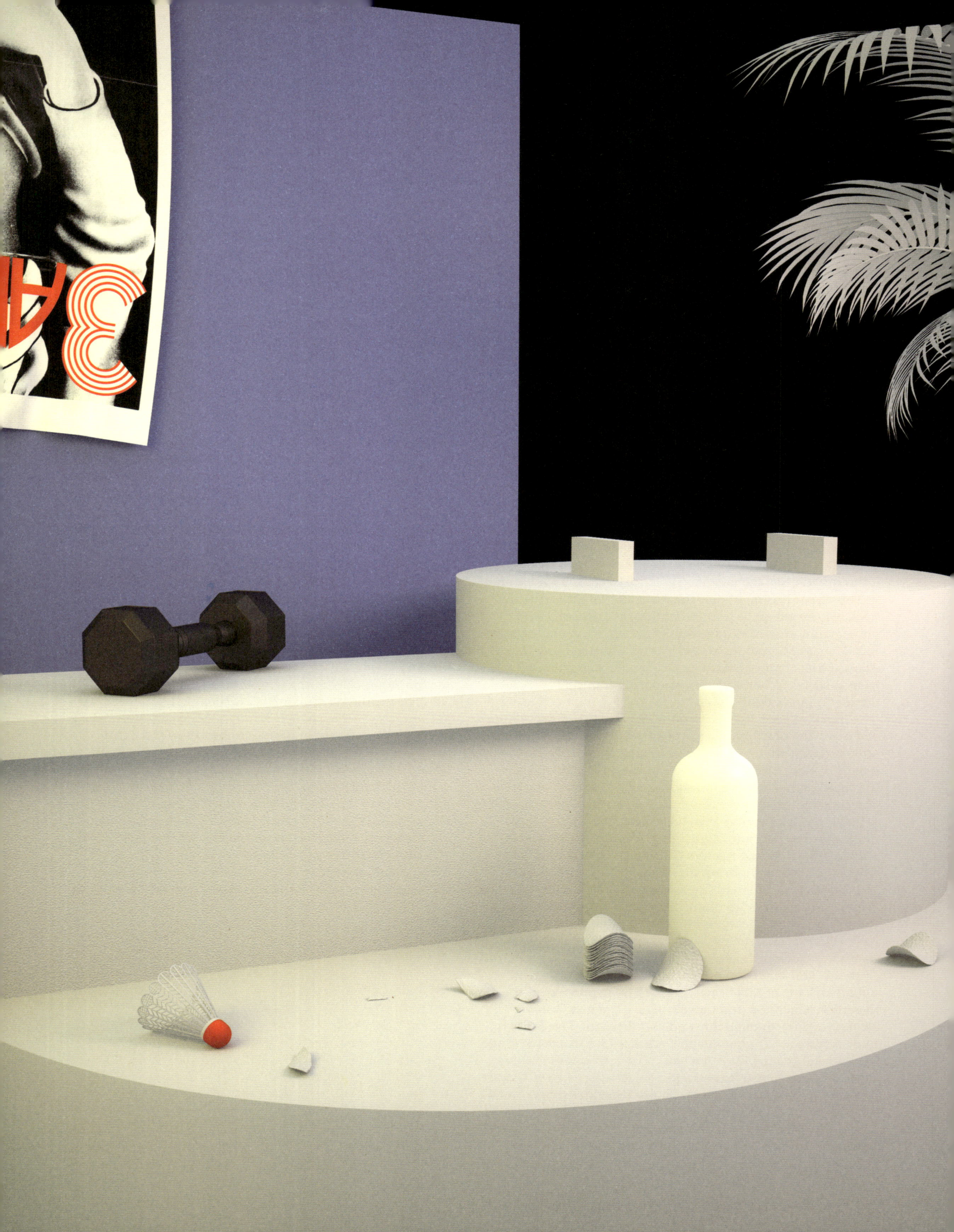

Opposite:
Takeshi Murata, *3 AM*, 2012
Courtesy the artist
and Salon 94, New York

Murata's computer-generated series of photographs, *Synthesizers*, begins with backgrounds "sculpted" by the artist using 3-D software he learned to use through online tutorials. The "sets" are then filled with readymade 3-D elements purchased online.

Photo.edu
Toward a New Curriculum

Arthur Ou

"The camera has offered us amazing possibilities. [...] We are only beginning to exploit them; for although photography is already over a hundred years old it is only in recent years that the course of development has allowed us to see beyond the specific instance and recognize the creative consequences." This proclamation, made by László Moholy-Nagy, one of the progenitors of contemporary photographic education, resounds perhaps even more meaningfully now than when it was uttered in 1925. Nearly a century later, photography is again at an unprecedented historical threshold: a moment unlike any in its 170-year history.

At this juncture, the role and definition of photographic education are of particular concern. What is photographic education today? The question elicits a wave of differing, often contesting answers. While it is generally understood that photography is teachable, the spectrum of pathways by which it is approached—as an art, as a medium or a set of techniques, as a field or an industry—complicates the pedagogical strategies that lead to a cohesive answer. And there are of course the inevitable debates within the realm of photographic education: the viability of analog processes, the necessity of the printed image, commercialism versus artistic expression, photography's relation to other media, documentation versus invention, the question of upholding a medium-specific curriculum, and so on. Such ongoing arguments have led to a variety of distinct educational philosophies and curricular programs in the United States and abroad. And certainly the most complicating factor in all of these discussions is that the definition of photography itself has, in recent years, been wondrously, perturbingly, bewilderingly altered.

The history of photographic education is admittedly rather brief, not counting the many instances from the medium's inception in which techniques were taught through apprenticeship and training, evolving into photo-clubs and photo-societies. The first institutional instance of photographic education occurred at the Bauhaus, where Walter Peterhans was appointed to teach courses in photography in 1929. A decade later Moholy-Nagy brought photography to the Institute of Design at the Illinois Institute of Technology in Chicago, after the Bauhaus was forced to cease operation by the Nazi regime. In 1946 he invited Harry Callahan to the I.D. to teach photography; Callahan made a lasting impact during his Chicago tenure and was subsequently appointed head of the newly established photography degree program at the Rhode Island School of Design in 1961. Other seminal photography programs were established in the 1940s: at the California School of Fine Arts (now San Francisco Art Institute) by Ansel Adams and Minor White; at Ohio University by Clarence White, Jr.; and at Indiana University by Henry Holmes Smith. Needless to say, BFA and MFA programs in photography have proliferated ever since.

It is illuminating to note that many of these pioneering photographic programs were housed not in art academies but within umbrella schools and programs focused on industrial design and technology. A sampling of contemporary programs offered in the United States shows that degrees in the "practice" of photography can be found in departments of art, design, media, journalism, and fashion, as well as technology and science. Not surprisingly, the study (and research) of photography in technology programs is on a radically changing path today. To explore the medium through such vehicles as computational photography, imaging research, and computer vision brings us closer to the societal and cultural uses of photography; furthermore, these modes in turn are broadly shaping the medium's current applications and practices, while also pointing toward photography's future.

How do we tackle a medium in the process of breakneck evolution in the photography classroom today? We now live in a world full of photographs, or, more precisely, the world is rapidly becoming a totality of photographs. To expand on this claim, we need only consider two related trajectories in the area of "mechanical vision." One is the eventuality of photography replacing human perception. It is not a stretch to imagine, in a not-too-distant future, mechanical vision (and the recording and presenting of this vision) reaching an event-horizon, ultimately replicating in exactitude the sensations and experiences of our biological eyes. Secondly, photography will surpass human vision. Already, something *resembling* photography—not quite the medium as it is defined—is replacing what we have long understood as photography. When computer-generated processes can "pre-image" something that will eventually be actualized—when photographs "imagine" the future or another reality—how do we define this type of image in the photographic lexicon? Who or what is the photographer? Where does a photograph begin? Where do photographs end?

These are pertinent pedagogical questions that programs providing photographic education now have an obligation to address. The teaching of photography—beyond application-centered focuses such as "fine art," "documentary," or "fashion" —has a new duty to encompass not only philosophical but technological engagements with the larger curriculum. (This is truer with photography than with other media since photography is *always* intertwined with the technological.) Above all, it would seem to be necessary for programs in photography to instill a sense of experimentation, more so now in this uncharted period in the medium's history. One thinks here of Harold Edgerton, professor of electrical engineering at the Massachusetts Institute of Technology from the 1940s to the '70s, whose extensive experiments with stroboscopic photography greatly impacted our understanding of time (and its photographic capture), and the possibilities he would have inspired in a classroom full of photography students. Such curricular crossovers are clearly even more exigent in our time.

•

When considering photographic education today, one might look further back than the history of the photographic medium itself, to ponder the forty-thousand-year-old human impulse to replicate our perceptual experiences. The first prehistoric cave paintings—the earliest "proto-photographic" pictures—gave the viewer an alternate (and unprecedented) version of the experience of seeing animals that were not actually there. They also provided a means to share the experience of seeing with others. These ardent impulses—to preserve experience and to share seeing—led to photography's invention, and have been driving the myriad developments of photographic technologies and theories throughout its history. It is not the amalgamation of processes, both obsolete and emerging, that defines photography, but rather the impulse to record, to depict, to share.

In recent decades, however, our understanding of these impulses has undergone important transformations. As early as 1965—still in the initial stages of institutionalized photographic education—anthropologist Pierre Bourdieu stated in *Photography: A Middle-Brow Art*: "Photography owes its immense diffusion to its social function. [...] More than any other cultural practices, the practice of photography appears to respond to a *natural* need." The power of the medium's "social function" has been evidenced recently, of course, in the incalculable numbers of images taken and sent through mobile and networked devices by participants in historic events from the Arab Spring uprisings to the Occupy Wall Street activities.

The bulk of photographic images today are not "taken" so much as "computed"; this is one of the main concepts that differentiates contemporary photographic education from that of the past. We now take for granted premade software (such as Photoshop) and hardware (notably digital cameras and cellphones)—tools with a set of available features at our immediate disposal—without thinking of the vast predetermined programming that went into their design. To advocate for a medium-specific curriculum in photography today, this less-considered "back end" of photography will surely have to be addressed and incorporated into the course of study. What's hidden beneath the user interface or the sleek camera casing needs to be exposed, not only made visible and comprehensible to the photographic practitioner, but also taken apart, deconstructed, and mined for creative potentials.

Opposite:
Matthew Monteith,
***At the Light Box*, 2004.**
From the series *Art School*, 2002–4
Courtesy the artist

What's hidden beneath the user interface or the sleek camera casing needs to be exposed, not only made visible and comprehensible to the photographic practitioner, but also taken apart, deconstructed, and mined for creative potentials.

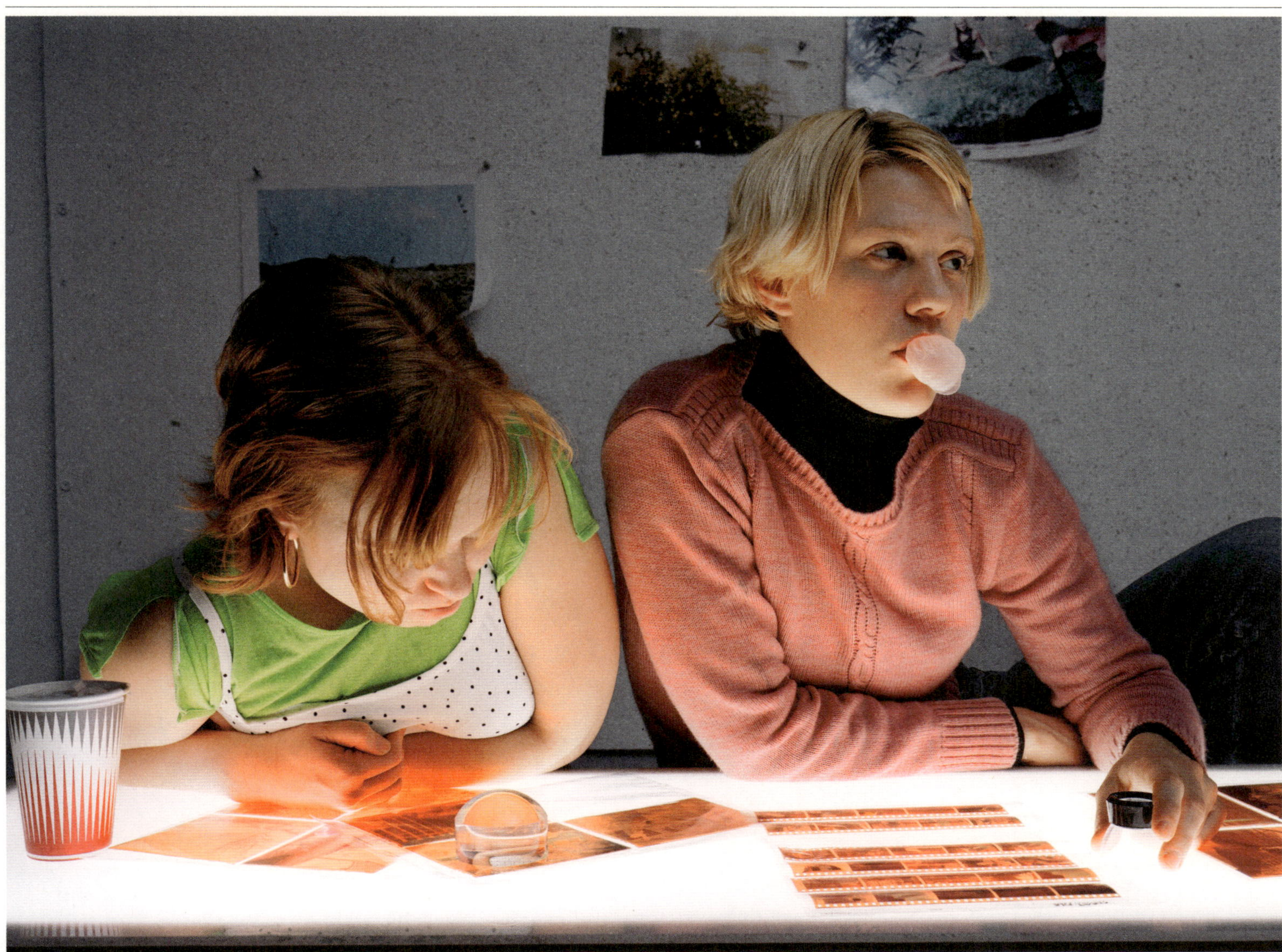

To do this, it is useful to look toward the research and projects being conducted in places like the MIT Media Lab and Stanford University's computer-science program, whose activities have been instrumental in advancing paradigmatic shifts in photography. As an example: the Camera Culture research group at MIT's Media Lab, in a departure from "line-of-sight" photography, is focusing on what is known as "femto" mapping—using extremely short and accurate bursts of laser light (photons) and tracing the movements of these photon particles in order to visually map what is around corners. For many practitioners and educators of photography, drawing such parallels between the medium and the realm of computation is unsettling; however, this is part of the reality we inhabit presently and for the foreseeable future. As computing power increases, new possibilities will upend what we have come to understand as photography and begin the process of charting out the still-unknown future of the expanding medium. These progressions are key to laying the groundwork for a new era in photographic education.

But technology is only one side of the pedagogical coin. The other necessary component in photographic education is to provide a context for these technologies within the broader cultural landscape and to remain constantly aware of their cultural impact. Much can be drawn from Vilém Flusser's notion of the "photographic program," explicated in his 1983 book *Towards a Philosophy of Photography*, a theory that totalizes photographic processes: the camera operator is but a small part in an all-encompassing mechanism. Today that mechanism encompasses everything from the manufacture of the capture and output devices to the photographic materials used to the eventual outlets (newspapers, magazines, the Web, and so on) through which photographic images are disseminated: channels that are increasing exponentially, at speeds unimagined at the time of Flusser's formulation of his theory.

A crucial aspect of teaching photography now is to inform students producing images with intention that the urgent task of the photographic producer is to acknowledge and counter the unending torrents of images, and to forcefully and meaningfully respond to their own individual impulse to record, to depict, or to render. Then, like the prehistoric cave-painters, they can share their perceptual experiences against the limits of what's possible.

Arthur Ou is an artist and writer based in New York. He is currently the director of BFA Photography at Parsons The New School for Design. His work was recently included in the 2012 Daegu Photo Biennial.

Ou is an organizer of the April 2013 Photographic Universe conference. See aperture.org/events

Akram Zaatari, a founder of the Arab Image Foundation in Beirut in 1997, has emerged as one of the most prominent commentators on photography of the Middle East. Overseeing AIF's mission to preserve and study the photographic culture of the region, Zaatari has, as both an artist and a cultural critic, pushed for more experimental approaches to understanding this collection. Through books, installations, and videos, Zaatari's visual studies provide new ways of seeing and thinking about images. This work parallels his long-term engagement with "the state of image making in situations of war," highlighted in his book *Earth of Endless Secrets* (2009). More recently, *Akram Zaatari: The Uneasy Subject* (2011) explores the way photography and other imaging practices capture vernacular expressions of masculinity and sexuality. The following interview with anthropologist Mark Westmoreland took place last October via email correspondence.

Akram Zaatari
Against Photography
Conversation with Mark Westmoreland

Mark Westmoreland: **You have played a fundamental role in the establishment and direction of the Arab Image Foundation. Today, AIF is one of the most interesting and significant photographic archives in the region. Can you talk about how this collection came to be?**

Akram Zaatari: AIF was created by many endeavors, with many movements in it. It could have ended up simply as an image bank. My involvement marked AIF's path after the first two years, and my interest in extensive fieldwork tied to the production of exhibitions dominated AIF's practice. Walid Raad has been of great support since that time, both in interpreting the collection and in debating with the other members.

The initial goal of the foundation was naïve, but not unproductive: we wanted to be able to recount, one day, a history of photography in the Arab region. AIF did not exist as an archive before individual artists expressed the desire to create a collection and work on it, with it. AIF reflects the concerns and desires of those behind it. Fundamentally, there is a difference between archives as collections of "sediment"—repositories of images of various practices in an institution—and what we do as individuals with AIF. If it is an archive, it is more an archive of research and collecting practices than an archive of photographic practices.

MW: **You touch upon something quite significant here. If we consider the Arab Image Foundation as a conventional archive, we might assume that your work at AIF and your work as an artist occupy two distinct registers. But by delineating research and art as separate facets of your work, we might miss out on important ways these two projects converge. Can you talk about these roles and what your work at AIF means for you as an artist?**

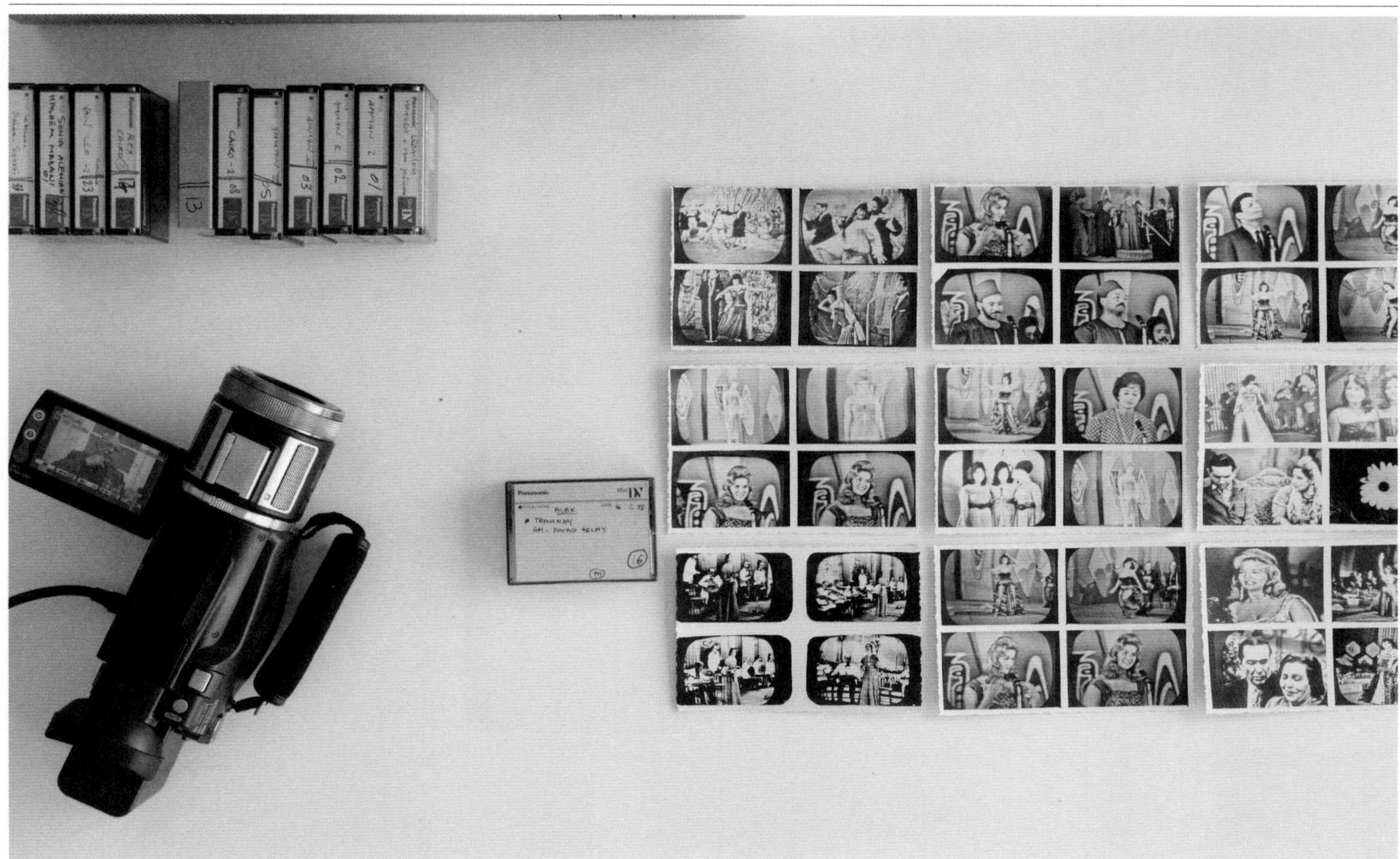

Still from the video
***On Photography People and Modern Times*, 2010**
Courtesy the artist and Sfeir Semler Gallery, Hamburg/Beirut

AZ: If we consider AIF's collection as an archive of a photographic heritage/practices, we do miss out on the personalized nature of that collection and its contemporary component. AIF is a product of a movement in contemporary arts, internationally and in Lebanon—particularly in the late 1990s—and seeing it today without this angle would be presenting a false history. Again, AIF started with a naïve propos to focus on important moments in photography's history in the region, but soon we came to recognize how important photography is in writing personal histories, multiple histories. Looking through photographs became a writing project—in the way that Siegfried Kracauer and John Berger undertook amazing readings of history through photographs. So the desire to write histories became a driving force behind expanding AIF's collection.

MW: **As an example, a substantial part of your research and collecting practices have focused on Hashem El Madani, a studio photographer in your hometown, Saïda (Sidon), Lebanon. You've published two books about his work, *Studio Practices* in 2005 and *Promenades* in 2007, and have organized numerous exhibitions. How did you begin working with him?**

AZ: I met Madani in 1998, and I became interested because he was not a perfectionist, "high-end" photographer. He produced many images that look poor from a technical perspective when compared to the work of his peers in urban centers like Beirut, Tripoli, Cairo, or Alexandria. Madani's compositions were not complex: his subjects were usually placed right in the center of the frame, shown from head to toe. He rarely bothered with mannered or excessive lighting. In his early years, his shadow would fall onto his subjects because he would photograph them with the sun low behind him. (I find it amazing to see a photographer make mistakes that directly affect the shape

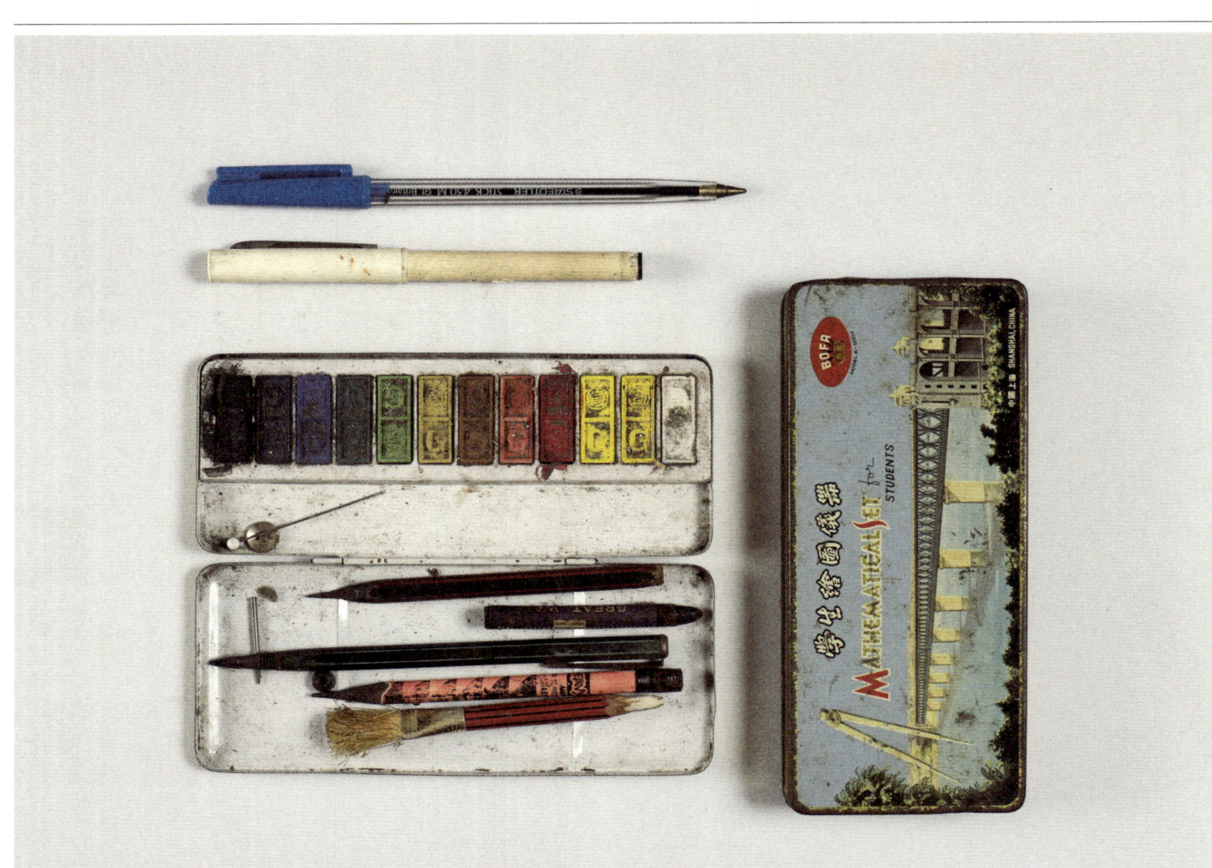

***Twenty-eight Nights and a Poem* (tools found on Hashem El Madani's desk), 2007–10. C-print**
Courtesy the artist and Sfeir Semler Gallery, Hamburg/Beirut

of images!) But then ... you could see him improving over time, learning more and more. Madani did his best to establish a kind of signature style to differentiate his product from other people's. He took as many photographs as he could, all the while expanding his address book and adding clients to his growing archive.

MW: **How did your interest shift from Madani's individual pictures to the workings of his studio?**

AZ: He took pictures both in the studio—Studio Shehrazade—and outside, in public spaces or workplaces. He photographed by day and developed by night, seven days a week. He took pictures of weddings, burials, circumcision celebrations, festivities, political demonstrations, election rallies; he traveled with people who wanted a photographer along on daytrips. He cared about the quality of the image, his prints were well developed, and he wanted his prices to compete with other studios in town—so he privileged the 35-millimeter camera over heavier photo gear, and relied on this format for most of his outdoor photography.

A few years after I met him, I realized that my own interest in researching photographs was shifting, and that I was not looking for individual images of particular significance only; rather, I wanted to understand *how* Madani worked and how he made his choices. I was interested in how he used his studio, how he treated his clients, what kind of transactions took place there. I was also trying to understand why this profession was dying. This is how I decided to take his entire studio as a repository of transactions and records, and to target it with projects, a series of exhibitions, publications, and videos that would communicate an understanding of how photography has mixed with society throughout modern times. Studio Shehrazade still exists today partly because of an art/study project that considers describing his collection, preserving it at once as capital and as study material.

MW: **Recently, you have entertained the provocative idea of being "against photography." Your position entails a critique that challenges photography's privileged status among other imaging practices, the presumed importance of preservation, and the burden of carrying collections into new and unintended economies. Particularly striking is your counter-preservationist suggestion to "give it all back"—to return original photographs to their owners. But, while *against* can mean simply contrasting, the term also carries the connotation of physical abutment, or collision, or even ideological opposition. What does this oppositional gesture mean for your future work with photography?**

AZ: "Against photography," as you say, has a double meaning. Today, it would make a great title for a magazine on photography—better than, say, "*Aperture*." On the surface, it is a statement in opposition to the paths that photography institutions have taken. But indeed, "against photography" also means leaning against photography's history in order to move elsewhere, where we can save photography from its fate.

My relation to photography is mainly one of study; it is a medium I rely on in my art practice: I am an image maker. Having explained how I admire photography's ability to overthrow dominant historical narratives, to present us with multiple histories, even contradictory narratives, I want at the same time to stress that what stimulates me in this study is being able to look at documents with critical distance (both temporal and situational) and being able to compare them with other documents. But that's the kind of cultural-studies perspective that marked much of my work in the 1990s. The idea behind the Arab Image Foundation was to establish a collecting mechanism and a study platform. For me, it was meant to be first a learning experience, culturally, and then a preservation project. When I started traveling, looking for photographs, I was eager to discover what was out there that had been inaccessible to me. I was guided by the possibility of discovery.

I recently proposed to the board of AIF that we should offer to return collections to their respective families. There are many facets to this proposal. With passing years, I realized that the foundation does not need original documents to write history, especially now that scanning technology allows us to do what was difficult to do in the mid-1990s. We always insisted that we were interested only in originals, because our interest lies in photographic preservation. I don't believe in this anymore, because I don't see the preservation of photographs as preservation of material only. It would be interesting to determine what exactly is essential to preserve. If emotions can be preserved with pictures, then maybe returning a picture to the album from which it was taken, to the bedroom where it was found, to the configuration it once belonged to, would constitute an act of preservation in its most radical form. I made a video in 2010 titled *On Photography People and Modern Times*. It is about my sense of discovery while researching photography's history in the Middle East, and my more recent reservations about photographic preservation. The video closes with an interview with Armenian-Egyptian photographer Van Leo, during which I try to convince him to donate three additional pictures to AIF while he is trying to avoid answering. Van Leo's hesitation communicates a fear of parting from his images, perhaps because he knows he will soon die: should he agree to give away his archive while he's alive, or stay with it, at the risk of it being dispersed after his death?

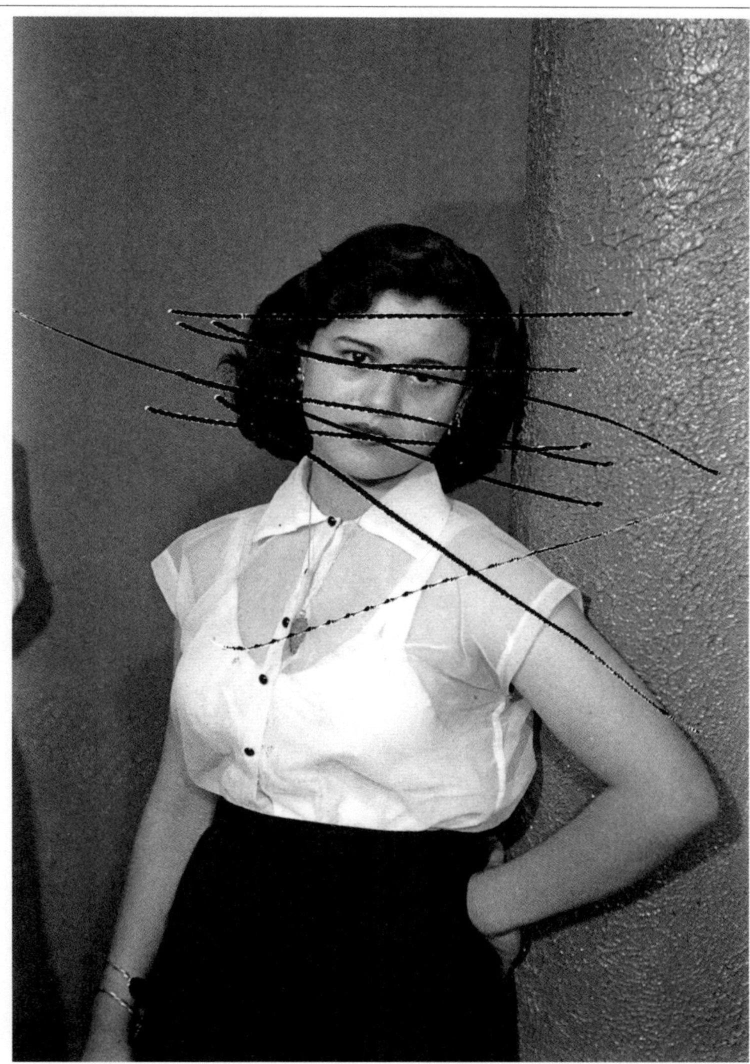

***Objects of Study/Hashem El Madani/Studio Practices/Scratched Portrait of Mrs. Baqari. Saida (Lebanon), 1957.* Modern gelatin-silver print, 2006**
Courtesy the artist and Sfeir Semler Gallery, Hamburg/Beirut
© Arab Image Foundation

MW: **Critics often remark on the archaeological motifs in your work, but this idea of discovery strikes me as more alive with possibilities than the mere search for artifacts. Your video *In This House* (2005) and the related work *Letter for a Time of Peace* (2007) superbly demonstrate the nuance of excavation. The video records the search in the garden of a house in southern Lebanon for a letter buried by former resistance fighter Ali Hashisho, who occupied the house from 1985 to 1991. Can you elaborate on the idea of discovery in that work and in *Letter for a Time of Peace*?**

AZ: When I started digging, looking for Hashisho's letter, which had been buried twelve years earlier in the garden of a house that he and his military group had occupied in Saïda, I was not really after the letter itself, but I was enjoying the *possibility* of finding it, and what might have been the experience of excavating it. I have the actual letter today in a drawer at my home in Beirut. The letter is not the work. The work lies in all that has surrounded its excavation, in what was constructed around that story, gesture, or performance—whatever you might call it. This is exactly how I would like to refer to the collection of the Arab Image Foundation. They are there as records, but also as traces of research, and they are not there as final pieces by themselves.

"Against photography" also means leaning against photography's history in order to move elsewhere, where we can save photography from its fate.

MW: **How does this relate to the world of photography?**

AZ: The world of photography, and the direction in which I see it heading, interests me less and less. I do not think that the platforms dedicated to photography—schools, journals, exhibition spaces, museums, funding organizations—have done enough to challenge definitions or to reenvision or reinvent the medium today. I am glad that Hasselblad Awards were recently given to Sophie Calle and Walid Raad, two artists who have expanded our notion of photography—but I can't see many other examples of forward motion, to be honest.

Look at how the notion of dance has changed in the past fifty years, and you will understand my argument against photography.

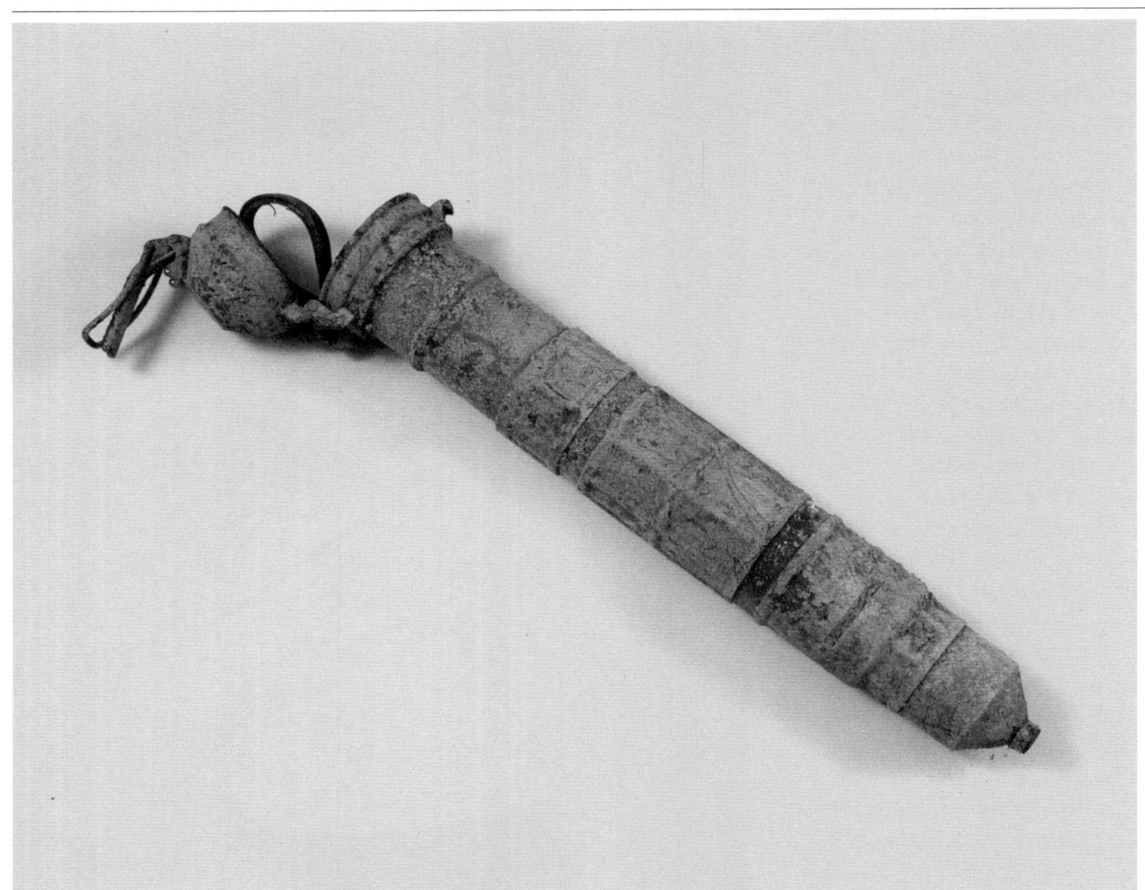

***Letter for a Time of Peace* (the mortar capsule that housed Ali Hashisho's letter), 2007. C-print**
Courtesy the artist and Sfeir Semler Gallery, Hamburg/Beirut

Why, in comparison to dance, has the notion of photography not evolved? In my opinion this lack of progress is largely due to the cult of the original, and the glorification of the image as an object—not as an element in a larger protocol—that makes photography an object of speculation. It is speculation that ties a photographic object on one hand to a market and on another hand to a tradition of conservation. We are told that a photograph needs constant maintenance to keep it alive. Is it because dance is based originally and fundamentally on protocols that it is liberated from definitions, from material objects and the kind of capital that is linked to them? I think this question needs reflection, and I would have loved for the Arab Image Foundation to take it on, but I am afraid it is not yet ready.

If emotions can be preserved with pictures, then maybe returning a picture to the album from which it was taken, to the bedroom where it was found, to the configuration it once belonged to, would constitute an act of preservation in its most radical form.

MW: **Can we extend these ideas to your work at last year's Documenta, as an instance of thinking "against photography"—and ironically against preservation?**

AZ: Instead of *ironically*, let's say *metaphorically*. My work at Documenta 13, *Time Capsule, Kassel* and the film *The End of Time*, imagines scripts/models for radical preservation designed for the Arab Image Foundation. These models consider nonscientific paradigms and recognize the necessity of timely withdrawal—as a gesture of radical preservation—of documents and artifacts in times of risk. The project was inspired by an act of the National Museum in Beirut at the outbreak of the civil war in Lebanon in 1975, when the museum director had most of the museum's collections of archaeological objects and artifacts sealed up inside huge concrete blocks, which remained onsite in the museum's main hall until the end of the war in 1991.

MW: **This parallels the work in your 2009 project *Earth of Endless Secrets*. Your videos *In This House* and *Letter to Samir* foreground the "gestures" of opening and sealing,**

Letter to Samir, 2008.
C-print
Courtesy the artist and Sfeir Semler Gallery, Hamburg/Beirut

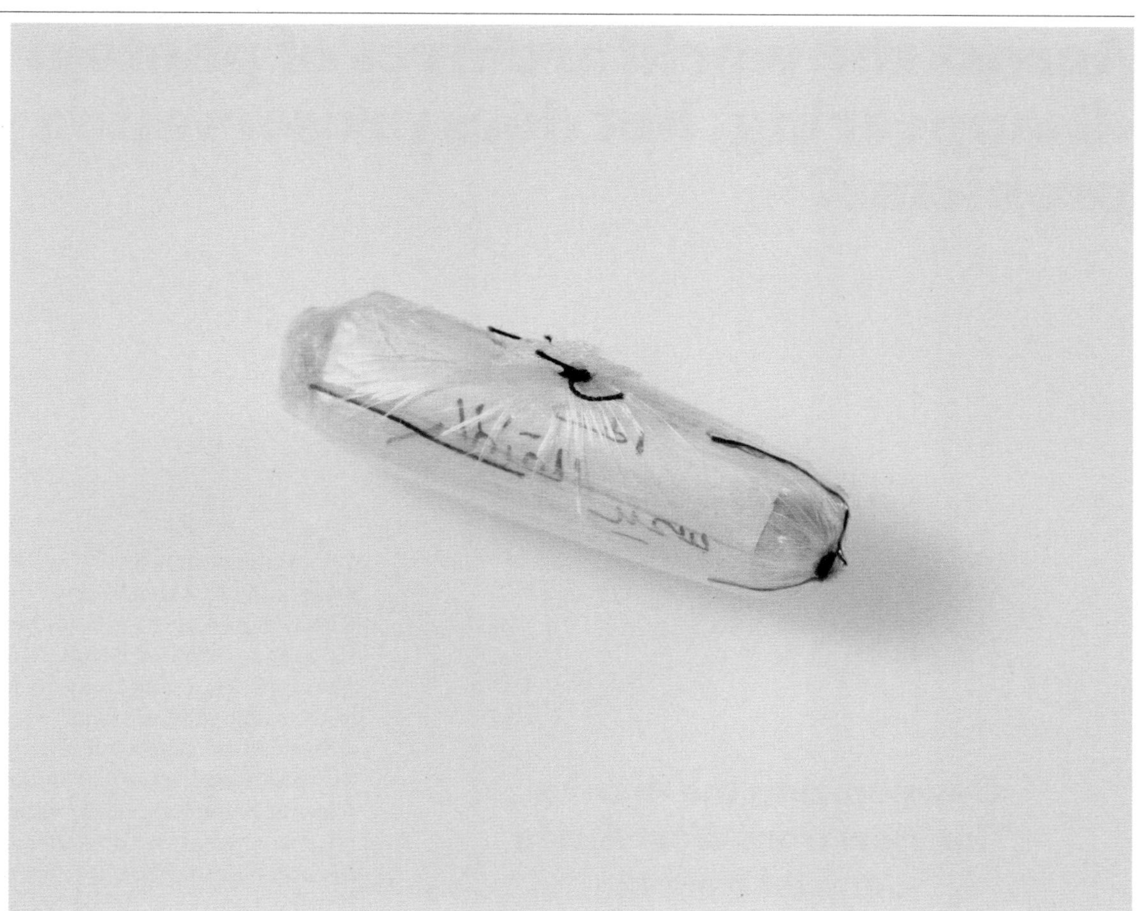

burying and unearthing, and so on. (*Letter to Samir*, of 2008, is a video that depicts the writing of a letter, kept secret and sealed into a capsule, from Lebanese resistance fighter Nabih Awada, a former prisoner-of-war in Israel, to Samir al-Qintar, a prisoner in Israel for thirty years, upon Samir's release in 2008.) In this way, *Time Capsule* strikes me as an extension of your interest in the "habits of recording" during times of war. In what ways does this project relate to your earlier work and in what way does it suggest a new approach?

AZ: I agree that time capsules are ways of recording, and consider the Earth to be the ultimate archive, the ultimate recording; hence the title *Earth of Endless Secrets*. Certain forms of recording—including my diaries, photographs, and audio recordings while living through the Israeli invasion of Lebanon in 1982—are messages for time, but they are not totally time capsules. The work I did for Documenta borrowed the form of the time capsule as a medium to make a statement, to express my take on photography and on archives and on the future of the Arab Image Foundation.

You're right that *Time Capsule, Kassel* draws from other works, notably *Letter to Samir*. *Time Capsule* takes the shape of an underground reinforced concrete foundation, whereas *Letter to Samir* takes the form of a letter-capsule that prisoners make and give to other prisoners to swallow before leaving prison, to send messages out without censorship. For me the form that any time capsule takes—its tectonics—is essential in the work, not only what's inside it. I would even say it *is* the work. I considered leaving *Time Capsule, Kassel* empty—but at the last moment I decided to have it carry painted photographic objects, inspired by different photographic film formats: a reference to a photographer losing sight, hence producing monochromatic paintings. In parallel, *Time Capsule, Kassel* imagines institutions parting from their collections, and photography relieved from the institution.

Akram Zaatari is an artist dedicated to researching and studying photography in the Middle East. His work will be presented this summer at New York's Museum of Modern Art, as *Projects 100*. Zaatari will represent Lebanon at this year's Venice Biennale.

Mark Westmoreland is an anthropologist currently writing a book titled *Catastrophic Images*, about experimental documentary practices in Lebanon.

Across the world archives of photographs are disappearing, but does preservation pose its own problems?

Decolonizing the Archive
The View from West Africa

Jennifer Bajorek

A museum director and friend in Saint-Louis, Senegal, once said to me when I asked her if it was true that large numbers of negatives had been dumped into the Senegal River: "Si ce n'est pas de poissons, c'est des clichés" (There may not be fish, but there are negatives). Her comment refers to the contemporary crisis in the local supply chain caused by overfishing in Atlantic coastal waters. It also refers to the fact that large numbers of negatives have been destroyed, or disposed of in ways that have led to their destruction, in this city, as in several other coastal West African cities, over the years. Owing to the particular geography of Saint-Louis, whose central districts are located on an island in the mouth of the Senegal River, negatives—including whole crates of glass-plate negatives—have become trapped in the mouth of the river, which is separated from the Atlantic by the island and by the long, thin sandbar known as La Langue de Barbarie. This sandbar, which has amassed what I sometimes refer to as the "submarine archive," has played an unexpected role in what we might call the archival situation in Senegal. In Ghana, by contrast, negatives disposed of in a similar fashion have simply washed out to the open sea.

Although Saint-Louis boasts a history of photography that goes back to the nineteenth century (the first known daguerreotype studio opened in the city in 1860), most photographs of that vintage are long gone. The jettisoning of negatives—mostly studio archives from the mid-twentieth century—appears to have peaked in the mid-1980s. This is the same period that, not incidentally, saw the closure of hundreds of black-and-white studios owned and operated by African photographers, as a result of the transition to color.

Along with my work in Saint-Louis, I have in recent years been doing research in several other cities in coastal West Africa with rich histories of photography: Dakar, Senegal; and Porto-Novo and Cotonou, Benin. In all these places large numbers of photographs, dating from the first half of the twentieth century to the mid-1980s, are in advanced states of decay. Some are closer to dust than to photographs. But I am also very aware that photographs have been destroyed or are missing for other reasons. Some have been carried away to distant cities and other continents with relatives. Whole swaths of archives are missing because they have been sold to European collectors. Other images were deliberately destroyed in the years before the collectors came. My research has sought to frame what is called "archival loss" (the term favored by international archivists' associations and UNESCO) in a new perspective in Africa, where the practical protocols and infrastructures of the archive are fraught with colonial legacies. In a formal and institutional sense, they have been imposed largely by those in the West and North, who continue to control the purse strings even of projects initiated from Africa.

Not all instances of archival loss are the result of dramatic acts of destruction, but stories such as that of Saint-Louis's "submarine archive" add considerable nuance to our understanding of "loss." As my friend's sly reference to the contemporary geopolitical situation reminds us (the blame for overfishing off the coast of Senegal lies mainly with Europe and particularly Spain), the African studios that were forced to shut their doors in the 1980s were put out of business by foreign competition: new color labs, owned by Lebanese or Koreans. The outlays of cash required to buy color film-processing machines were beyond the reach of ordinary Africans. The submarine archive is, among other things, an allegory of the loss of cultural sovereignty. At the very moment that Africans were supposed to be seizing control of their destiny in the postcolonial period, photographers who had fought to maintain both creative and economic control of the photographic apparatus during the colonial period found that it could be suddenly taken away. Such stories are also, however, about the survival of photographic memory. They point to forms of resilience—and resources for writing, or transmitting, history—that have allowed these communities to remember their lost photographs, and an earlier period of photography history, even when the images are no longer visible or tangible as photographs. As such, the submarine archive encourages us to rethink the relationships among history, memory, and photography in ways that can seem downright prophetic or at least ahead of their time, given that twentieth-century photographic prints and negatives are disappearing all over the world today.

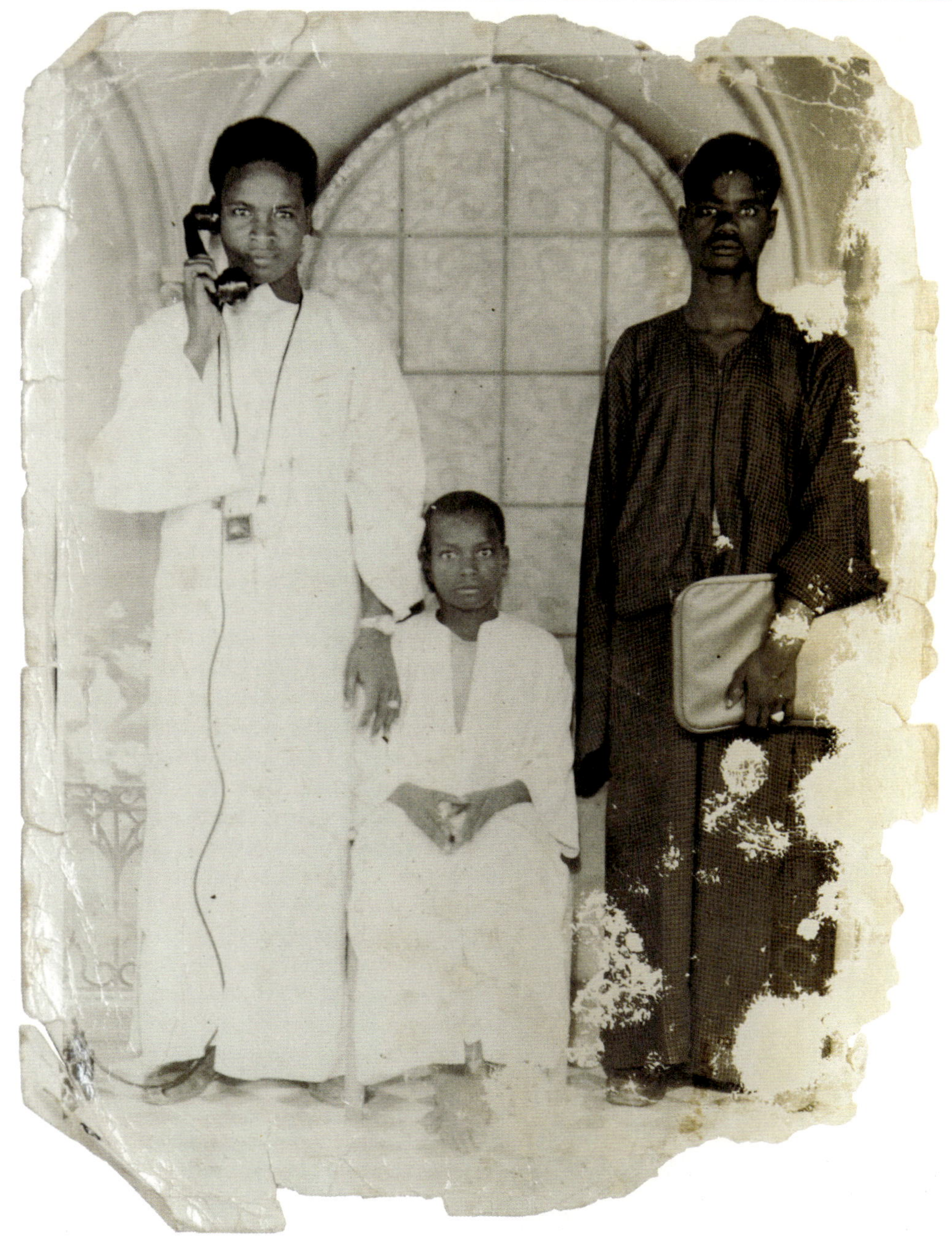

Portrait of three young men with wristwatches, briefcase, and telephone, Dakar (Médina), Senegal, early 1960s. Photographer unknown
Private collection of Dédé Ly, Dakar, Senegal. Rephotographed by Leslie Rabine

I was first drawn to West Africa by distinctively local aesthetic concerns that deliberately engage with the ephemerality of the photographic image. Longstanding notions about the fixity of the photographic reference have been challenged throughout the region from a very early date. Common practices—such as writing, drawing, and painting on photographs, with charcoal, graphite, and gouache, and the repeated reproduction of prints through serial rephotography over many generations—seem openly to address ephemerality and decay, aesthetically and conceptually, and to inscribe a conscious engagement with photographic materiality within the visual frame. Scholar Erin Haney has written beautifully about photographs in early twentieth-century Gold Coast (present-day Ghana) in which the image of a given individual would be carefully removed from a photograph, or a new one introduced—effecting the substitution, for example, of one wife for another within the photographic frame. Another widespread practice, also in Ghana, consists of marking an "X" on the surface of a photographic print above the head of anyone who has died. Several years ago, while looking through photographs in the archives of the New York Public Library's Schomburg Center for Research in Black Culture, I came across a photograph of a West African delegation

A delicate "X" had been discreetly marked, in black ink, above the head of the representative from Ghana—an indication that the man was dead, and that the photograph […] had passed through Ghanaian hands.

to the United Nations, in which a delicate "X" had been discreetly marked, in black ink, above the head of the representative from Ghana—an indication that the man was dead, and that the photograph, which had been taken in New York and had very likely never left it, had passed through Ghanaian hands.

Such practices alert us to dormant material qualities of the photograph, and heighten our awareness of the photograph's inherent capacity for modification, right on the surface of the print. If the hair or other features of the photographic subject have been inked in, it is often because the photograph was faded. In other cases, photographs have been repeatedly inked over many years, or various lines and features darkened with charcoal or redrawn, in open acknowledgment of fading and disintegration: actions that underscore both the photograph's impermanence and its vulnerability to deterioration, and that engage with it in creative ways.

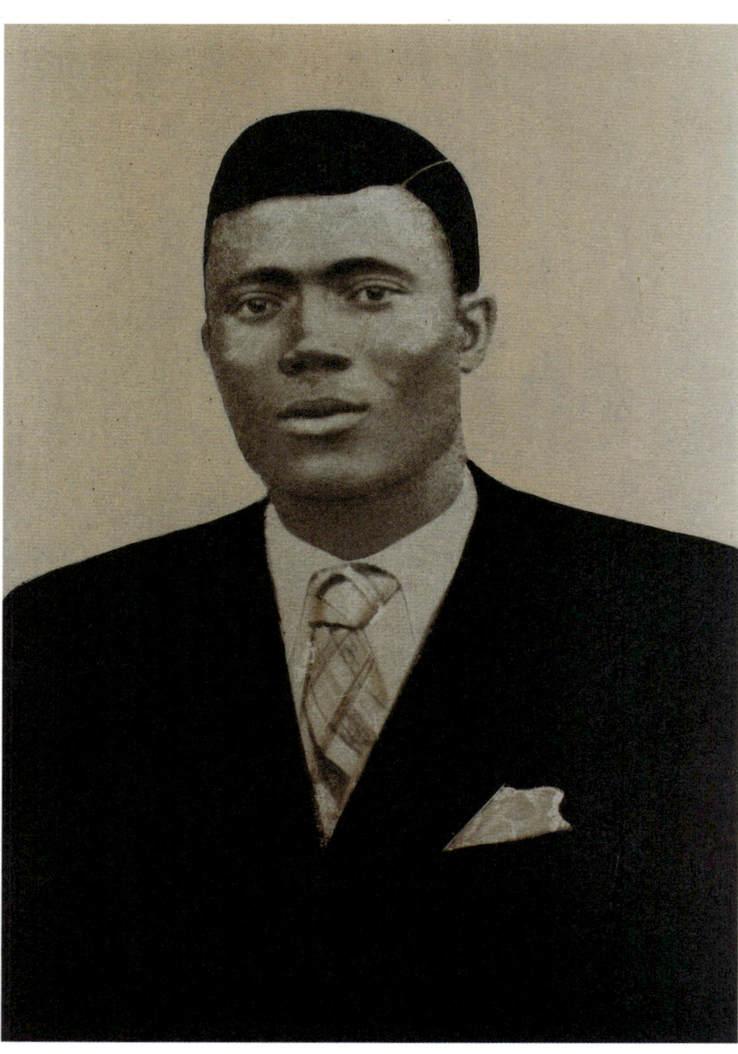

Edouard Méhomey, unknown sitter, Porto-Novo, Benin, mid-1960s. Photograph overpainted with gouache and ink
Private collection of Ida Méhomey, Porto-Novo, Benin. Rephotographed by Ida Méhomey

This same vulnerability is naturally a major preoccupation of the keepers and sponsors of photographic collections and archives. As a consequence of my research, I have also become involved in projects focused on creating, and funding, archives and other institutions for photography in Africa. Substantive reflection on the politics of the archive is, when it comes to these types of practical projects, urgently necessary—and sadly elusive. Digitization—which, it was widely thought, would make possible new modes of preservation, even if it cannot ensure a photograph's survival—has offered few solutions here. International digital archival standards, explicitly imposed by Northern and Western grant makers, stipulate that archival masters should be produced from negatives, and that prints should be included only if they provide "contextual information" (writing on the verso, a name, date, or caption)—thereby disregarding concerns with both the ephemerality and materiality of photographs as objects that are central to African histories. The equipment essential to local management of a digital archive (servers, backup systems, and the generators needed to run them in the absence of a reliable electricity supply) is considered to be "infrastructure" by these same grant makers—and therefore not covered under their funding guidelines.

These guidelines are based on a utopian vision of industrial modernity that is, at best, irrelevant to contemporary African realities. They are furthermore incapable of grasping the intention of a photograph such as the one in these pages of Oumou Khady Guèye. What archive, analog or digital, in existence or imaginable today has the protocols of preservation, the equipment, and indeed the infrastructure in place that would allow us to valorize ephemerality, transience, and decay in a way that would be faithful to this photograph? How do we archive a photograph that in turn archives the progress of its own decay, and that chronicles a quintessentially photographic experience of ephemerality and loss? Rarely does one find in West Africa a photograph of great value that has not been rephotographed, and in which cropping, retouching, or other postproduction manipulation after multiple episodes of rephotography have been used to *conceal*, rather than to highlight, the fact of decay. As for the idea that the equipment necessary to the archive is "infrastructure," and is therefore the responsibility of the state, this assumes a certain understanding of state sovereignty, and of the state's responsibility to its citizens—an understanding that is regrettably narrow.

Visual anthropologist Liam Buckley directs us to an important crux in this discussion. Buckley has argued eloquently for what he calls "the right to allow for decay," a right that is, he maintains, central to the cultural practice of archiving. Buckley is responding to the anxieties of (mostly non-African) researchers regarding the conditions of advanced decay that they have found in African photography archives, even in formal institutional settings. While they may be unsettling, Buckley's arguments are exemplary of a series of more radical decolonial strategies, and they become clearer when we consider the complicated relationships among photographic archives and colonialism from a postcolonial vantage point.

Whereas in most of Europe, the birth of the modern nation-state took place before the invention of photography, in most of Africa, photography predates the implantation of the state form by more than a century. Not only was photography witness to the birth of the postcolonial state in Africa (1960 in francophone West Africa, where my own research is focused), it was deeply bound up with it. Collections connected with the rise of African liberation movements and with the inaugural moments of decolonization nonetheless remain squarely outside official and state-sponsored institutional spaces—in washtubs, under beds. The situation is vexed by the fact that the official or state-sponsored archive is in most of these places a colonial institution, inaugurated by Europeans as part of their colonial projects.

As Buckley astutely observes, in voicing their anxieties, foreign researchers often continue these projects unwittingly when they collude with the ruses of development discourse and other discourses calling for the "modernization" of African states. Buckley suggests that letting certain things go—literally, letting them rot—in the existing institutional contexts may itself be a sign of modernization, and the supreme expression of sovereignty.

In those rare cases in which postcolonial African states have taken a more active interest in curating their own archives and shaping an explicitly postcolonial archival legacy, further questions about the materiality of the archive crop up. Political scientist Achille Mbembe, in his 2002 essay "The Power of the Archive and Its Limits," writes compellingly about the attempts on the part of states to destroy or suppress certain archives—for example, of myriad liberation movements or, in South Africa prior to the transition to democracy, of the struggle against apartheid. Such gestures are, in a sense, the flipside of the right to allow for decay. They are not identical to the exercise of state sovereignty, yet they cannot be wholly separated from its conditions. Mbembe notes that, all too often, when these states have succeeded in destroying the material support of the archive (by destroying actual photographs or documents), they have ended only by strengthening the power of collective memory, which lives on in, and defines, a community. These attempts demonstrate, again, that more general questions about the exercise of state sovereignty are essentially bound up with the *materiality* of the archive even more than with its contents. "The final destination of the archive is," Mbembe writes, "[...] always situated outside its own materiality."

The image of the world's waterways clogged with discarded photographs is a haunting one. But it is not possible for me or any other scholar or theorist to prescribe when, or whether, a given archive should be preserved, or conversely left to rot, or deliberately destroyed. On the contrary, to take it upon myself (or to leave it to any other foreign researcher) to decide which photographs should be preserved and which merely remembered would be to further the loss of cultural sovereignty discussed at the start of this essay. It would also be to ignore the more nuanced picture of the materiality of the archive, and of photographic memory, that emerges in the West African case. Few could deny that we now have both the historical distance and practical experience to know that images, like technologies, are neither culturally nor politically neutral. It follows that "archival loss" does not have the same meaning in all places. Nor should it. It remains an open question of what it will take to decolonize the archive in this context, and one that we are just beginning to explore.

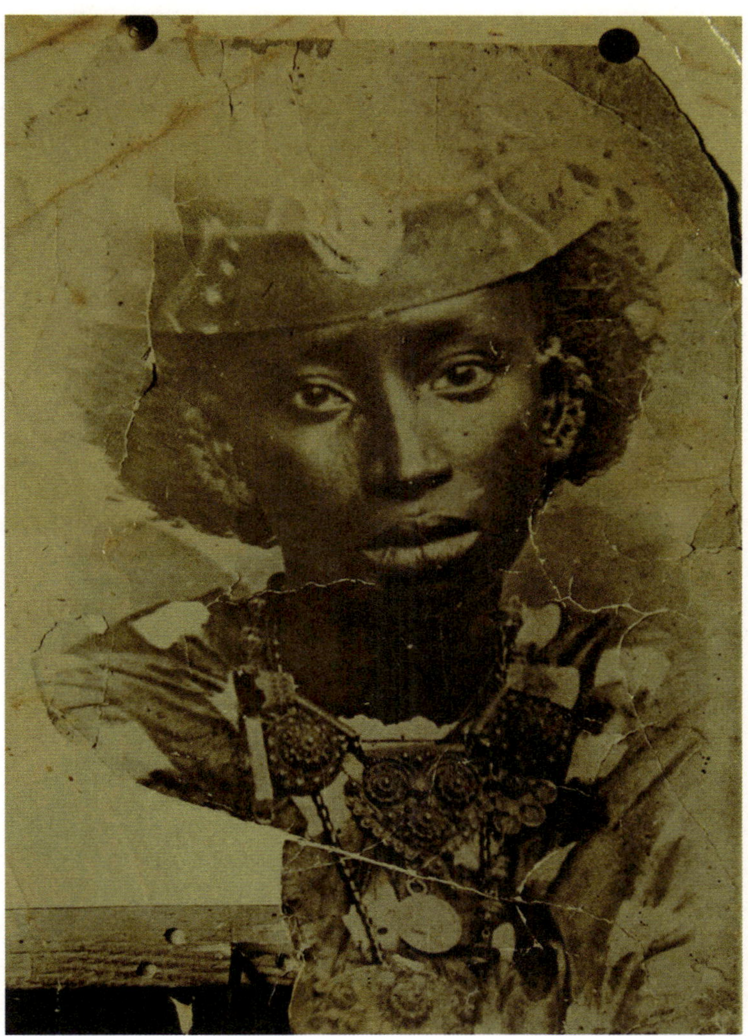

Portrait of Oumou Khady Guèye, Dakar, Senegal, early 1930s (first vintage print); 1958 (print that was rephotographed, using a digital camera, in 2007). Photographer unknown
Private collection of Ibrahima Faye and Khady Ndoye, Dakar, Senegal. Rephotographed by Leslie Rabine

Jennifer Bajorek writes and does research on literature, philosophy, and photography. She is completing a book on photography and decolonial imagination in Senegal and Benin.

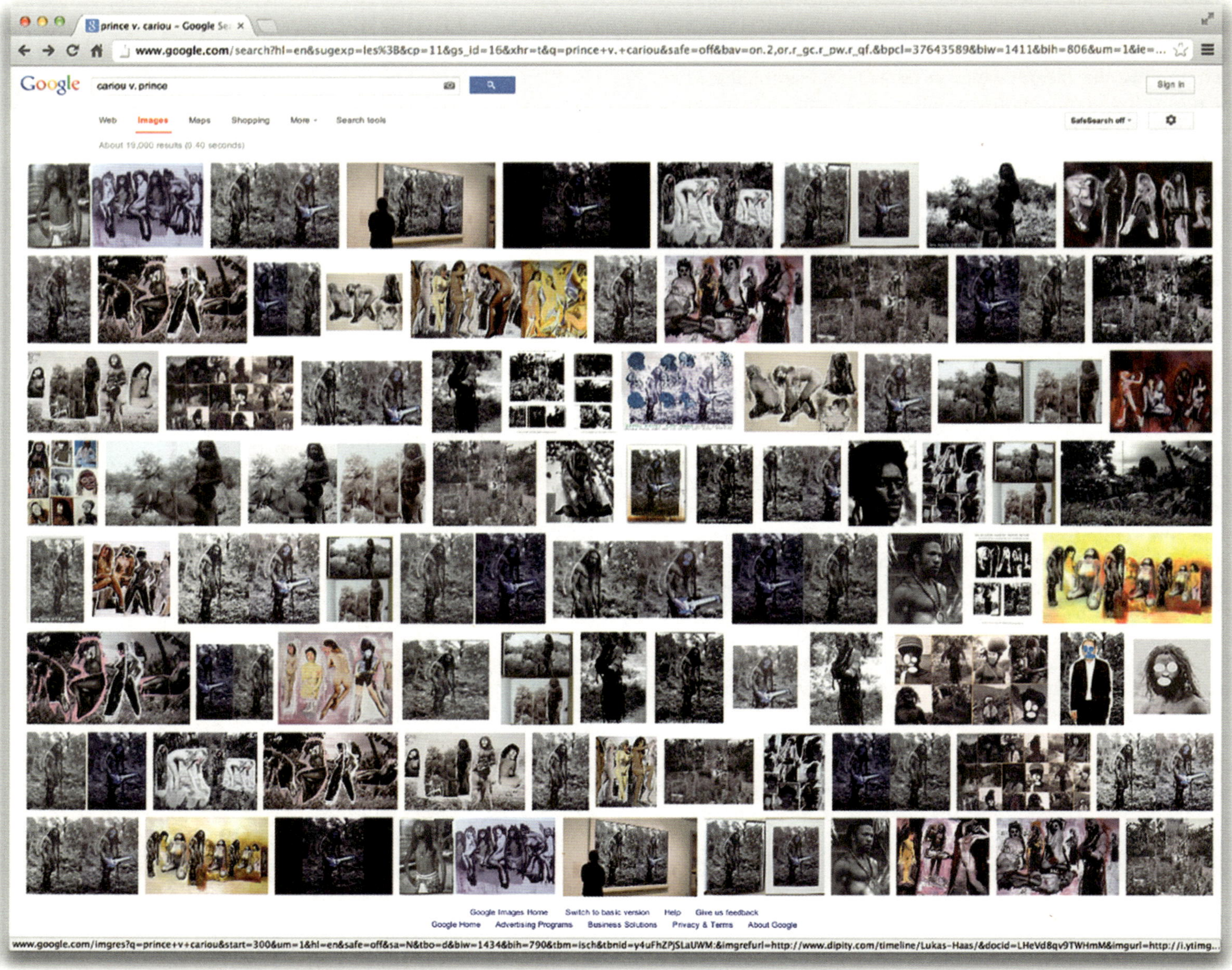

The Image World Is Flat

Penelope Umbrico in conversation with Virginia Rutledge

Virginia Rutledge and Penelope Umbrico, *cariou v.prince/Google Image Search on 11/07/2012*, 2012; digital collage of the first eighty-five images of photographs and paintings by Patrick Cariou and Richard Prince found on Google Images during a single "cariou v.prince" search.
Courtesy the artists

In 2008 Patrick Cariou brought a copyright infringement suit against Richard Prince. Prince had used images of Rastafarians photographed by Cariou and published in a photobook to create a series of collage paintings. At the trial level, Prince's use of Cariou's images was ruled infringing, and the case is now on appeal. Debates around appropriation raise a number of questions regarding creative freedom, fair use, and transformative versus derivative borrowing. However, a less examined aspect of legal cases involving art is the role played by visual evidence. Here artist Penelope Umbrico, known for her work with images sourced from various print and online contexts, speaks with art historian and intellectual-property lawyer Virginia Rutledge about the use of reproductions in our increasingly flattened image world. — The Editors

Penelope Umbrico: **I'd like to start with something you said recently on a panel about the *Cariou v. Prince* case. You mentioned that judges don't always see the art involved in litigation about copyright, but may only be looking at reproductions. I tried to imagine both Cariou's book-sized black-and-white photographs and Prince's giant color paintings reduced to standard 8.5-by-11-inch photocopies. It strikes me as absurd that people who aren't familiar with the actual works are asked to compare reproductions in order to make a judgment about them.**

Virginia Rutledge: It is absurd, but not uncommon, for courts to consider images of art rather than the art itself. Certainly there can be logistical challenges in making a direct examination of disputed artworks, if we're talking about bringing enormous paintings like Prince's into court or arranging judicial field trips. But the greater challenge is to see what is at stake if the only reference point is a set of reproductions! Maybe the concept of hearsay is useful here. Basically, hearsay is a statement made by someone out of court, so there is no witness to directly question or test for credibility or veracity. There are exceptions, but generally hearsay isn't admissible as evidence of the truth of what the statement asserts. Obviously we can push this analogy much too far, but reproductions of art are largely hearsay—they shouldn't be taken as evidence of the "truth" of the artistic statement.

PU: **Relying on reproductions as evidence seems particularly problematic in this case, since the finding of "transformative use" is so important in determining whether an appropriation of a copyrighted image is fair. How can a court understand where artistic transformation occurs if the documentation moves through generations of degradation entirely beyond the artist's control? There may be very little space between a photograph and its reproduction in a good print publication. However, an image of a painting in a book is always going to look like a reproduction of a painting—we are obviously looking at one medium seen through another. Seeing a photocopy of a photograph side-by-side with a photocopy of a photograph of a painting really doesn't give us any sense of what we are supposed to be looking at. Both sides of the evidence actually start to look alike.**

VR: That is a very funny and scary observation, not least because the charge of copyright infringement depends on the existence of "substantial similarity" between works, to use the legal term. I have to agree that reproductions can cause serious damage to the understanding of paintings rather more quickly than may occur with some photographs. But perhaps this is just a more insidious problem with respect to photography, and maybe the photobook in particular. Neither Cariou nor Prince is well represented by most of the images of their work that are circulating in the media at the moment. And in Cariou's case the images are completely severed from the context of the book in which they initially appeared.

PU: **Well, yes, and, if this is the argument, then any single image that is excerpted from Cariou's book is actually transformed by just that decontextualization alone.**

VR: That separation from the book context definitely alters my perception of the work, as it would if I saw the images printed and framed as separate objects. This is where vocabulary can be tricky, though. Showing a single image from Cariou's book does not necessarily "transform" it in the sense that's relevant for copyright. And with respect to art, it may be entirely relevant who does the decontextualizing and why. As we're talking to some degree about the artists' intentions, it's important that we credit how much the art world makes of how an image is presented and encountered. That understanding is central in the critical discourse about documentary photography, and it also underpins our appreciation of the meaning of artistic strategies involving appropriation of images, in all their great variety. Is it controversial to suggest that people who spend more time in studios, galleries, and museums are probably going to be more attuned to meanings produced by shifts in context and better at reading reproductions of art than people who spend less time? What can we reasonably expect of the average judge or juror who may not have the same experience of art, and the same visual expertise?

PU: **I began with this idea of the photocopy because I think the distance it represents equates with a lack of visual sensitivity. It points to the assumptions we make based on viewing images through such media of mass distribution.**

VR: It's curious. We all know certain musical scores or motifs, and we hear the musical work across different performances and different technologies of recording. But we are also very aware that the work is being realized at *this* moment in *this* way. The role of performance in the perception of "the work" is one of the things that makes music and sound different from the visual arts, and as contemporary art embraces hybrid media we can experience ever more powerfully when and why those differences matter. When we're looking at still images, however, it seems easier to lose sight of the work if we fail to see the mediation of reproduction. It's rather alarming to imagine judges comparing reproductions of different works of art and thinking that they are considering impartial evidence, when in fact what is most in evidence is the flattening effect of technologies of reproduction.

PU: **So the work itself becomes neutralized and leveled. It's not unlike what happens to images on the Web—where they have no physicality, place, or specificity. Though the screen itself is clearly a medium through which we see the image, the "object-ness" of the actual works is lost and so they can be moved from one setting to another with ease.**

VR: Yes, and without the right caption, so to speak, it is easy to mistake the image. This reminds me that some years ago when art history lectures still involved analog slides, I needed an image of Sherrie Levine's now-classic *After Walker Evans*. There was no easy-to-hand reproduction of Levine's work, so I made my own—by substituting an image of the Evans photograph. Of course neither work is adequately represented by a slide surrogate.

PU: **It's a good example of how invisible the medium is, and therefore how easy it is not to acknowledge its particularity.**

VR: Thus the danger of overreliance on reproductions of art in legal cases: it helps dumb down the fair-use analysis to an exercise in mere image recognition. The role of context in shaping meaning is disregarded, and visual connoisseurship is ditched. If the test for copyright infringement is simply "match the image," the first copyright holder will always win. Fortunately there's much more to fair use. What matters most is whether new expression or meaning is created. Fundamentally, that is

Left: Image cropped from a photograph captioned *"cariou's vs. prince's,"* found at http://www.tomorrowstarted.com/2009/04/richard-prince-copyright-infringement/.html; Center: Image of a scan of a page from the book *Canal Zone Richard Prince YES RASTA: Selected Court Documents from Cariou v. Prince et al by Greg Allen* (greg.org, 2011); Right: Image of a photograph captioned "Richard Prince, 'Canal Zone,' installation view, Nov. 8–Dec. 20, 2008, Gagosian Gallery, New York," found at http://www.artnet.com/magazineus/features/finch/richard-prince-copyright-3-21-11_detail.asp?picnum=2. Courtesy the artists

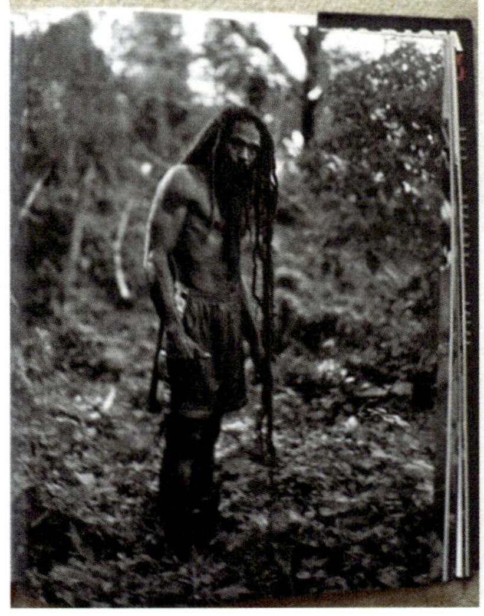

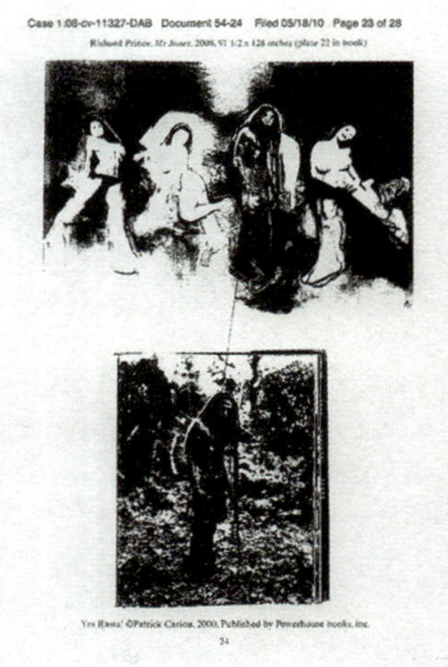

Case 1:08-cv-11327-DAB Document 54-24 Filed 05/18/10 Page 23 of 28

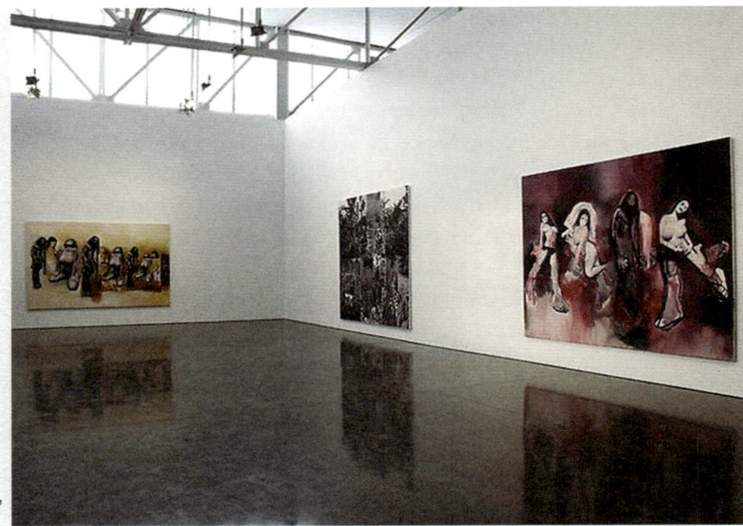

why *Cariou v. Prince* is so perplexing. It's easy to spot "Cariou's" Rastafarians in Prince's paintings, but even the Prince works that make the least visual changes to Cariou's imagery clearly make a different artistic statement.

PU: **And if the test for infringement is image recognition, then this tests our assumptions about who "authors" the recognizable aspects of the image. Why are they "Cariou's Rastafarians"? I'm not saying we should contest Cariou's authorship of his photographs, but if it comes down to the recognizability of his subjects, then shouldn't we?**

VR: It's an intriguing point, and suggests a huge discussion about "cultural authorship" and some additional legal rules—next time, perhaps! Let's return to your mention of the Internet as not only a distribution platform for this material, but also as a leveling mechanism. Consumed via the screen, images certainly can be subject to a kind of leveling not unlike what happens when reproductions of art are gathered for a set of legal exhibits.

PU: **So, we end up with an example like this image created for an article on the case published by Artinfo.com—a mashup of a relatively small Cariou photograph and a much larger Prince painting, inserted in what appears to be real space. There's no perceived physical difference, or distance, between the two works. Some people, including myself at one point, have mistaken this manipulated illustration for an installation shot of an actual work of art. And this image is now all over the Web, often with no attribution. Seeing it in the flat sea of other images is confusing.**

VR: Absolutely—although no one familiar with Cariou's photography could think for a moment that this is *his* work. So thank goodness there's a credit line for all those who may not happen to be in the know. Well, how very nice of "Flickr and the Artists" to allow their work to be reproduced in this way! Which just proves that context can be everything.

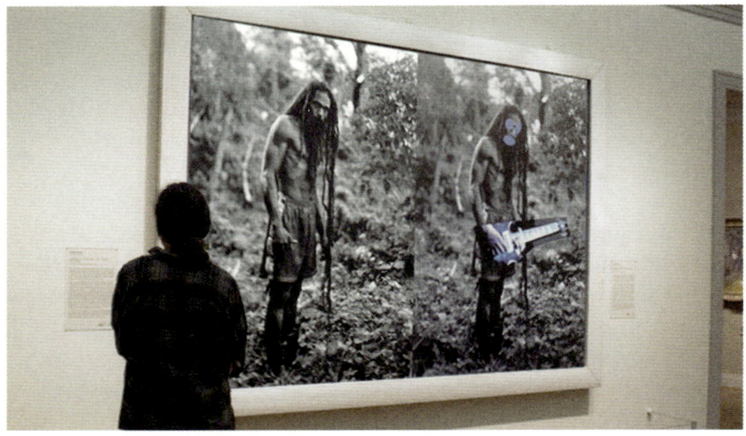

Courtesy Flickr and the Artists; Illustration by BLOUIN ARTINFO

Top:
Virginia Rutledge and Penelope Umbrico, detail from *Images and Texts*, 2012; digital collage of images and texts, output variable

Bottom:
An illustration as published on artinfo.com to accompany the article "Is Prince v. Cariou Already Having a Chilling Effect? Contemporary Artists Speak," by Julia Halperin, found at http://www.artinfo.com/news/story/758352/is-prince-v-cariou-already-having-a-chilling-effect-contemporary-artists-speak

Virginia Rutledge is an art historian and attorney based in New York. Formerly a curator for the Los Angeles County Museum of Art, a litigator at Cravath, Swaine & Moore LLP, and vice president and general counsel of Creative Commons, she is now in private practice focusing on intellectual property, contemporary art, and cultural organizations.

Penelope Umbrico is a visual artist based in New York. She currently holds a Guggenheim Fellowship and a Smithsonian Artist Research Fellowship.

***Penelope Umbrico (photographs)* was published by Aperture in 2011.**

Pictures

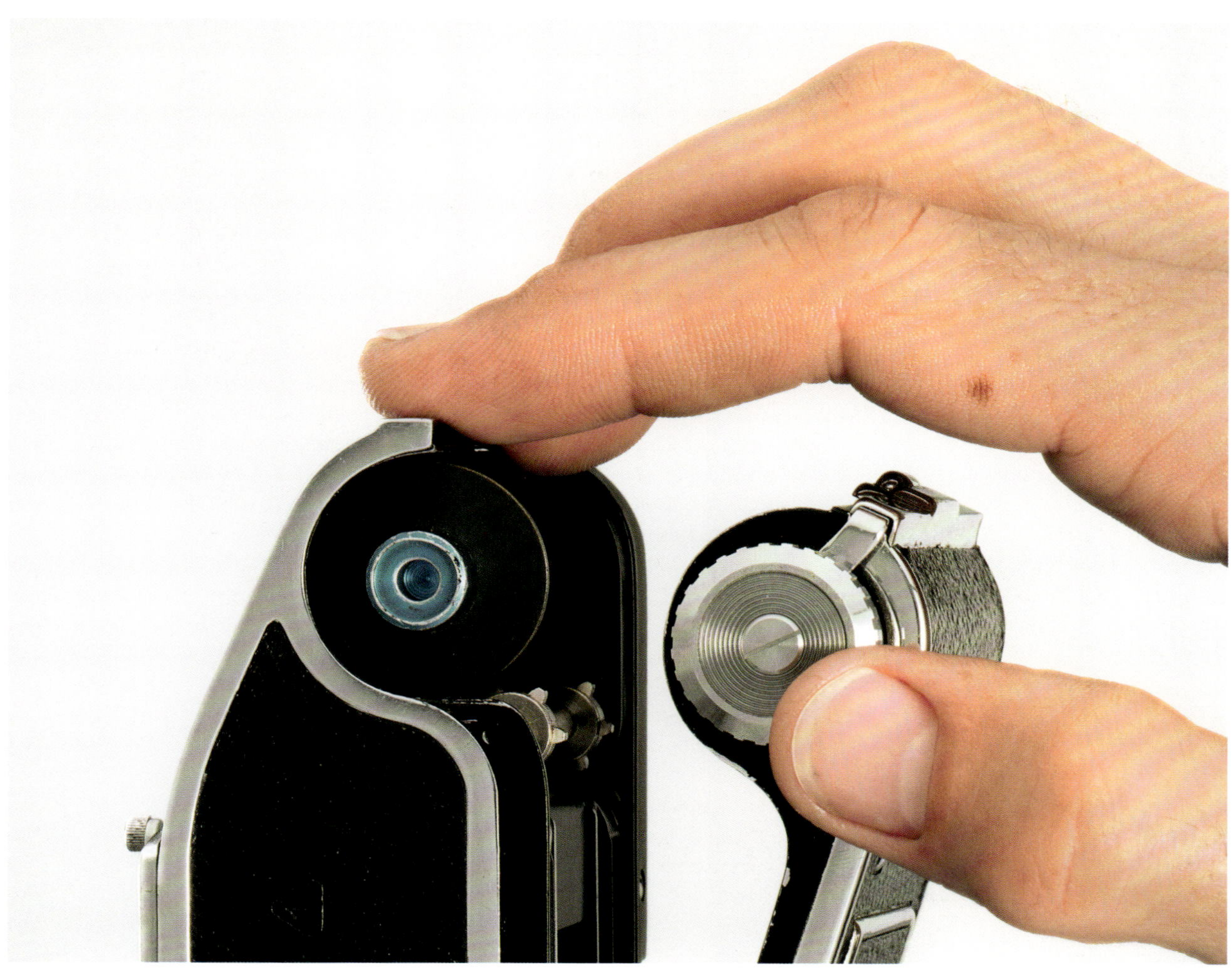

In 1960 the Dresden firm of Ihagee Kamerawerk brought out the third version of its Varex IIa model of the Exakta brand, the world's first 35-millimeter single-lens reflex camera. The initial model, marketed in 1936, expressed the link between still and movie cameras—reified through shared use of 35-millimeter film—in its name, the Kine Exakta. James Stewart, in the 1954 film *Rear Window*, had as his "co-star" an Exakta V (Varex) paired with a Kilfitt 400/5.6 extreme telephoto lens.

Sometime between 1966 and 1968, standing on a sidewalk in National City, California, John Baldessari had himself photographed in front of a palm tree. He had the snapshot enlarged on photo-sensitized canvas, then hired a sign painter to letter a single word underneath this image: *WRONG*. The work flouted conventions of painting, of course: photo-emulsion, not oils; banality in place of rapture; work for hire that doesn't pass itself off as free creation. But the most rebellious move in *Wrong* is Baldessari's turn for source material to art and photography manuals, which convey an unalloyed delight in codifying rules of composition. Don't pose people in front of objects taller than themselves, the experts like to write—it will look like the thing is growing out of their heads!

If ever there was a camera of which it could be said, "They don't build 'em like they used to," it is the Exakta VX IIa. [...] It is the epitome of German fine engineering, a Precision Instrument with capital letters. Those who are accustomed to more modern cameras may however breathe a short prayer of thanks at the fact that they don't make 'em like this any more. Compared with the vast majority of cameras past or present, many of the controls are upside down or backwards or both. It is not so much a camera with some eccentric features built in, as a collection of eccentric features with a camera hiding somewhere behind them.
— Roger W. Hicks and Frances E. Schultz, "Varex IIa," at rogerandfrances.com.

"The Exakta Varex is a valuable precision appliance, but it can satisfy all your demands only when it is always properly used," begins the manufacturer's instruction manual. Among the demanding and unusual features are a film advance lever that strips gears if not wound in one motion to its full, 270-degree extension; also, a hook-shaped knife attached to a pull-out rod that permits slicing film after any frame (and which can easily nick a carelessly placed finger during roll changes). This feature may have been helpful to Josef Koudelka, who shot some five thousand pictures in one week during the 1968 Soviet-led invasion of Prague using what a reporter for the *London Observer* later called a "primitive Exakta," which he stocked with lengths of salvaged movie film. True to form, Koudelka circulated barely one dozen of these images to the press, considering that more choices would be redundant or distracting.

The most unusual feature of Exakta cameras, common to all the models, is undoubtedly the placement of shutter release, aperture dials, and other important components on the left-hand side of the camera body. Ideological significance could be ascribed to this left-handedness for models made after 1945, when Dresden—along with Jena, home to lens manufacturer Carl Zeiss—became part of the Soviet bloc. Although it seems false to give radical political valence to a technological mechanism, particularly when the mechanism in question predates the corresponding political shift, such inventive readings were common in the part of Europe called "central" until 1945 and "eastern" thereafter. Even a simple advertisement for apples could, with the right lighting and in proper context, be understood to idealize socialist values, in opposition to values of the bourgeois era that directly preceded it. That era produced more than its fair share of studies of apples and apple trees, thanks to the legions of Exakta- and other camera-wielding enthusiasts.

Christopher Williams studied with John Baldessari and conceptual artist Michael Asher at California Institute of the Arts in the years around 1980. He has long worked using manufacturer manuals and showroom models as reference material for his photographs. Since 2008 he has been professor of photography at the Kunstakademie Düsseldorf. He lives in Cologne, Germany, and Amsterdam, The Netherlands.

Christopher Williams

Matthew S. Witkovsky

Matthew S. Witkovsky is the Richard and Ellen Sandor Chair and Curator, Department of Photography at the Art Institute of Chicago. He is collaborating with Christopher Williams; Roxana Marcoci, curator of photography at the Museum of Modern Art, New York; and Mark Godfrey, curator at Tate Modern, on a major show of Williams's works to be presented in Chicago and New York in 2014.

All Exakta camera photographs untitled as of 2012

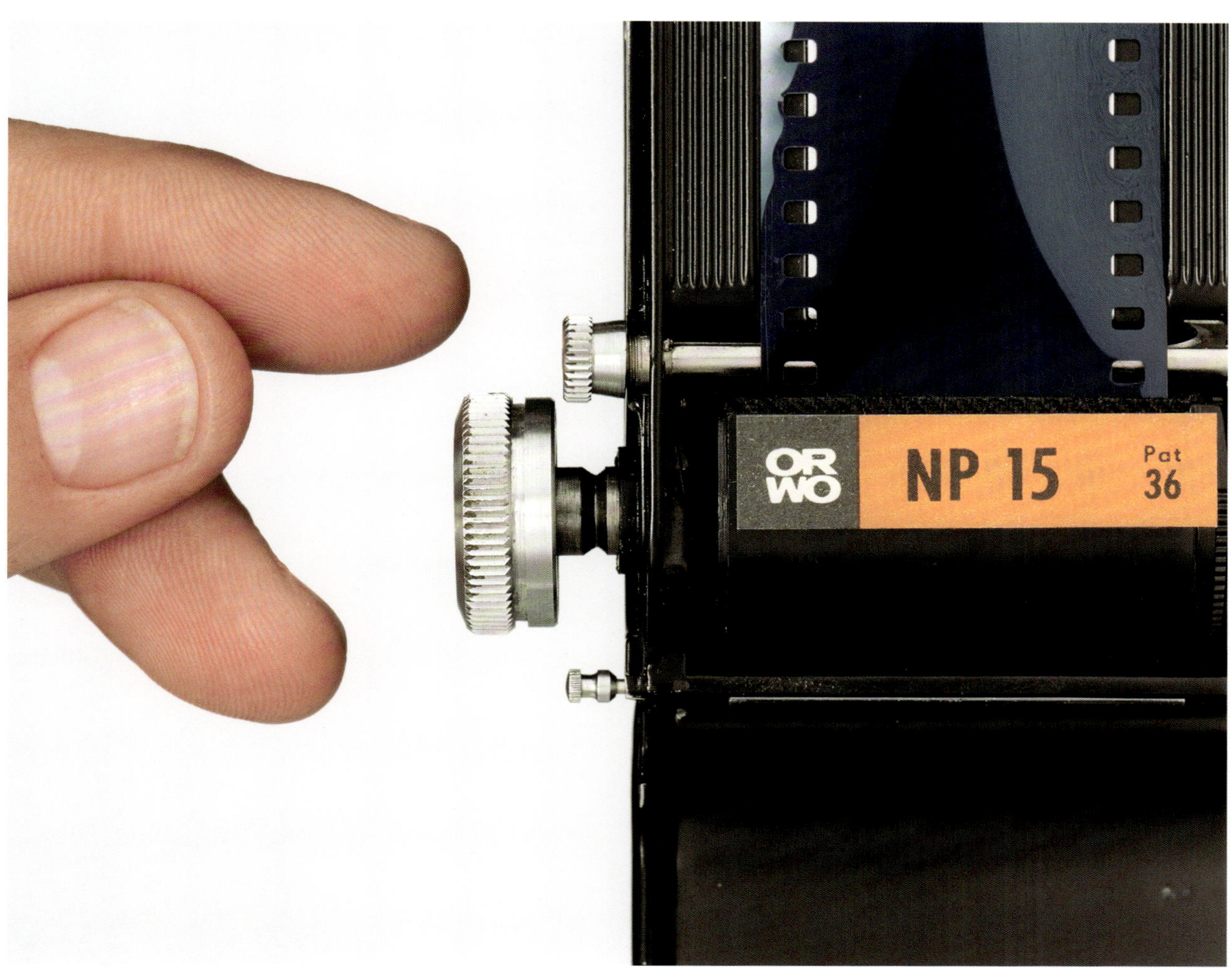

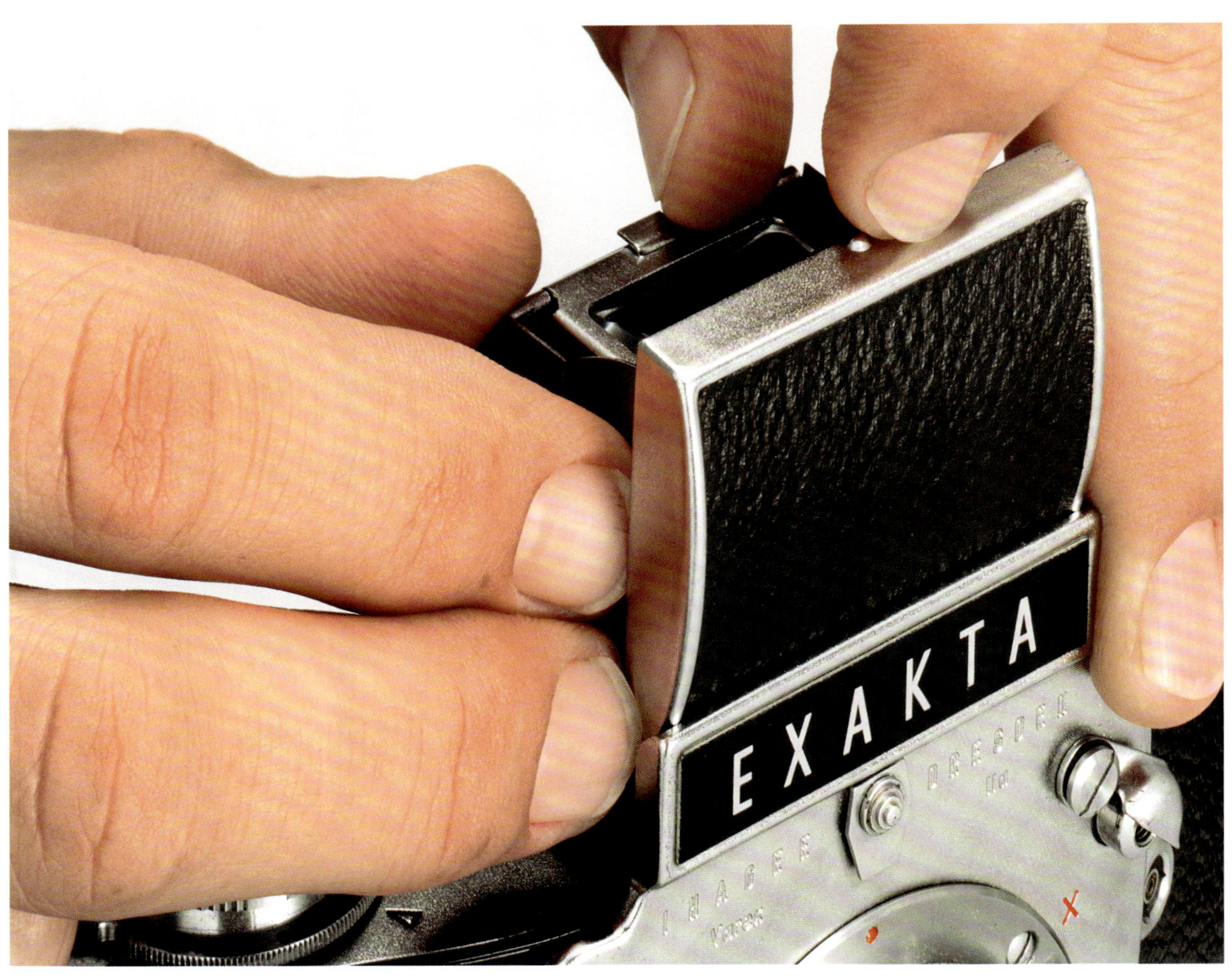
EXAKTA

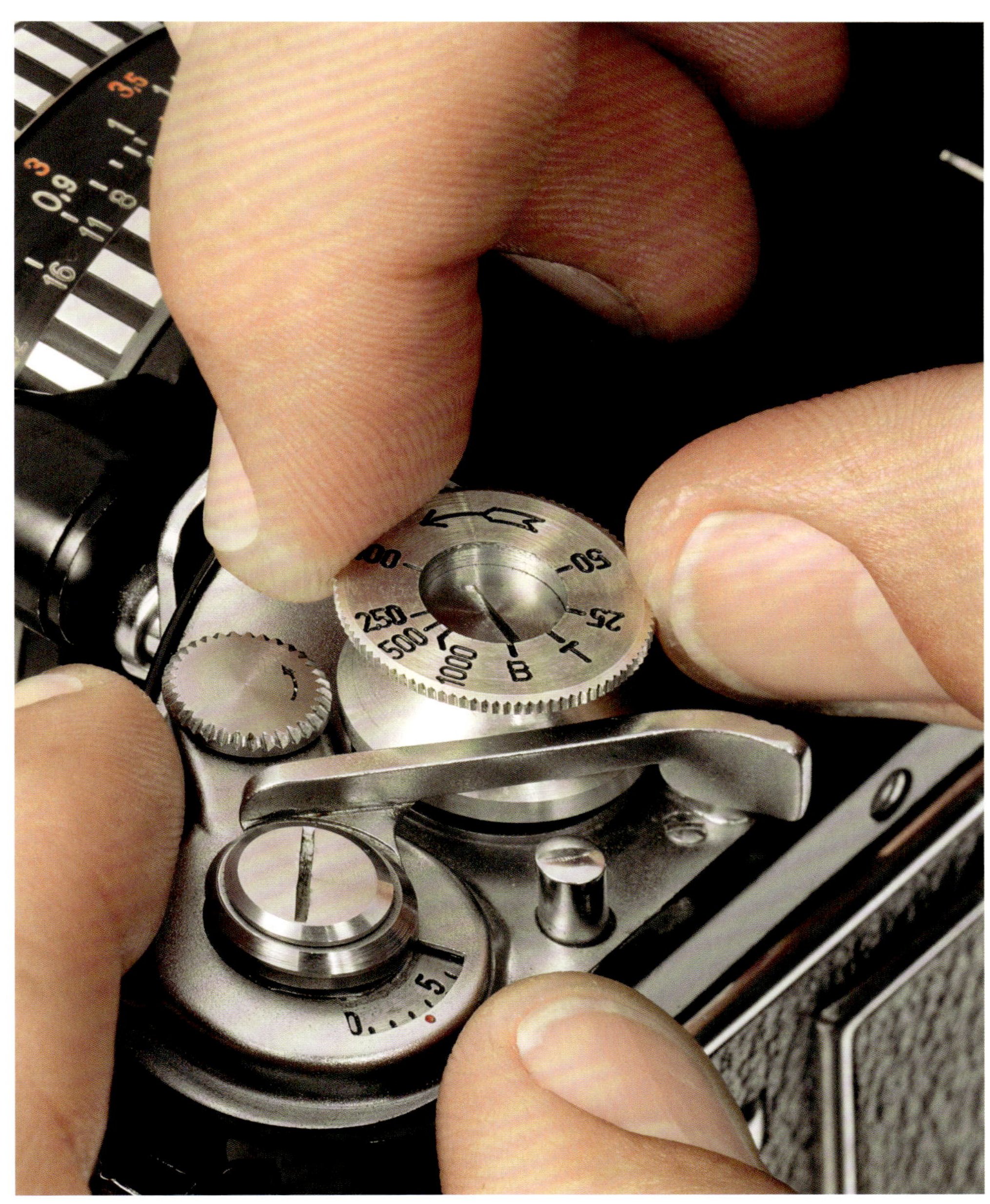
250
500
1000
B
T
25
50

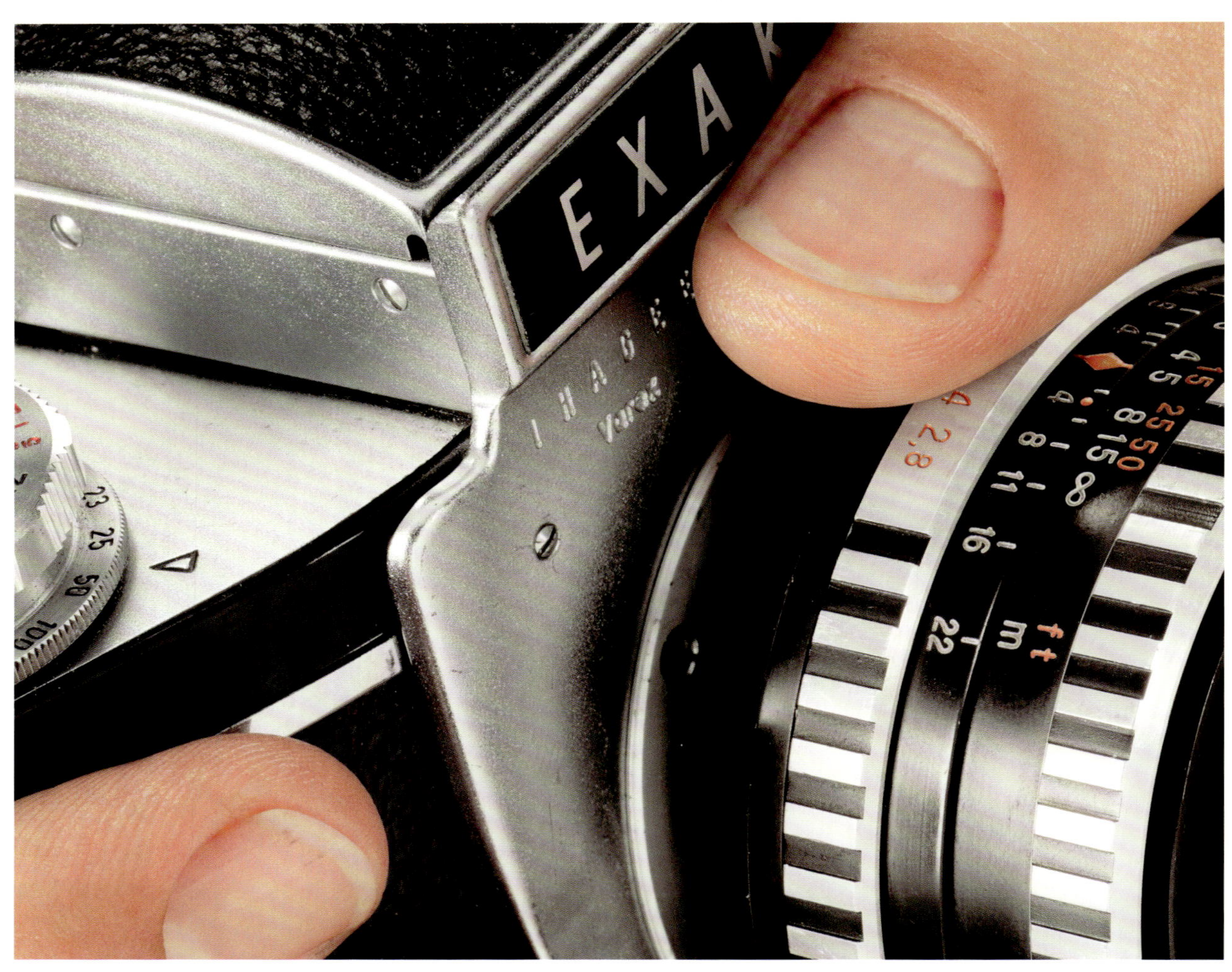

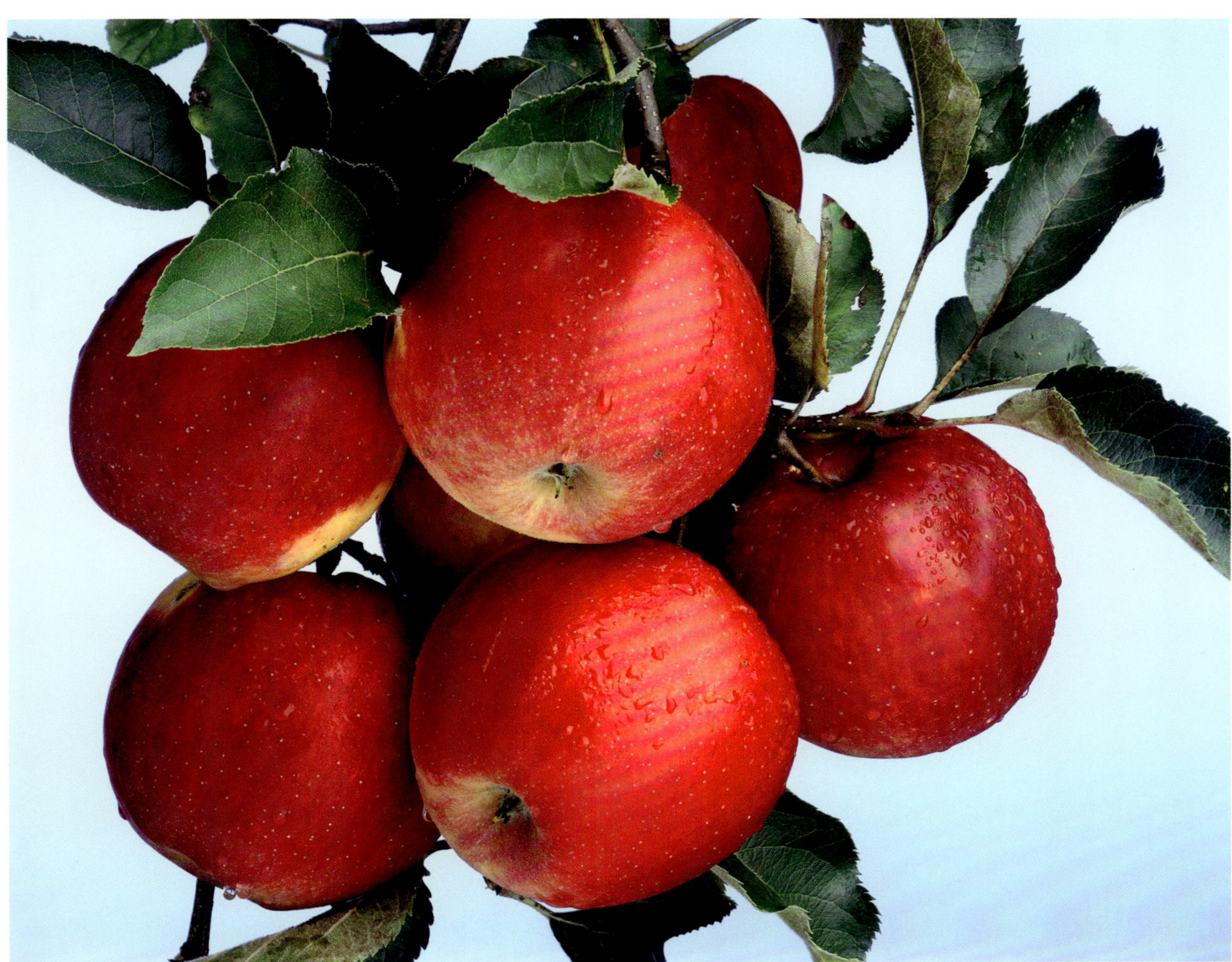

Bergische Bauernscheune, Junkersholz, Leichlingen, September 29th, 2009, 2010. All photographs courtesy Galerie Gisela Capitain, Cologne, and David Zwirner Gallery, New York/London

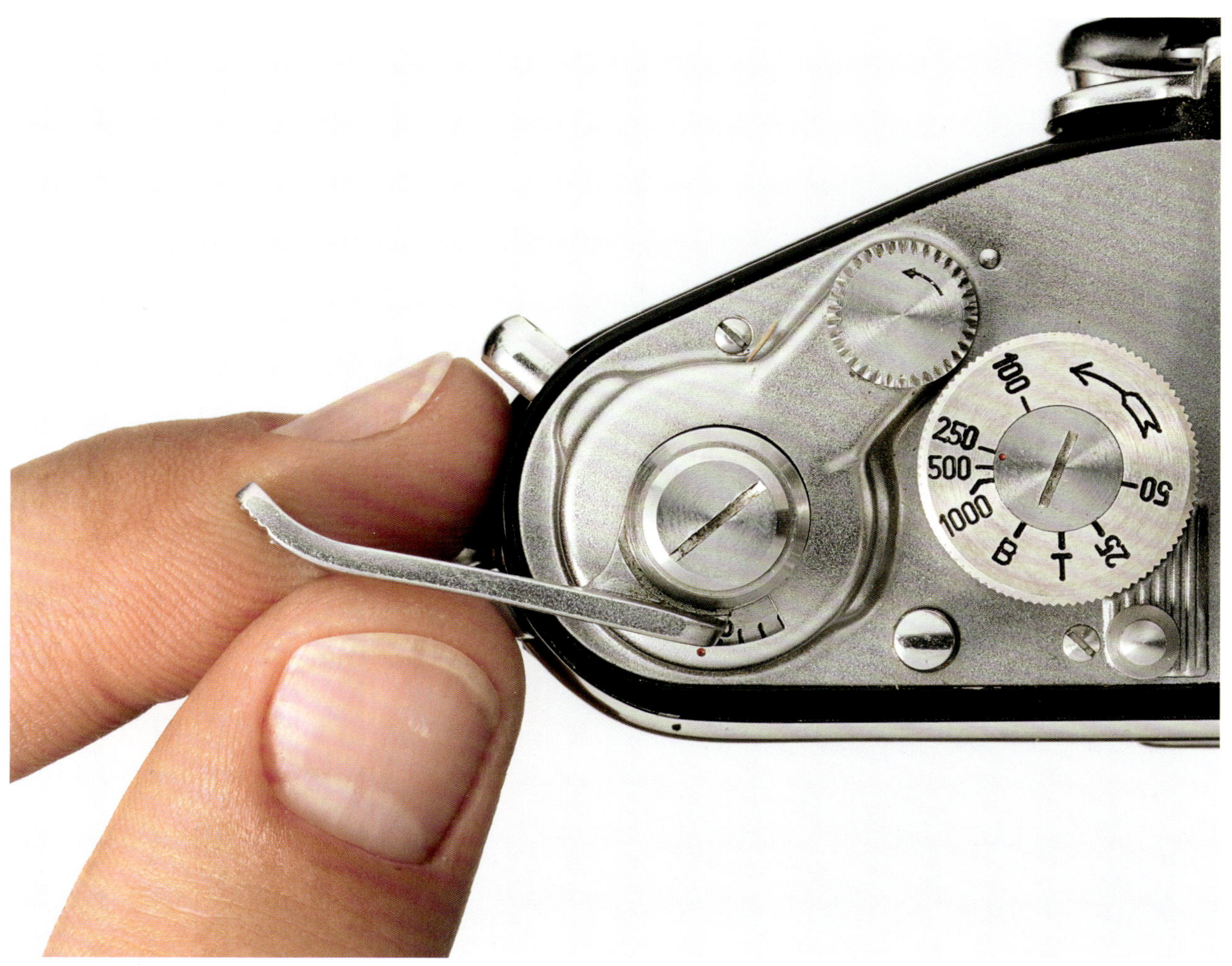
100
250
500
1000
B
T
25
50

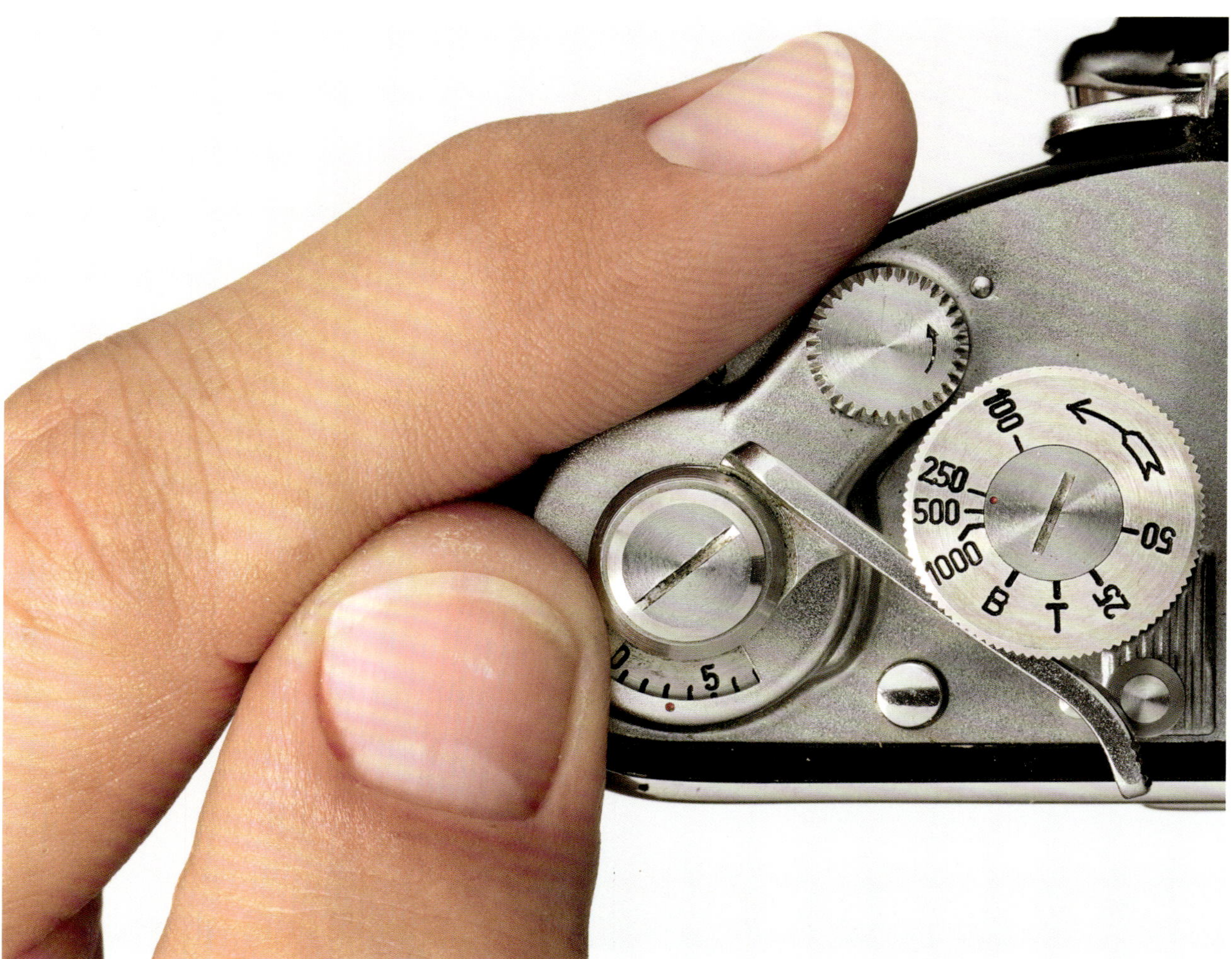
100
250
500
1000
B
T
25
50
5

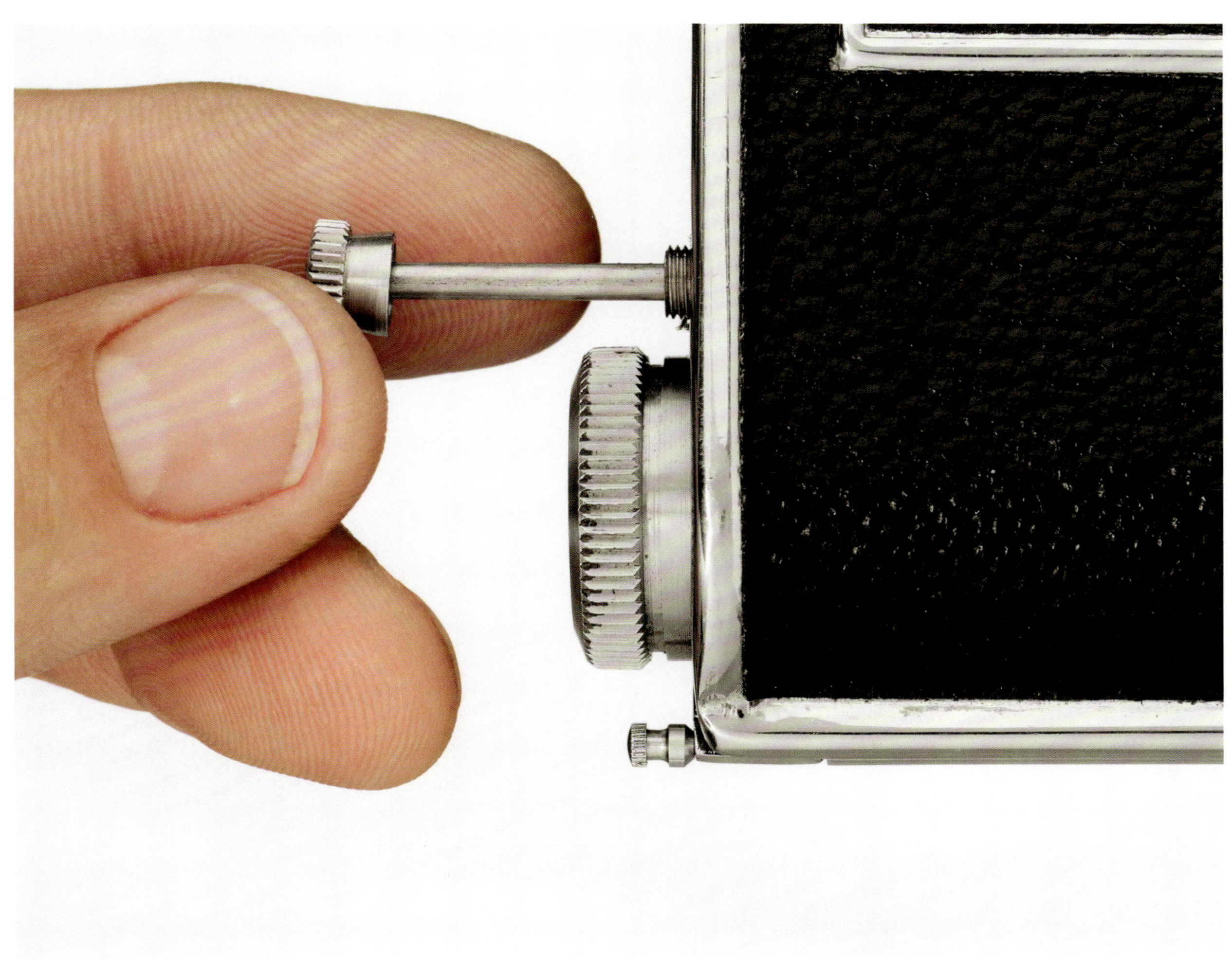

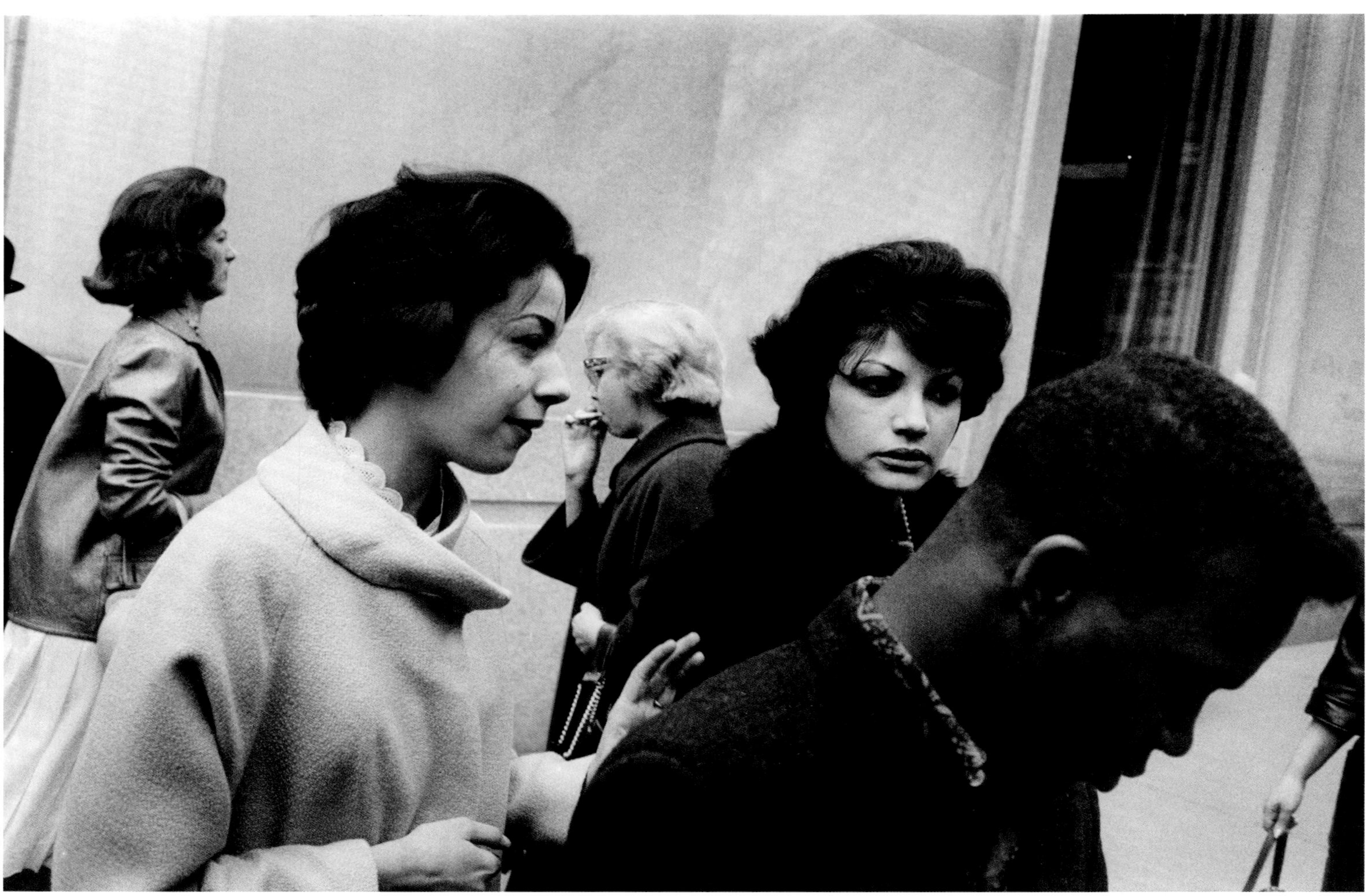

New York, ca. 1960

For many years, an aura has surrounded the Garry Winogrand archive. The photographer, who died in 1984 at age fifty-six, left behind more than six thousand rolls of unedited film and numerous photographs that had been marked on his proof sheets but never printed. Over the past three years, photographer Leo Rubinfien has been working for the San Francisco Museum of Modern Art and the National Gallery of Art in Washington, D.C., as guest curator of the first Winogrand retrospective since the mid-1980s, re-editing these materials —in collaboration with curator Erin O'Toole (SFMOMA) and Sarah Greenough (NGA)—and supervising the printing of many never-before-seen images, some of which appear in the accompanying pages. The exhibition *Garry Winogrand*— accompanied by a major publication —will open on March 9 of this year at SFMOMA, and will subsequently travel to the NGA; the Metropolitan Museum of Art, New York; the Jeu de Paume, Paris; and the Fundación MAPFRE, Madrid. Here, photographer Philip-Lorca diCorcia (known as PL) speaks with Rubinfien about the complexities of Winogrand's work, which has often been mischaracterized as "street photography," the legacy of curator John Szarkowski, and the new meanings we may discover today by revisiting this influential photographer. — The Editors

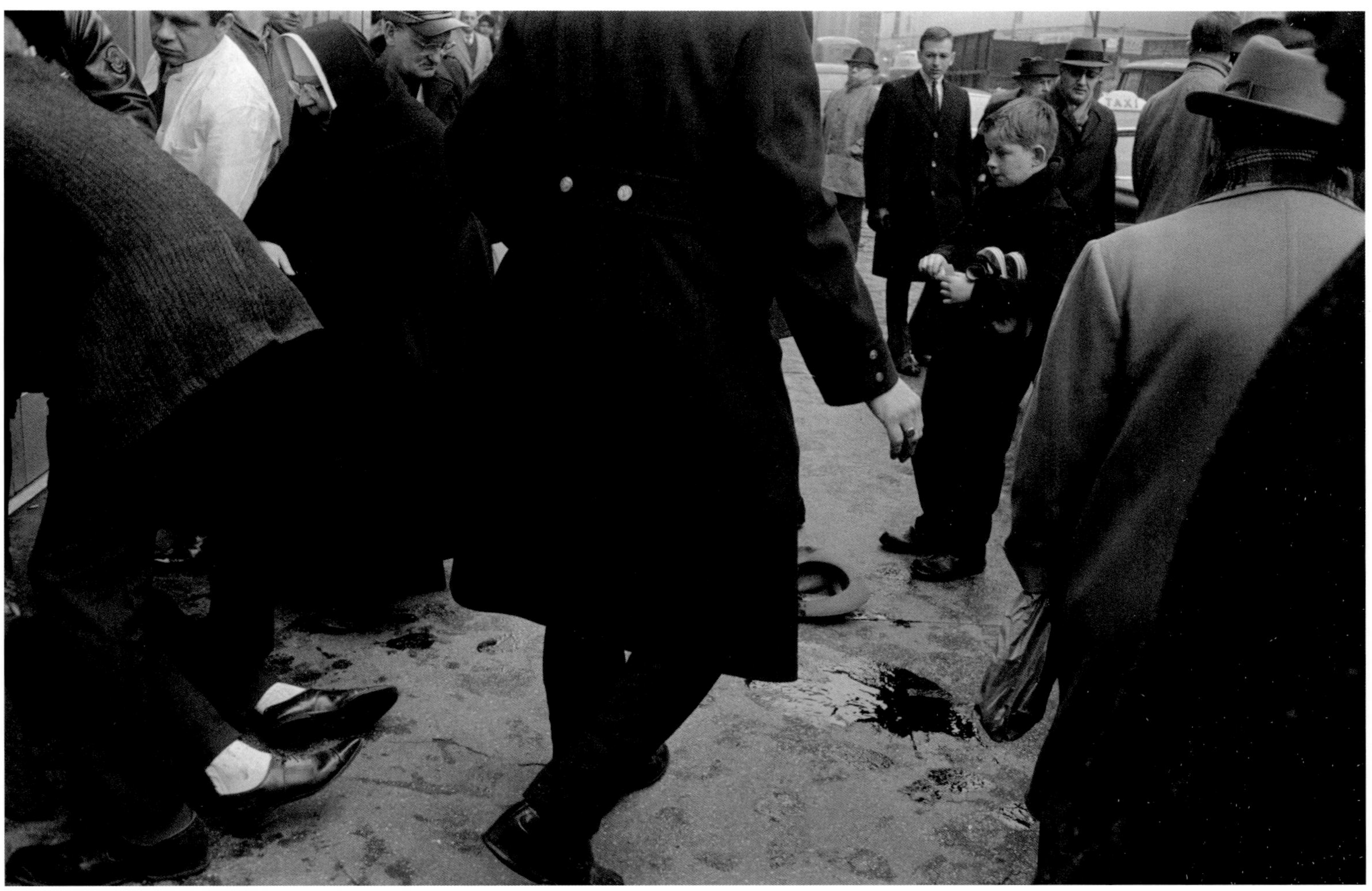

New York, ca. 1960

Revisiting the Garry Winogrand Archive

Philip-Lorca diCorcia in conversation with Leo Rubinfien

Top left:
New York, 1960

Bottom left:
New York, 1961

Top right:
Grand Central Terminal, New York, 1964

Bottom right:
New York, ca. 1963

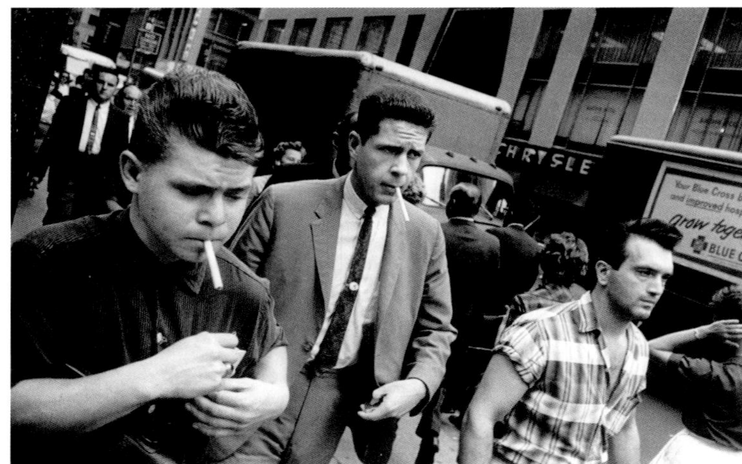

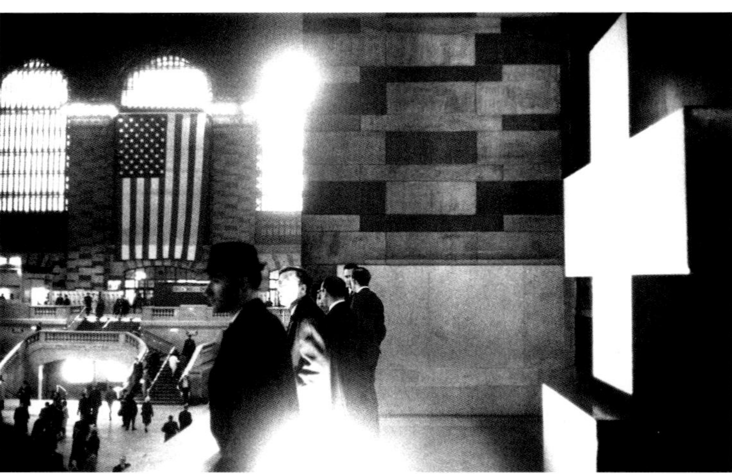

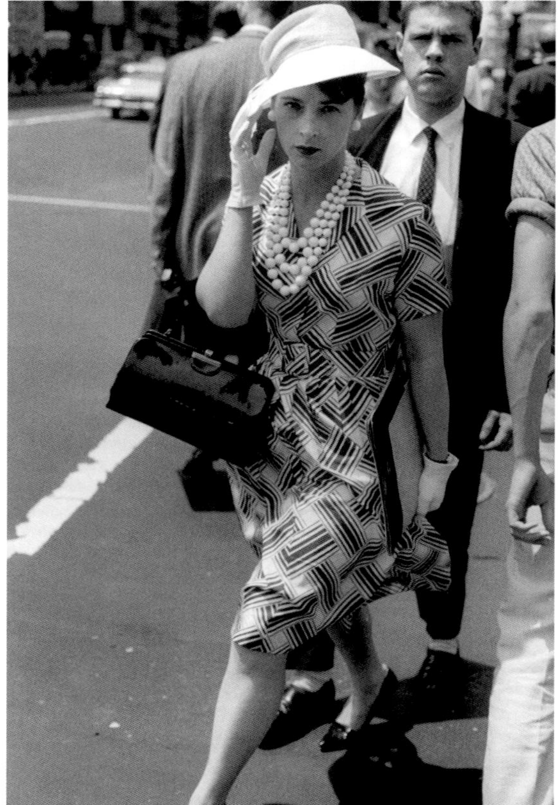

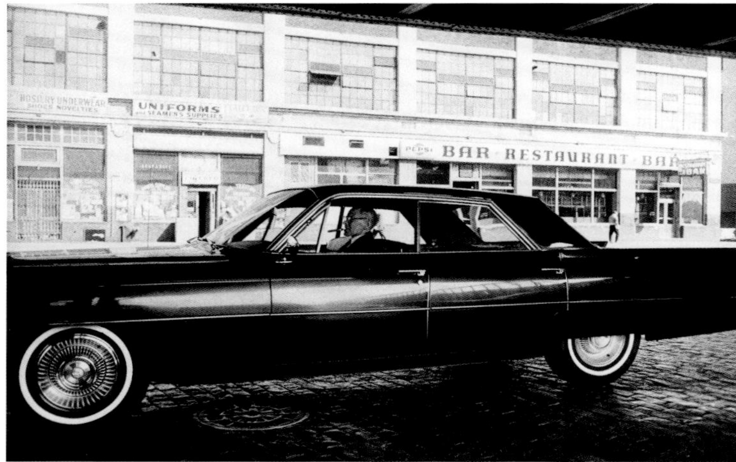

Philip-Lorca diCorcia: **As someone who went to Yale in the late 1970s and had Tod Papageorge as a professor, I resisted Garry Winogrand. By '78, he was a cult; there was an orthodoxy around him at that time.**

Leo Rubinfien: There was certainly a circle of people associated with Winogrand—mainly photographers, but not exclusively. They had intense convictions about the value of his work—and other people's work, too—and also about how photography should be thought about and discussed, but to say that a cult formed around him seems harsh to me. These were thoughtful, intelligent people, and each one had reasons for being present. Did an orthodoxy develop? Maybe so, but slowly. The photographers connected with Winogrand in the 1960s were drawn at least partly by the sense that there was more freedom in his approach to photography than they could find anywhere else. Later, they had to defend themselves and if there was some dogmatizing, that was only human.

PL: **Of course, the arbiter of photographic quality at that time was the Museum of Modern Art. There was a pantheon there, and Winogrand was one of them. With that pantheon came certain attributes —for instance, black-and-white work. I remember going to MoMA and the only color photography that was up at that time was by Irving Penn.**

LR: When MoMA showed the color work of Eggleston and Stephen Shore in the mid-1970s it was news, although I'm not sure that noncommercial photographers were doing a vast amount in color before that, anyway—before C-printing made it affordable. As a matter of fact, though, one component of MoMA's famous 1967 *New Documents* exhibition was a slide show, in color, by Winogrand.

It's true of course that Winogrand was openly supported by John Szarkowski and the Museum of Modern Art, and that Szarkowski had his own case to make, and didn't compromise it. He dismissed a lot of work, and that made many people resentful. But if somebody asked: "What's the simplest explanation you can give of what Szarkowski did?" I would say that it was to move photography out of the world of journalism and into the world of the fine arts. The old picture magazines were dying. They had dominated the practice and the dissemination of photography for three decades, and now their culture and their mode of thinking were fading away. Szarkowski didn't just bring a gang of photographers across the street from the Time-Life building to the Museum of Modern Art; he replaced one set of values with another, one way of looking at photographs with another. Journalism had demanded pictures that explained the world "clearly," in well-accepted ways, but Szarkowski said that photographs explain almost nothing, and that this was not a defect, but a virtue. And Winogrand's work demonstrates that the ambiguity of photography can be one of its great strengths.

PL: **In terms of the legacy in museums, the Szarkowski world is disappearing. The Museum of Modern Art has a new director of photography, Quentin Bajac, who has nothing to do with that world. Is this major project about Winogrand— one of the core figures of that school —in some way marking the end of that era?**

LR: I didn't work on the Winogrand retrospective to make a statement about MoMA, but to better understand Winogrand. Although it's true that since shortly before Szarkowski's death, his prime protégés have been having retrospectives—Arbus, Friedlander, Eggleston, Robert Adams— and that these have inevitably re-evaluated Szarkowski's work. The SFMOMA Winogrand project is the most recent one. Is it the end of something, or the beginning of something else? Maybe it's both. Today, the debates of the Szarkowski years have mostly expired, or turned into other debates, so maybe an artist like Winogrand can now be set free of them. The SFMOMA book and show say: "Let's go back and look again at what Winogrand did." It's particularly interesting to do this because he died young and until now his work has never been thoroughly explored. A lot of what's in SFMOMA's book and show has never been seen before, or has rarely been seen, and it presents a somewhat different Winogrand from the one we thought we knew.

PL: **There was presumably a reason that so much work was left behind, unprocessed and unedited. Is there any sense that that was the way it should have been left?**

LR: Well, I didn't think the work should be left in the closet or I wouldn't have undertaken SFMOMA's project. The unfinished work was unfinished because Winogrand died not only young, but suddenly, and he had no time to prepare anything for posterity. In December 1983 he thought he had years to live. In March 1984 he was gone. There are many reasons why he didn't edit and print more of his work, and they're all interesting. But would those pictures be better left unseen? We're speaking of one of the finest photographers there has been, and of work that changes the way we understand him. It's work of great beauty and depth that will nourish anyone who lets it in. So no, I think it would be arbitrary, rigid, and shortsighted to hide it away.

PL: **Every epigram that is attributed to Winogrand seems to be an evasion of a question. It's hard to say, when someone's work has an aspect of evasion and alienation in it, whether this is social commentary or an expression of an artist's own feelings. But the man obviously was not comfortable with the world and with himself. Do you think his investigation of class was a manifestation of his own insecurities? In his pictures at the Whitney and the Metropolitan Museum you can't help but think that he's being judged by the same people that he's photographing. And there's his own not-too-subtle criticism in most of those images.**

LR: Winogrand was often combative and sometimes defensive, and his evasiveness sometimes expressed this. But more importantly, he understood how untranslatable a photograph is, how it says something that can't be said in speech. I think that the main reason he resisted explaining himself was that he didn't want to smother under a pile of words that special, poetic ambiguity that makes a photograph beautiful.

I don't believe that he felt himself an outsider in the way that *The Americans* suggests that Frank did. The world in Winogrand's photographs is his own world. His pictures from the streets of Manhattan in the early '60s—the beautiful women, the businessmen, and so on—to me they describe a world that Winogrand is contemplating joining, or that he is in the process of joining even if he's horrified by many things he sees. Beauty and ugliness, order and chaos, are inextricable in Winogrand's work.

PL: **Was he carpet-bombing the visual realm—shooting everything in sight? Why settle for one frame when you can have twenty?**

LR: The idea that he was an extraordinarily prodigious shooter, a "carpet-bomber," is actually a myth. I didn't know that until I worked on SFMOMA's project. From the time he started up until 1971 (twenty-one years—and most of his best pictures were from that period), he was shooting five hundred rolls of film a year on average, which is not very much: a roll-and-a-half a day. The large numbers came much later. In fact, when they did come, that's when the quality of the work fell off sharply—

Los Angeles, ca. 1980–83

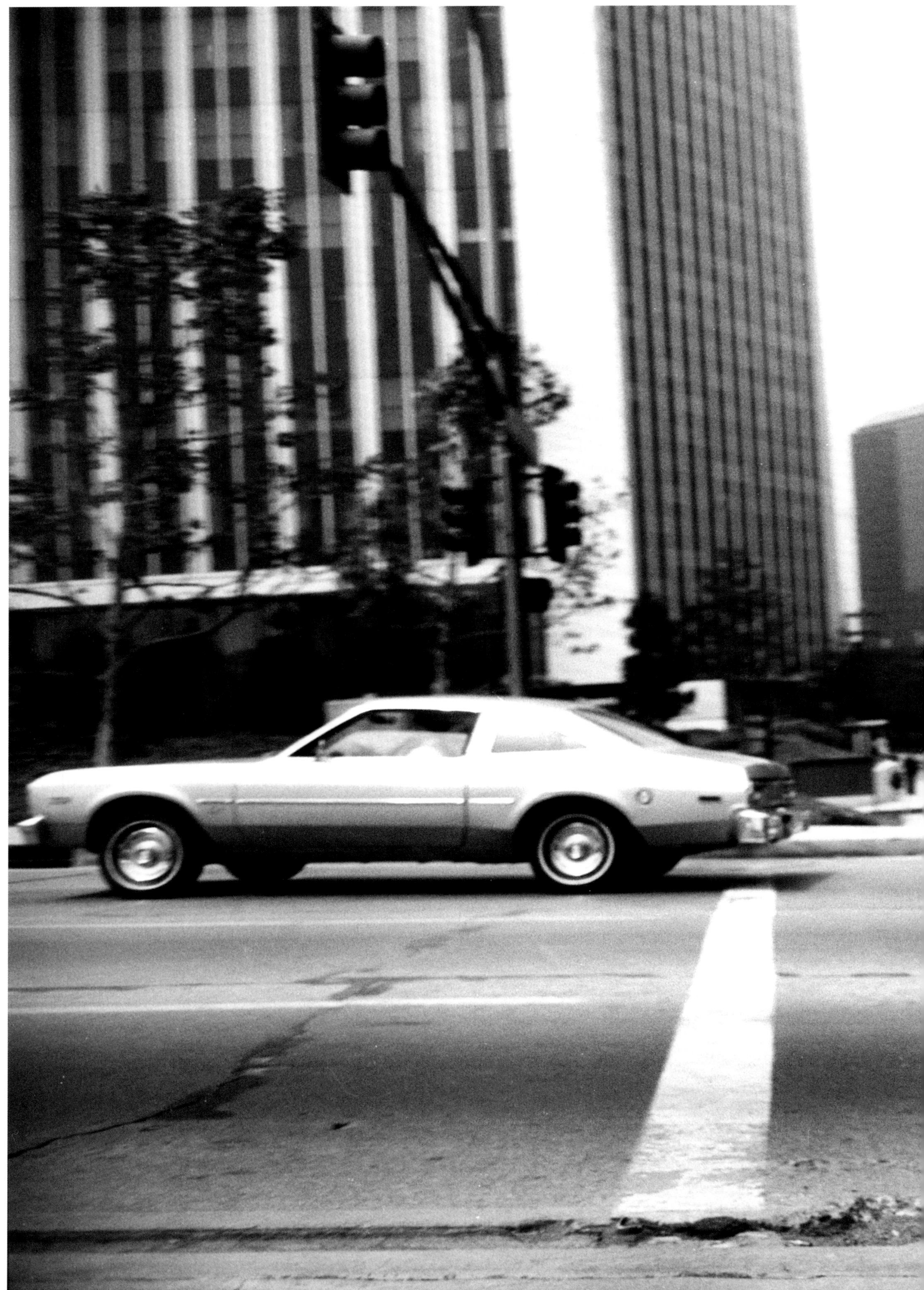

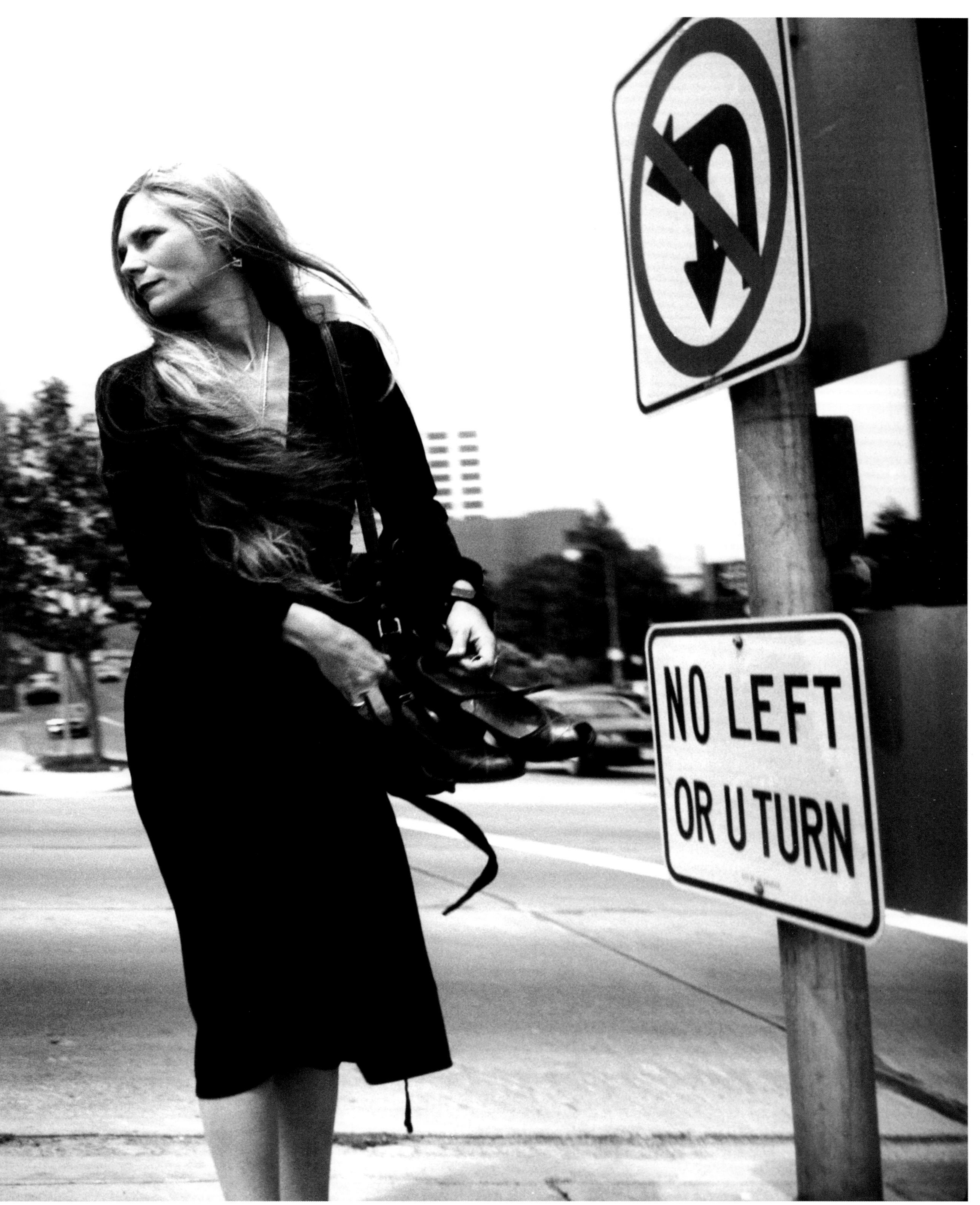
NO LEFT
OR U TURN

almost as if Winogrand knew that he was weakening and was struggling furiously against it.

PL: **Winogrand's narratives are so elusive that they sometimes seem quite modern. But some of his work was almost corny, in the "tale told" way. I think as his picture structure started to fall apart, so did the conclusions to be drawn from the suggested narratives. And that's where, for me, he becomes really interesting and surreal.**

LR: He began in the world of magazine journalism, where pictures were functional and illustrative. But he resisted this from very early on, and by the '60s he was working in an anti-narrative way and arrived at a kind of ambiguity that he found enlightening and beautiful. He would ultimately say: "There is nothing as mysterious as a fact clearly described," as if the picture might stand in front of you like an apparition. It would be strange. It would be surprising. It would be disconnected from the rest of the world as you knew it, and from whatever story you expected it to tell. In the late work, in the 1970s and the early '80s, there's not only no narrative, there's almost no *event*. The pictures are about the way faces look. They're about space. And you could say that he learned how to find beauty in a picture in which you can't tell what's happening at a moment in time—the 1960s—when the entire American nation couldn't tell what was happening in life itself. And so his way of picture making came to speak not just for him but for a vast collective experience.

PL: **The street provides a constantly changing set of possibilities. The pushback that the world throws at you when you attempt to wrangle from it some sort of meaning with a camera is significant.**

LR: In one way, Winogrand's work is all about how the world coalesces, and then dissolves, about how chaos threatens to overtake order again and again. He often talked about himself and his work in relation to photography in general. He'd say: "I'm interested in the problem that a piece of material sets for the medium," or "I'm interested in the contention between content and form." Szarkowski, too, among others, argued that Winogrand was saying various things about photography itself with his work.

But another aspect of his work is a ferocious attention that I associate with portrait making more than with most photography of the street, even though Winogrand brought it to the street, to crowds of people in motion. He looks at those people with a fierce grip, and he asks, *What's that hat you're wearing?* and *Why does your foot turn the way it does?* and *Who are you?* At one point he said: "You could say that I'm a student of photography, and I am, but really I'm a student of America." At another time, he said to a close friend of his: "You know why your pictures are no fucking good? Because they don't describe the chaos of life." These two comments are the best guides I can think of to what Winogrand's work is about. In the end, I think the street was just a site. The point was what he saw in the street—and what he saw there was a great many pieces of evidence that teach us serious things about the character of American people, about the evanescence of seeing, about the transience of life itself.

PL: **There's a reductiveness to photography, of course—in the framing of reality and the exclusion of chunks of it (the rest of the world, in fact). It's almost as if the act of photography bears some relationship to how we consciously manage the uncontrollable set of possibilities that exist in life. I think that, more than any other photographer, Winogrand expressed the fact that everything is held together by the thinnest of threads.**

Strangely, I doubt that anybody in a photo program right now thinks of Garry Winogrand as their prime motivation, although the current practice of photography does have a certain relationship to his work, which could now seem outmoded. I think part of what he did, which is today a process in contemporary photography and art, was to break assumptions.

LR: Well, maybe that's one reason why people should look at him again now. The work is very free, and it remains fresh. It's powerful but it refuses to make grand declarations—it's powerful partly *because* it refuses to do that. It's only outmoded if one thinks that art progresses in a linear way, and that this year's art disqualifies last year's. But I don't believe that there is any such progression. That kind of thinking is a fiction of certain criticism and of the art market. If a work of art is alive, it is alive, no matter when it was made.

There is something tremendously open-ended about Winogrand's work. It's there picture by picture, and in the overall body of work. It's a quality of Winogrand's, but it was a quality that artists often sought in the 1960s. Fellini once said: "To make a movie that has an ending is immoral." It's *immoral*. It's to lie to the audience. Because life has no endings; life is all flux and discontinuity. Life has no solidity at all. It's chaos. You have to try to capture that, Fellini said. There was more than a little of the same feeling in Winogrand.

PL: **Well, I like the Jean-Luc Godard quote, when he was asked: "Does a movie have to have a beginning, a middle, and an end?"**

LR: What did he say?

PL: **He said: "Yes, but not in that order."**

LR: And Winogrand might well have said: "Beginning, middle, and end—how do you know which one is which?"

Philip-Lorca diCorcia's work is the subject of many books, including *Eleven* (Damiani, 2011), *Thousand* (Steidl/Dangin, 2007), *A Storybook Life* (Twin Palms, 2003), *Heads* (Steidl, 2001), and the forthcoming *Hustlers* (Steidl/Dangin, 2013).

Leo Rubinfien is the author of *A Map of the East* (Godine/Thames & Hudson, 1992) and *Wounded Cities* (Steidl, 2008), and co-author of *Shomei Tomatsu/ Skin of the Nation* (SFMOMA/Yale University Press, 2004). The book accompanying his Winogrand exhibition will be co-published by SFMOMA and Yale University Press.

Wyoming, 1964

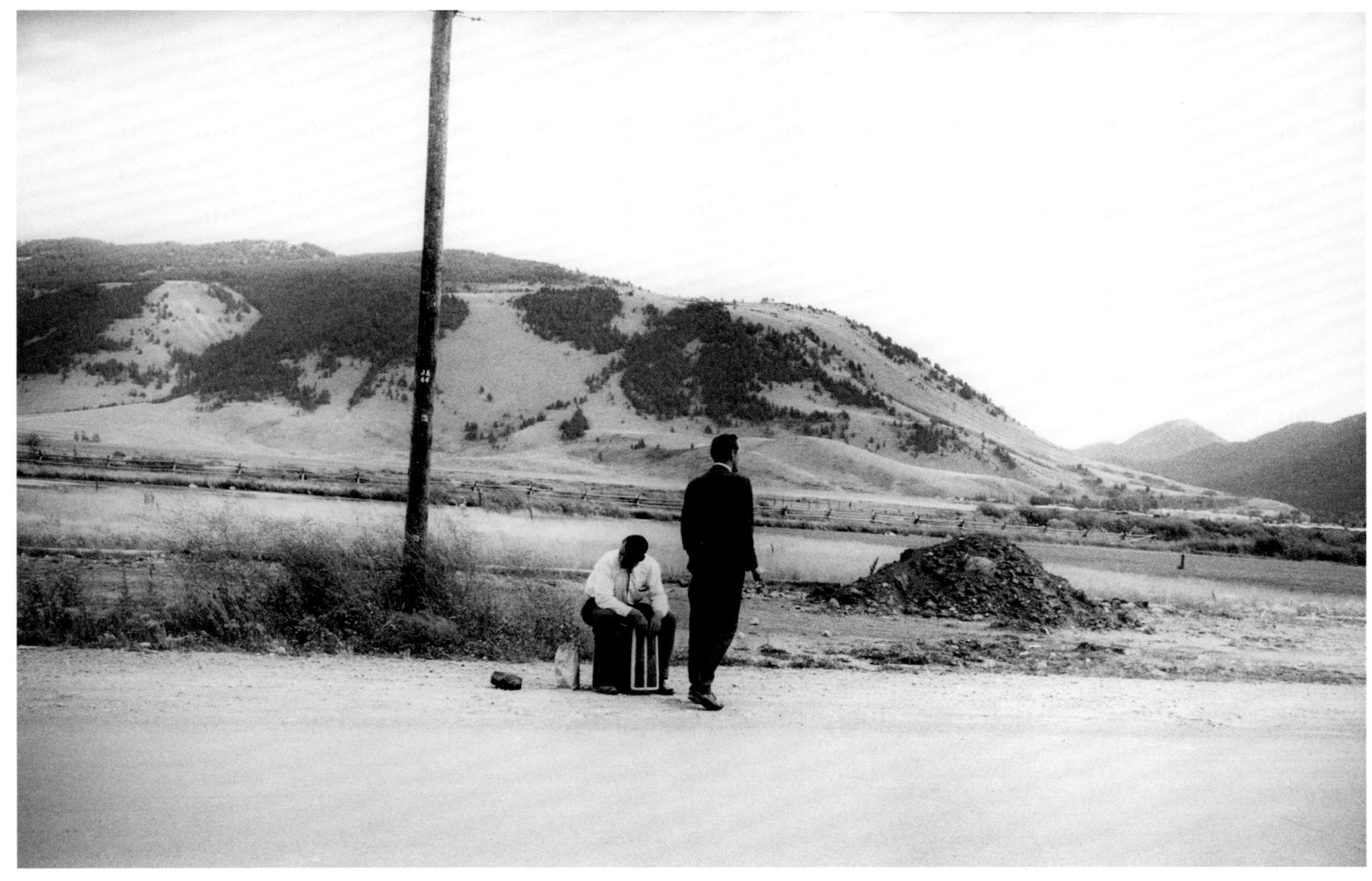

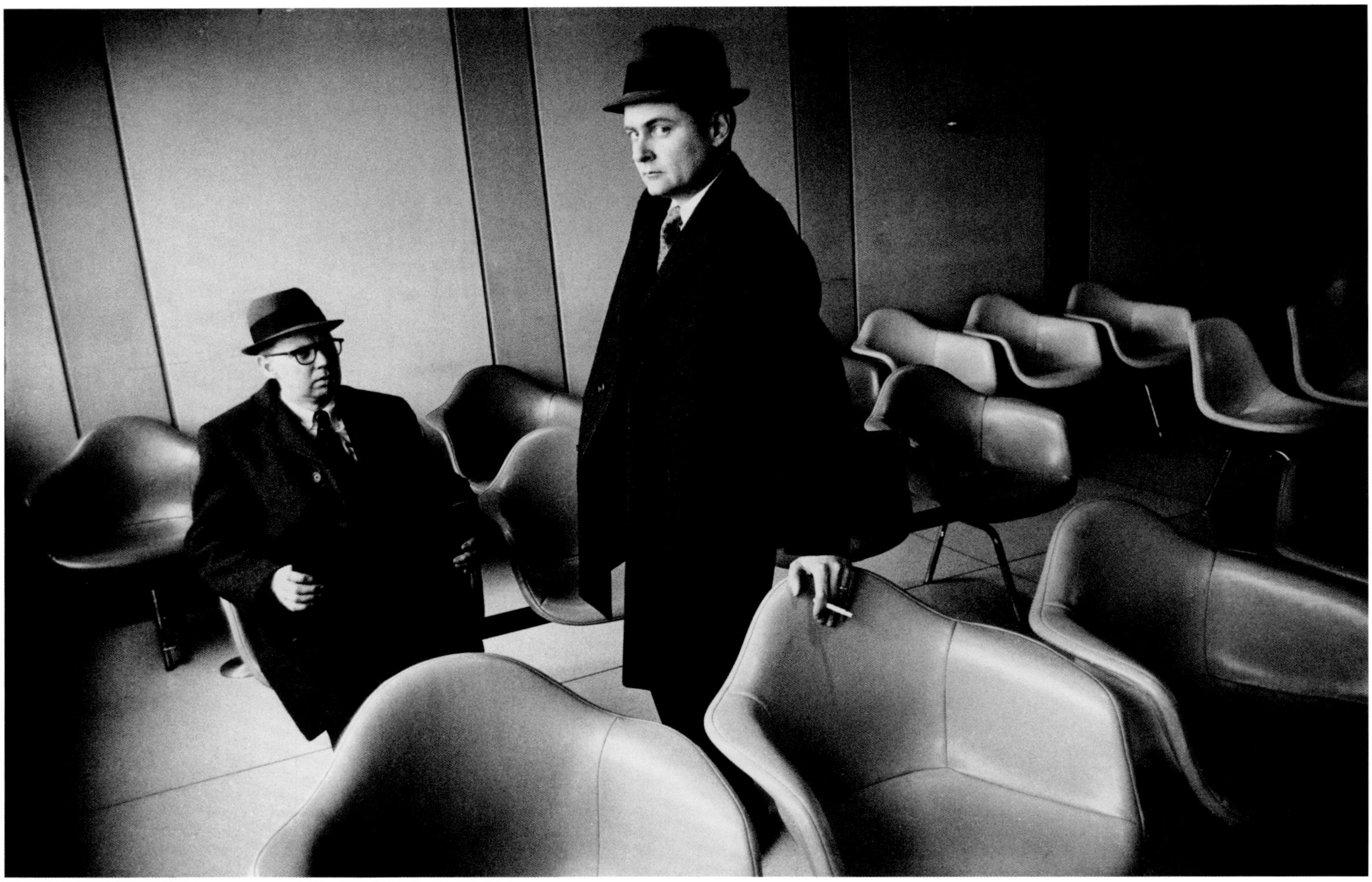

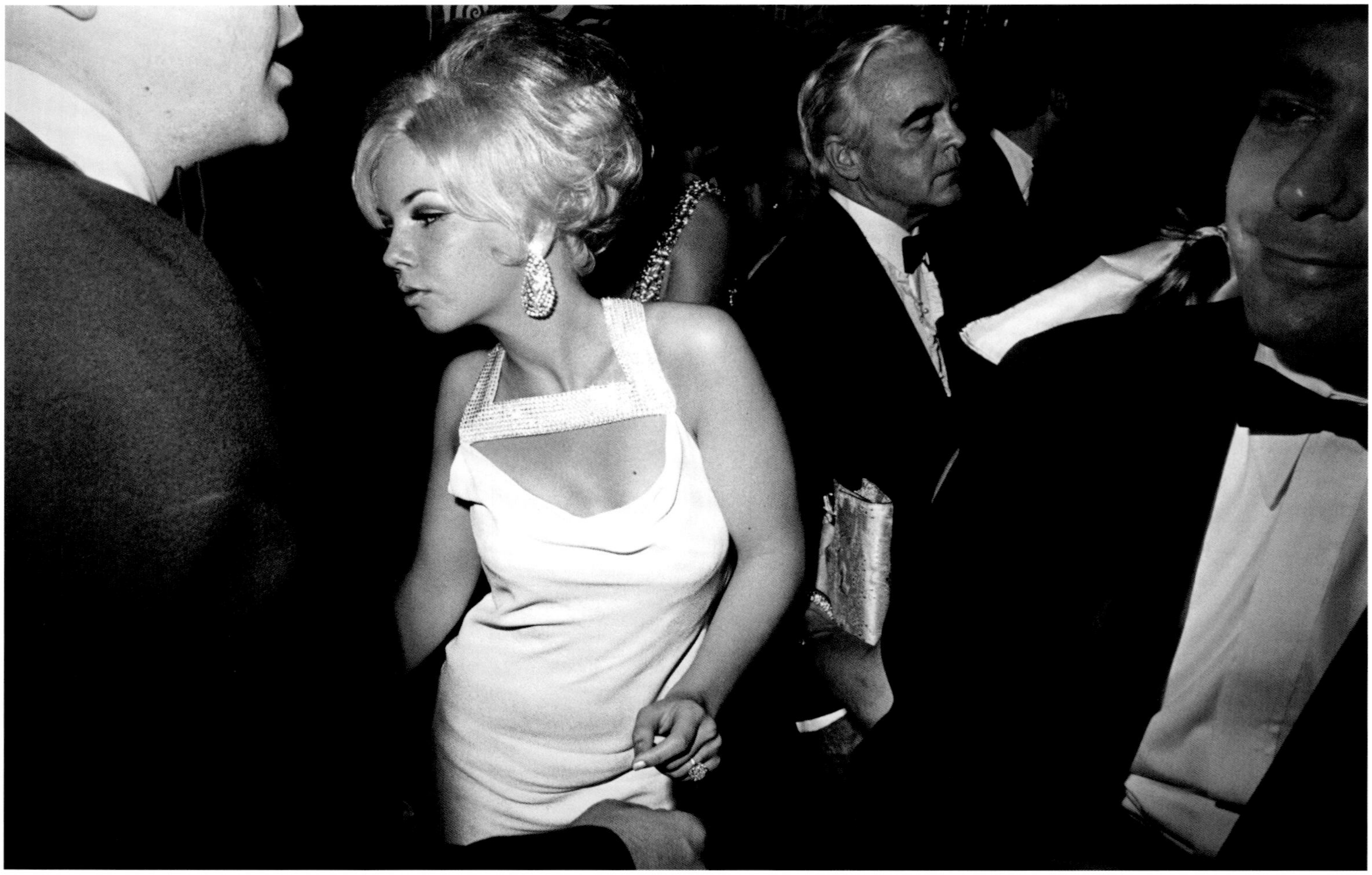

Opposite, top:
La Guardia Airport, New York, 1968

Opposite, bottom:
Centennial Ball, Metropolitan Museum, New York, 1969

Below:
State Fair of Texas, Dallas, 1964

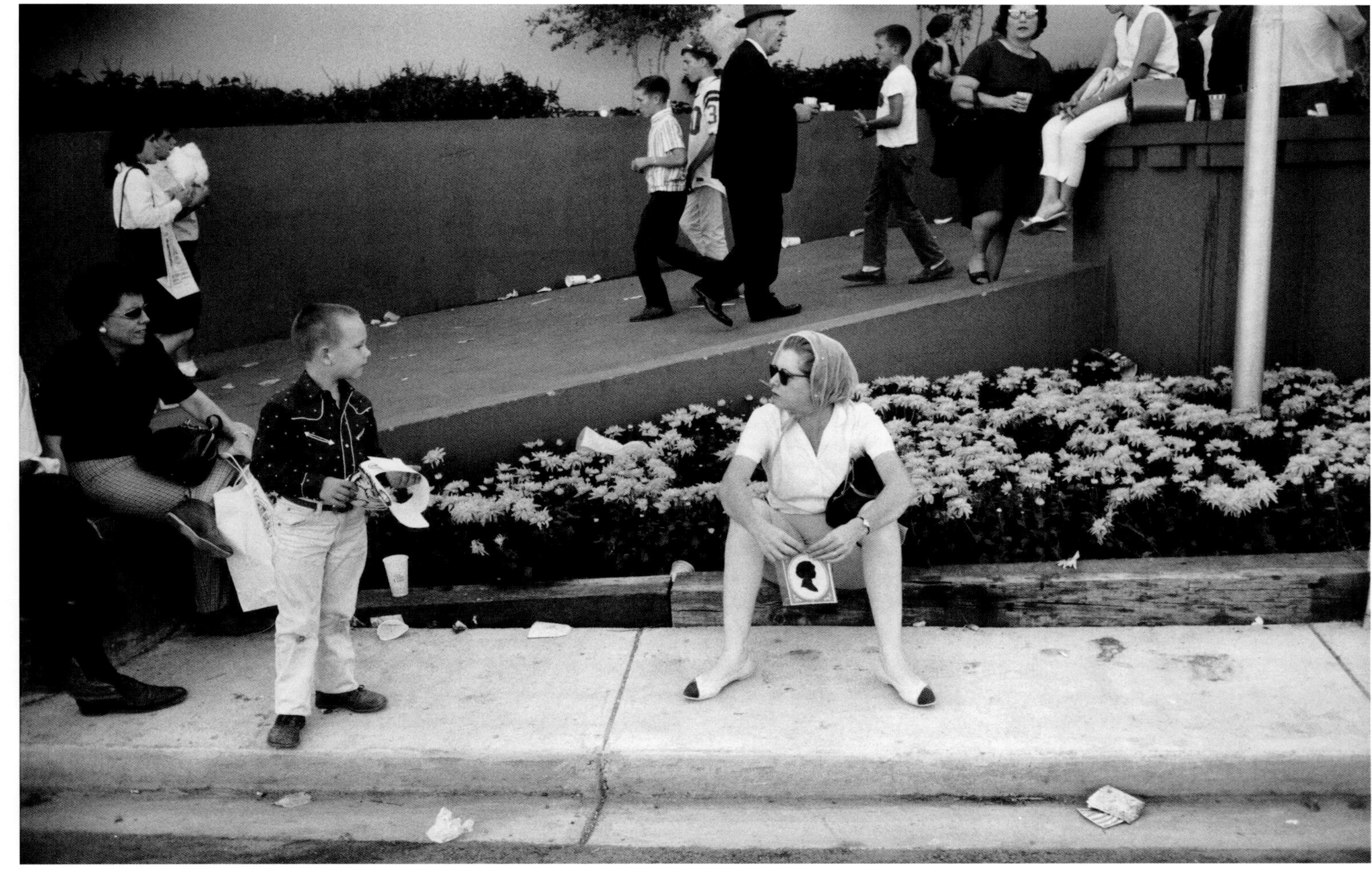

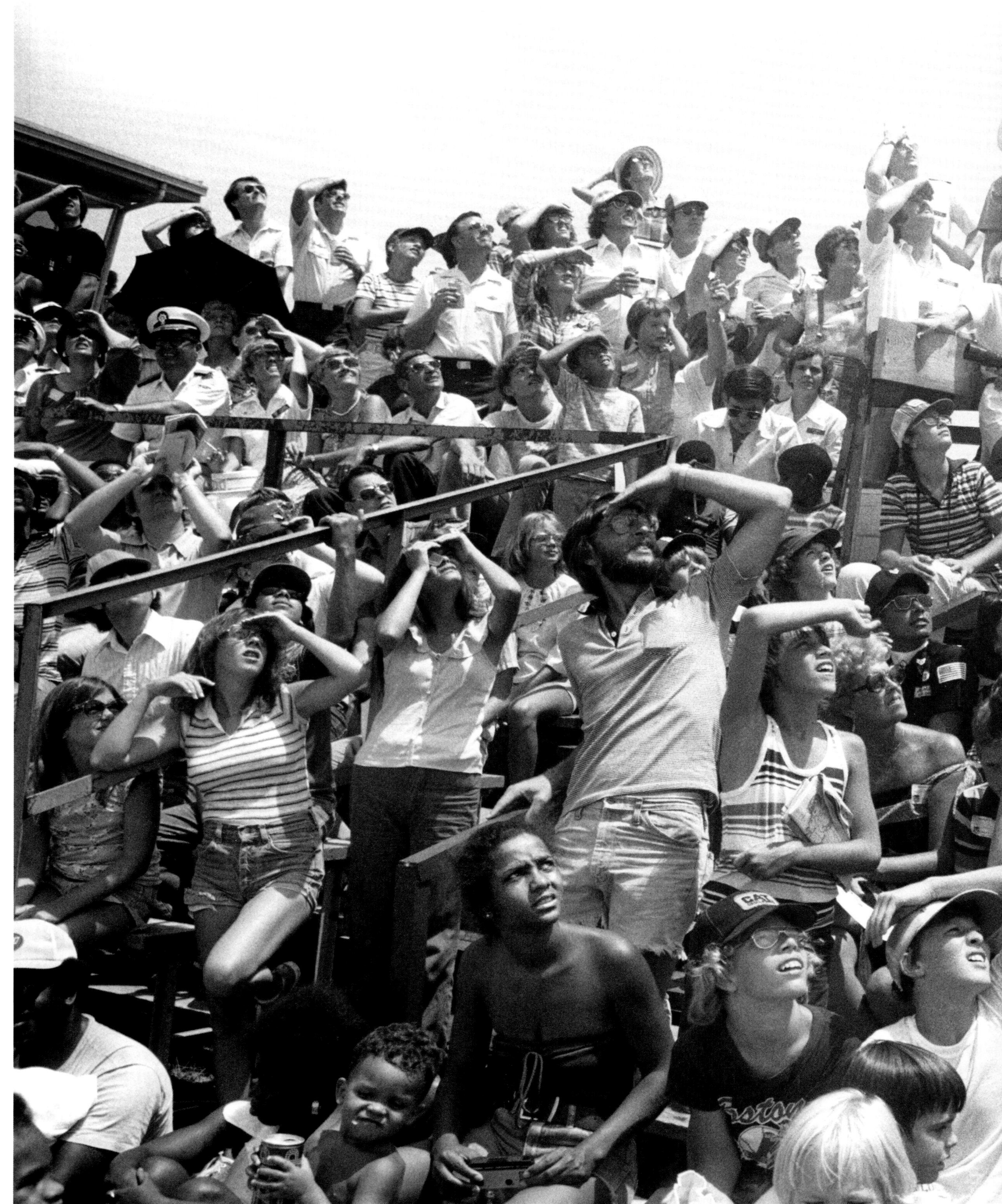

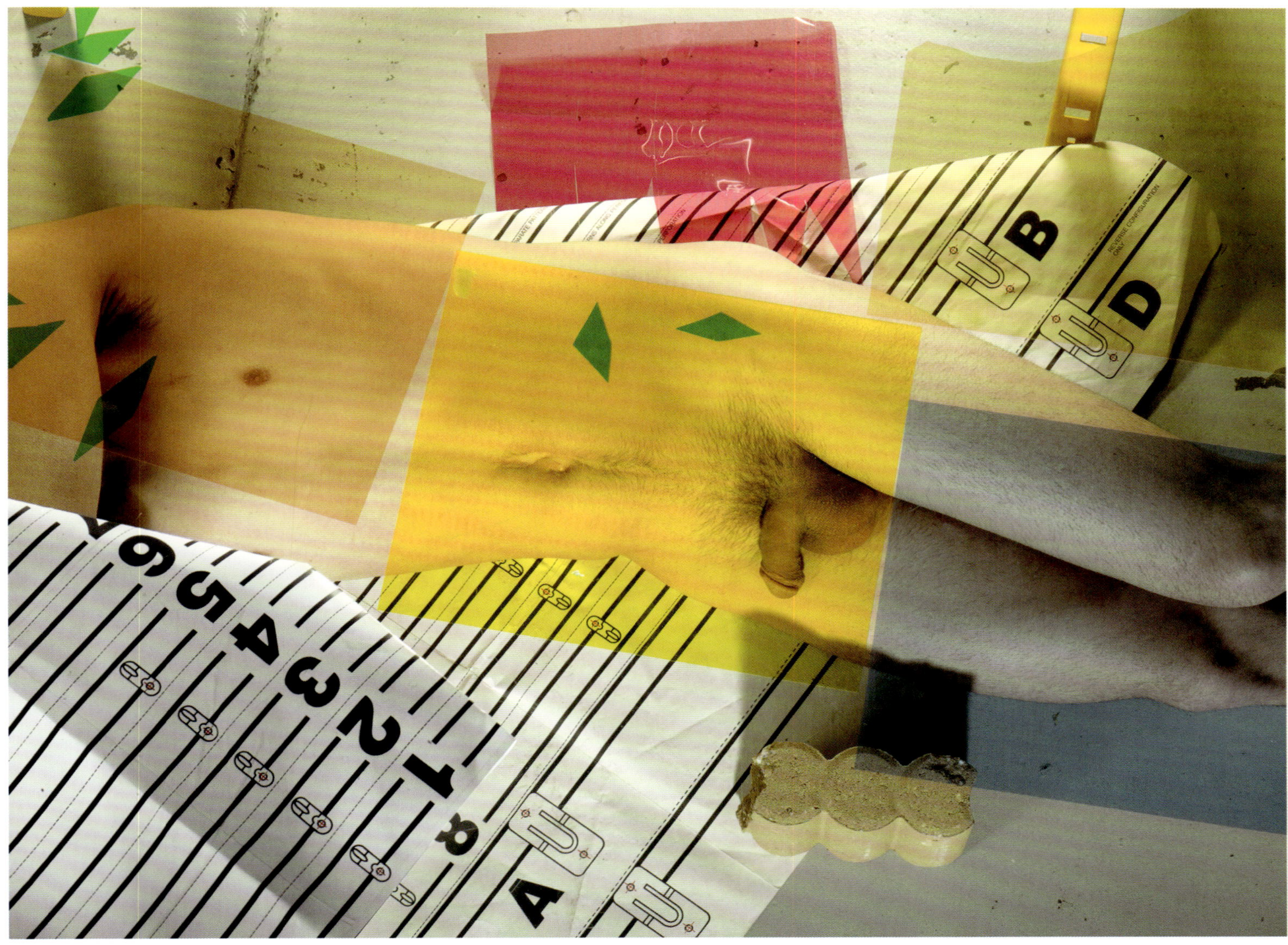

Fuchsia, Yellow, Green, Blue, Numbers, Man, Cement, Paper, 2010

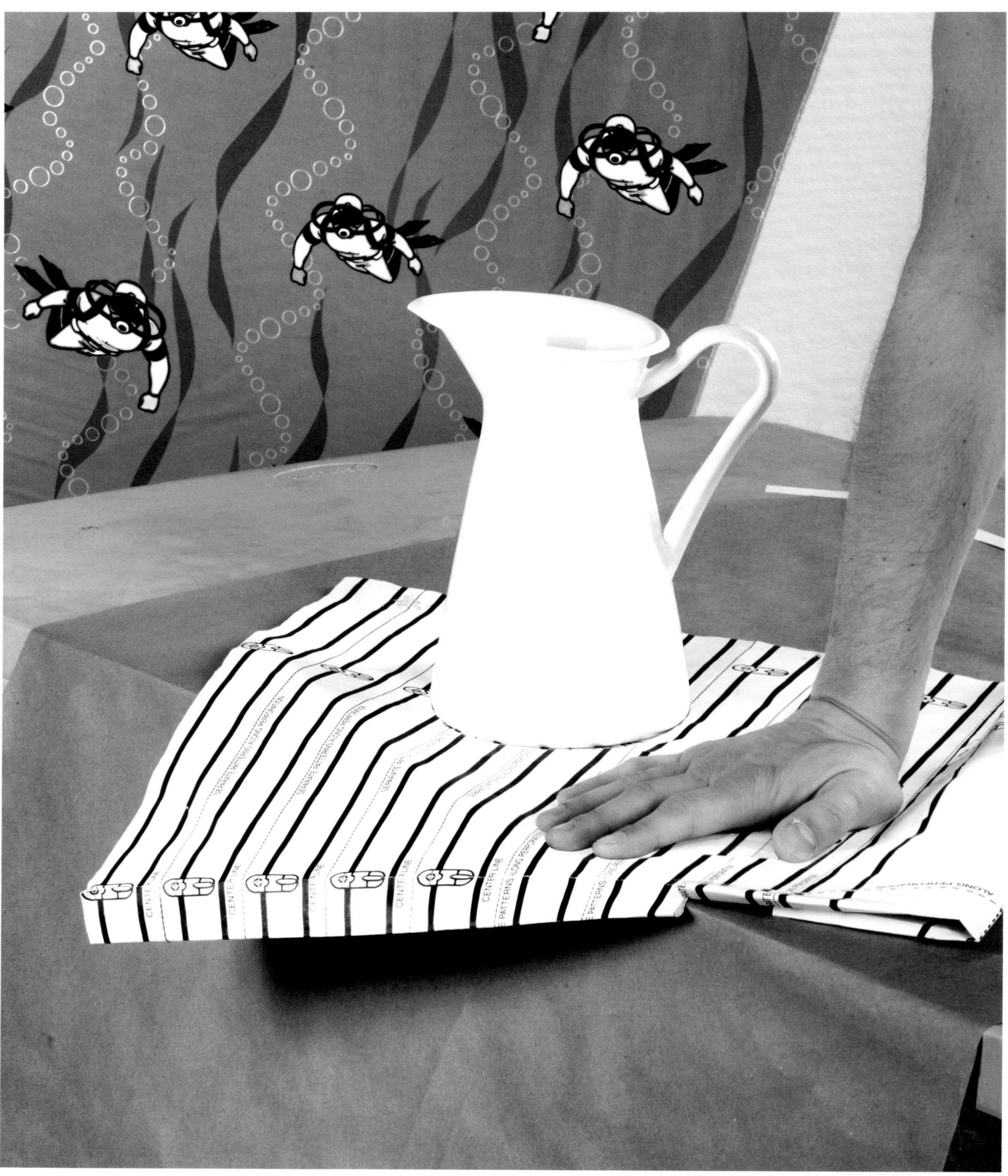

This page: *Pitcher, Paper, Arm, Scuba, Lycra*, 2011

Opposite: #4, 2012

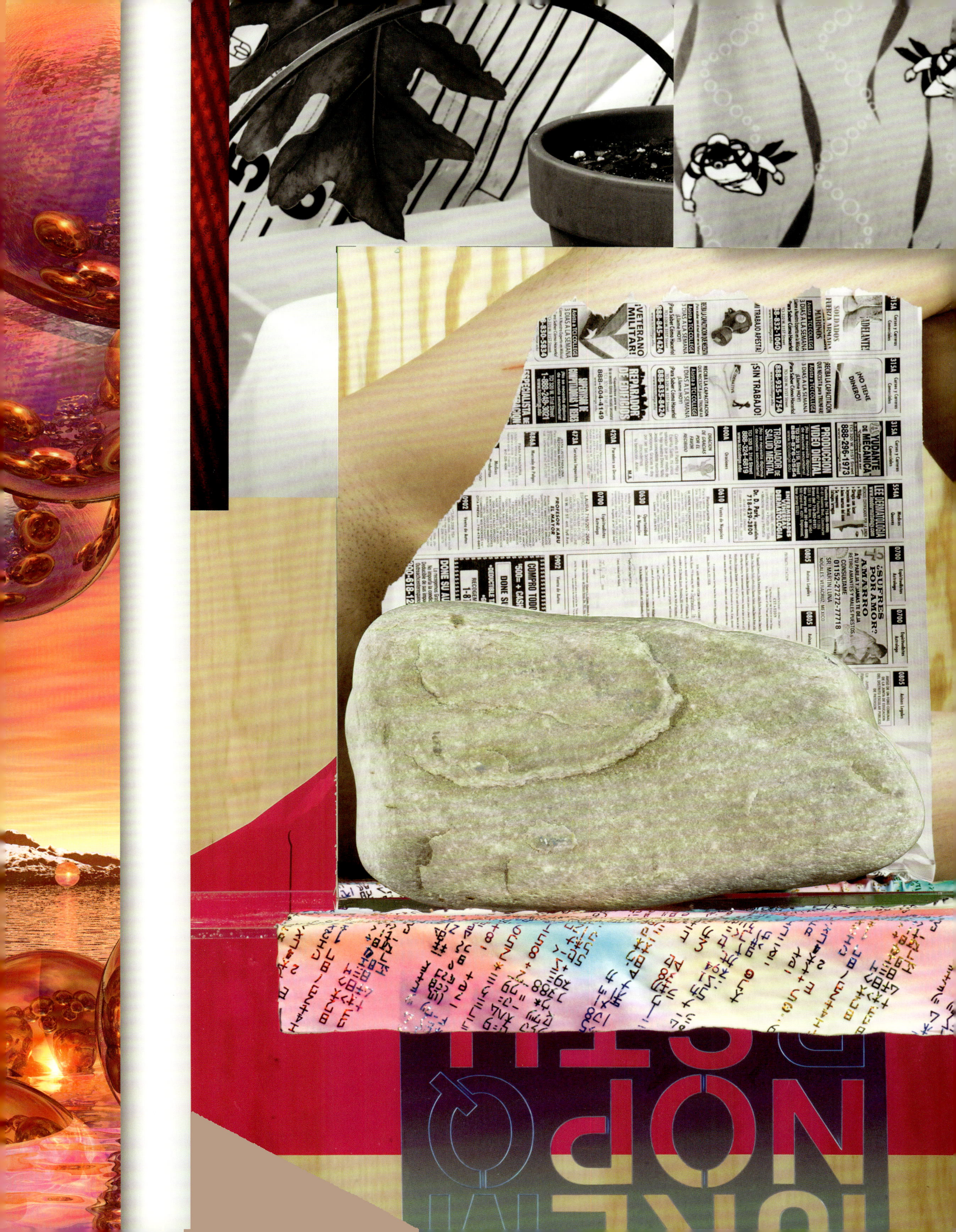

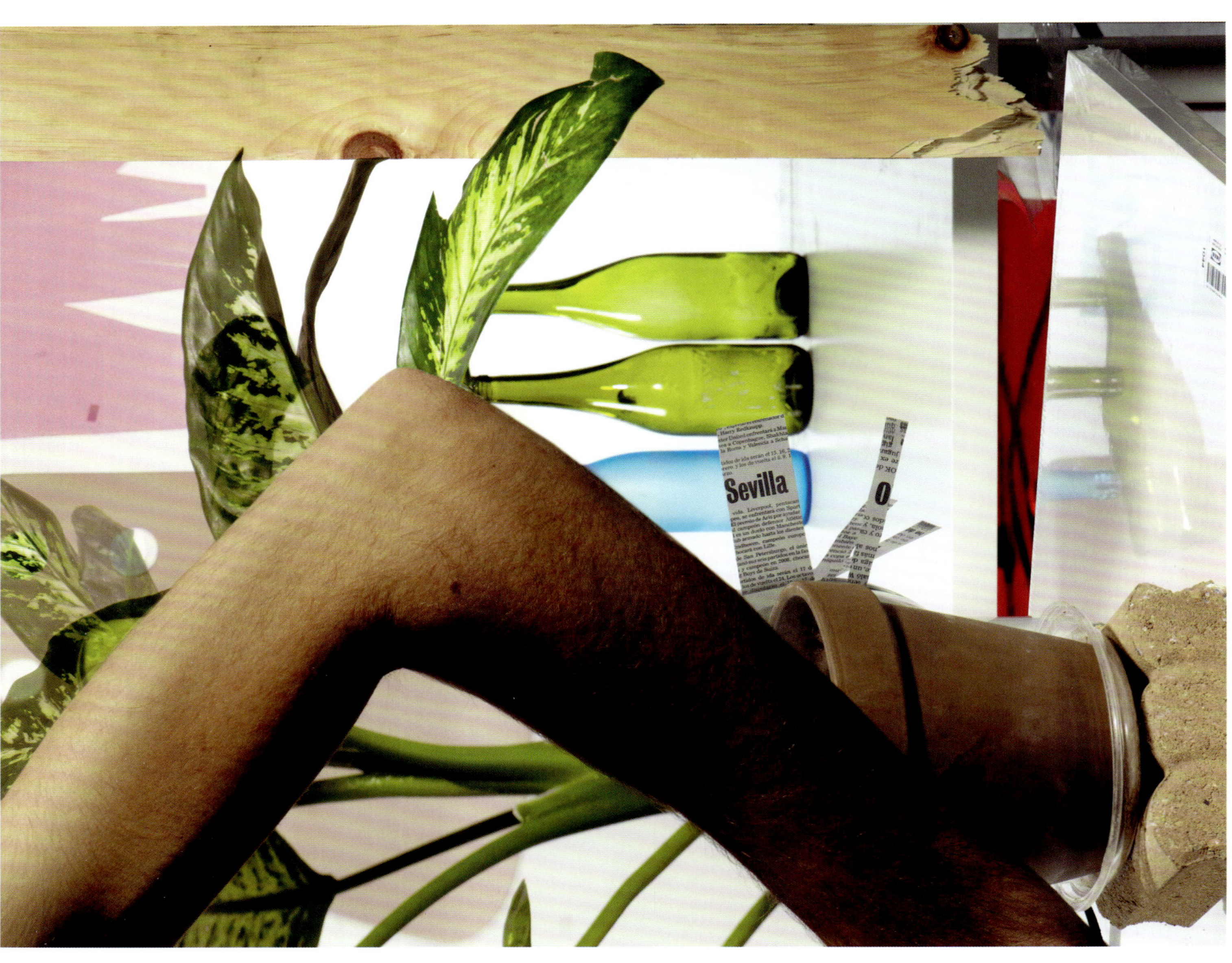

This page: *Arm, Plant, Bottles, Wood*, 2011

Opposite: *Not So Optimal*, 2010

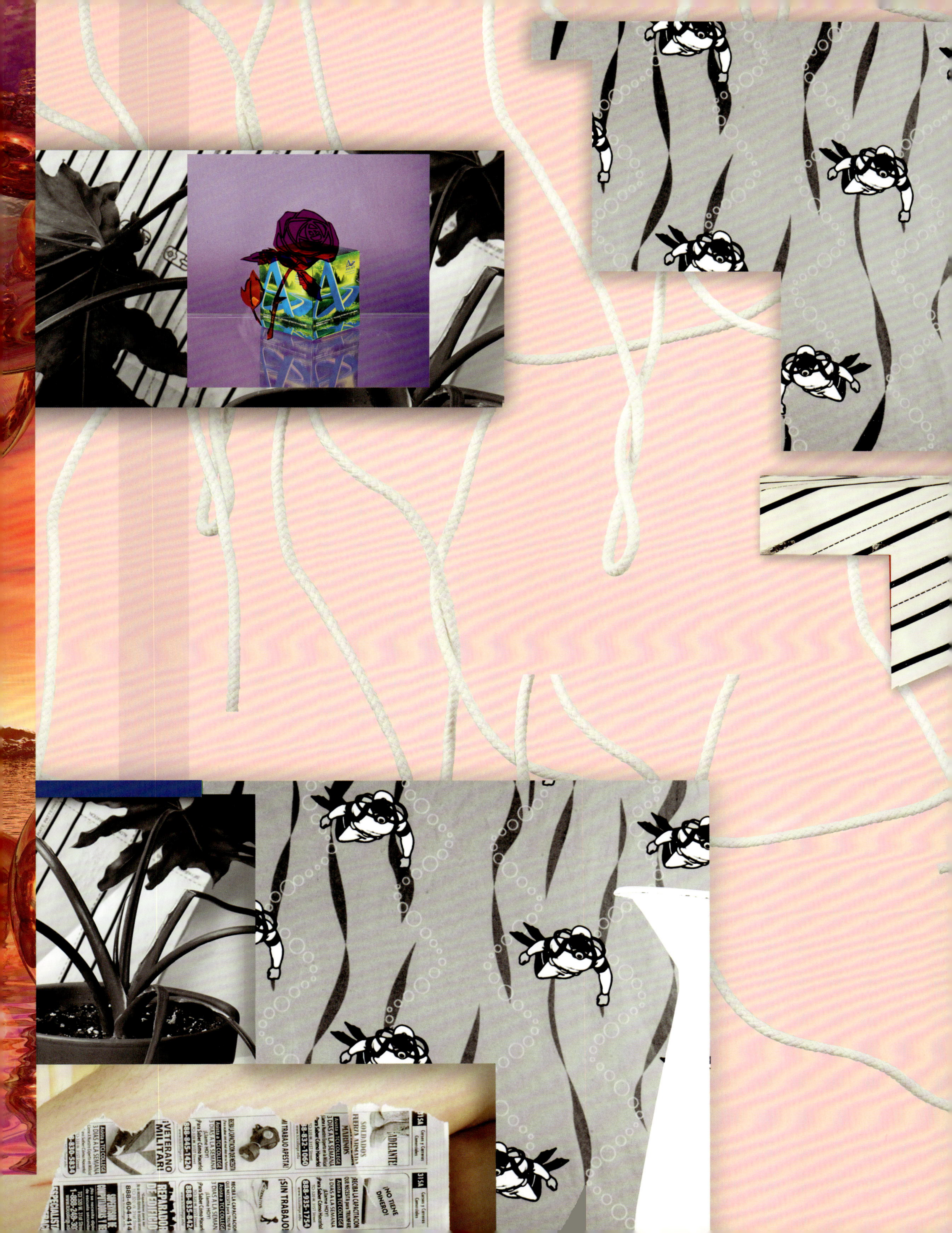
¡VETERANO MILITAR!
¡SIN TRABAJO!
¡ADELANTE!
¡NO TIENE DINERO!

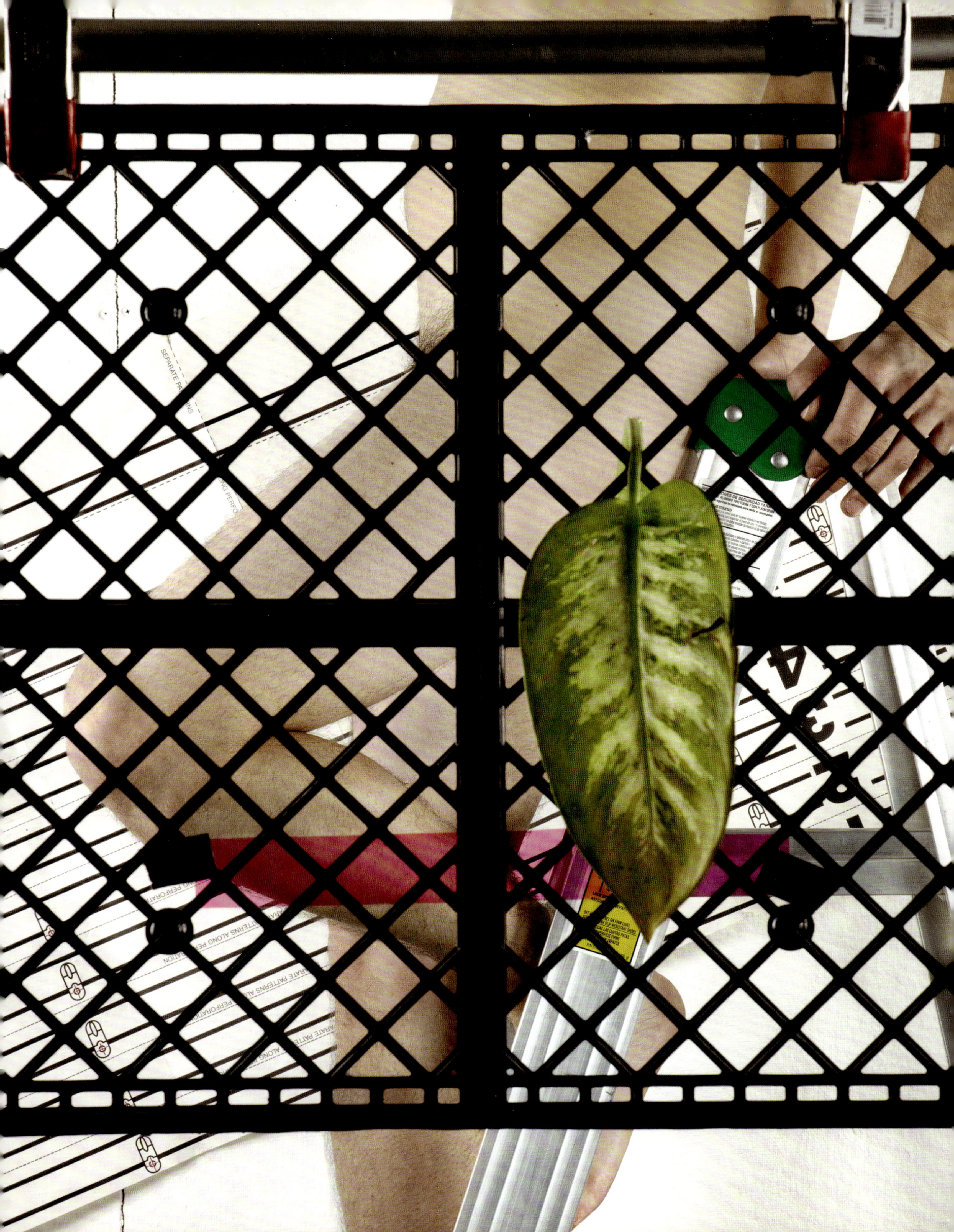

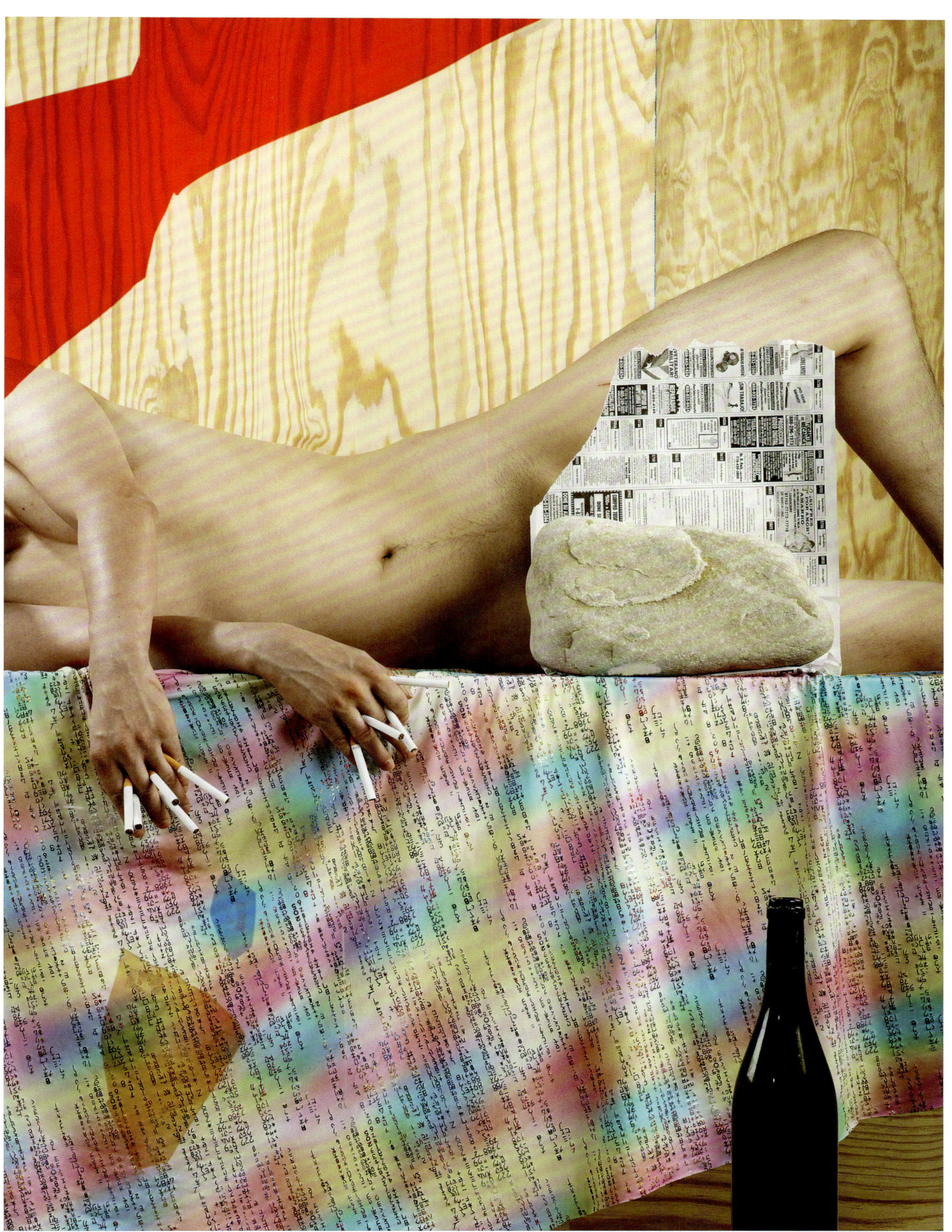

Opposite: *Leaf, Grid, Ladder, Black, White*, 2011

This page: *Red, Rock, Cigarettes, Newspaper, Body, Wood, Lycra, Bottle*, 2011. All photographs courtesy the artist and 47 Canal, New York

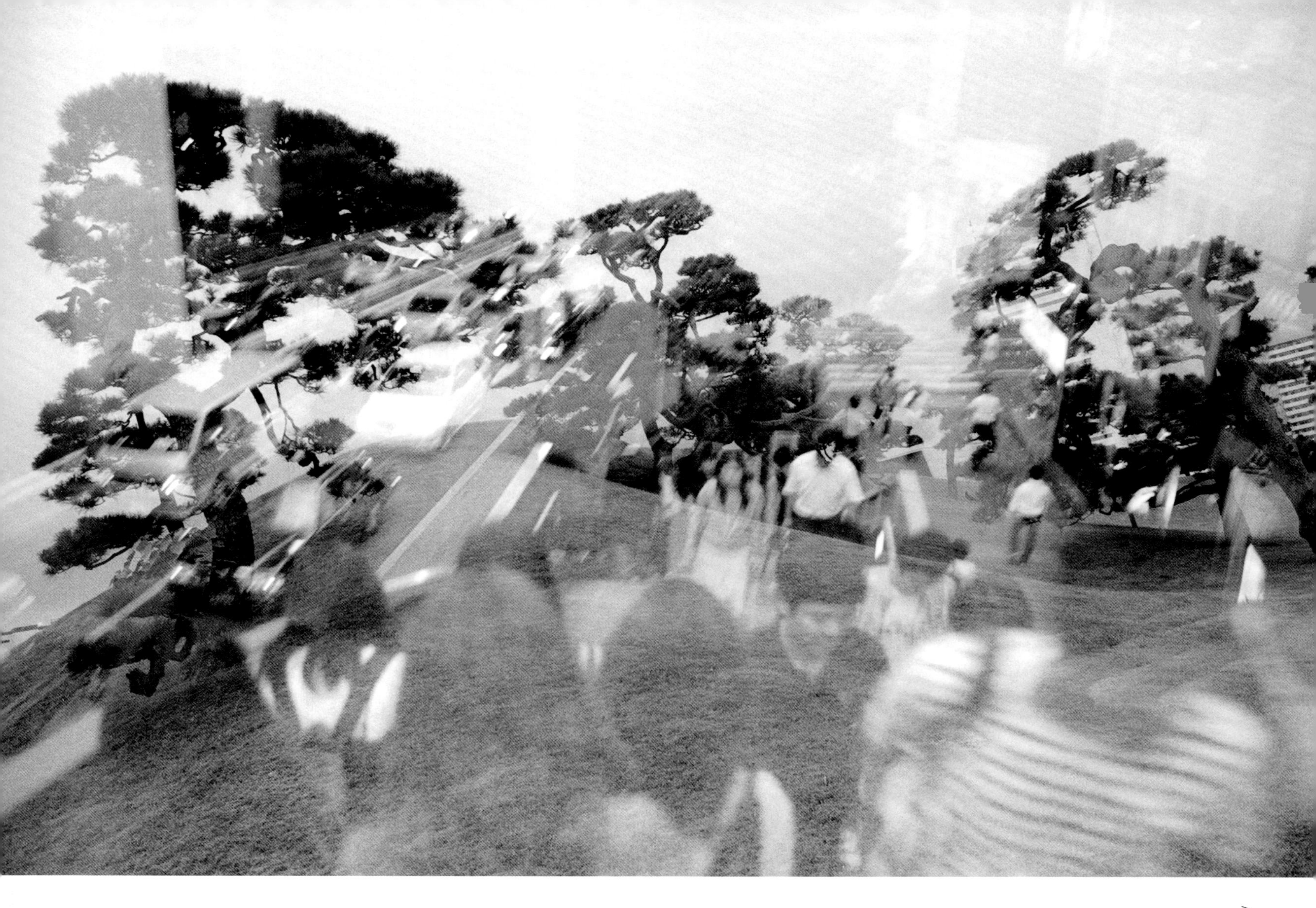

Jason Evans

NYLPT

Aaron Schuman

Aaron Schuman is a photographer, writer, editor, lecturer, and curator. Most recently, he exhibited his photographic series *Redwoods* at Flowers Gallery (London), wrote the foreword for Melinda Gibson's *The Photograph as Contemporary Art*, and curated *In Appropriation* for the Houston Center of Photography (2012).

Walking with Jason Evans—through city streets, across a university campus, or even around his own home—one realizes that he is a truly voracious looker. His eyes will frequently light up, a camera will appear in his hand, and the journey will veer in a new direction, even as the conversation maintains a steady flow. These forays provide an instantaneous insight into the interior reality, the internal experience, of Evans in that moment. "Essentially, I'm just a street photographer—a traditional, very boring flâneur," he maintains, "[but] I'm capable of being a human being with a camera, not just a photographer."

What often distinguishes Evans's work from that of other practitioners is this multilayered and definitively "human" approach to photography. The emphasis is not only on what occurs in front of our eyes (and cameras); his work is also engaged in exploring the psychological power that is embedded in the act of seeing. Established in 2004, Evans's thedailynice.com is a webpage on which a single new photograph appears every day, and no archive is maintained. Partially intended as a therapeutic exercise for Evans himself, the site also provides both photographic and emotional stimuli for its audience—he regularly gets emails from fans who have found reassurance there. "I'd rather see something than look at it," Evans recently commented, "but you can only see by looking. When you really see something you get the feeling ... We see when we look, and then we feel."

Over the course of the past eight years, during trips to various cities known for their street-photography heritage—New York, London, Paris, Tokyo—Evans has compiled images for a new body of work, *NYLPT*, which again internalizes the photographic act, both technically and figuratively. (The project was published in book form last year by MACK, and as a progressively designed iPad app produced by MAPP.) Evans found it difficult to escape these cities' well-known photographic histories, which were embedded deep within his consciousness, so he began to shoot rolls of 35-millimeter black-and-white film in the traditional manner, then rewound and pocketed them. Later—days, weeks, months, even years later—he would pull out the same films in the same cities, and re-expose them, sometimes doing so up to five times without having a clue as to which images would overlap with one another. "I was missing that in photography: chance, happy accident, luck," he says. "The 'decisive moment' was no longer out there waiting to be hunted down. It had moved behind the lens, onto the film plane." The results are kaleidoscopic—as if a thousand-piece jigsaw puzzle had been tipped out of its box, and into each frame—and yet every photograph conveys a multilayered "feel" of its city, an amalgamation of Evans's own photographic experiences of each place with their combined effect on his psyche.

In a technical sense, by coopting the fundamental materials of street photography—35-millimeter black-and-white film—and then treating each frame as one might expose a digital sensor, Evans layers historical and current street-photographic strategies upon one another. As he wrote in his 2008 essay "Online Photographic Thinking": "In the inevitable and frankly tedious digital versus analog debate, my position is one of either/and. Both systems offer distinct possibilities, but I ultimately believe that they are just different sides of the same coin."

"The flâneur [...] is bombarded by a plethora of stimuli that cannot be completely assimilated," wrote Charles Baudelaire. "Accordingly, [he] must remain alert, vigilant and constantly on guard lest he experience psychological disintegration and loss of coherence." By surrendering his guard, by committing to the incoherence of contemporary experience, and by internalizing the "decisive moment" and then overlaying the resulting film plane with that of the mind, perhaps Evans proposes a new order—and new possibilities—for photographic observation; we feel when we see, and then we look.

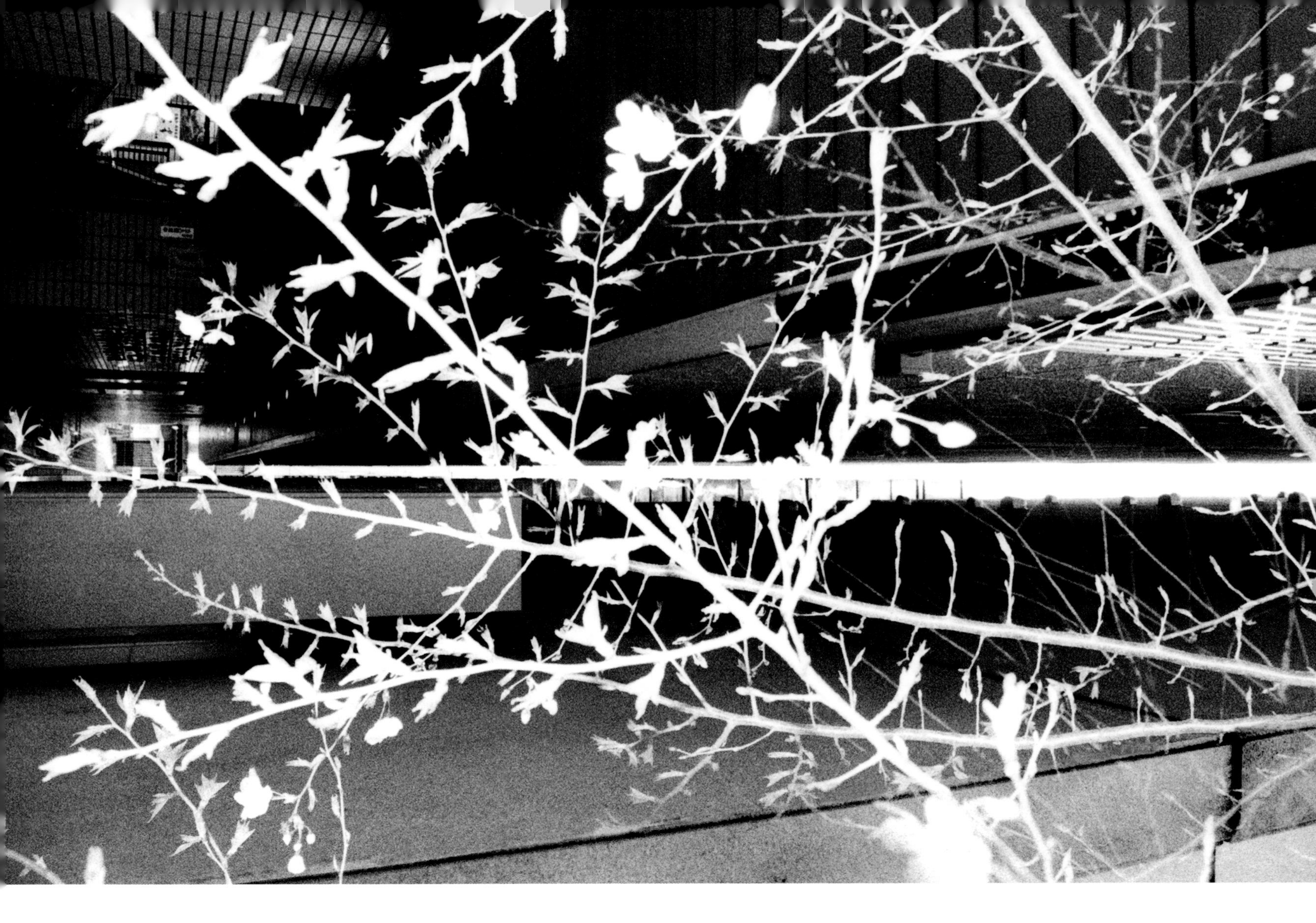

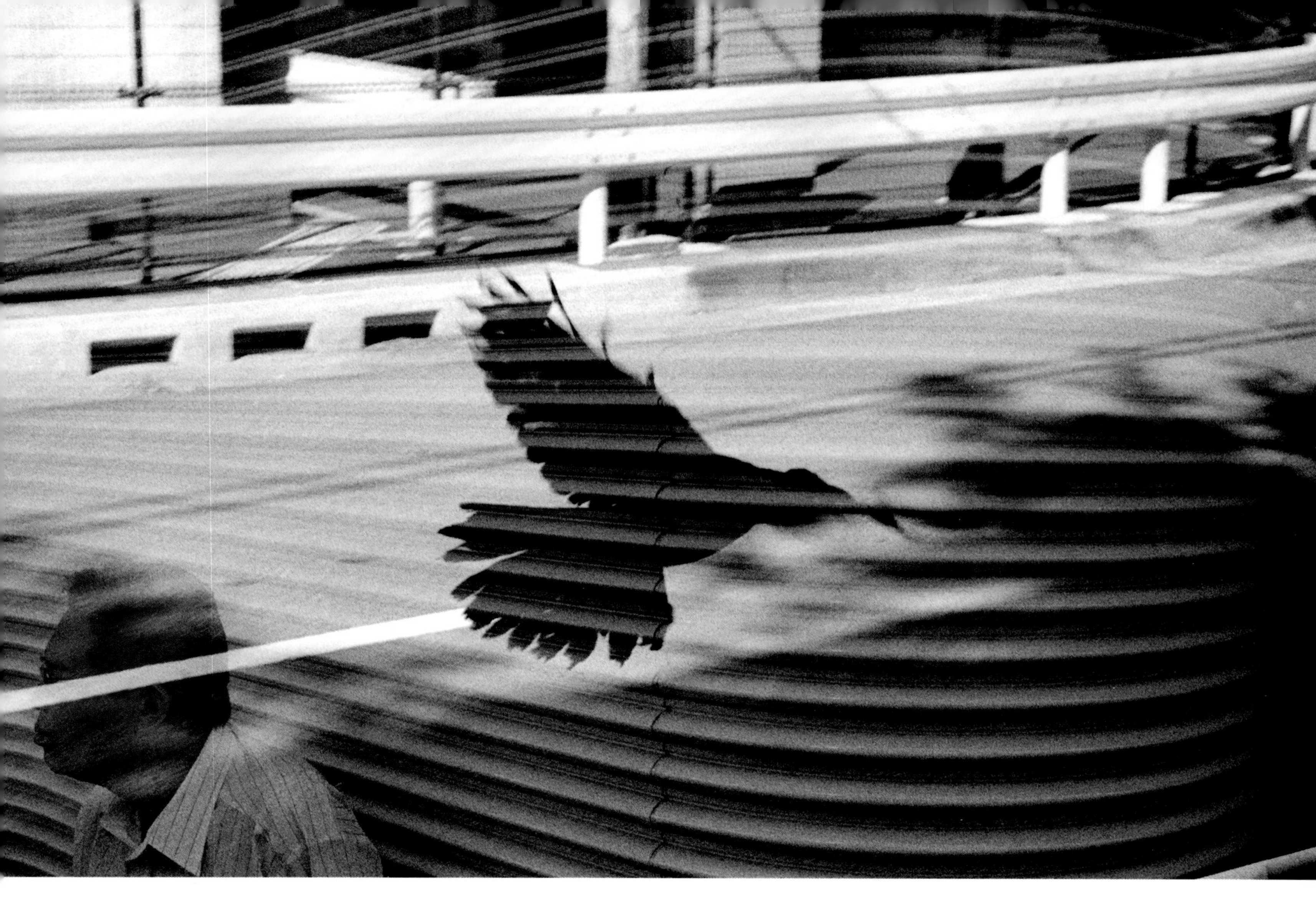

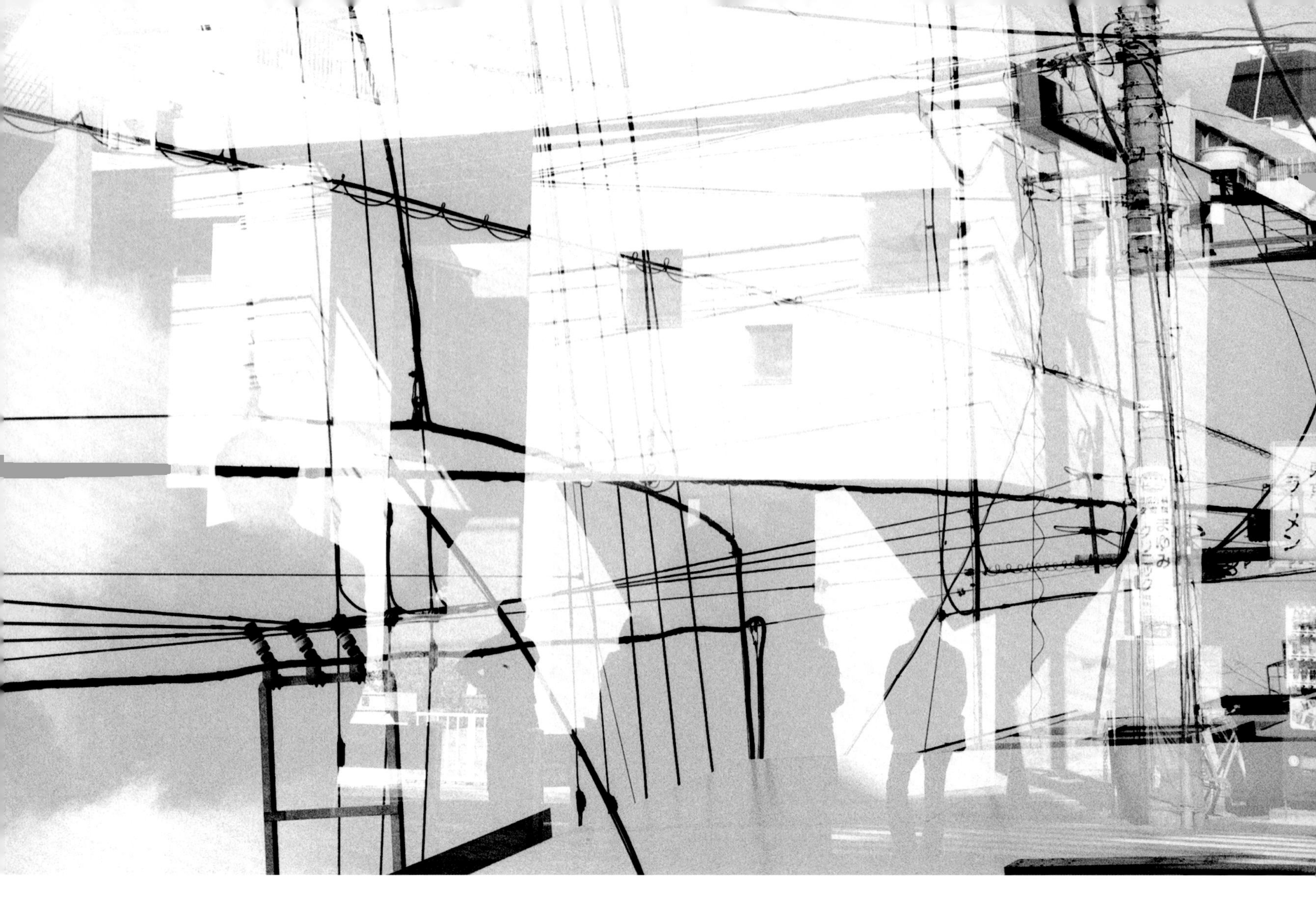
まゆみ
ラーメン

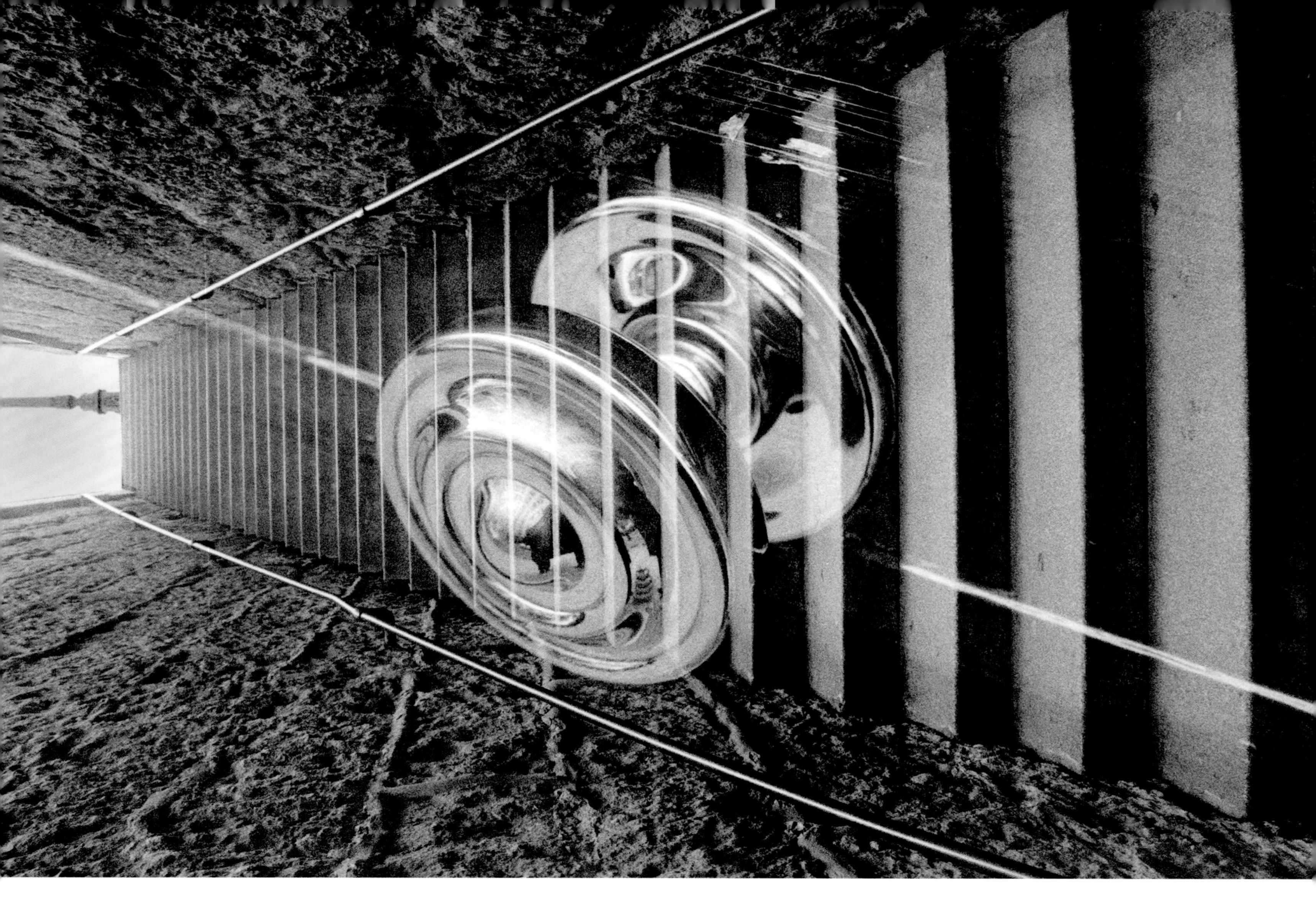

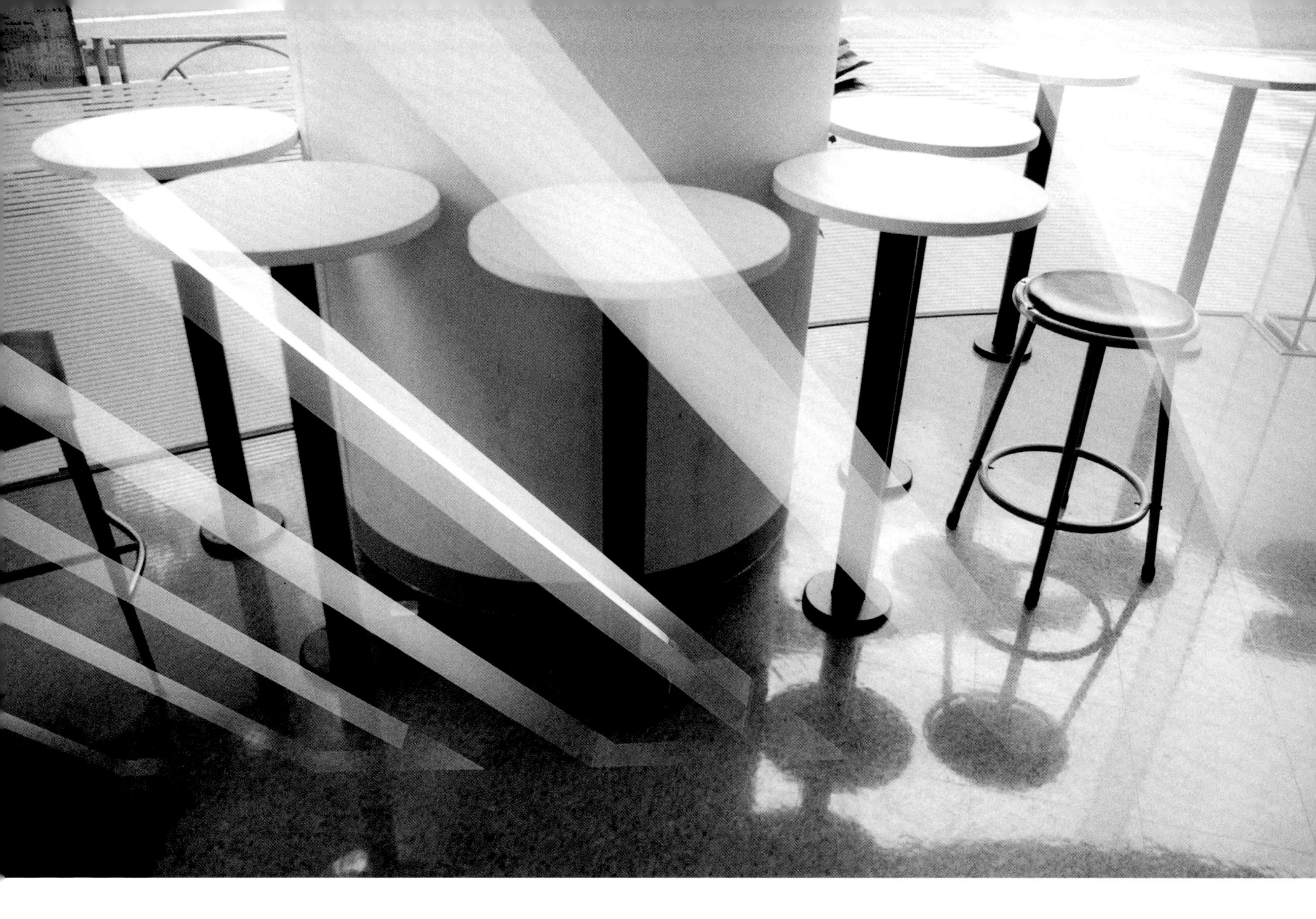

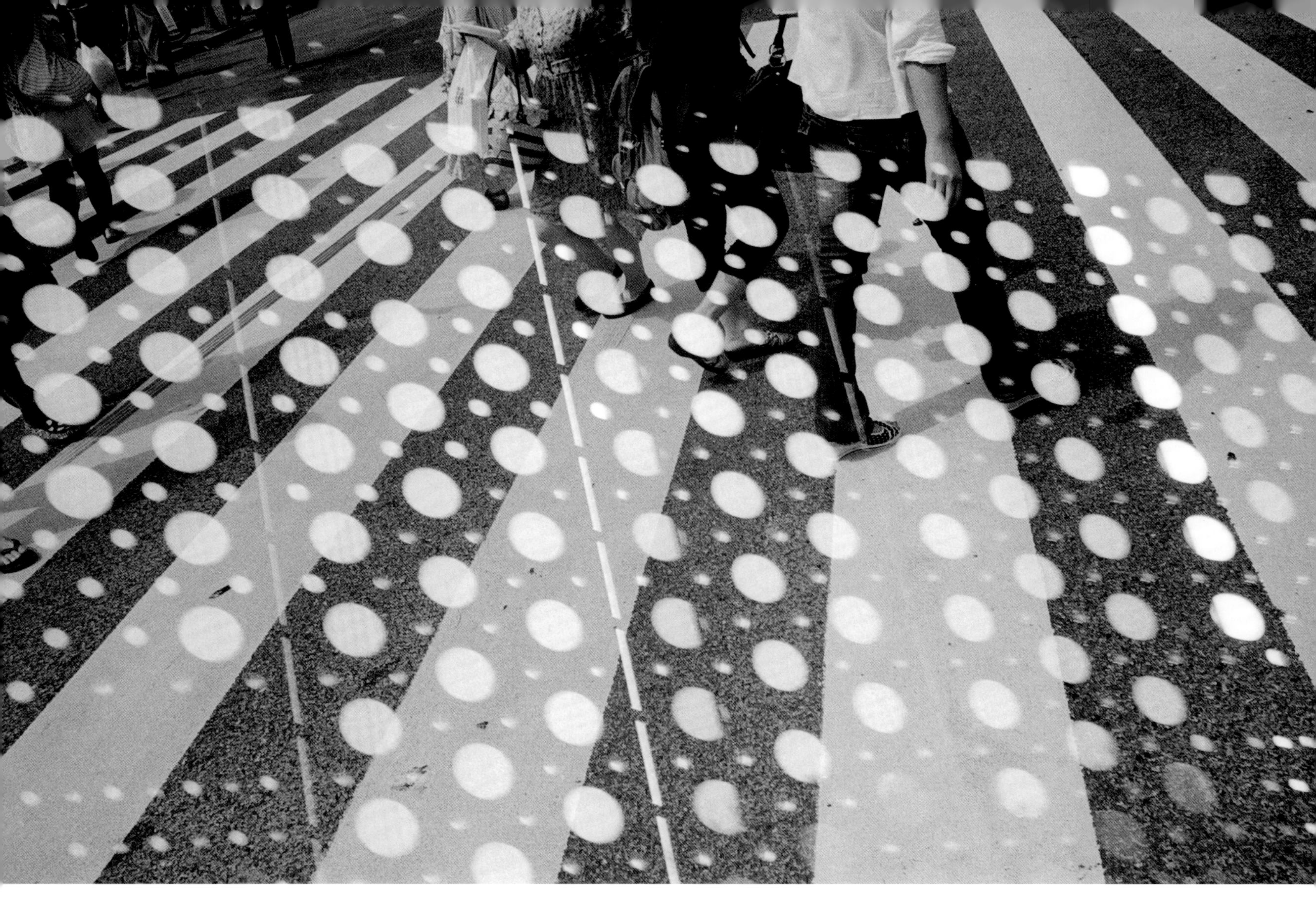

A decade ago, documentary photographers and visual journalists relied for production funding on their agencies and representatives brokering a path to primary (assigning) and secondary (resale) markets. Now publishers' ability to invest in visual storytelling or pay re-use fees is seriously diminished, while photographers increasingly reach their audiences directly. The agency in between has been squeezed. Highly specialized micro-agencies and multinational aggregators can yet thrive. The rest must reinvent themselves.

Magnum Photos, the sixty-five-year-old photographers' agency, has much reinvention to its historic credit. Its marketing-genius founder Robert Capa forged a new kind of contract between publishers and photographers, licensing territorial rights to photographic stories for "guarantees" and flat fees as an alternative to the prevalent assignment model of the 1940s, trading job security for freedom. Capa's mechanism for funding production became the norm for photojournalists' agencies over the following fifty years. In the 1960s and '70s Magnum was at the forefront of cultivating the corporate market for photojournalists' work. During the downturn in magazine fortunes in the 1990s, the agency leveraged its brand in Europe to develop and exploit the "cultural market," serving civic and nongovernmental clients with bodies of work disseminated via exhibitions and books alongside associated press coverage.

With the ongoing *Postcards from America* project, which began in May 2011, Magnum photographers are developing another new model, every bit as inventive. The principle is similar to the group project of Magnum's civic-storytelling practice, and has roots in older projects such as *People Are People the World Over*, which was shot by an international team of photographers for *Ladies' Home Journal* in 1948. Now, however, neither magazines nor institutions act as the funding client. Instead, projects build on the success of individual photographers who have engaged audiences directly, employing crowd-sourced fundraising, attracting customers with offers of limited-edition books and prints, and connecting with more people through Facebook, Flickr, and Tumblr. *Postcards from America* aggregates the individual audiences of several photographers, as well as Magnum's thousands of online followers, with additional sponsorship and logistical help provided by corporate, cultural, and educational supporters. This new model involves Magnum's photographers working *together* as photographer-publishers.

The subject of the project is the social and economic fabric of the United States. A group of photographers heads out on the road, or to a particular place, with a coordinated plan and a common subject—in the installment featured in these pages, it is Florida during the 2012 presidential election. Each photographer follows his or her own artistic agenda, but works with the others to offer a range of editioned products. For an organization that has always valued artistic freedom, this model allows the photographers to share control of all editorial and production decisions. It bypasses the usual agency mediation, relying on the photographers themselves to speak directly to the work's audiences. This requires the commitment of the photographers to each other but only minimal administrative input from the agency's staff. The model suggests a distinct Magnum path through the crisis facing documentary photographers: a light infrastructure to sustain connections with broad audiences (and photography-buying collectors), but little of the traditional baggage of the photo agency.

The Magnum team characterizes *Postcards from America* as "a series of collaborative projects aimed at discovering a polyphonic visual sound." It is a project that aspires to what writer and theorist Ariella Azoulay terms a "citizenry of photography" (in which no photographer, subject, or viewer is sovereign). Fueled by seductive ideas about democracy and collaboration, as well as sound economic sense and an independent spirit, this model will likely appeal to photographers and agencies for years to come, and far beyond Magnum.

Postcards from America

Jim Goldberg, Alessandra Sanguinetti, Alec Soth, Zoe Strauss (with Ashley Thompson), Mikhael Subotzky, Donovan Wylie

Introduction by Chris Boot

Chris Boot is executive director of Aperture Foundation. He worked for Magnum Photos from 1990 to 1998.

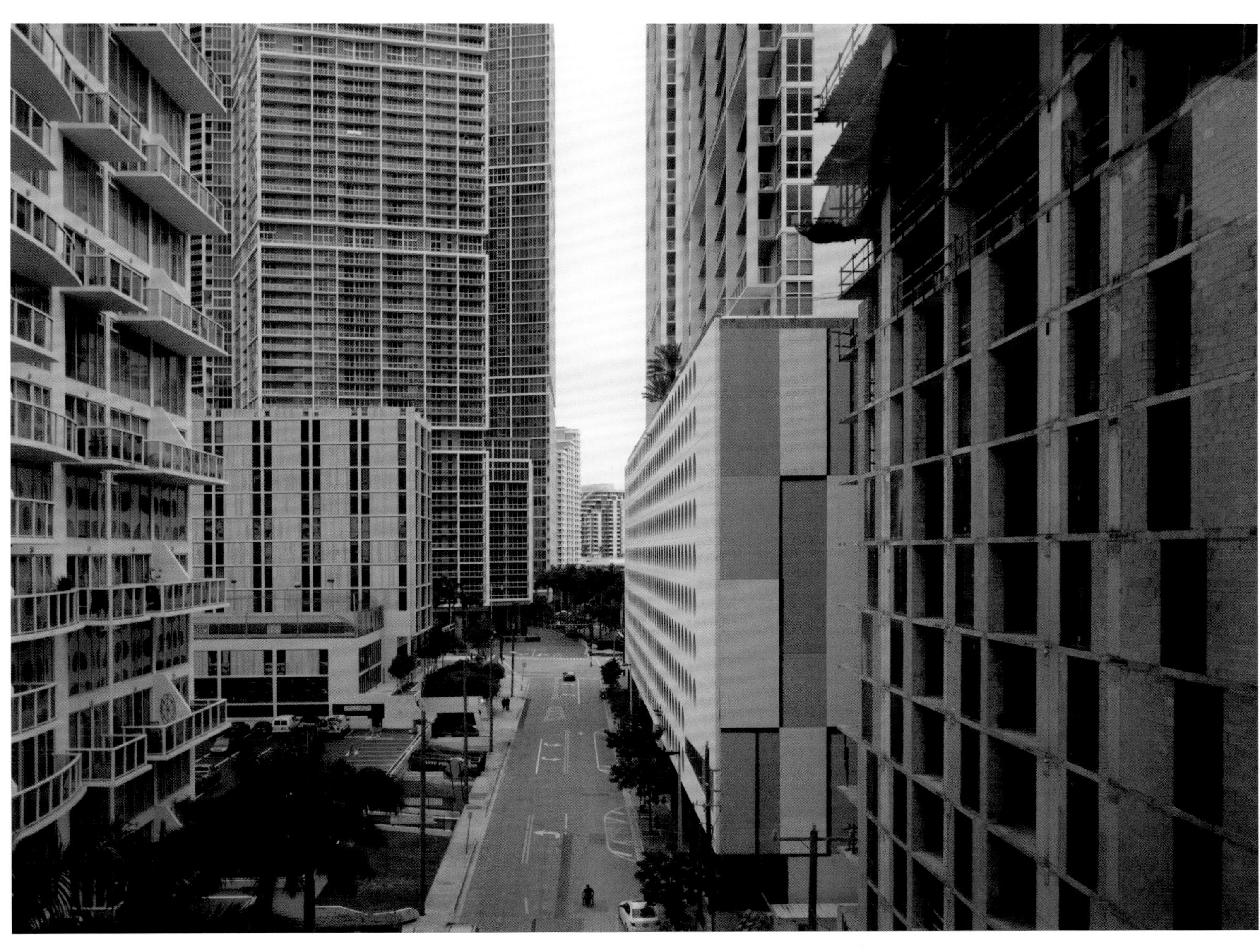

Donovan Wylie, Citizen,
from the window of a train
passing SE 5th Street, Miami,
Florida, 2012

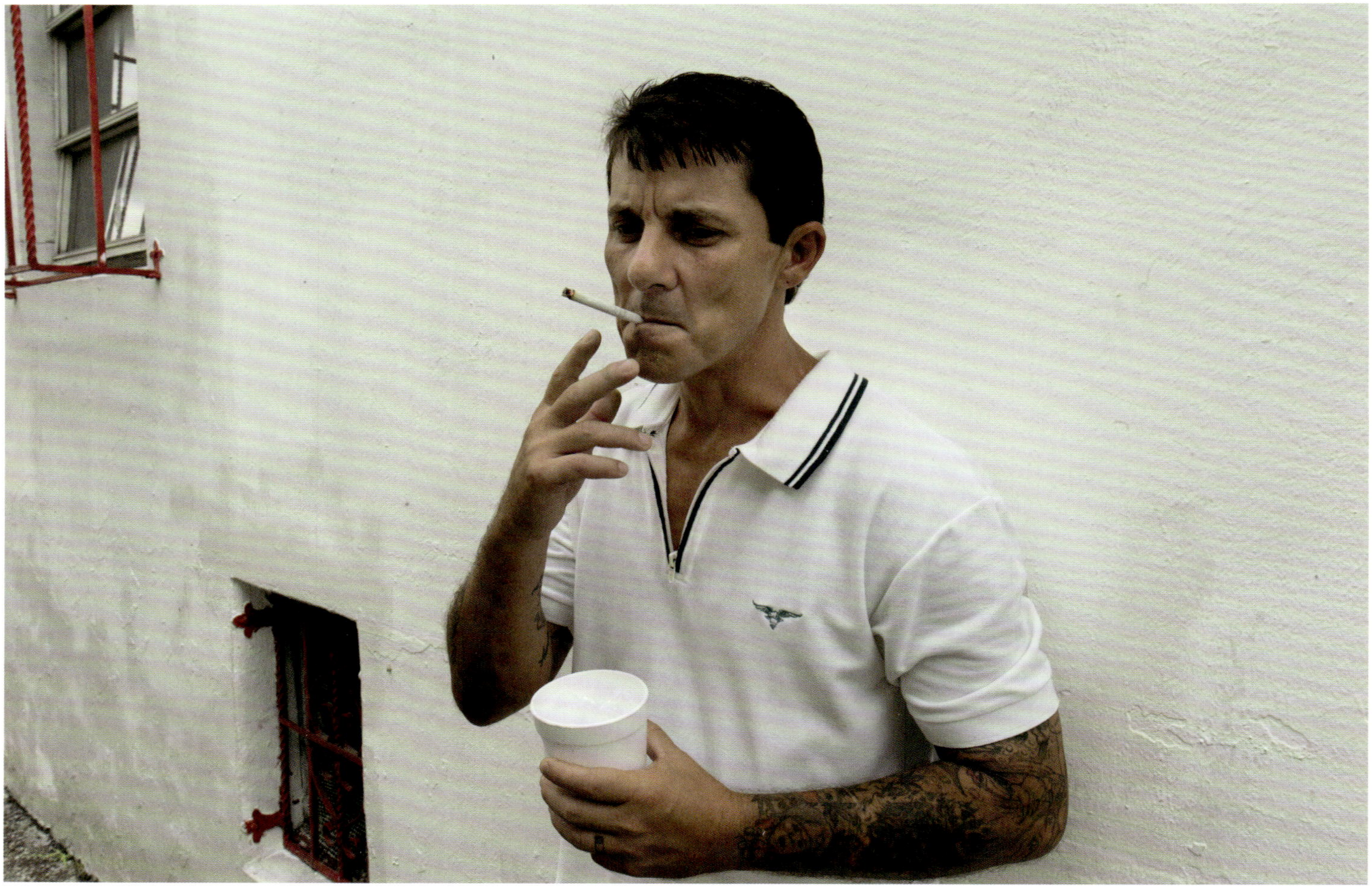

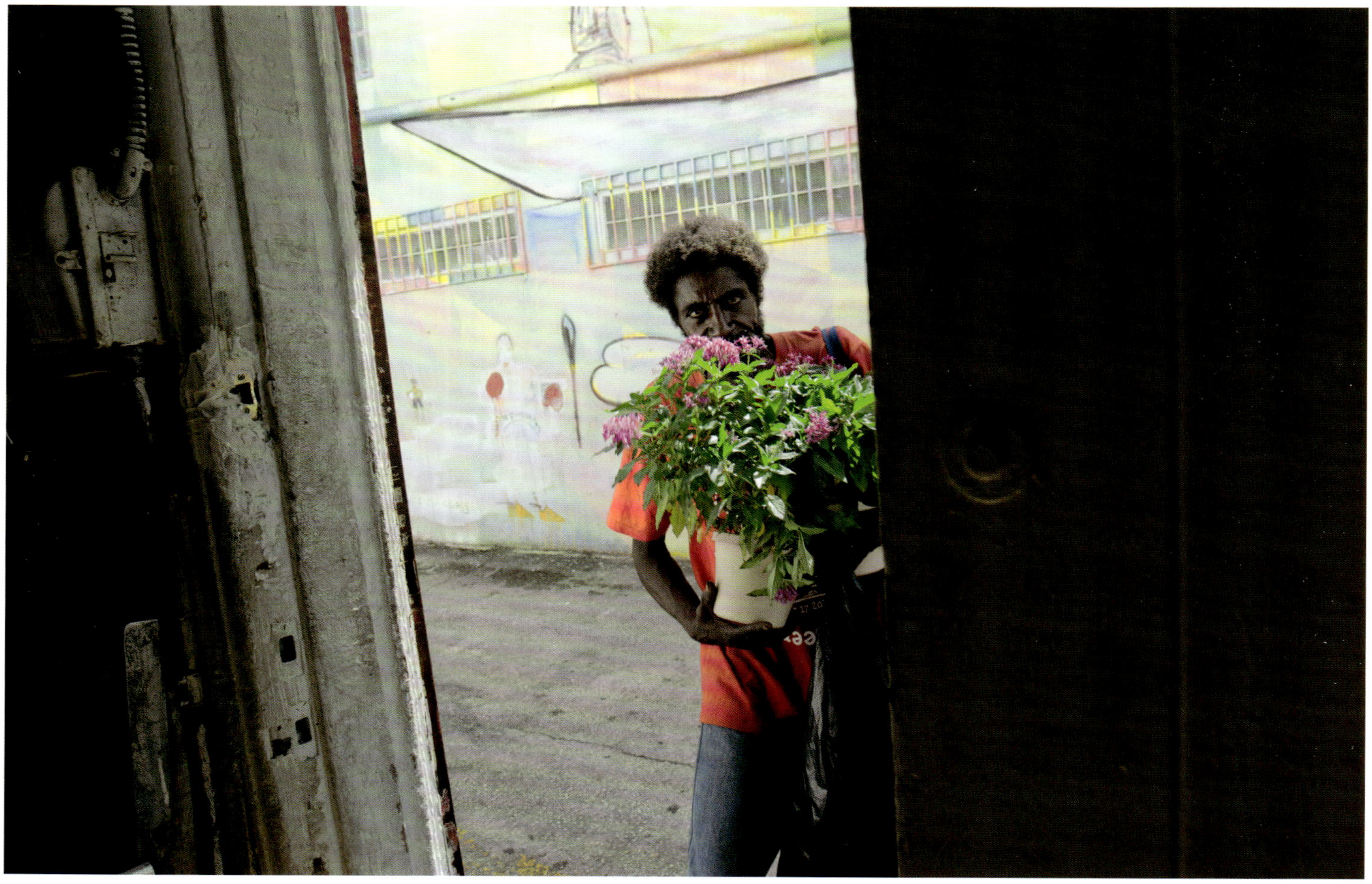

Opposite:
Mikhael Subotzky,
Steve outside
the S & S diner,
Miami, Florida, 2012

Mikhael Subotzky,
Flower seller outside
the S & S diner, Miami,
Florida, 2012

This page:
Alec Soth,
Home Suite Home
Motel, Kissimmee,
Florida, 2012

Alec Soth,
Magic Castle Inns and
Suites, Kissimmee,
Florida, 2012

Outside the gates of Walt Disney World in Orlando, many of the motels that once catered to tourists now shelter homeless families. On U.S. Highway 192, sixty-seven motels house more than five hundred homeless people.

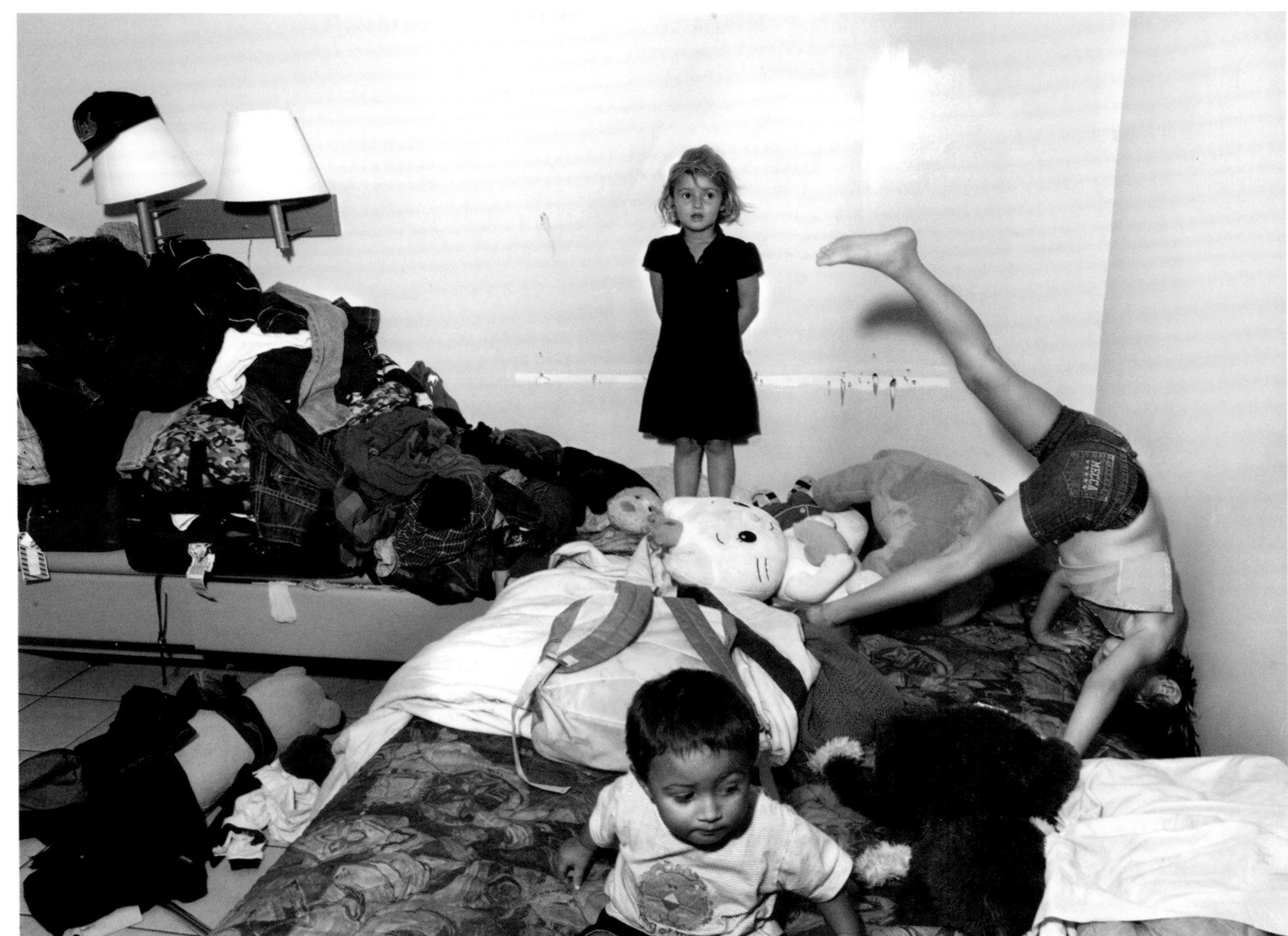

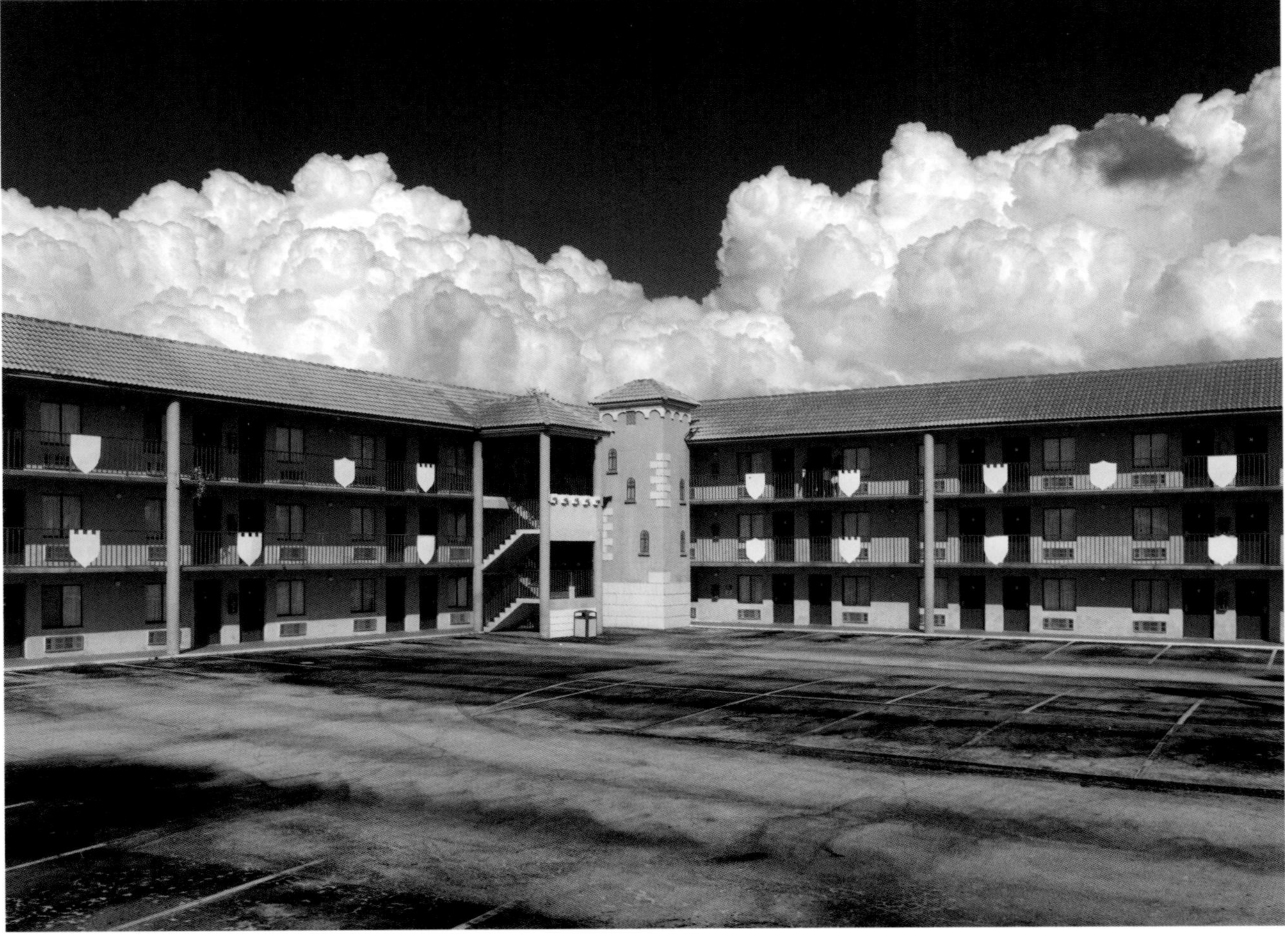

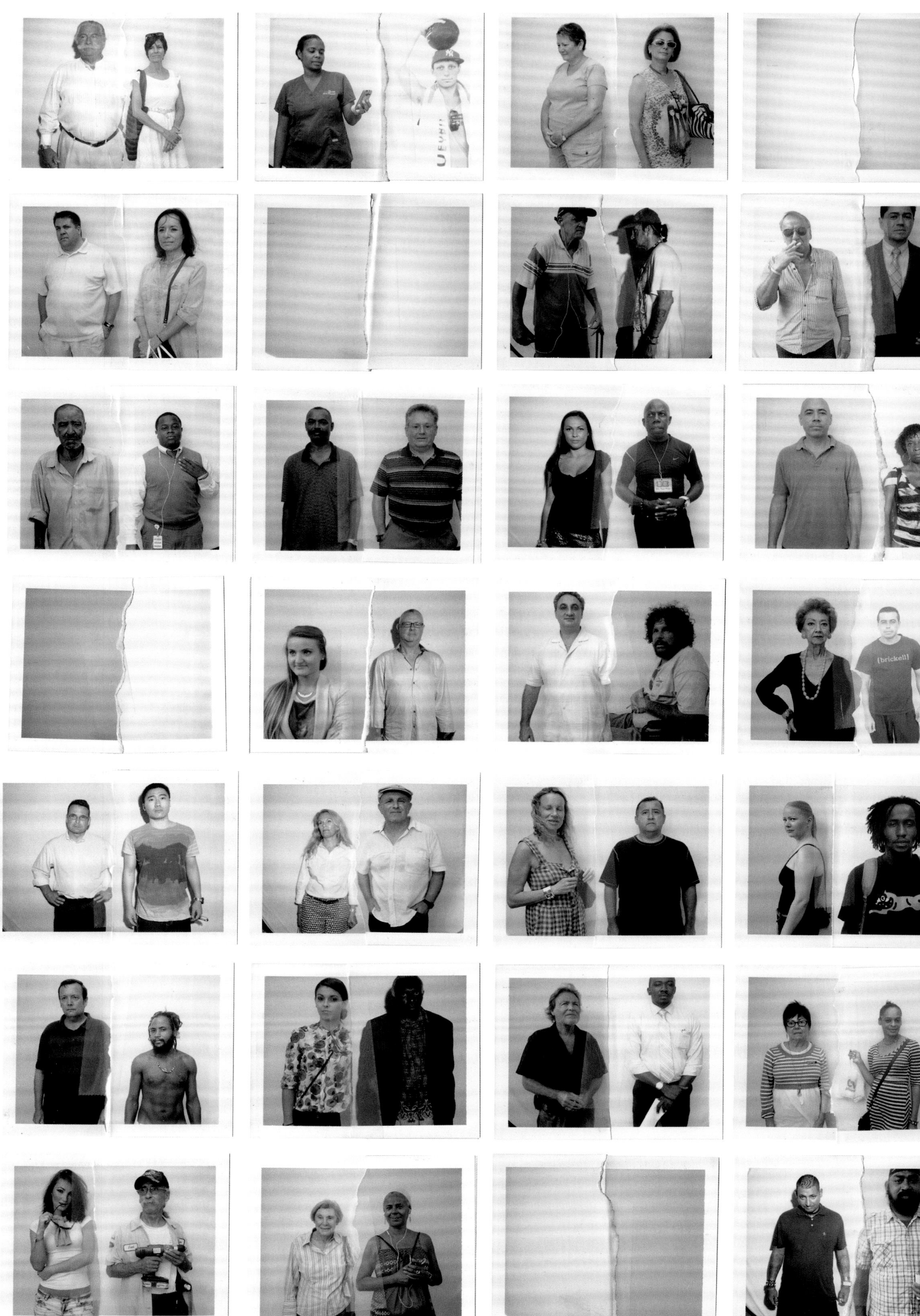
{brickell}

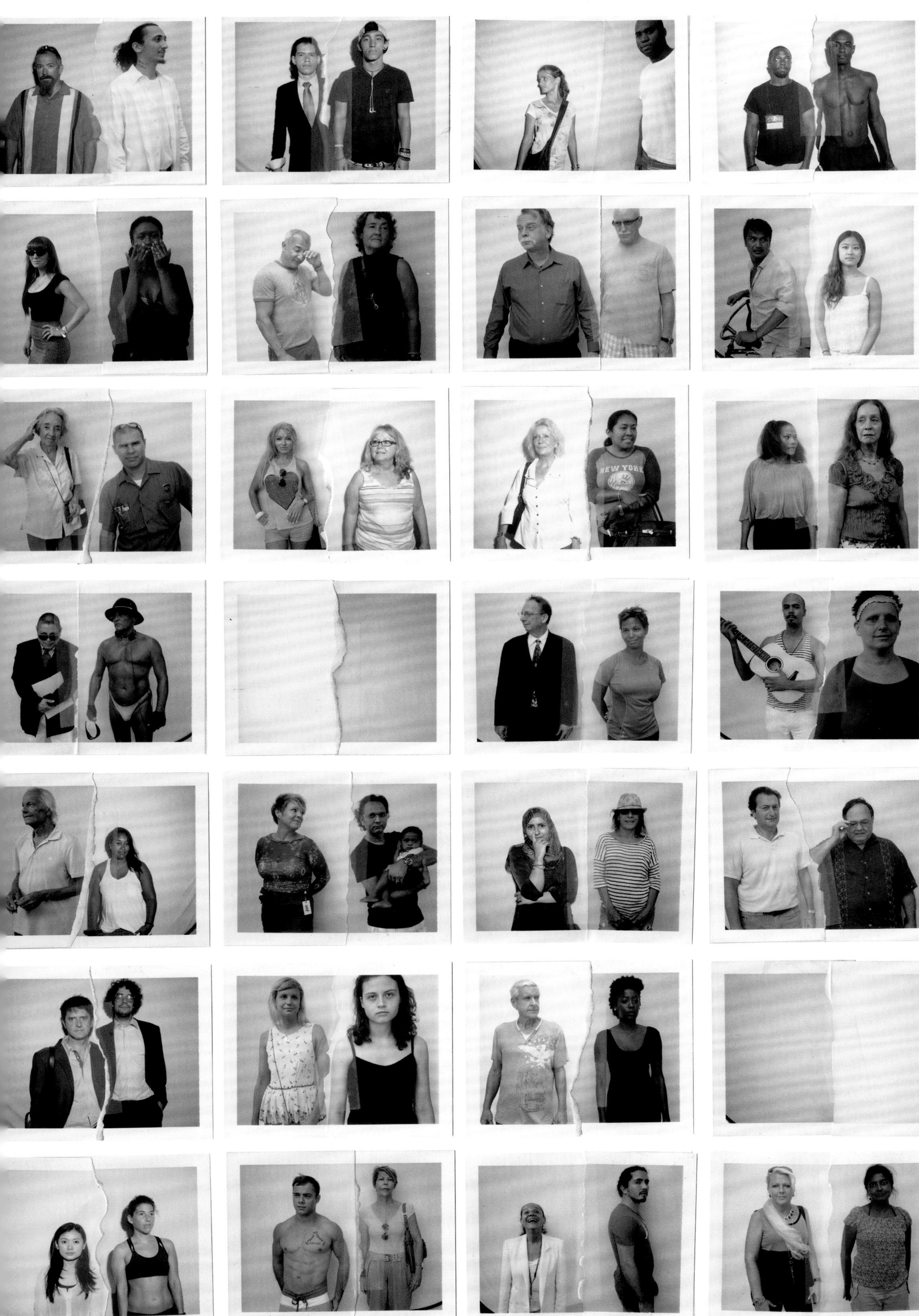

Previous spread:
Jim Goldberg, *50/50*, 2012

Goldberg says of this work: "I wanted to explore the evenly split divide of our nation's voters into Republicans and Democrats. To do this, I collaged Polaroids together into the same frame—half-Democrat and half-Republican."

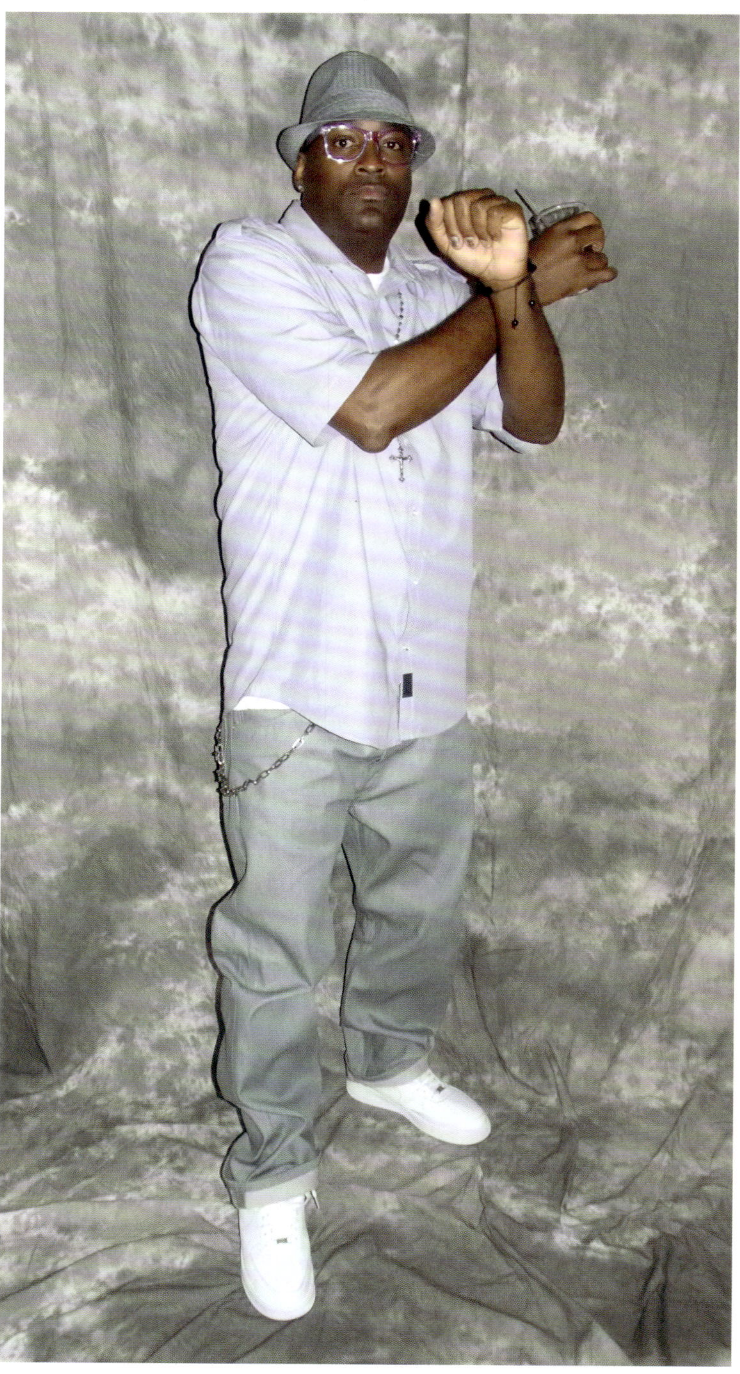

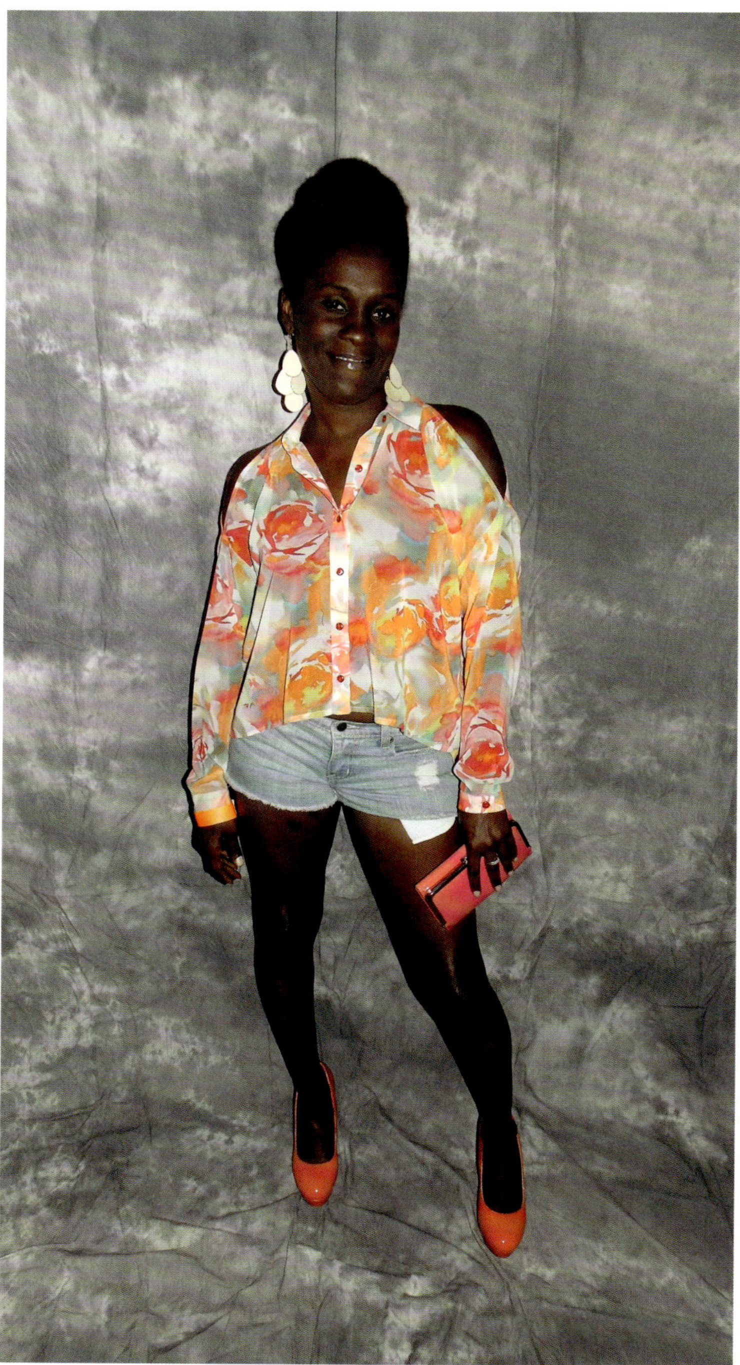

Ashley Thompson, Sarasota, Florida, October 2012

From the *Citizen 941* project: images of disenfranchised voters from Sarasota and the surrounding area. Thompson, himself a felon who has now completed his jail term, no longer has the right to vote. Zoe Strauss met Thompson while making her photograph of Presidential Pawn. The two photographers then began a collaborative project on disenfranchised voters.

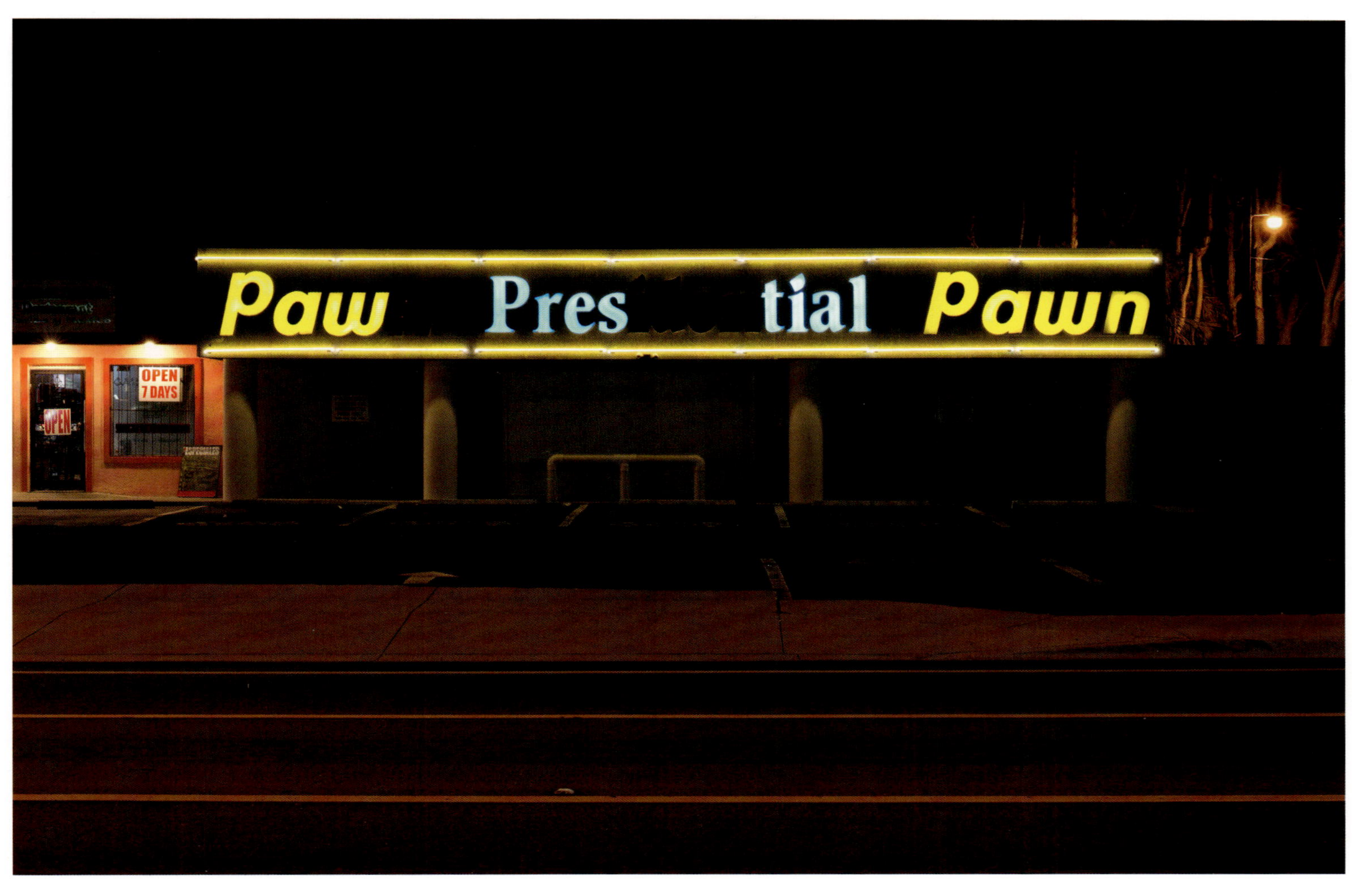

Zoe Strauss, Presidential Pawn, Sarasota, Florida, October 2012

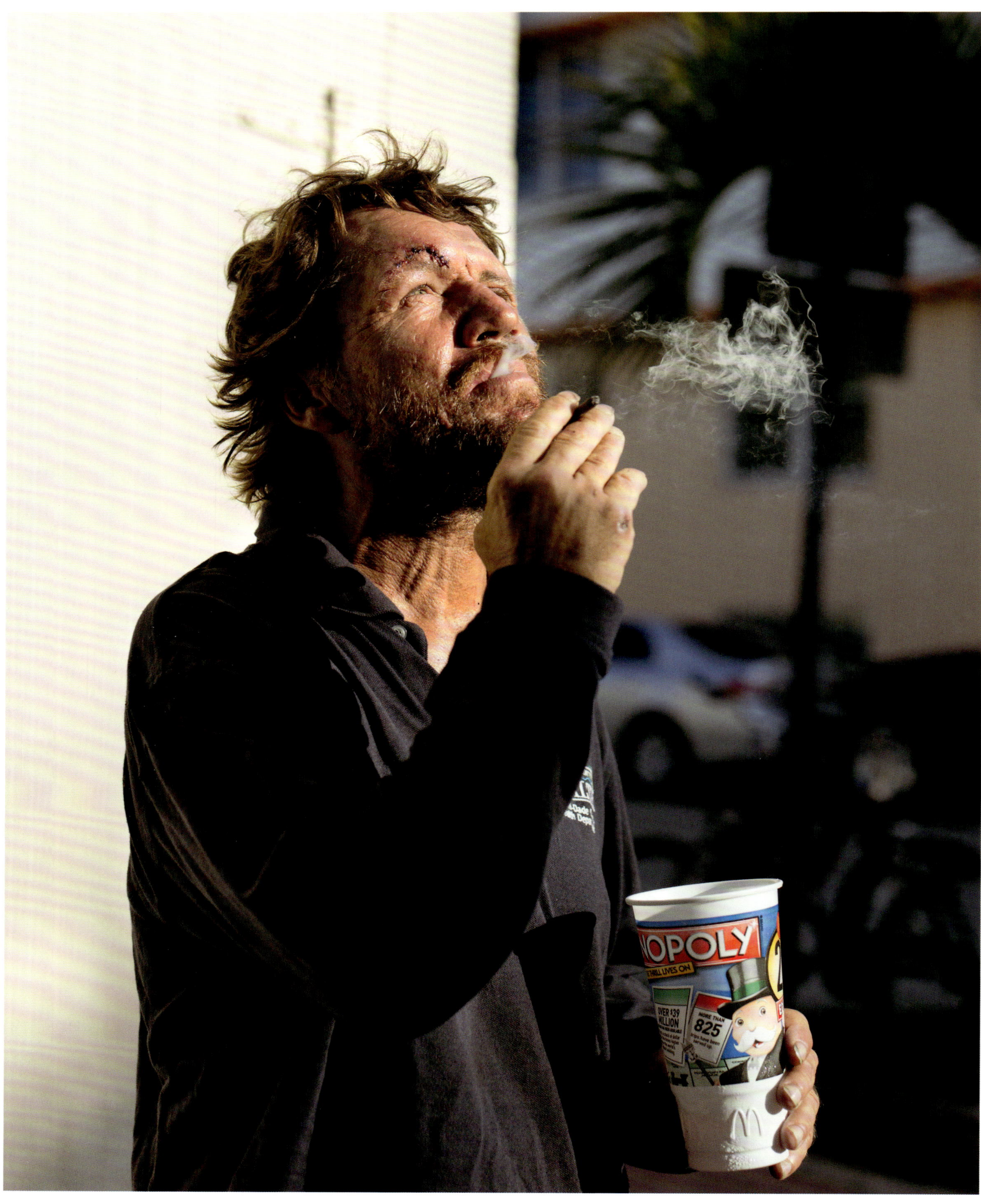

Alessandra Sanguinetti, Ocean Court and 9th Street, Miami, Florida, October 2012

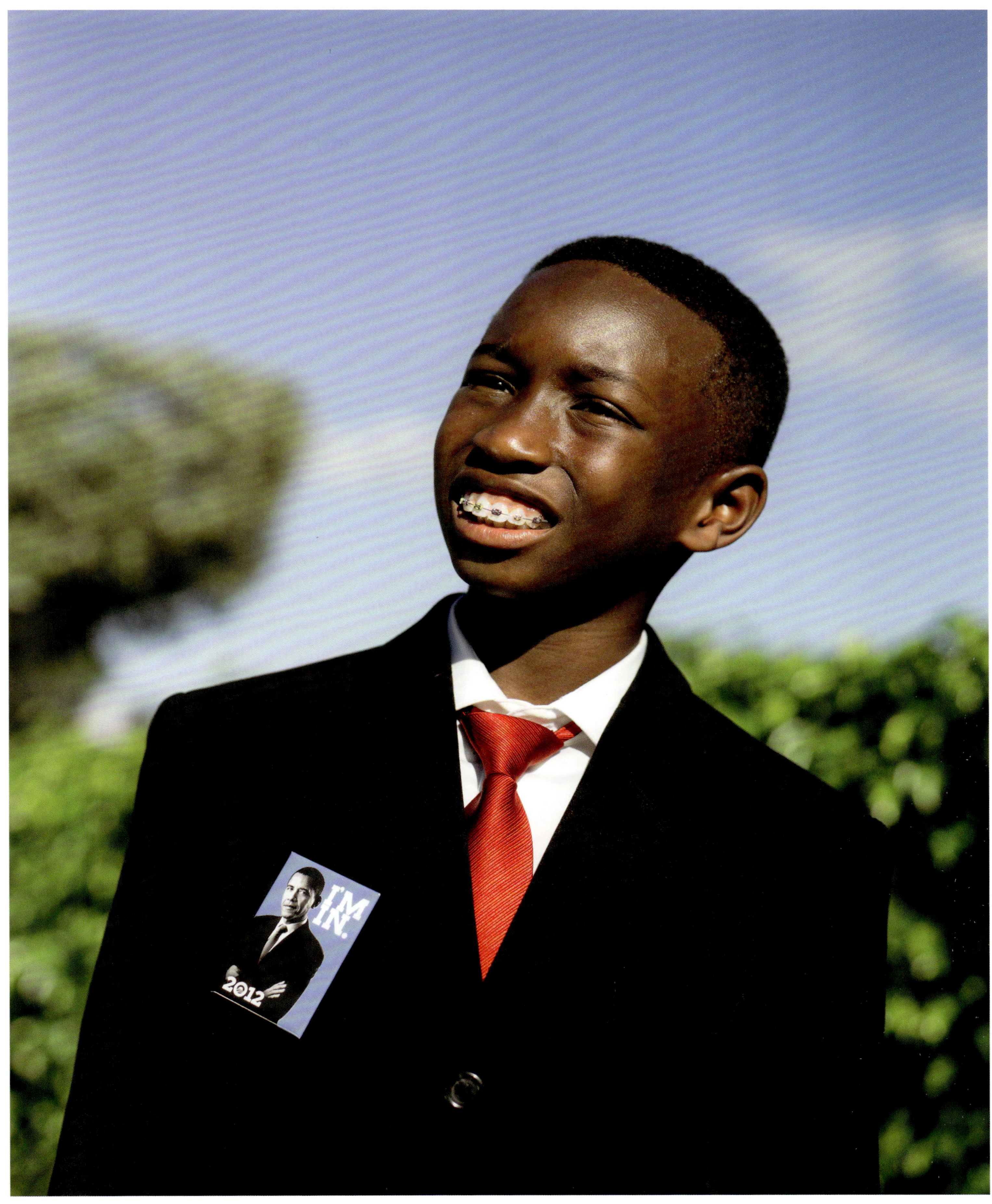

Alessandra Sanguinetti, Guerby Mertil, Jr. after seeing Barack Obama speak at a grassroots event in Coral Gables, Florida, October 2012

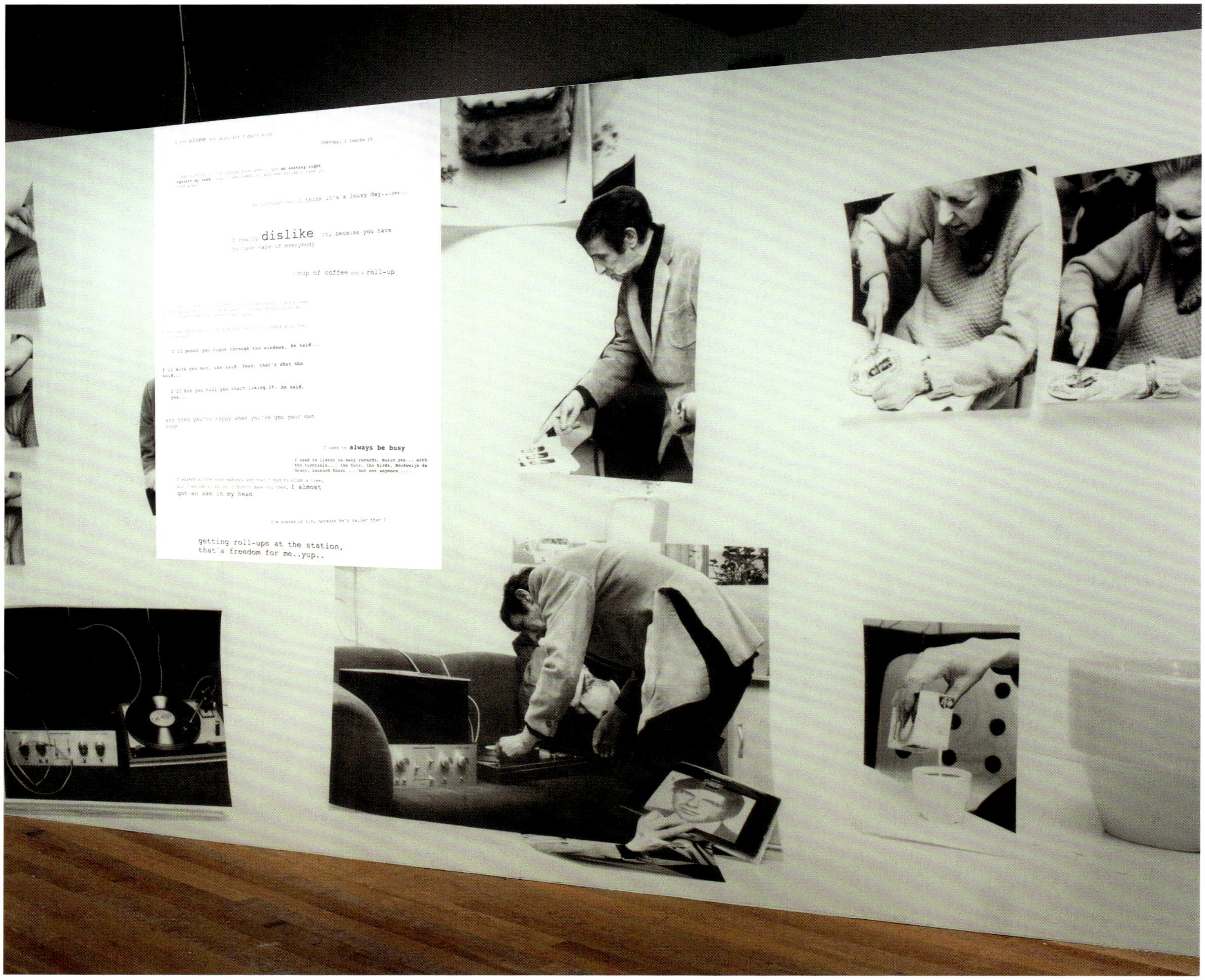

Lang Zal Ze Leven/Happy Birthday to You (wallpaper), 2012. Installation view of the exhibition *Dutch Doc Award 2012* at Tropenmuseum, Amsterdam, 2012

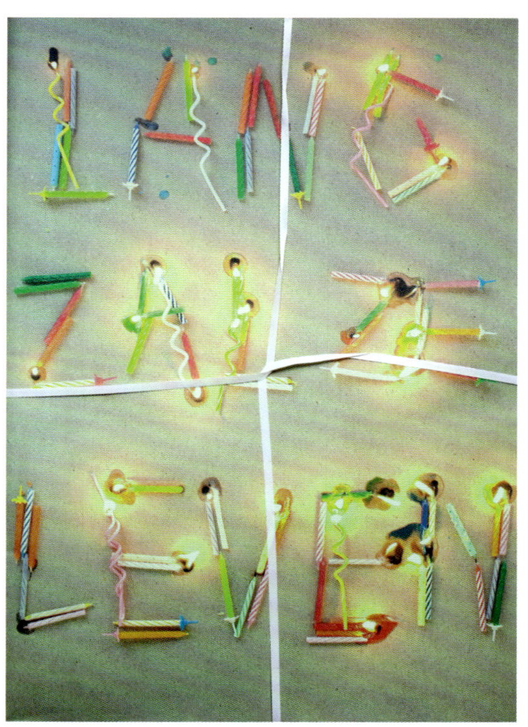

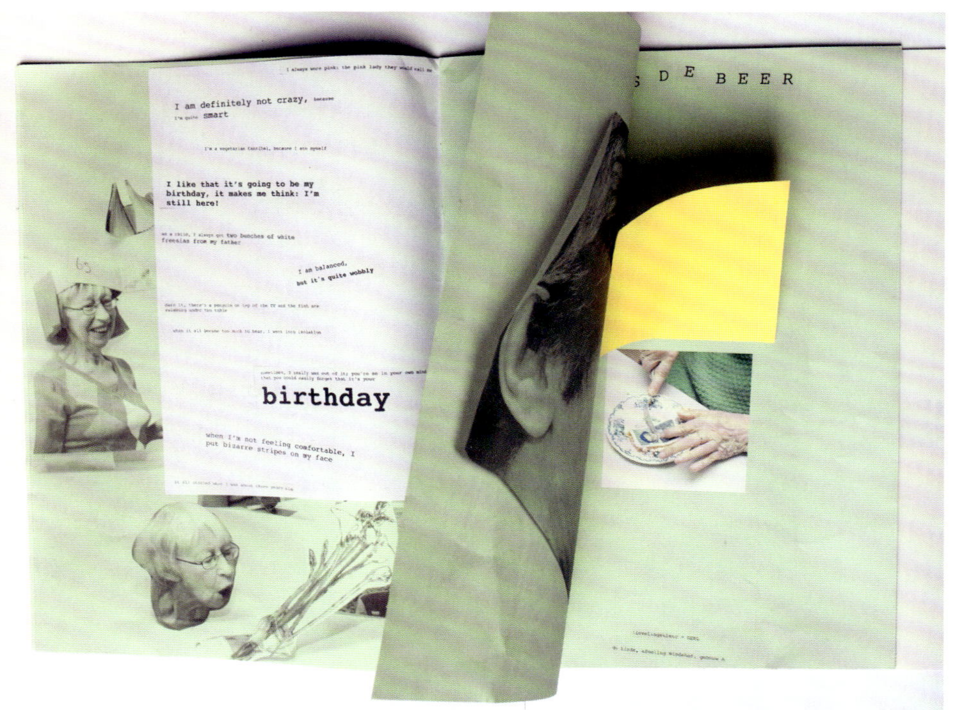

Lang Zal Ze Leven/Happy Birthday to You, 2011. Cover and inside view of the publication

Anouk Kruithof

Lesley A. Martin

Anouk Kruithof works with photography: she works through photography, around photography. The stand-alone image is rarely, if ever, the point. More critical are the events that result in photographs—actions that lead to photographs, which lead to installations, books, and videos; projects like *Lang Zal Ze Leven/ Happy Birthday to You*; *Playing Borders: This Contemporary State of Mind*; and *Untitled (I've Taken Too Many Photos/ I've Never Taken a Photo)*.

Lang Zal Ze Leven (2011) was created during an artist's residency at a progressive psychiatric hospital in Den Dolder, Netherlands. During her stay, Kruithof interviewed a group of patients about what they wanted for their birthdays and did her best to fulfill those wishes, including baking each of them a cake featuring an edible printed-frosting portrait of the recipient. Kruithof photographed her interactions with the group, and each of the patients participated in creating collages from this material. The resulting collaborative works, incorporating snippets from conversations as well as images, form the core of a book and subsequent installations. The foundation of the piece is consciously transactional—the photographs would not exist without the artist's interaction with the patients; the interaction itself may not have happened without the intention to document it. Photography acts as a connective tissue, a binding agent that also provides a record of these individuals and their birthday wishes, and as a means for Kruithof to explore the fine lines between compulsive, "abnormal" psychologies and those considered "normal."

Another series, *Untitled (I've Taken Too Many Photos/I've Never Taken a Photo)* (2012), offers an experiment in call and response between photographer and viewer. In preparation for a show at the Festival International de Mode et de Photographie in Hyères, France, Kruithof sought someone in her adopted Brooklyn neighborhood who had ostensibly never taken a photograph. A young man named Harrison was enlisted to select images for an installation of Kruithof's work, and determined as well the size of each print in the final presentation. The point of this exercise was to find a person who might bring a fresh, unjaded perspective to an archive of three hundred images, conflating the role of curator and viewer and destabilizing the notion of the artist as an auteur fully in command of every tiny detail of creation. Further inverting the traditional logic of exhibition making, eighty selected images made by Harrison were installed on the ceiling, with viewers asked to experience the exhibition via mirrors, much as tourists are given mirrors for better viewing of frescos on the ceilings of Venetian cathedrals.

The installation turns viewers into performers, a role played by former office workers in *Playing Borders: This Contemporary State of Mind,* a series Kruithof began in 2008 at the site of an abandoned office building. The improvised performances and interventions in the space give shape to an absurdist commentary on the average workplace in the face of collapse. On one hand, *Playing Borders* is a document of today's workforce and work sites; on the other hand, it's a performance piece enacted amid a series of incongruous still lifes. Kruithof's restlessness and disinterest in categories is reflected in both installations of the work (one of which took place in the emergency exit of the Nederlands Fotomuseum in Rotterdam) as well as in the subsequent book, a series of unbound spreads of various sizes.

The installations and publications that emerge from these and other of Kruithof's projects underscore her interest in visceral, physically interactive experiences of the work as well as a commitment to pushing beyond the conventions prescribing the creation and display of a body of photographs. In today's socially mediated world, in which interpersonal interactions are frequently created, measured, and validated by the act of taking a picture, Kruithof generates her own network of action and photographic reaction.

Lesley A. Martin is the publisher of Aperture's books program and of the *PhotoBook Review*.

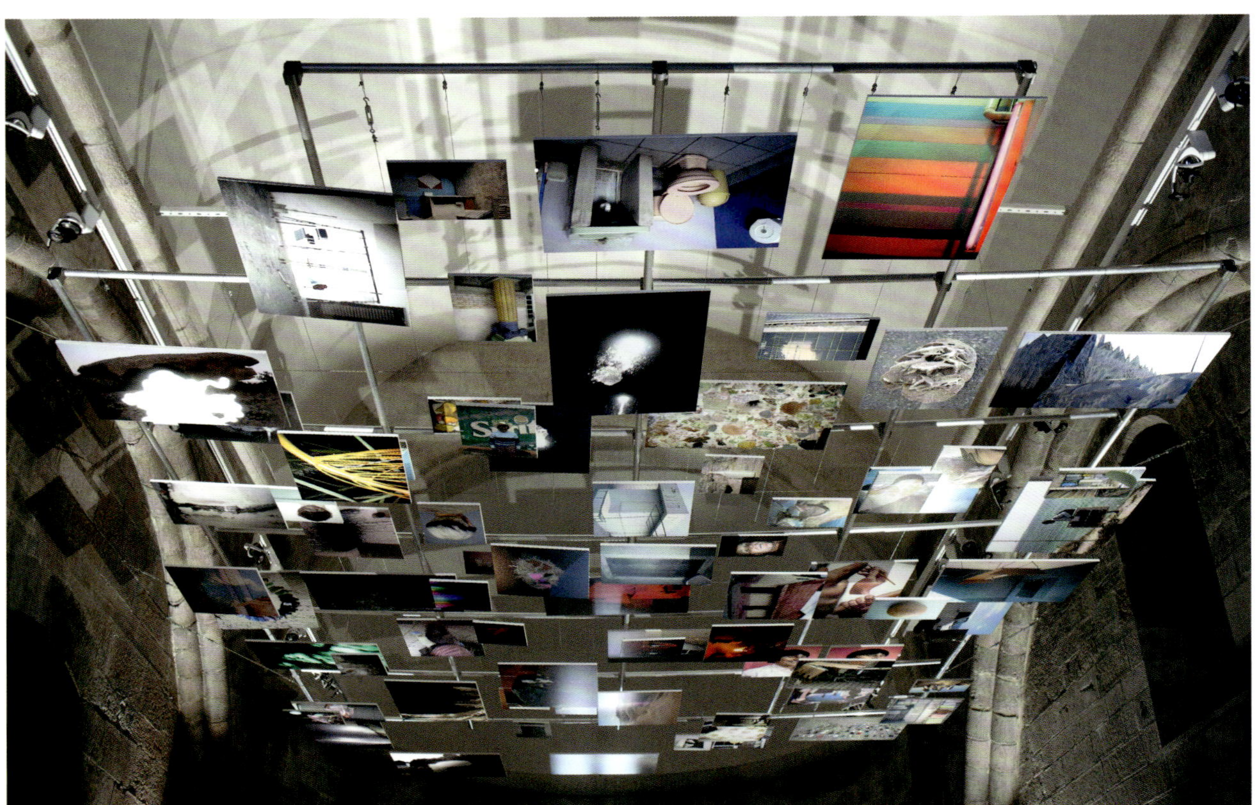

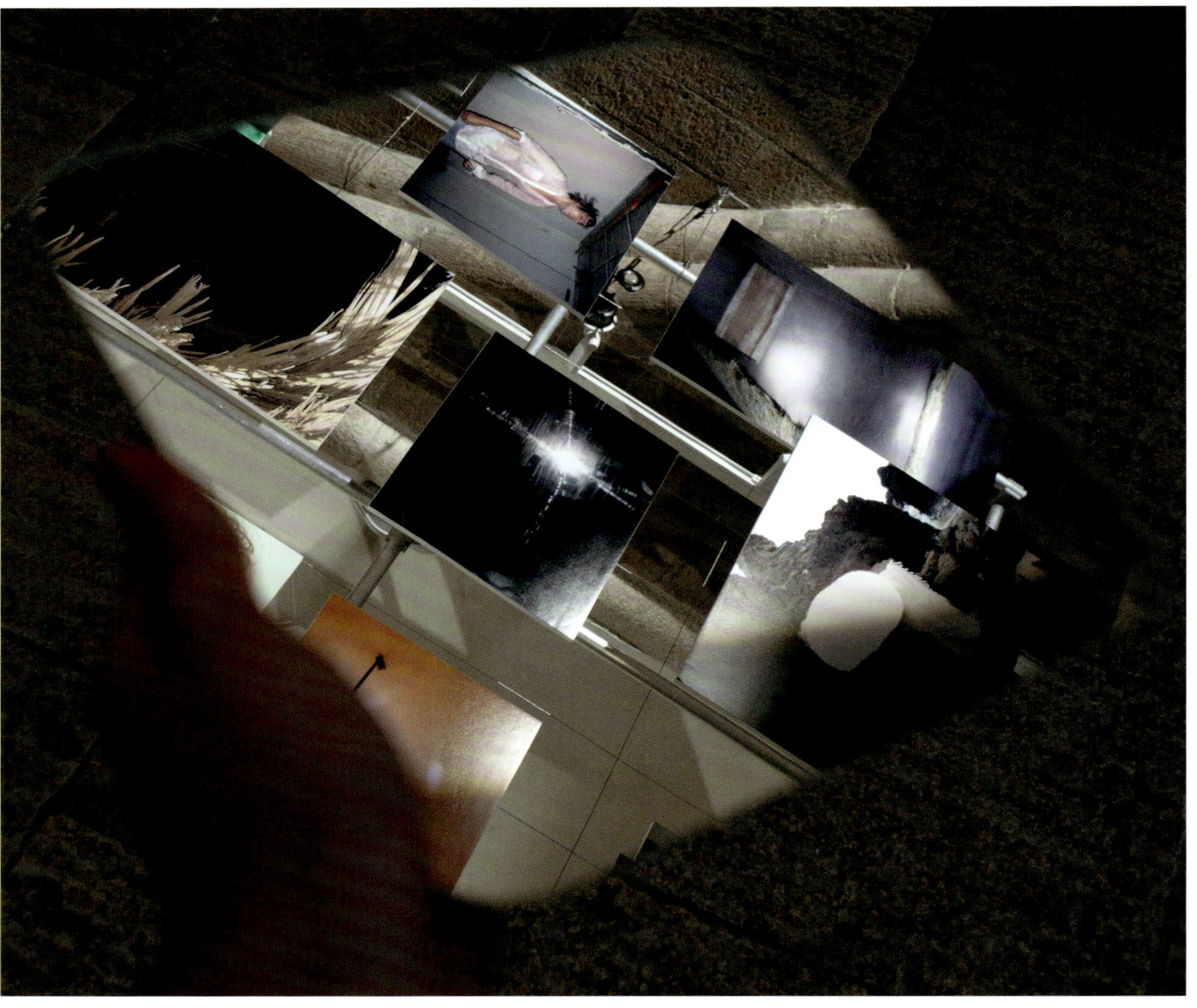

This page, top:
View of ceiling photography installation of Kruithof's solo exhibition *Untitled (I've Taken Too Many Photographs/I've Never Taken a Photo)* at Tour les Templiers, Festival International de Mode et Photographie, Hyères, France, 2012

This page, bottom:
View of mirror used to look at photo installation

Opposite:
Detail of the poster available at the exhibition, which features images from Kruithof's picture archive, accompanied by excerpts from a conversation between Kruithof and a young man, Harrison—said to have never taken a photograph himself—who edited, rated, and offered his commentary on the images.

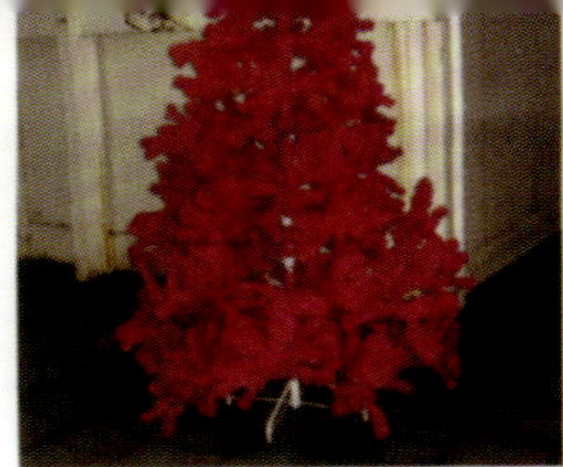

HM: 7, 7, 8, out, in... yes no I will go back to it ok? This is very nice, in and definitely 8, this one out. Medium: 7
HM: That's a masterpiece.

AK: So... That's a compliment...

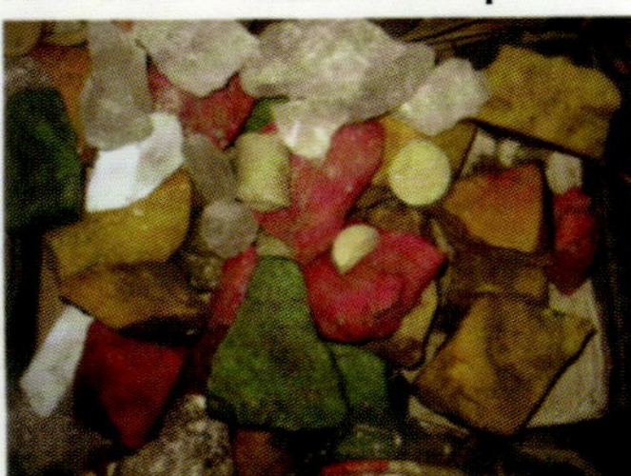

HM: Because it makes you think forever. Here you see part of a leg. The photo makes you come back to it, spend one-to-one time with it. The picture is now your brother or sister. The picture can be your girlfriend. Like the picture is part of you now. You start a relationship with it.

AK: Wow, ha-ha, what a philosophy!
HM: Yes that's my philosophy about it: I will make this a 6 but it should be seen.
HM: Pass, that's got to be a 7. I am from Coney Island, believe it or not.
HM: Pass, pass, pass, 6, 8, pass, 7, 7, pass, pass, 7, 6, pass...
HM: That's just a bag, floating in the sea. It's too simple.

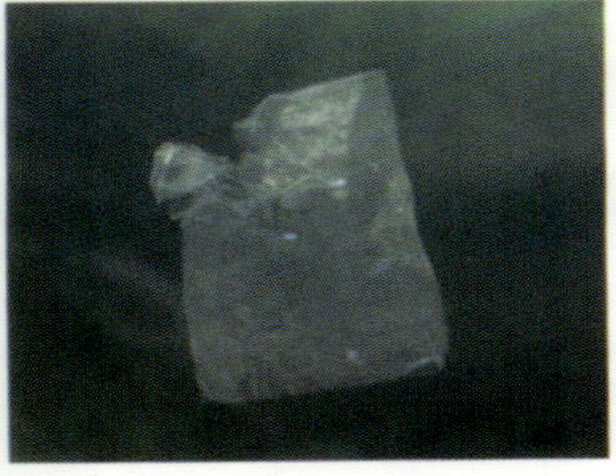

AK: Yes I know it's simple, do you think it's beautiful or not? HM: No not really... **AK: Why not? I get a bit mad now...** HM: Because it is too simple, leave it out please. It is nothingness, it is blank and it is blue. I'm trying to explain this to you to the best of my ability.
HM: I have to pass this. And this too, this one is too simple too. I have to pass, pass, pass, pass, pass...

AK: Ok.
HM: This should be small: 6. HM: mmm... this is nice: 7. It looks like a refrigerator, but also like a toy rock. This takes me back to my childhood; it might take a lot of people back to a good place, so it's a good picture: 7!

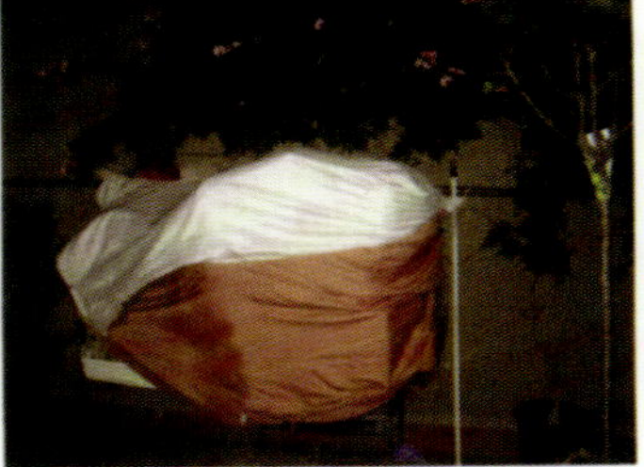

HM: A classic!
The desert: Vegas. Like Las Vegas

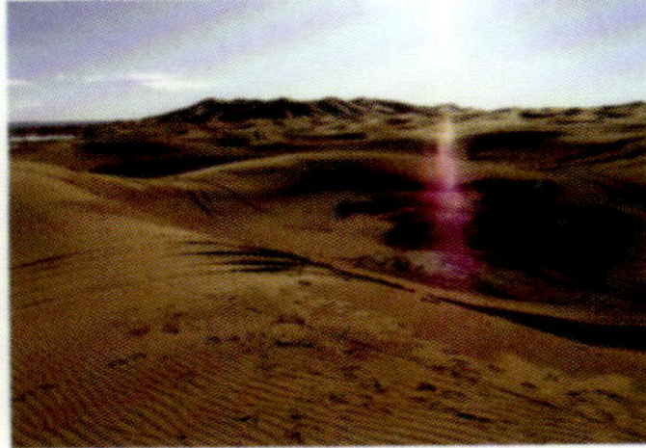

Looks like somebody's house in Africa...

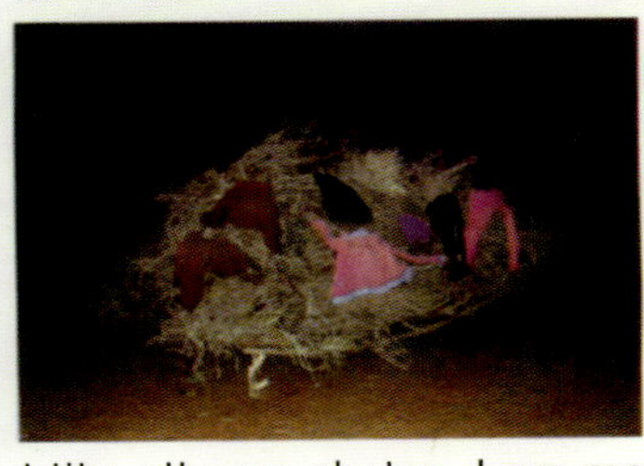

I like all your photos, I am mad, because I like all of them. The colours of the clothes. I guess I like bright colours, because they bring me back to childhood. Right now, life is a little hard, because I have to help my mother out with money. She relies too much on me; I am the only one who has a job.

AK: It is just the wall of a house.

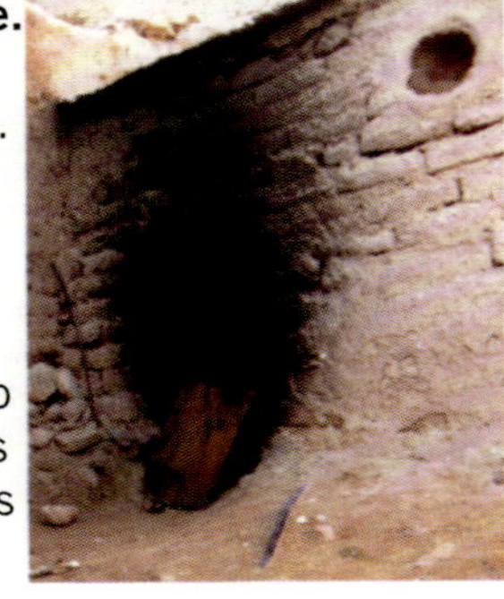

HM: It's the face of a wall.
He is surprised: he is like this...
He is surprised you're taking a picture of him.
So he is basically speaking to you. He is screaming, so you put that thing over his mouth so he'll be quiet, right? Yeah it has to be in; we could not make this too small: 8!

HM: This is too regular, because there are people in it: out.
HM: Another one of these thinkers. Where are you? On a train? In a plane or just insane? Uhmmmmmm... out. This looks like an 'out' too.
HM: We'll have to put it in, because it so weird. It's so beautiful as art because it's weird.

HM: This is a depressed picture: 'I have to work... Where am I? What am I working for? I am working for free. They hardly feed me...' He's like... 'What am I doing here? What position am I in? How can I get out of here?' That's what he's thinking. They don't care about my feelings anymore... This picture relates to society. Lots of people are stuck in a bad position, sort of like myself. This is one of my favourites, because it is me on the picture. I am that donkey and a lot of people can relate to the donkey and also feel like he feels. He thinks: 'I am not getting paid human dollars... I don't have a family and what if I want to venture out? ... Meet a donkey wife, make donkey kids, become a donkey grandfather.' This donkey is stuck in a position he can't escape from.
Just like me, so let's make it an 8.

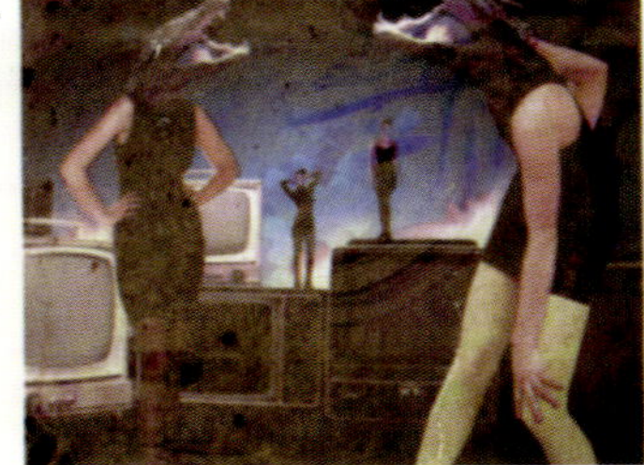

HM: Pass it: looks like a zebra.

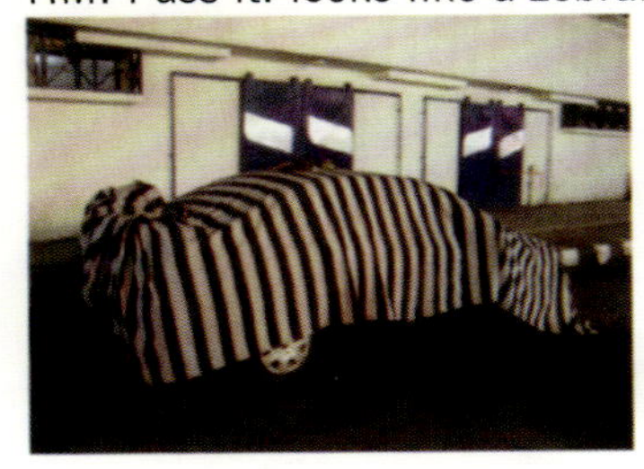

This is nice: 6, 7, 6 , pass, pass, that has to stay, this is real nice: Great wall of China: isn't it?

AK: No.
HM: Pass.. pass it's funny. Haha, the girls are crocodiles: they eat you raw.

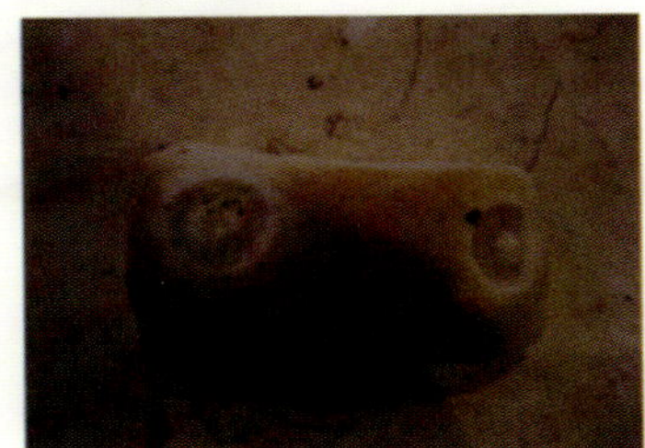

AK: Do you see girls as crocodiles?
HM: Yes, some girls can be like crocodiles: like my friend, she's real mean. It has to be in: size 7
HM: I don't get the concept of this: out, out, no it has to go in: 8. I take both of them out. Nice: 6, out, out, out, out, 6, out, uhummmmm 7: out, out!

HM: Nice! Like a piece of bread, hotdog bread, ah it's so nice because it has eyes: it looks like an alien. Ahhhhhh it's sort of as if you brought it to life: 8.

HM: Small, jail.

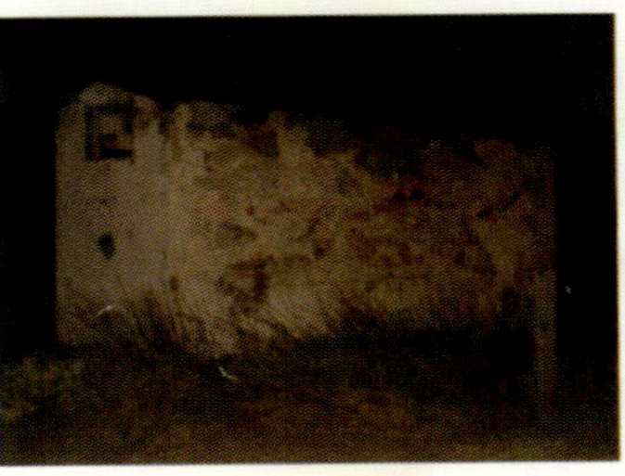

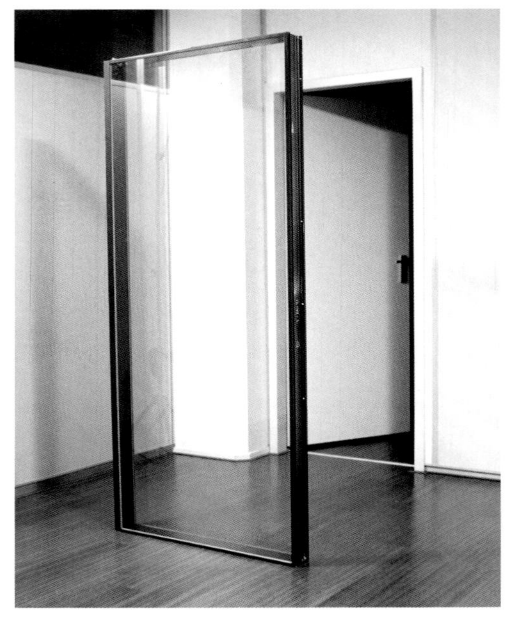
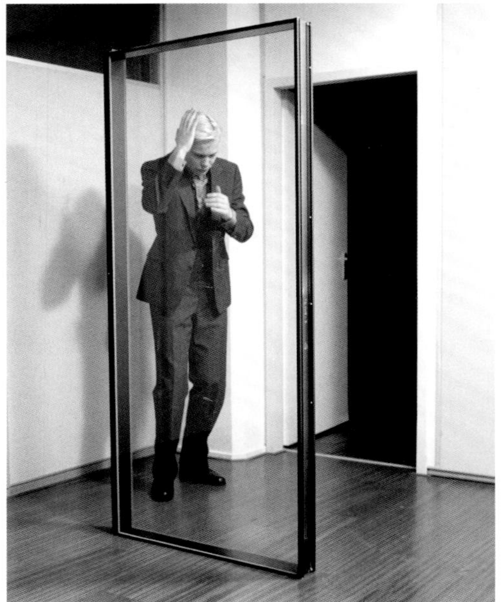
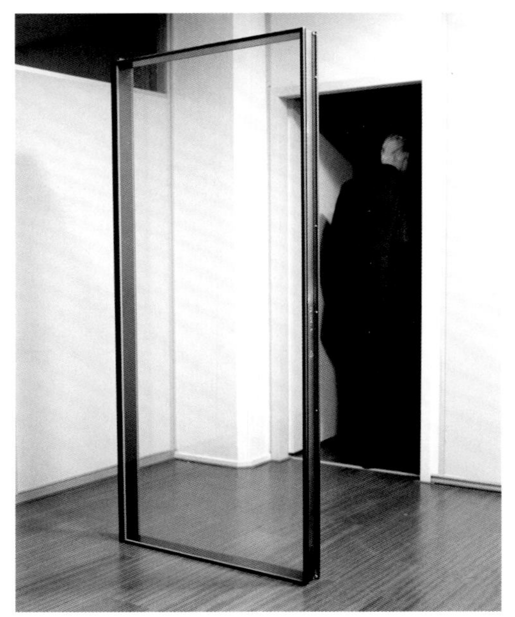
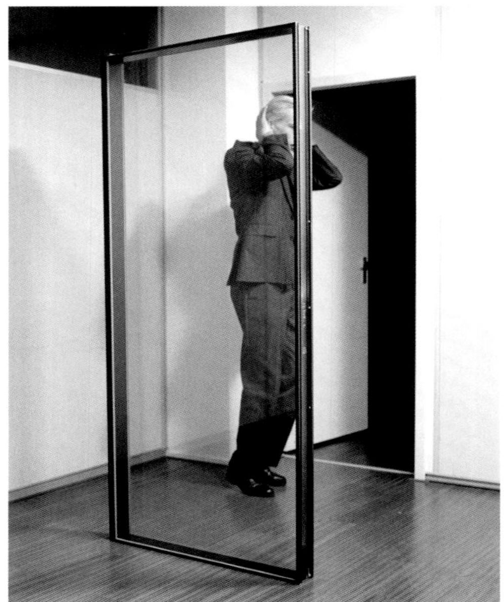
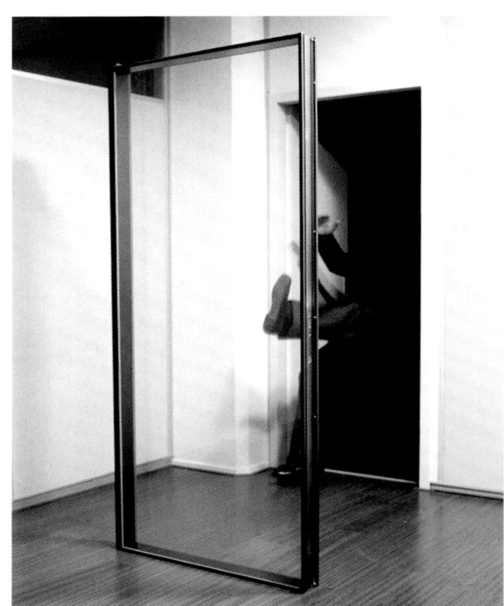
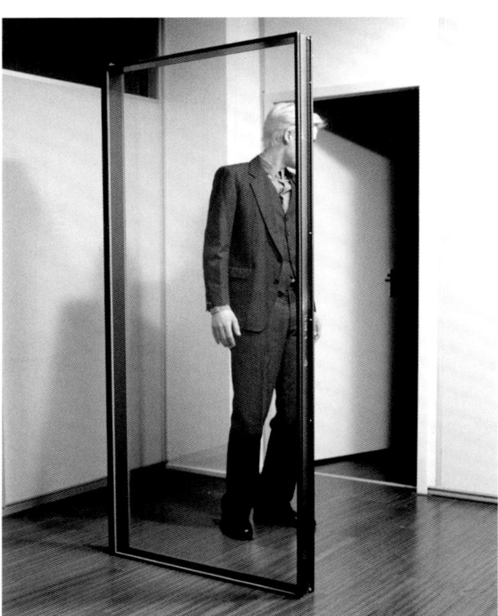
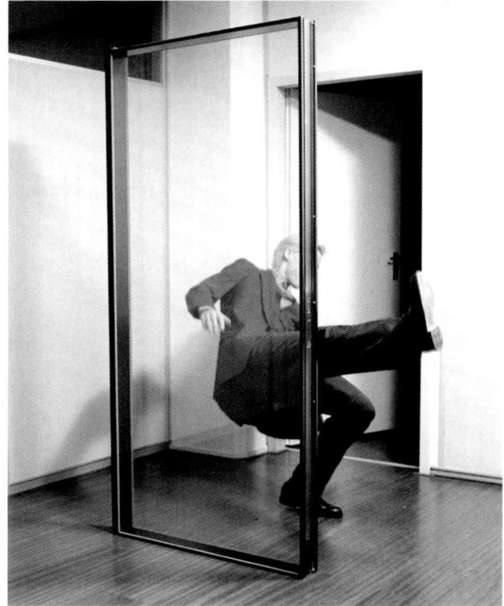

Fall 1–7, 2009, from the project *Playing Borders: This Contemporary State of Mind*

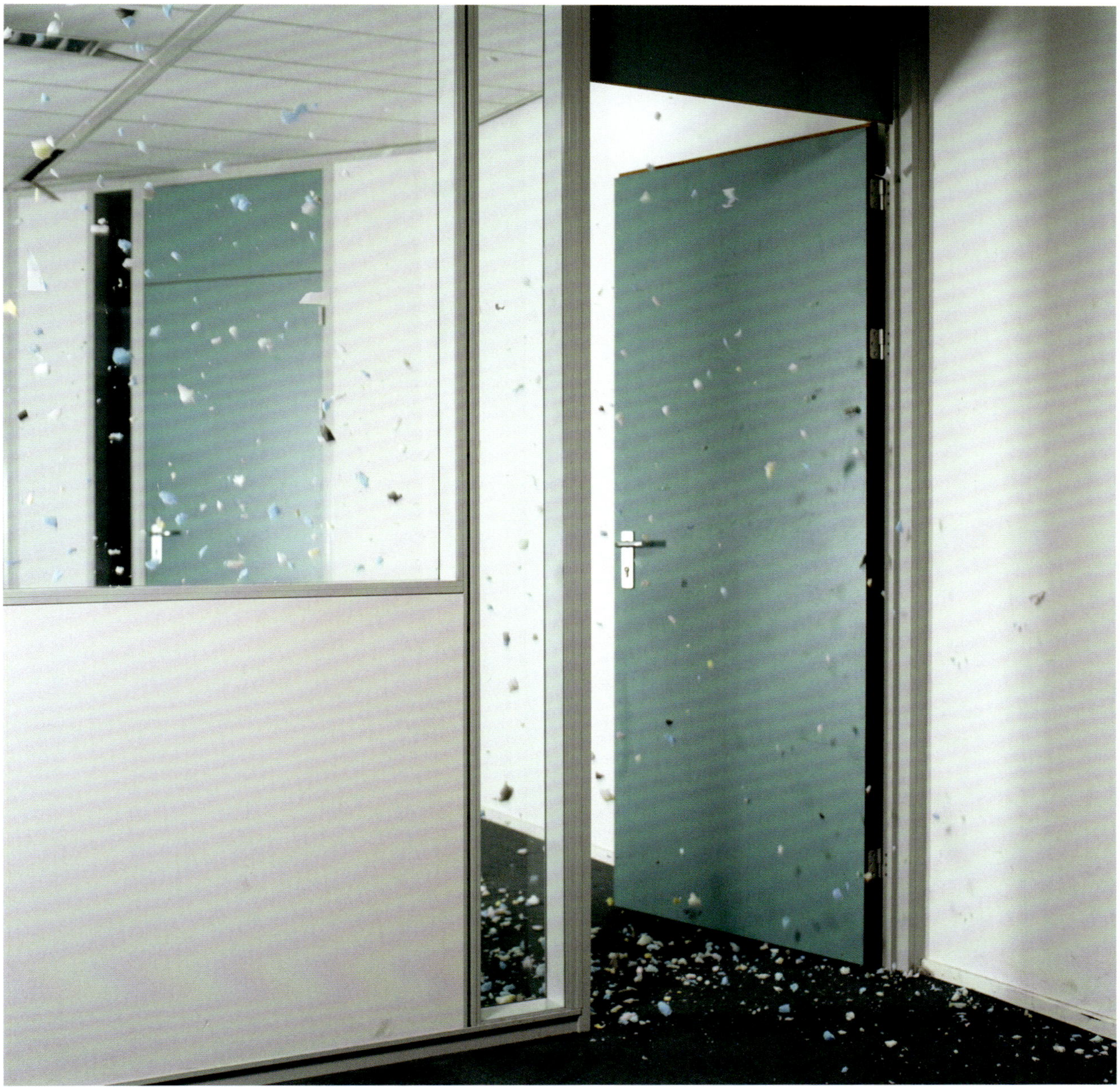

Business Explosion, 2009, from the project *Playing Borders: This Contemporary State of Mind*

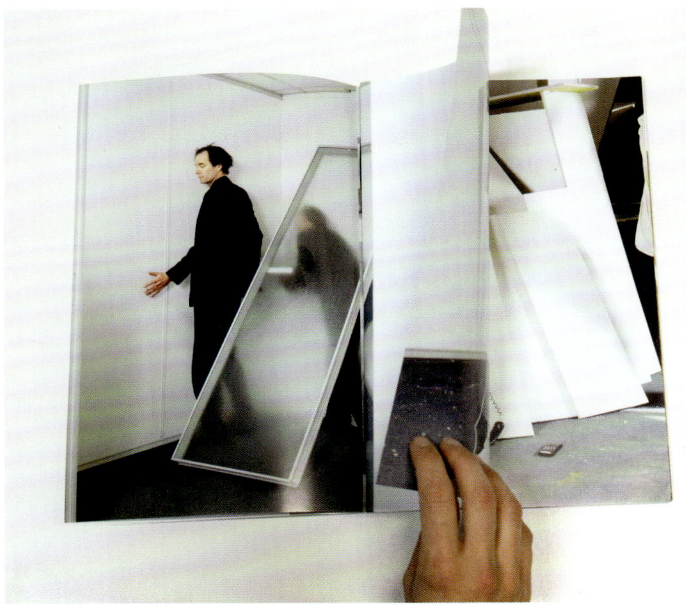

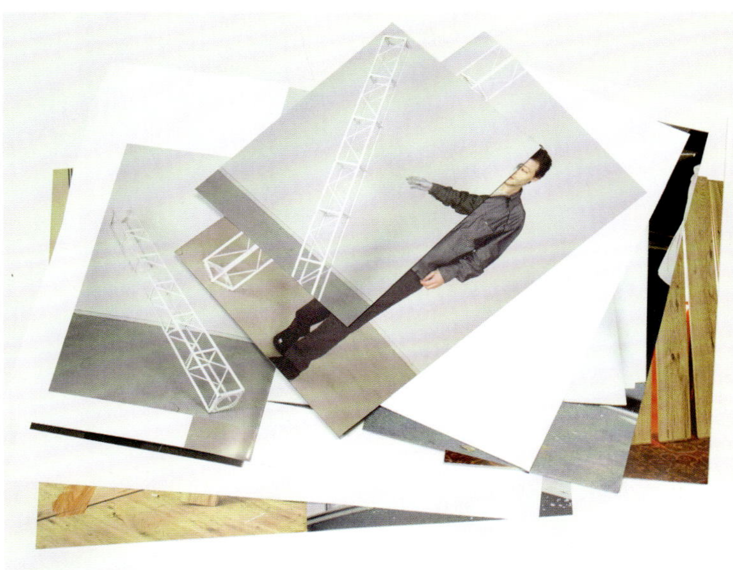

Playing Borders: This Contemporary State of Mind (Revolver Publishing by VVV, 2009). Interior views of the publication. All photographs © and courtesy the artist.

Andrew Norman Wilson

ScanOps

Conversation with Laurel Ptak

Andrew Norman Wilson's *ScanOps* project examines the systems, people, and processes behind Google Books. Here he speaks with curator Laurel Ptak about the project.

Laurel Ptak: **Tell us about your recent photographic series *ScanOps*. How did the project develop?**

Andrew Norman Wilson: I have been collecting "anomalies" from Google Books for a couple of years: images in which software distortions, the imaging site, or the hands of the Google employees doing the scanning are visible. The fingers and software distortions obscure the information in the books—which complicates the notion of universally accessible knowledge.

LP: **Where does the title *ScanOps* come from?**

ANW: It's the departmental name for Google's onsite book-scanning operations at their headquarters in Mountain View, California. I'm pretty sure the name "ScanOps" was never public—I found it searching around Google's Intranet.

In 2011 I made a video called *Workers Leaving the Googleplex*. I worked for a year in 2007–8 on Google's campus. While there, I wore a red badge—like most other contracted employees. The fulltime Google employees wore white badges, and interns wore green badges. In the video, these "classes" of employees are seen passing by, entering and exiting buildings at the Googleplex. Some of them ride Google loaner bikes; some are seen getting into a Google limo shuttle headed toward San Francisco. Some of them are leaving work, some may be walking to another building to exercise in one of the Google gyms or pick up their laundry, some may be just arriving at the Google campus to eat a free meal from one of the twenty gourmet cafés after a day of working at home.

But from my office, I noticed a fourth class of workers operating in the building next to where I worked; they wore yellow badges. They stood out on the Google campus because of their races—many are people of color—and their attire, which was not that of the usual tech worker. In the *Workers Leaving* video, the yellow-badge employees are seen leaving the one building they are allowed access to. They all leave at the same time every day—2:15 PM—because their superiors have asked them to. It is a separate departure time from the other workers, so their exit is its own "movement."

LP: **Can you talk about the films by the Lumière brothers and Harun Farocki that influenced you in putting your film together?**

ANW: In Farocki's 1995 film *Workers Leaving the Factory*, he discusses how in the Lumière brothers' film, also called *Workers Leaving the Factory* (1895), the primary aim was to represent motion; in particular to create an image of a *work force in motion*, organized by the work structure (a temporal construct), the factory gates (a spatial grouping), and the filmmakers' choreography of this time-space relationship. But of course moving images don't only represent movement, they can also grasp for concepts. This is what Farocki's film is about—how signs and symbols are taken from reality, as if "the world itself wanted to tell us something." He uses a particular motif in film history—that of

Andrew Norman Wilson lives and works in Brooklyn, New York. He is currently working on a ScanOps book to be published by Art Metropole, and lecturing on ScanOps and *Workers Leaving the Googleplex* in his PowerPoint performance *Movement Materials and What We Can Do*.

Laurel Ptak is a New York-based curator. With artist Marysia Lewandowska, she is currently co-editing a book titled *Undoing Property*, examining relationships among artistic practice, intellectual property, immaterial production, and political economy, to be published this year by Sternberg Press.

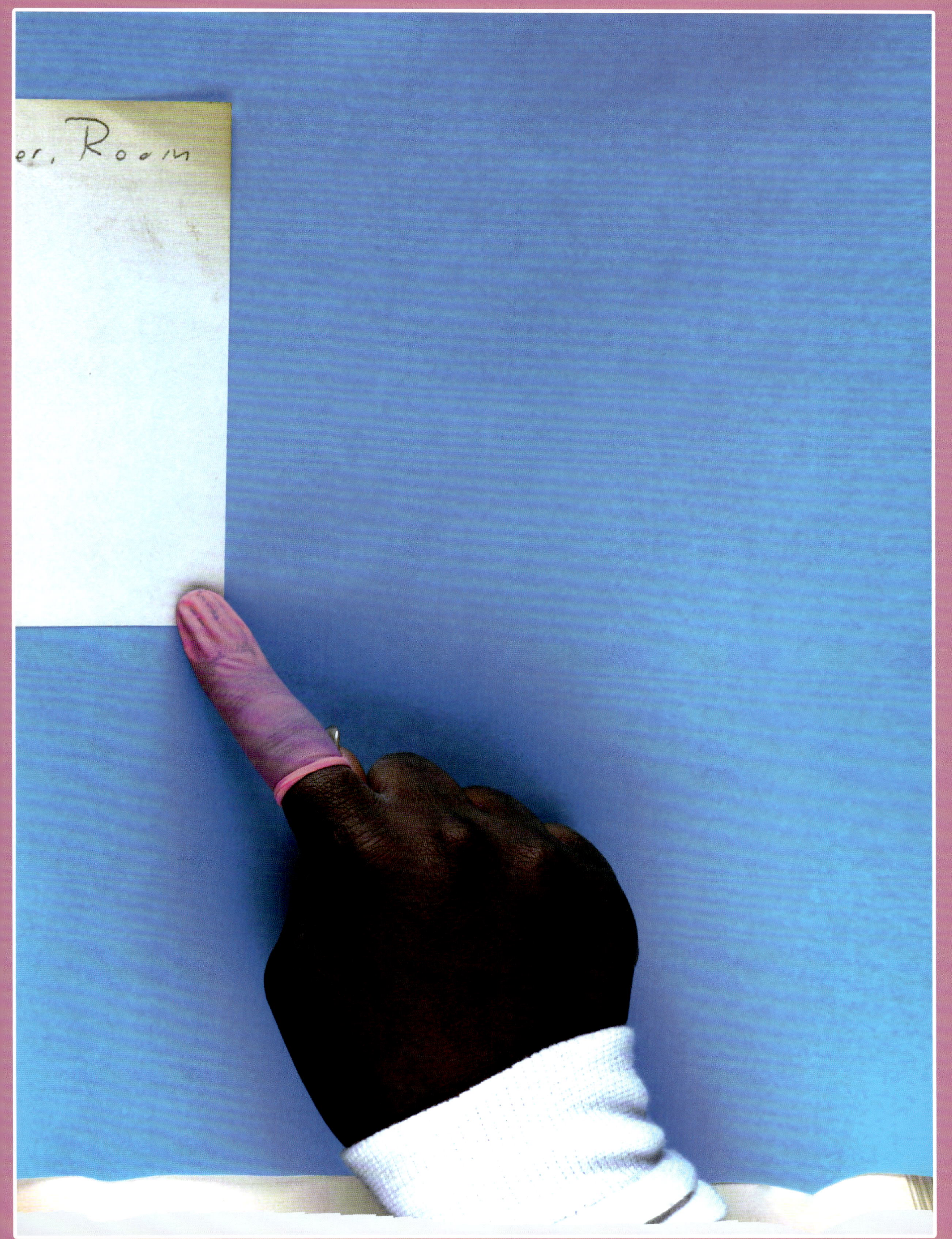
er, Room

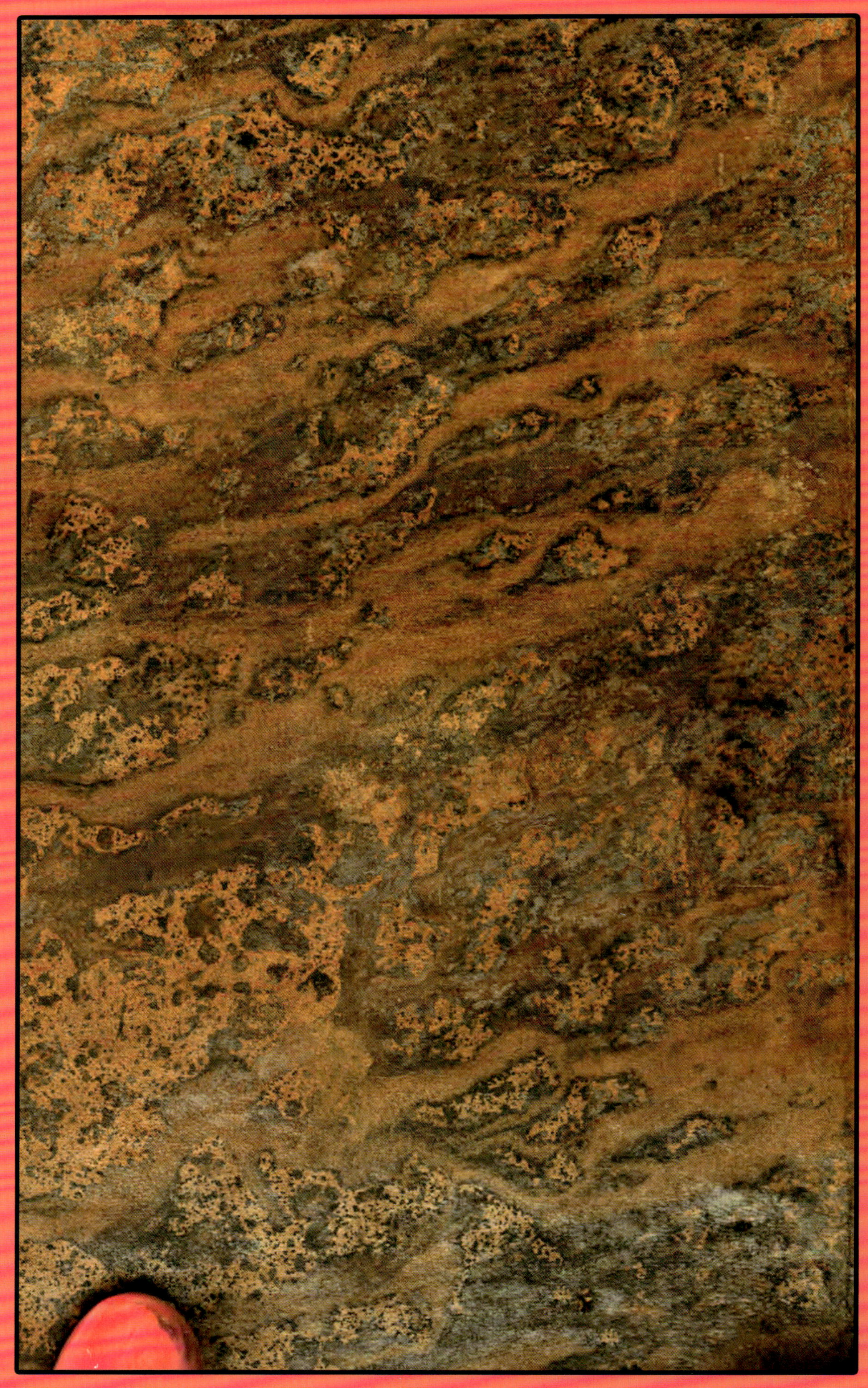

workers leaving the factory—to interpret what the world is telling us.

The Lumières' *Workers* and my own each present the social and technological conditions of their time. Both represent movement—but in my representation of movement, we see clearly defined tiers of workers ... so the movement is "scripted" by what class they are in.

LP: ***ScanOps* continues to follow these Google Books workers in another way.**

ANW: While I was working as a video editor and videographer at Google, I started to document and talk to the ScanOps employees—but was fired rather quickly. It was intended to be a larger project, but it ended up being quite simple and limited because I wasn't left with much more than my footage and my account of what happened.

At some point later I heard about the scanning mistakes and accidents that occur in Google's book-scanning operations and decided to look closer. The work of the ScanOps employees is an interesting hybrid—it is a labor of digitizing informational materials that requires no cognitive involvement with the content of those materials. The labor process is quite Fordist—press button, turn page, repeat.

The workers compose part of the photographic apparatus, which in a broad sense includes not only the machinery but the social systems in which photography operates. The anonymous workers, Google founders Sergey Brin and Larry Page, the pink "finger condoms," infrared cameras, the auto-correction software, the capital required to fund the project, the ink on my rag-paper prints, me—we're all part of it.

LP: **Would you discuss the thinking process behind your photographic work?**

ANW: Each stop along the way in my work involves machines and humans. I like the idea that my work is part of a living, expanding process, and I am trying to underscore the fact that we are all complicit in and responsible for our social and technological arrangements. I want to dispel any notion that we are passively, subjectively impacted by foreign objects and systems.

LP: **Take us through the steps in your work's production, the logic of each decision in *ScanOps*.**

ANW: Production starts before I get involved. The books are photographed at the libraries where they are stored, or are shipped to the Google Books facilities to be photographed. Software auto-corrects and converts the images and uploads them online. I browse for images that fulfill my criteria, download them, convert the pages I want, and edit out the Google watermark. There's no resizing or additional editing.

Next I have them inkjet printed to scale, they are mounted and sent to the framers, who make a custom frame for each print. Then I bring the prints to Home Depot, and pick a color from each print for them to match. They mix up the paint in that color and I bring everything to an auto-body shop, where the frames are sprayed in their respective colors. It's a whole production line.

I'm choosing materials and production processes—some of them subcontracted to other people—that allow the materiality of the work to be emphasized. There are also preexisting conditions that communicate that for me, and I let them alone—for instance, leaving the images at their original size keeps them in direct correlation to the printed matter they came from. In a gallery or on the page of a magazine each work occupies a unique volume of space, and so when put together their spatial/sculptural qualities are emphasized.

LP: **It's compelling to think of *ScanOps* as a kind of update to the tradition of documentary photography, but for the online image.**

ANW: I do look toward the work of certain documentary photographers—Dorothea Lange, Jacob Riis, Lewis Hine, and so on—whose socially engaged, journalistic photography represents marginalized populations, and in particular their labor.

In addition to the work engaging photography's materiality and an interest in the abstraction that the anomalies can present, I like to think of each image —whether it contains accidents or not— as a view of the world. They reveal traces of the humans and technology that produced them.

LP: **We most often encounter digital recordings of books as scans, but you refer to these as "photographs"—why is that? Who are the photographers here?**

ANW: Mass-market books can be sliced open and fed into scanners, but the books I'm looking at come from library collections and can't be dismantled; they need to be photographed with a camera from above. The fingers we see in some of the images could mistakenly be called the photographers' hands—but their actions have been dictated by superiors at Google, so really *they* are the camera operators. The photographers are Sergey Brin and Larry Page, who proposed the digitization of all the world's books when Google was just a fledgling startup. Because the copying of an entire book violates copyright, the photographers have been faced with lawsuits from the Authors' Guild, the Association of American Publishers, and more.

Google is in the sole possession of the means of search and distribution for most of the books published in the United States in the twentieth century. For the first time, elements of public library collections are offered for sale through a private contractor, with additional revenue coming in from the ad space for sale next to the online books.

Everyone who uses Gmail, Google Docs, Google Books, Blogger, YouTube, etc. becomes a knowledge worker for the company. We're all performing freelance data entry. Where knowledge is perceived as a public good, Google gathers its income from the exchange of information and knowledge, creating additional value in this process. Google, as we know it and use it, is a factory.

Page 127:
The Inland printer-164, 2012
Opposite:
An Inquiry into the Nature and Causes of the Wealth of Nations-365, 2012
Page 130:
The Rainbow Girl-9, 2012
Page 131:
Simon Newcomb-10, 2012
Page 132:
Mechanick dyalling: teaching any man, to draw a true sun-dyal on any given plain, however scituated-60, 2012
Page 133: *The Inland printer-152*, 2012

All photographs courtesy the artist

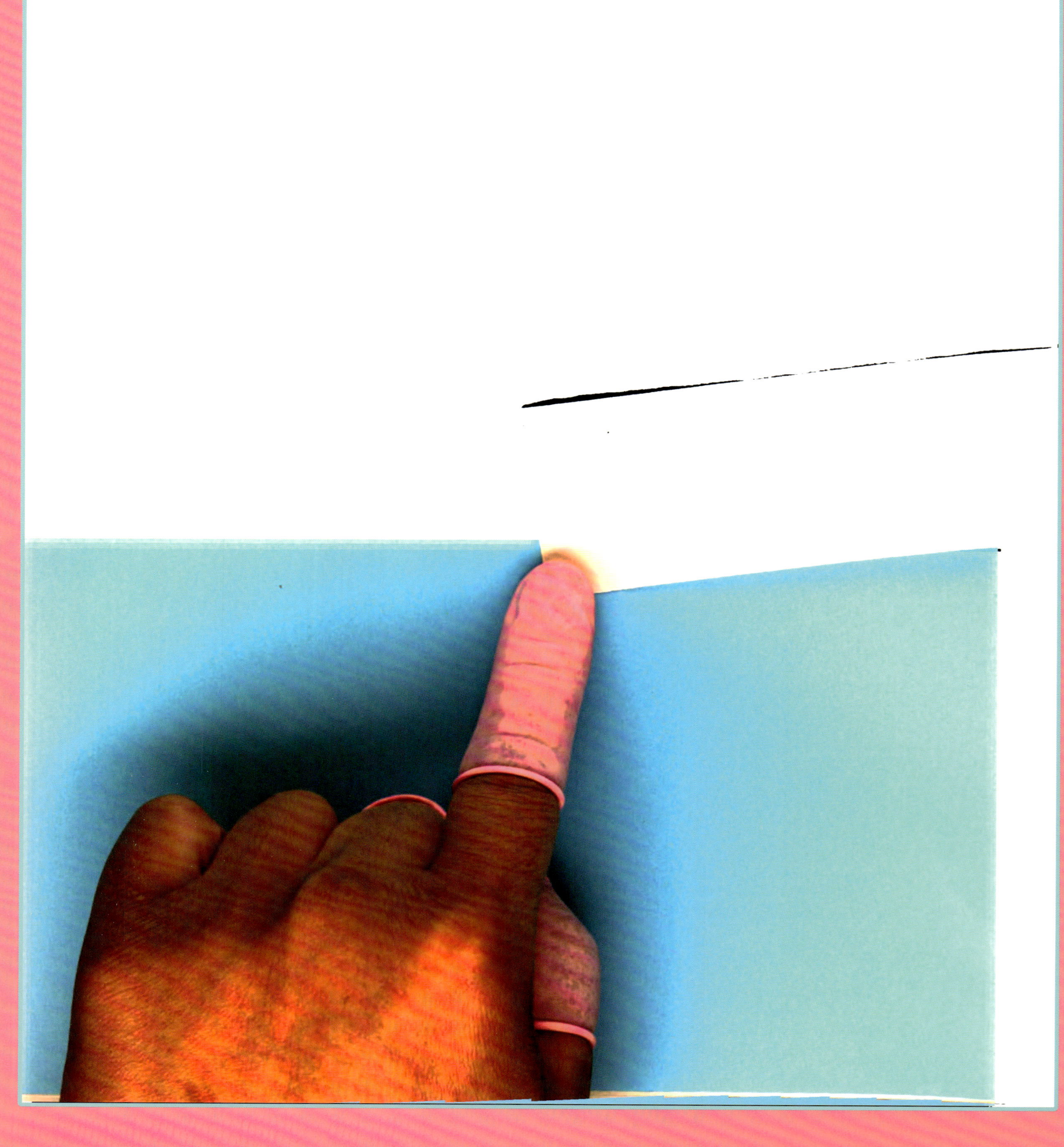

Compliments of
The Society

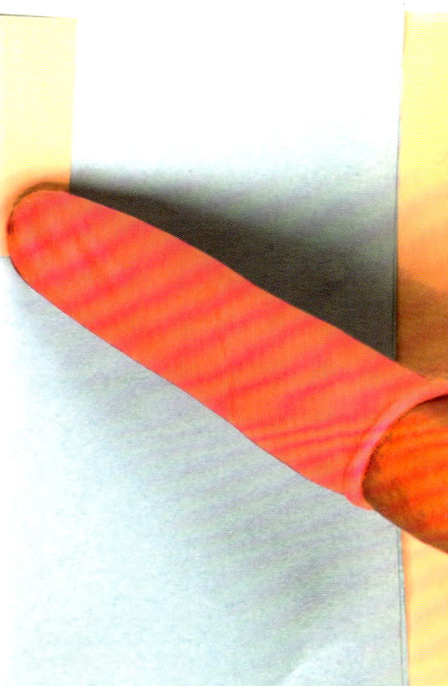

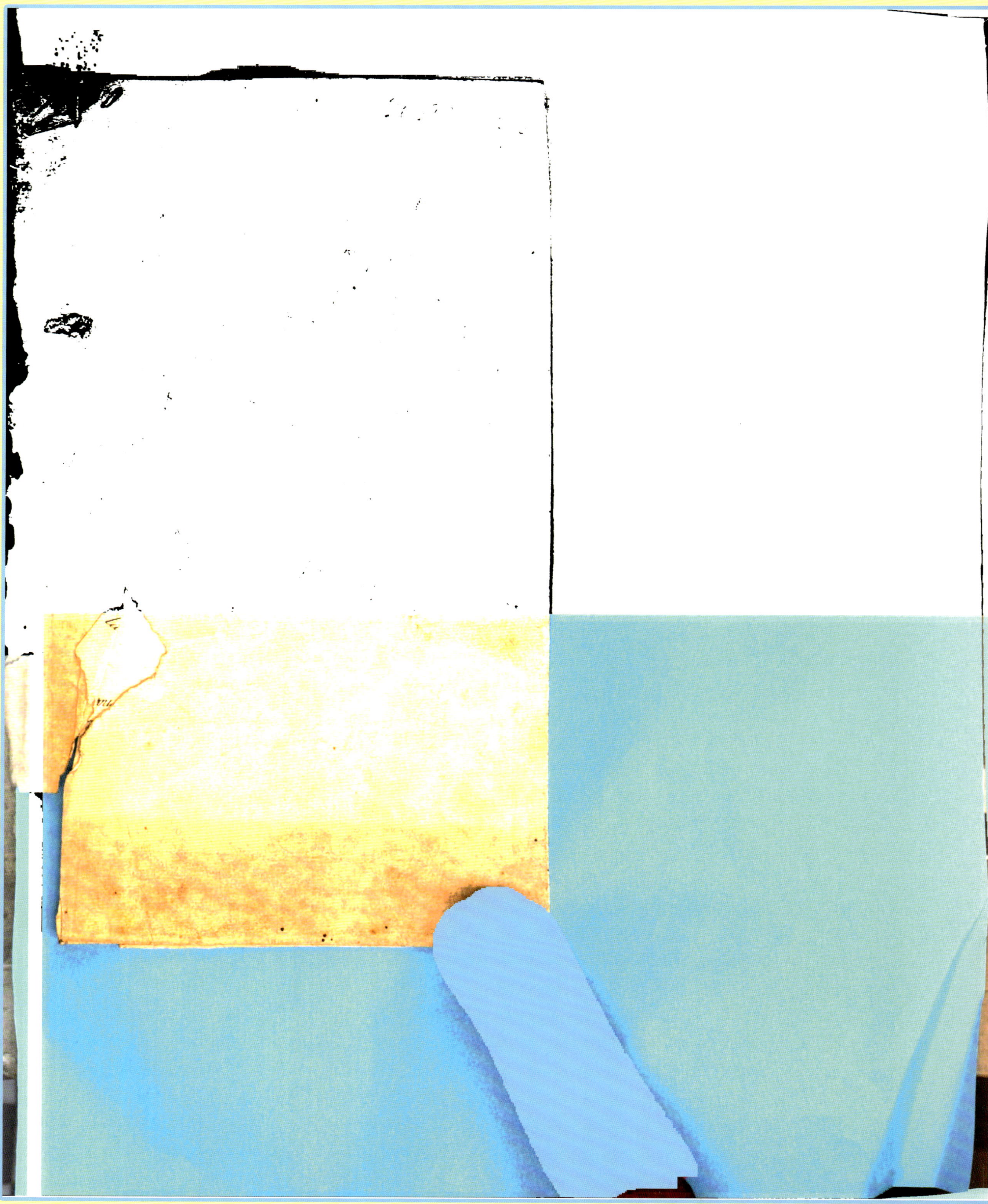

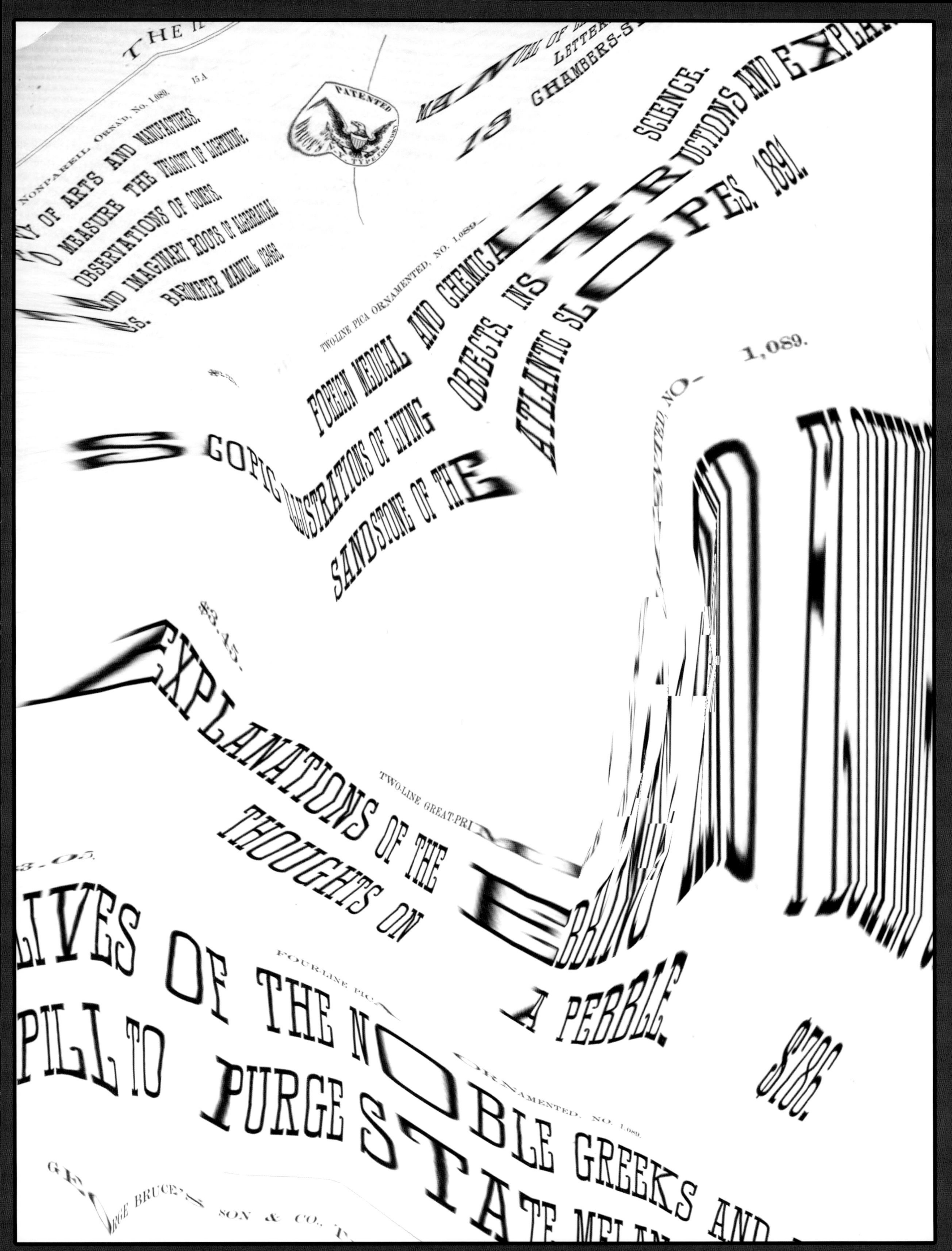

THE
15A
NONPAREIL ORNA'D, NO. 1,089.
PATENTED
OF ARTS AND MANUFACTURES.
MEASURE THE VELOCITY OF LIGHTNING.
OBSERVATIONS OF COMETS.
IMAGINARY ROOTS OF ALGEBRAICAL
BAROMETER MANUAL
SCIENCE.
TWO-LINE PICA ORNAMENTED, NO. 1,089.
FOREIGN MEDICAL AND
OBJECTS.
ATLANTIC
1891.
OF LIVING
SANDSTONE OF THE
1,089.
$3.45.
OF THE
THOUGHTS ON
LIVES OF THE
A PEBBLE.
PILL TO PURGE
BLE GREEKS AND
ORNAMENTED, NO. 1,089.
SON & CO.

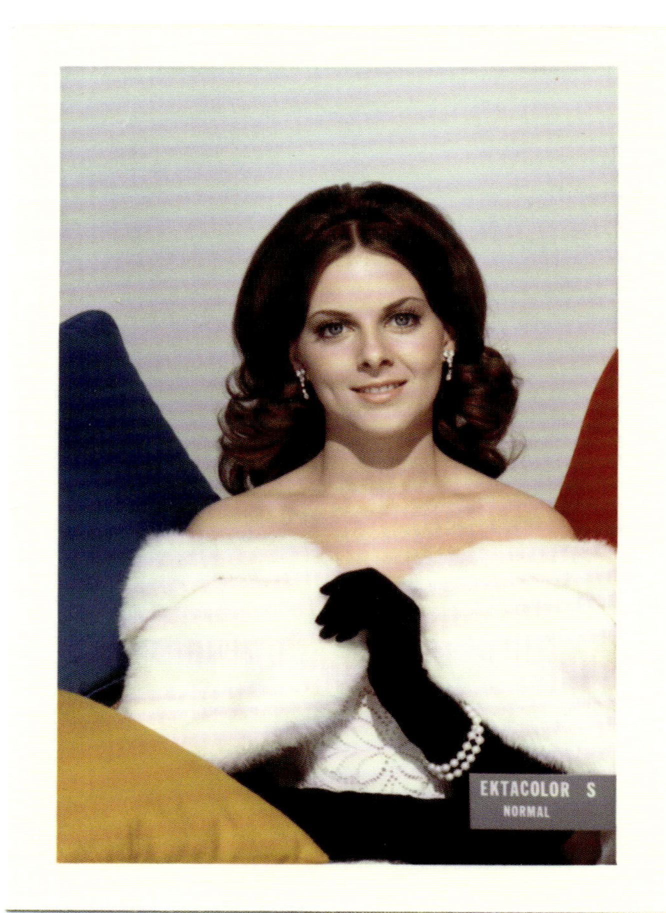

Shirley, 2012. C-41 photographic print

Adam Broomberg & Oliver Chanarin

To Photograph the Details of a Dark Horse in Low Light

Brian Dillon

It is said that she (or rather her first incarnation) worked at the Kodak factory in Rochester, New York, in the 1950s—though the story has never been verified. Her name is Shirley, and she is something like an embodiment of photography's tendency to dodge and blur distinctions between the generic and the particular. For decades images of "Shirley" were dispatched to Kodak labs around the world as a visual reference, the original model being replaced by a succession of more or less elaborately dressed and coiffed avatars. In the version chosen here by Adam Broomberg and Oliver Chanarin, Shirley's white evening wear, the gray backdrop, and the oddly invasive primary-color soft furnishings are meant to demonstrate a color balance and dynamic range labeled "Ektacolor: Normal."

Shirley and her successors were for many years solely Caucasian. Color film was designed for a narrow range of skin tones, and it was notoriously difficult to include black and white faces in the same frame. This despite the complaints, for example, of photographers in the 1960s who, following the desegregation of U.S. schools, had trouble rendering the faces of African-American students in class photographs. Institutional memory at Kodak has it that it was only when manufacturers of wooden furniture and chocolate complained they could not adequately photograph their products that the corporation began work on a new range of films with which, internal descriptions assured, one could "photograph the details of a dark horse in low light."

Broomberg and Chanarin's project—which includes photographs of Bwiti initiation rites, made as part of a recent commission in Gabon, remnants of a darkroom donated to the artists, and fragments from the photographic life of "Shirley"—takes its title from that curiously euphemistic suggestion as to how Kodak's new film might be employed. But the images presented here are points in a constellation with a more ambitious extent in terms of the history of photography and the medium's urge to extract generic meaning from knotty specifics.

Some orienting fragments of backstory: in the late 1970s the filmmaker Jean-Luc Godard was invited by the Marxist government of Mozambique to advise and collaborate on a new state television channel. Among the problems of representation that he touched on in the course of the project (ultimately abandoned) was that of Kodak's "racist" film stock, which Godard refused to use. No footage exists from Godard's time in Mozambique—only some photographs he took (with non-Kodak film) of his local collaborators coming to grips with TV technology.

In their travels in central Africa, Broomberg and Chanarin worry at the notion—which pertains to the history of Kodak, Godard's Mozambique project, and the tradition of anticolonialist photography—that each act of representation is somehow revelatory of a certain "typical" racial Other. The category of test images is essential to that aesthetically and politically vexed history. The artists here explore these experiments using darkroom equipment and reference images that belonged to a friend's late father, one Dr. Rosenberg. Among the photographs in this project is Broomberg and Chanarin's sole success among many tries with a batch of medium-format film that expired in 1978. Underexposed and color-shifted to weird magenta, the image, of a palm leaf, stands for the idea of a stable photographic reference and the wayward reality of the medium.

Brian Dillon is U.K. editor of *Cabinet* magazine and a tutor in critical writing at the Royal College of Art. His books include *I Am Sitting in a Room* (Cabinet, 2011), *Sanctuary* (Sternberg Press, 2011), and *The Hypochondriacs* (Farrar, Straus & Giroux, 2010).

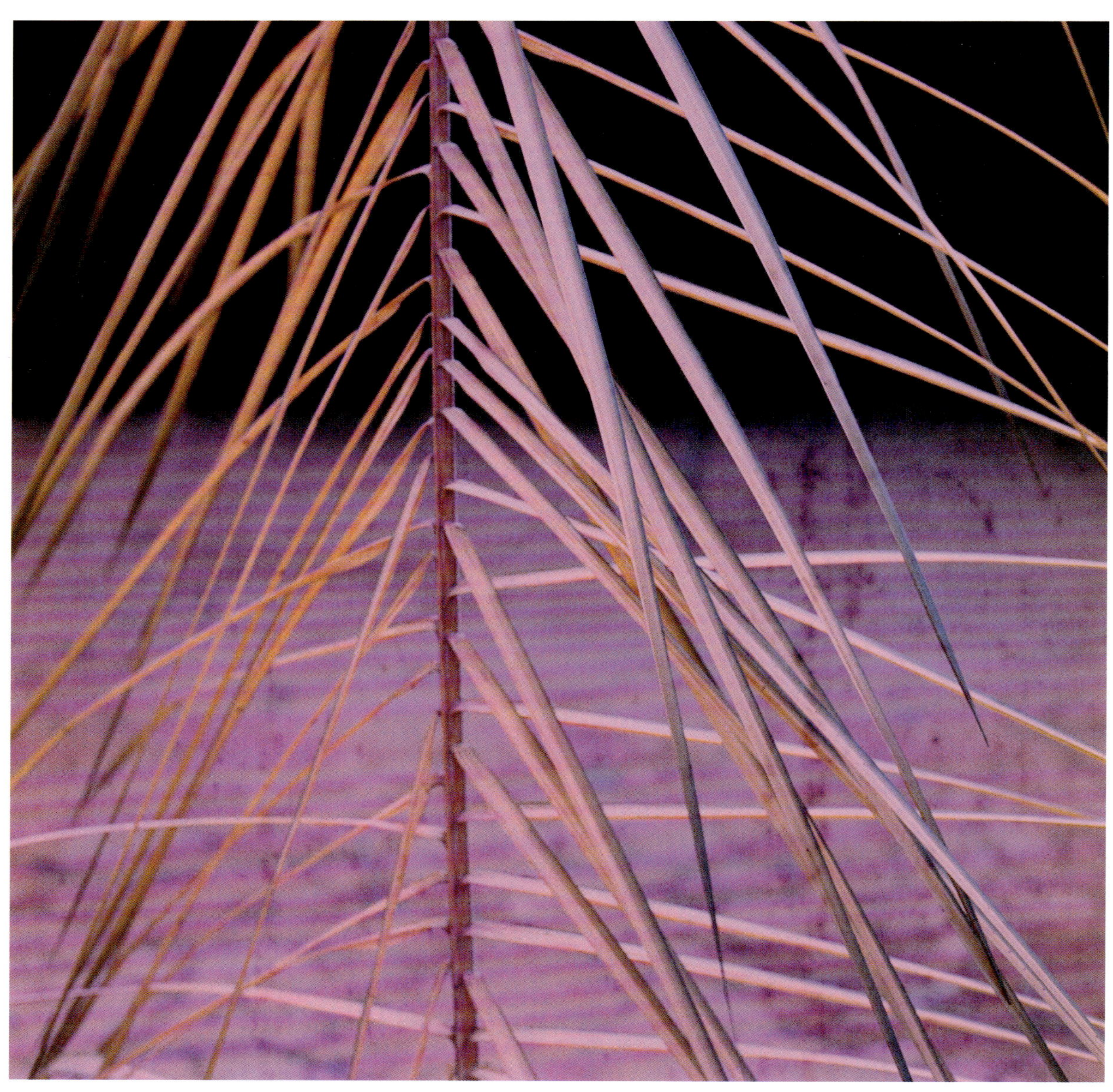

***Kodak Ektachrome 34 1978 frame 4*, 2012.**
C-41 color print
This image of a palm leaf, captured during a rare Bwiti initiation ceremony in Gabon, was photographed on film stock that expired in 1978. Color film from this period was designed to render a range of Caucasian skin tones, but was not suited for accurate depictions of dark skin. This is the only legible image to survive from the many rolls of out-of-date film stock that Broomberg and Chanarin exposed during the ceremony.

From Dr. Rosenberg's archive: *Untitled (Color Test)*, photographic print, and *Untitled (Darkroom Notes)*, work on paper
Broomberg and Chanarin were given the darkroom equipment of a friend's father, Dr. Rosenberg, an anatomist and amateur photographer, after he passed away. Among Rosenberg's belongings they found early color tests. Below is the anatomist himself in a dual role as both photographer and subject (curiously rigged up to electromagnetic-monitoring equipment). Broomberg and Chanarin's receipt of Rosenberg's materials and tests coincided with the artists' own research into the history of color photography.

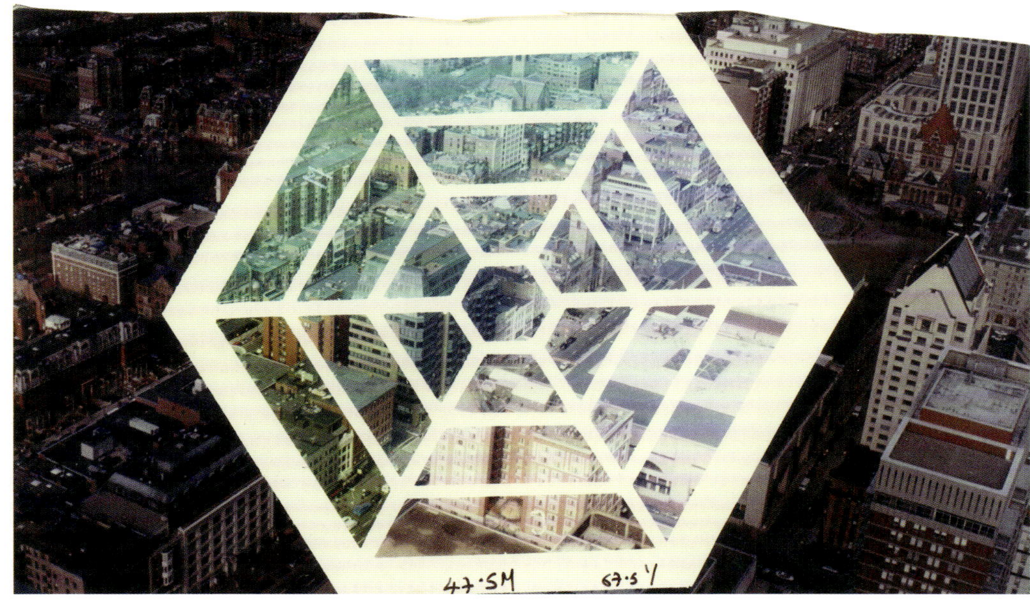

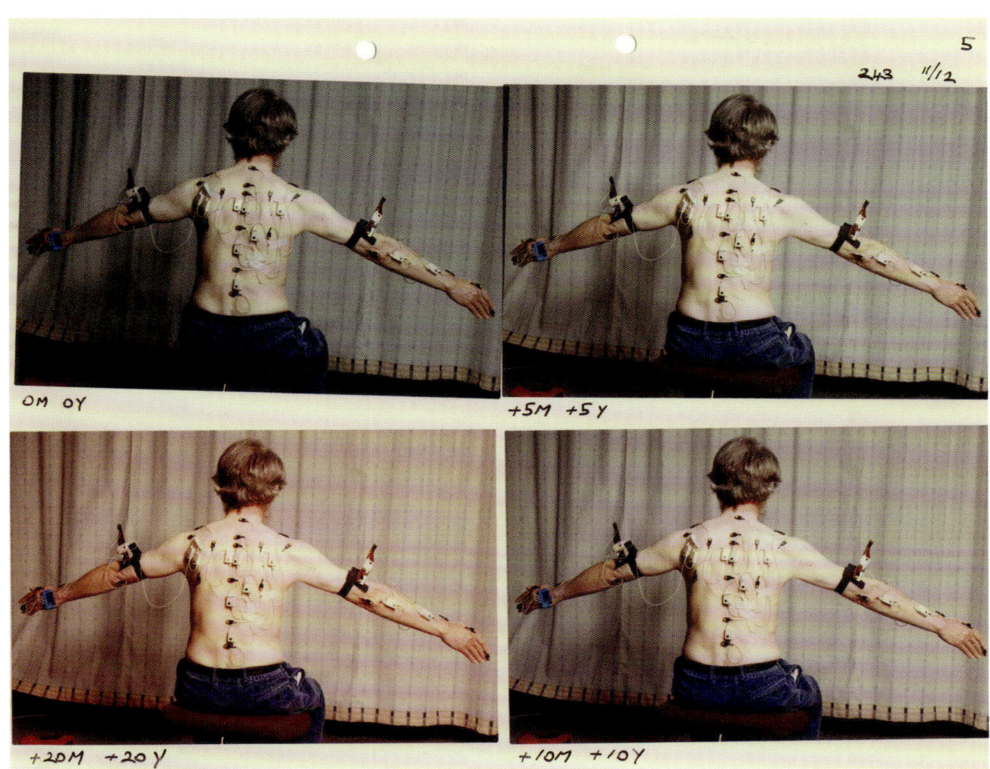

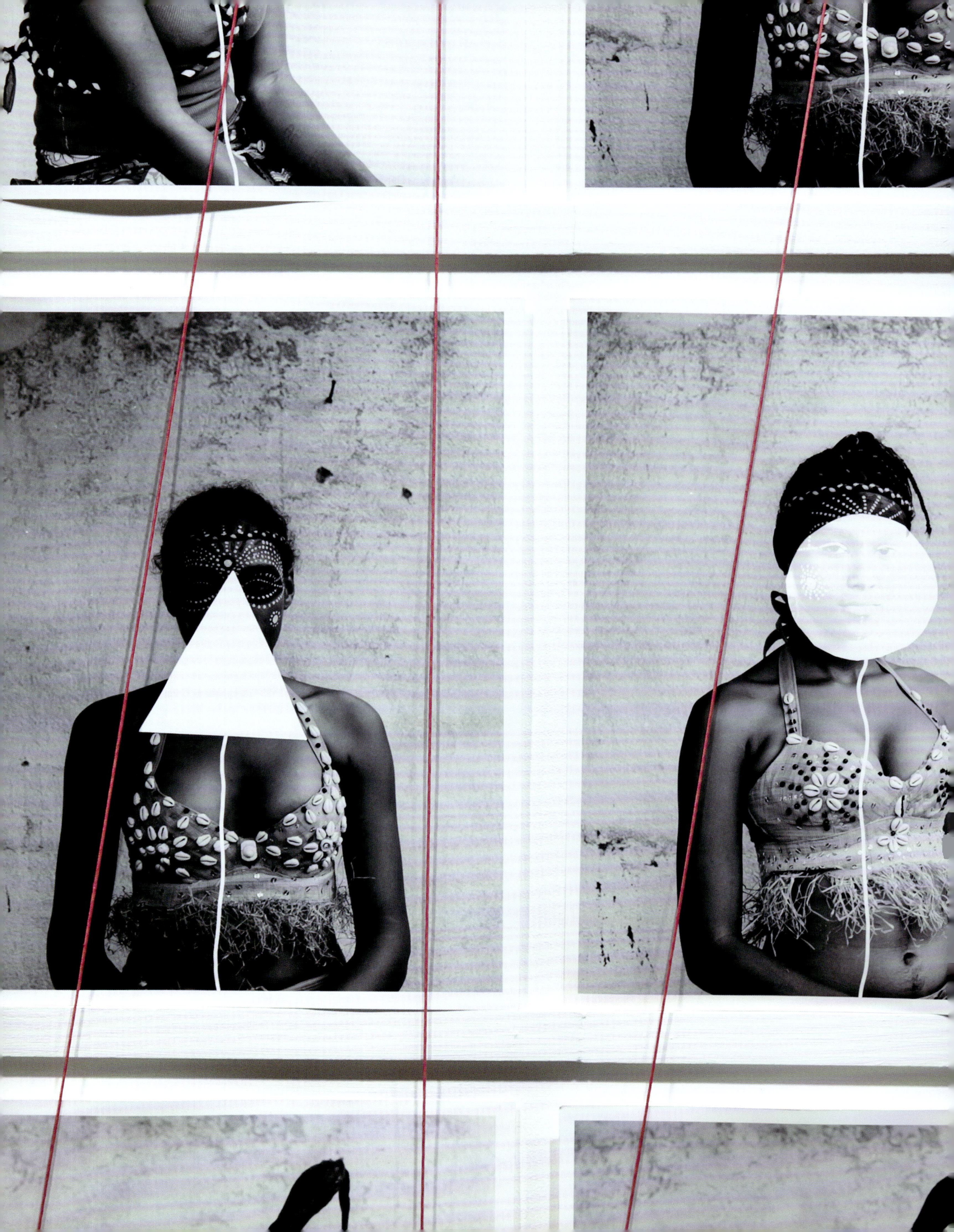

Opposite and below:
***Untitled* (from *165 portraits with dodgers*), 2012.**
Site-specific installation views, unique photographic hand prints on fiber-based paper
A *dodger* is a darkroom tool commonly used to control the exposure of selected areas of an image. The tool, constructed from a piece of cardboard with a handle of copper wire, has an indexical relationship to the photograph for which it is designed: the shape of the card reflects the shape (head, torso, mountaintop) in the photograph that the printer wishes to affect. Here Broomberg and Chanarin have placed the dodger directly against the photographic paper to create "masks."

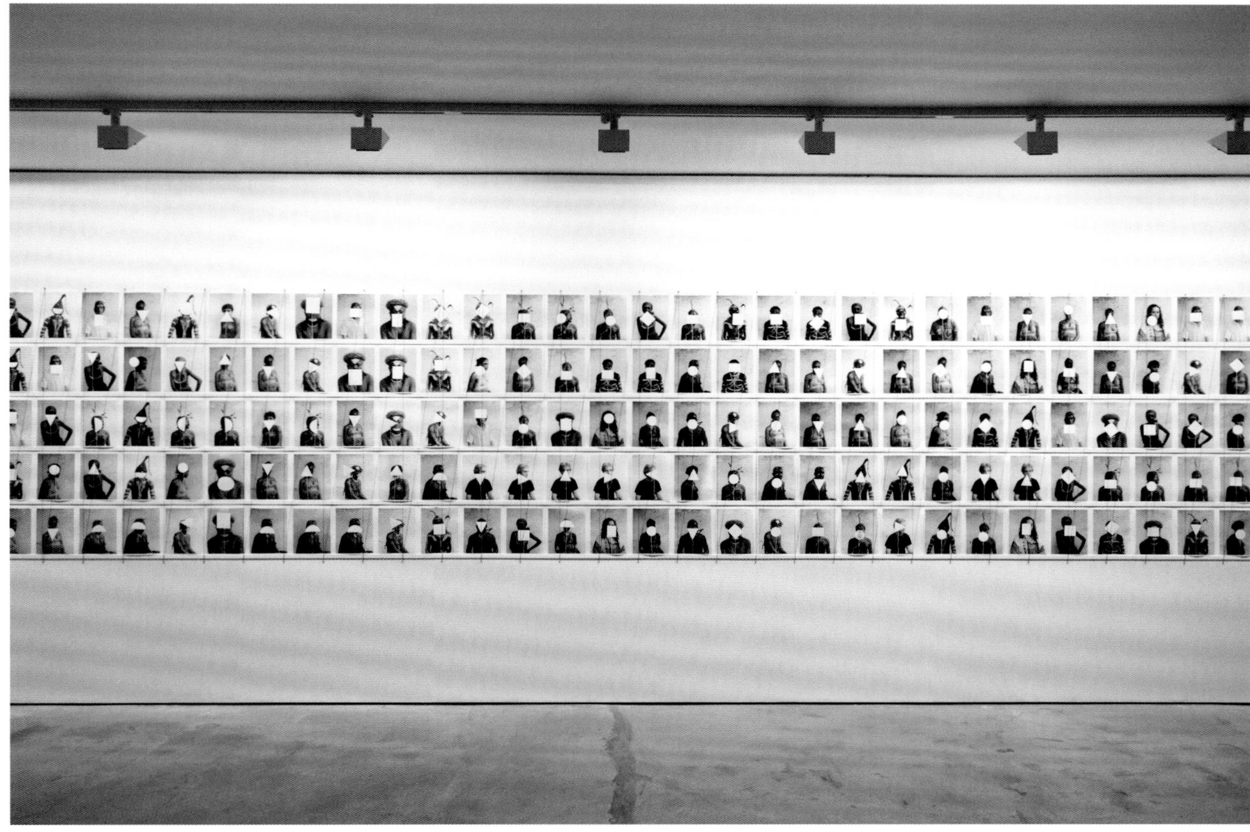

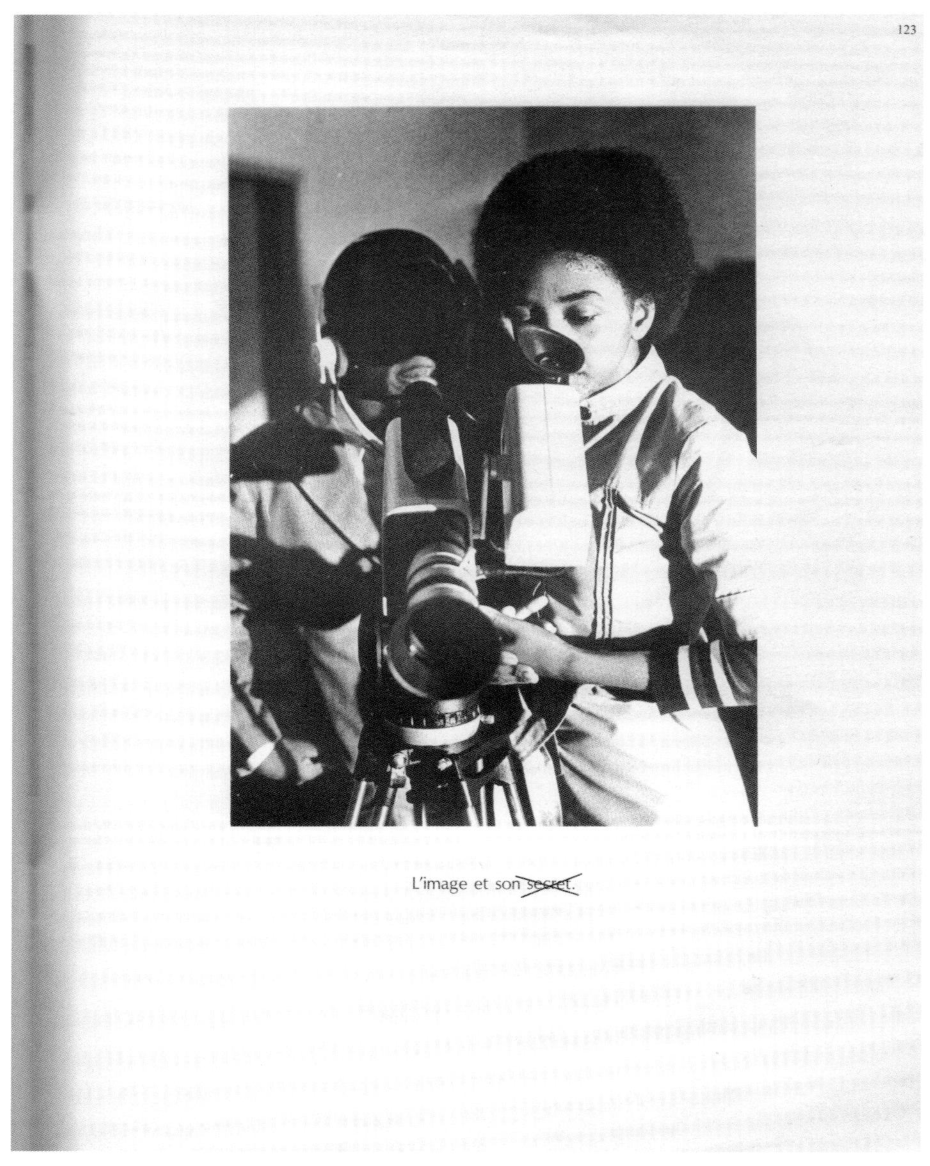

123

L'image et son ~~secret~~.

Page from *Cahiers du Cinéma*, no. 300, May 1979. The caption under the photograph reads: "The Image and Its Secret."
In the late 1970s Jean-Luc Godard was invited to Mozambique to start a television station for the new Marxist government of Samora Michel. Godard famously refused to use Kodak film, claiming that it was inherently racist, and turned to video instead. The project ended in failure and no trace of his video exists. However, Godard guest-edited issue 300 of *Cahiers du Cinéma*, which he devoted to his diaries from these experiments in Mozambique.

Strip Test 4, 2012. Photographic print on fiber-based paper
Following a weeklong Bwiti ceremony, this pygmy initiate is heading back to the city. Bwiti, a traditional religion in Gabon, is organized around *eboga*—a powerful hallucinogenic root that is ingested during the ceremony. Tucked into her robe is a Blackberry mobile phone.

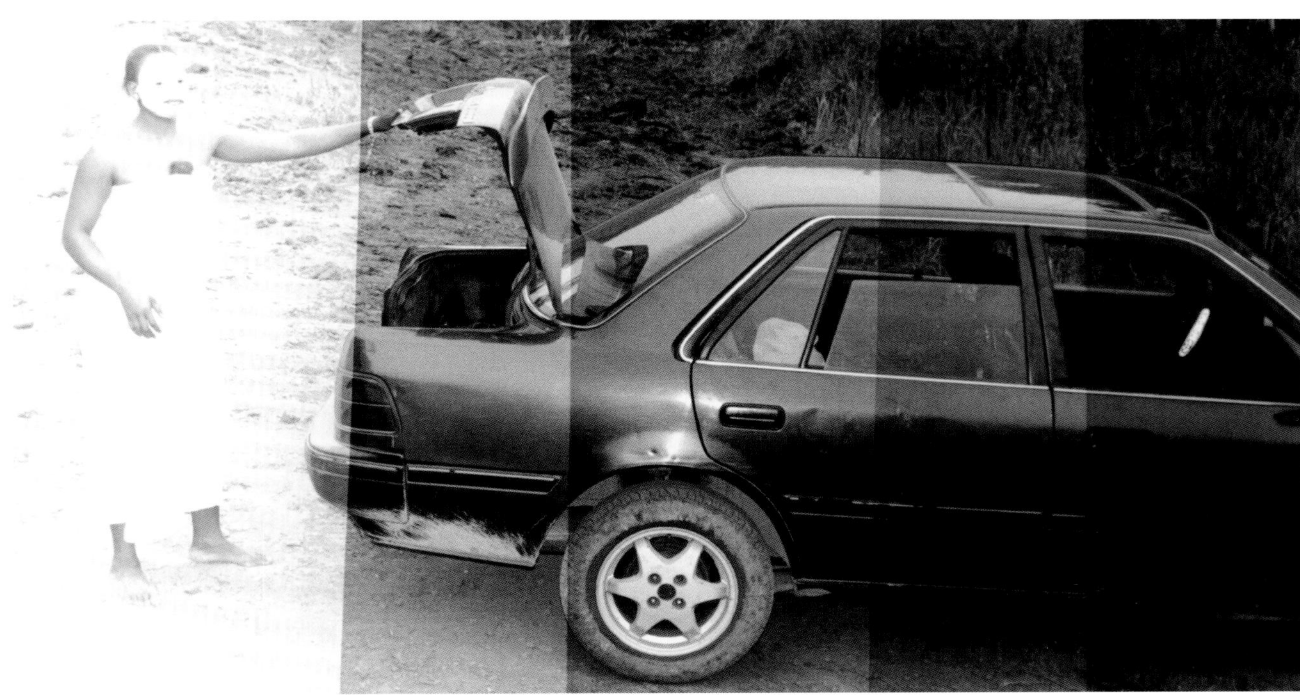

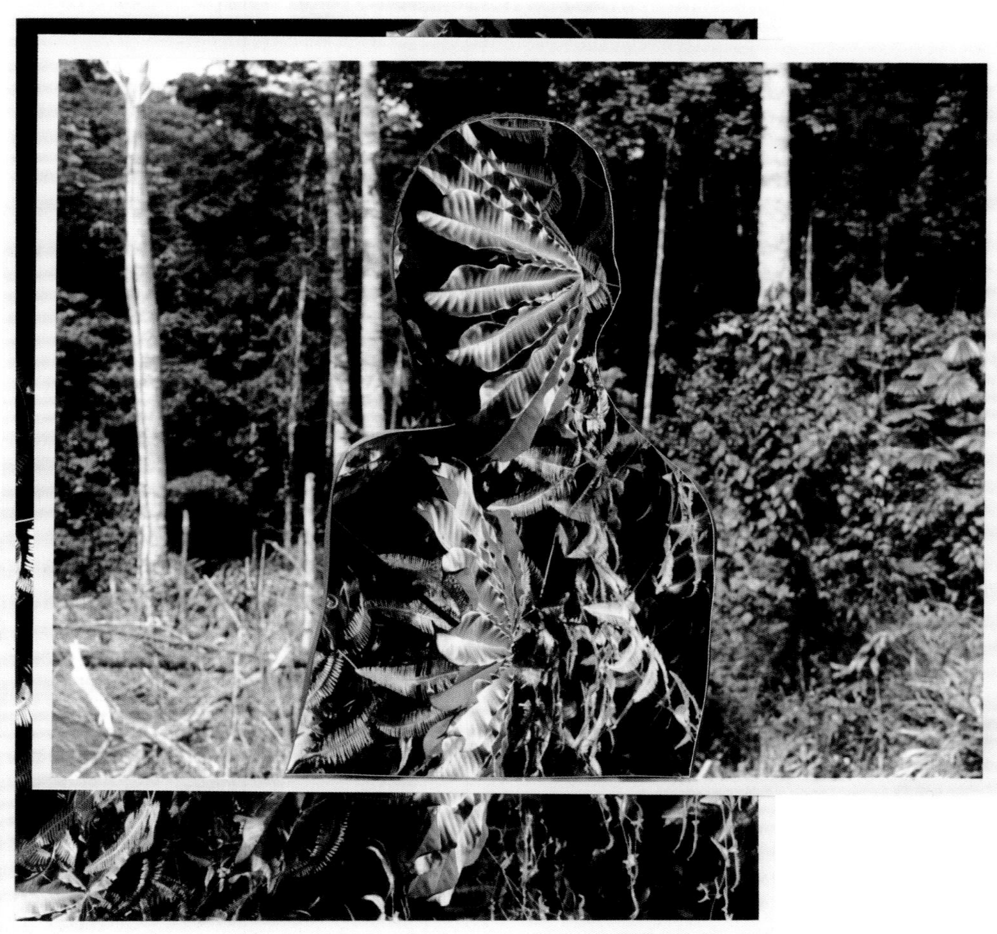

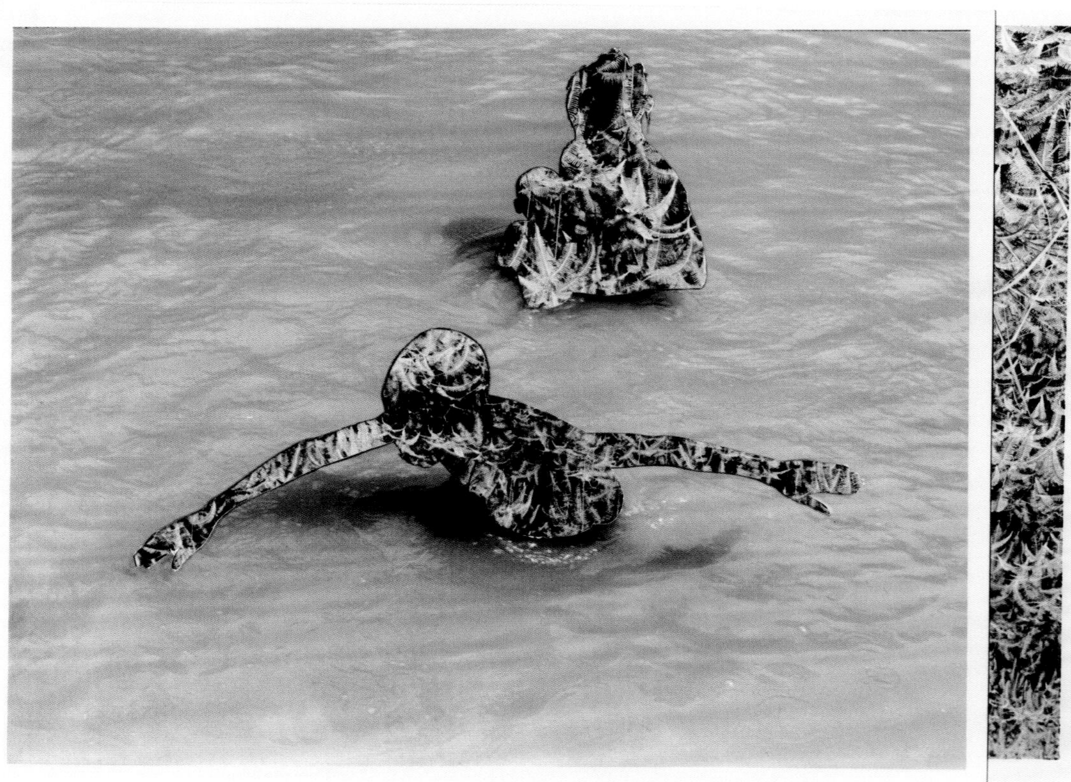

This page and opposite: *Magic and the State #6*, 2012. Collage, hand prints on fiber-based paper (unique prints)
This series of collages shows the outlines of young Bwiti initiates who asked to remain anonymous.

All photographs courtesy the artists

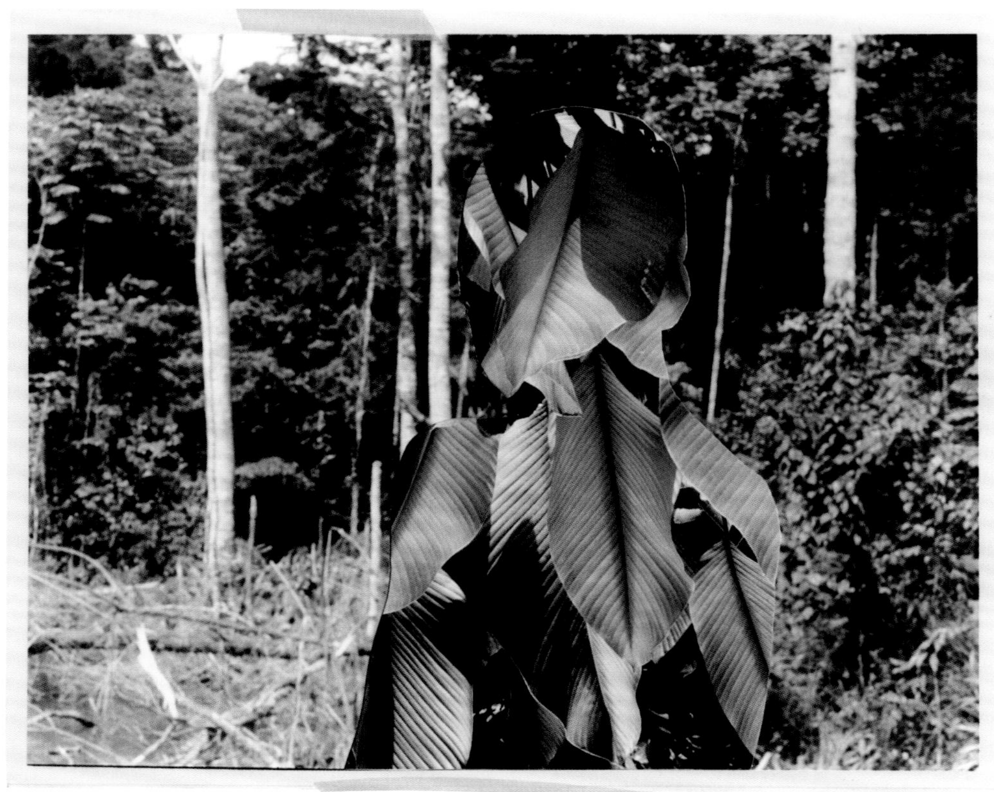

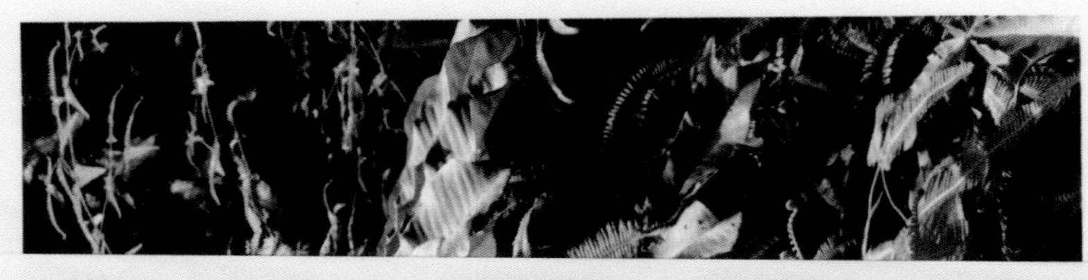

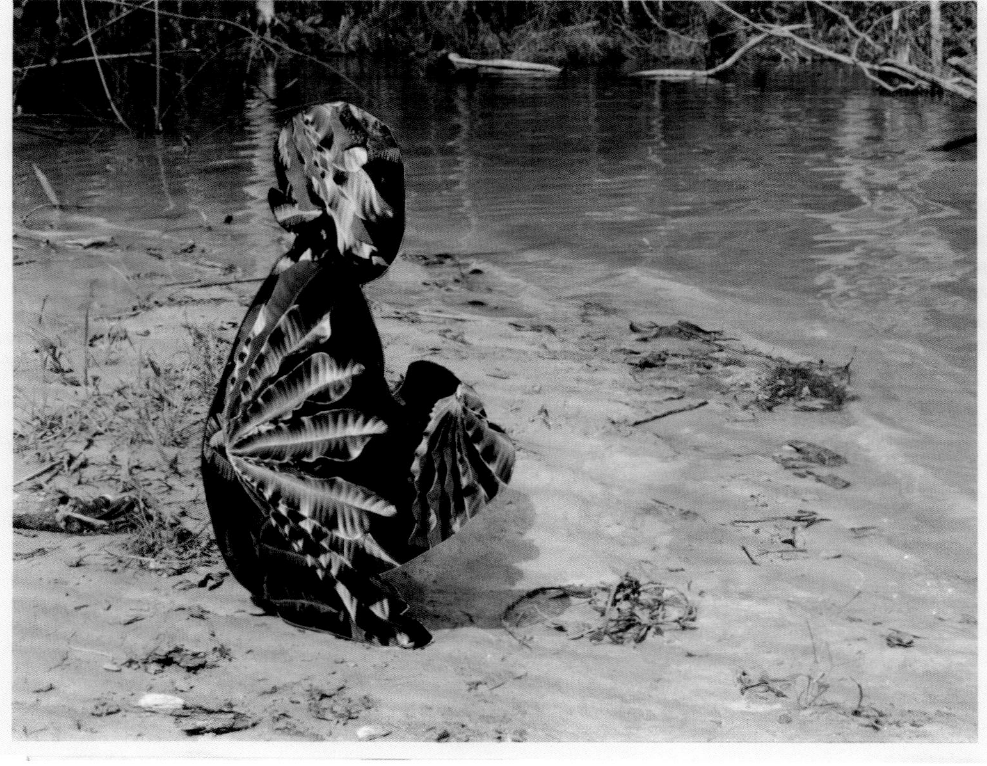

Phil Chang

Cache, Active

Conversation with James Welling

Phil Chang's unfixed photographic prints disappear in the light required to view them. Here he speaks with photographer James Welling about genre, the performative dimension of his work, and algorithmic realism.

James Welling: **Will you talk about how you view genre? The idea of genre came to mind when I saw your series *Cache, Active* (2010–12). When understood together, the subjects you work with—portraits, still lifes, abstractions, appropriated images, landscapes, and shots of your studio—strike me as embarking on an analysis of the idea of genre in photography. Am I wrong?**

Phil Chang: You're absolutely correct. Your work has been formative for me in coming to terms with how genre operates. The way in which you both rely on and expand aspects of genre in your practice has been invaluable. On another level, I've been interested in the various organizing systems that have been historically imposed upon photography. Genre was one of these systems, and it functions to order the trillions of photographic images that exist. It has a lasting and codifying effect on the medium in how it produces a tight correspondence between the subject and object of the photograph. If someone thinks that you make landscape photographs, then it's not difficult for that person to conclude that the subject matter is landscape or relates to physical space. What I enjoy about making photographs in the context of art is being able to complicate what is typically a tight correspondence between a photograph's subject and object.

For *Cache, Active*, I chose to include diverse genres in order to ensure that a viewer wouldn't become too closely fixated on the disappearance of a *particular* image since the light needed to view each one causes them to transform to a reddish-brown monochrome. If I were to present only portraits that transformed to a monochrome then the connection to mortality and death would be too strong. If I were to present only abstract photograms that transformed to monochromes I thought there would be too much of an insistence on themes relating to modernism and opacity. A range of genres became a way to preempt what I viewed as pre-existing conditions related to the history of photography and to what I anticipated as potential responses from viewers.

JW: **Could you talk about your sense of photographic materiality?**

PC: In addition to using photography as a depictive medium, I actively try to find ways to explore its material conditions. The idea of duration resides not only in shutter speed, for example, but also in the longevity of the materials I use. This aspect of duration has allowed me to be able to raise questions about the presentation of photographs in the exhibition context.

JW: **All photographs involve and/or perform activity, both in "taking" and in materializing or printing. With *Cache, Active* you are, in a sense, performing the "taking" side twice at the same time, namely in making digital internegatives for the contact prints on the outdated paper. In this work, printing a new negative becomes part of taking the image. Performance in your works is not a simple translation of intention.**

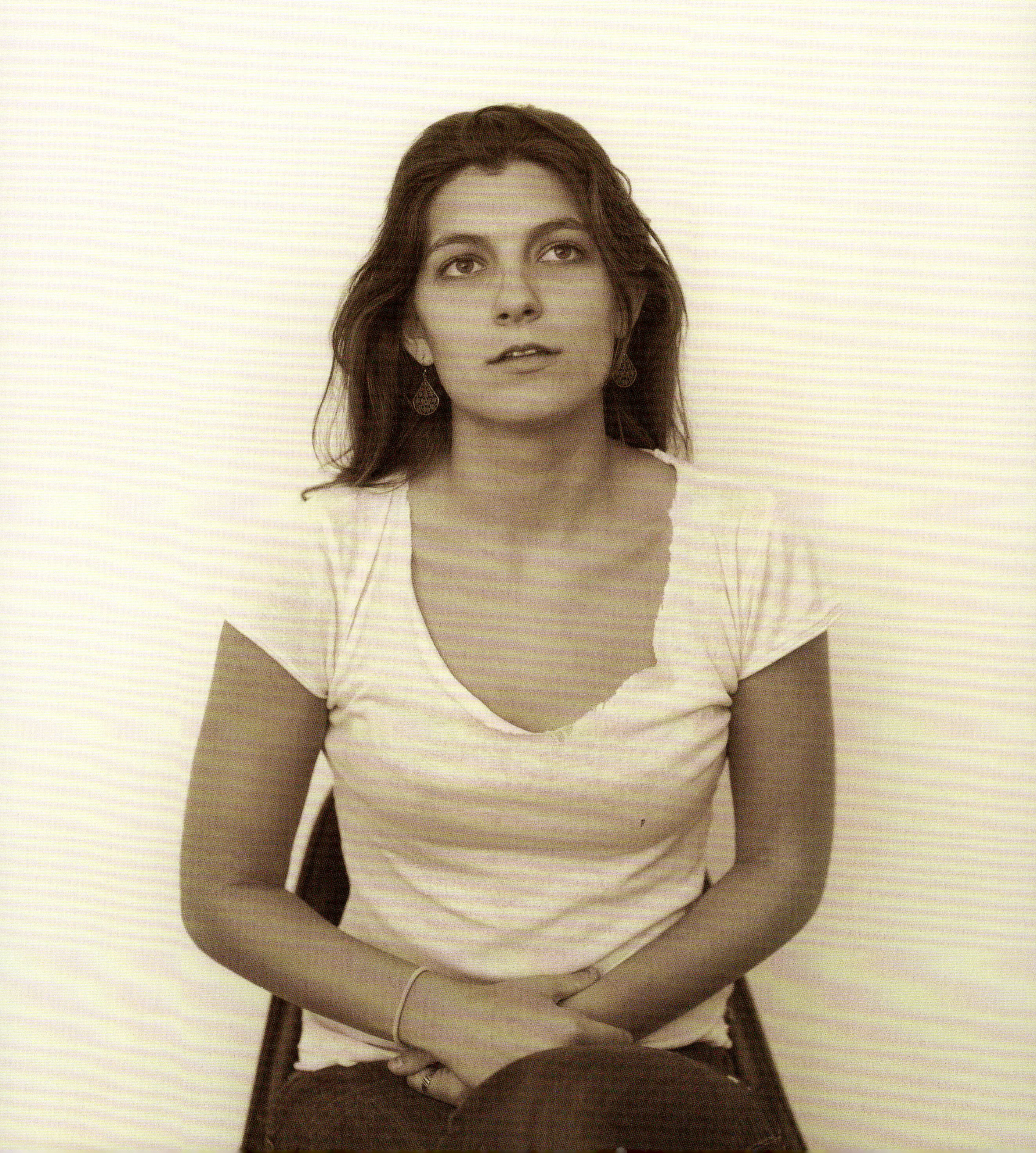

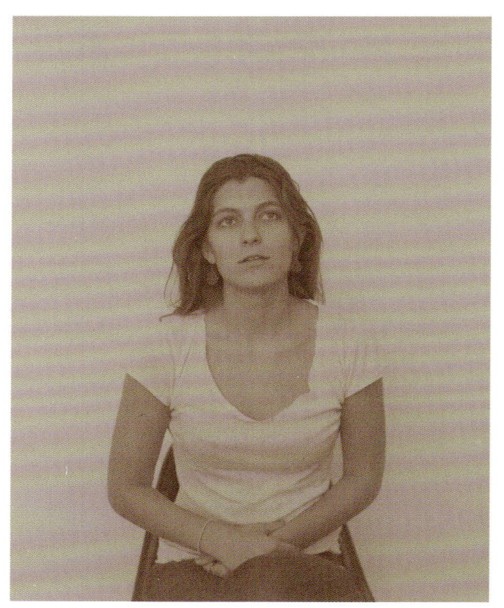
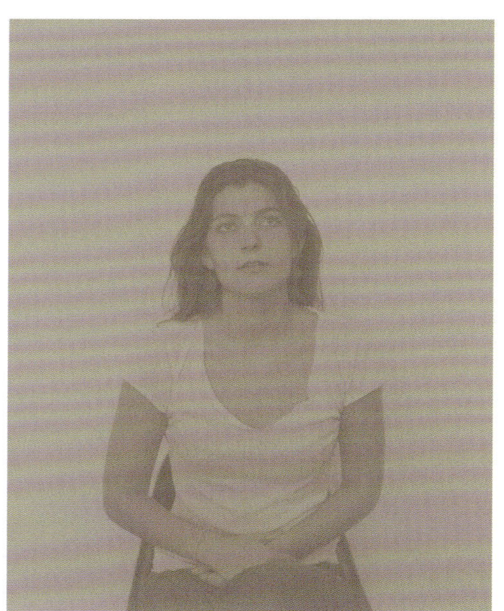

This page and previous: *Woman, Looking*, 2011. Unfixed gelatin-silver print, at different stages of exposure

PC: The photographs on view are themselves "performative" because they are unstable. They transform, over time, from a discernible image to a monochrome due to the photographic paper being unfixed and expired. The light necessary to view the work also makes the image disappear. In my play with photographic permanence I'm seeking a twofold outcome. On the one hand, I am interested in proposing an alternative to the incessant online archiving and caching of images by producing works that require the viewer to be physically present at the exhibition. On the other hand, I want to call into question the response of the viewer/beholder, to emphasize that, though it's inevitable that one feels something in response to the works' inevitable change, this feeling is irrelevant to the works' meaning—or, for that matter, one's initial impulse to feel altogether. My understanding of the latter goal is greatly indebted to the work of literary theorist Walter Benn Michaels, who has asserted that focusing on a work's affective responses alone comes at the cost of its meaning.

JW: **I was interested in a claim made in a recent review of your show in Los Angeles that your investigations of the properties of photography are in some way a response to our image-saturated digital moment, when images are networked and ubiquitous.**

PC: I think the present moment offers incredible opportunity for artists. One cannot work today without addressing the fact that images are prevalent, relentless, and networked.

I'm interested in what I have taken to calling "algorithmic realism." The term refers to the Web-based process in which search relevance, indexing, and page ranking shape an understanding of the world. This is a form of realism that concerns itself less with standard depiction or pictorial conventions and instead relies on a function of visuality (that of the Web and digital content) and the notion of a linked social reality (that of the actual networks between entities that ensures relevance) in order to represent the world. Photography historically has been a mechanism to structure the world —its indexical function was a way to assert factual claims. Realism in this way pictures the world. I would argue that today the algorithm accomplishes this with greater immediacy and efficiency. It isn't that the algorithm is more truthful than photography; it is just more dominant. Its form of realism, however, pictures the world but also allows "users" to actively intervene and participate in it.

The relentlessness and accessibility of the imagery that gets indexed is one of the reasons I decided to present an exhibition of photographs that were unstable and that eventually all become the same thing—a reddish-brown monochrome. However, I feel that if we were to focus only on image saturation then we would be enacting a major oversight—not of my work, but of what this condition says about the incessant flow of capital and the acts of circulation and consumption that structure image production today. In fact, it's precisely the fact that the images all become the same thing that connects the work more closely to one review's insistence on how equivalence here can be, in the word of the reviewer, "liberatory." In this way, issues of economics, interchangeability, and the collapse of heterogeneity into sameness become more relevant ways to understand my investigations.

Phil Chang is an artist based in Los Angeles; he has had solo exhibitions at LAXART and Pepin Moore, both in Los Angeles. He is currently visiting faculty in the Department of Art at UCLA and a lecturer at Otis College of Art and Design.

James Welling's retrospective exhibition recently opened at the Cincinnati Art Museum and will travel to the Fotomuseum Winterthur, Switzerland, later this year.

The exhibition is accompanied by the Aperture publication *James Welling: Monograph*.

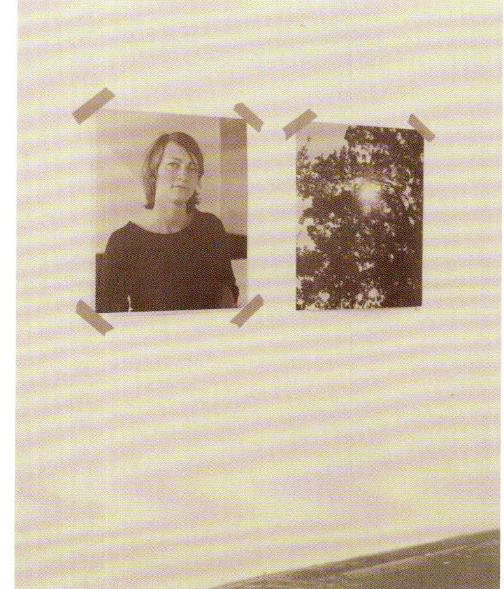

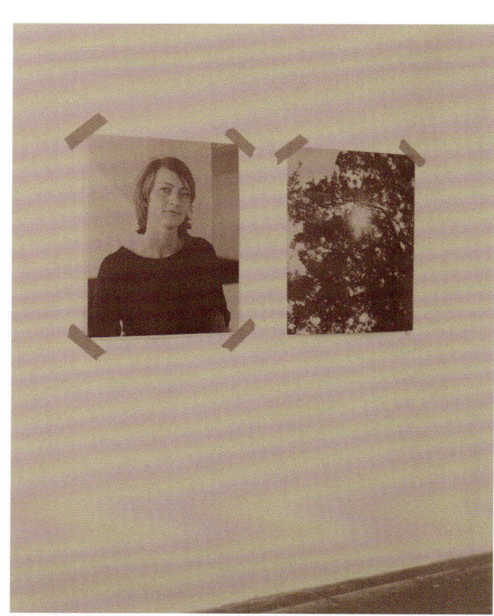

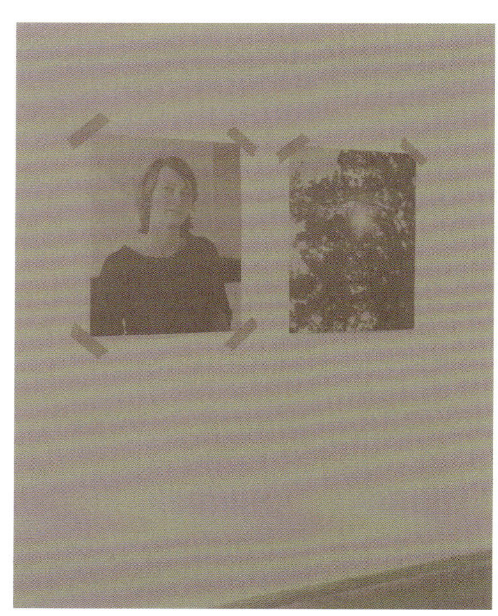

This page: *Prints Taped to Wall, Studio*, 2011. Unfixed gelatin-silver print, at different stages of exposure

Opposite: *Three Sheets of Thin Paper*, 2010. Unfixed gelatin-silver print

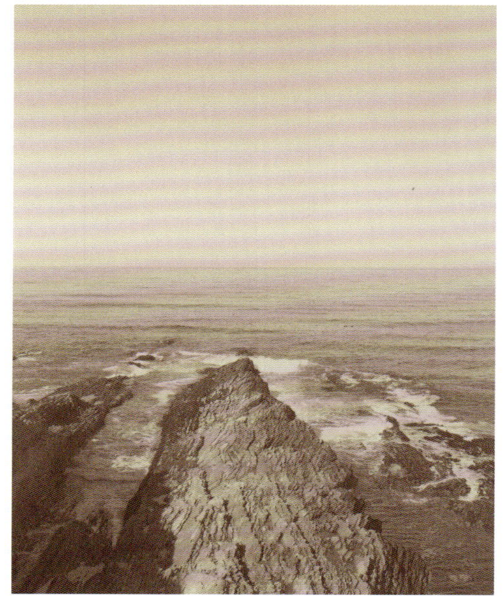

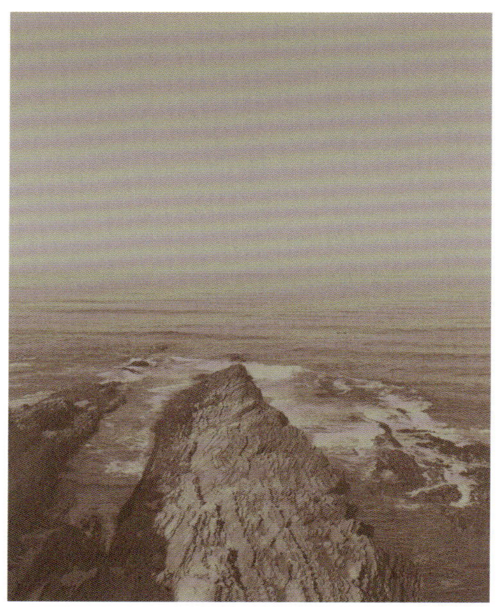

This page and opposite: *Sea #1*, 2011. Unfixed gelatin-silver print, at different stages of exposure. All photographs courtesy the artist and Pepin Moore, Los Angeles

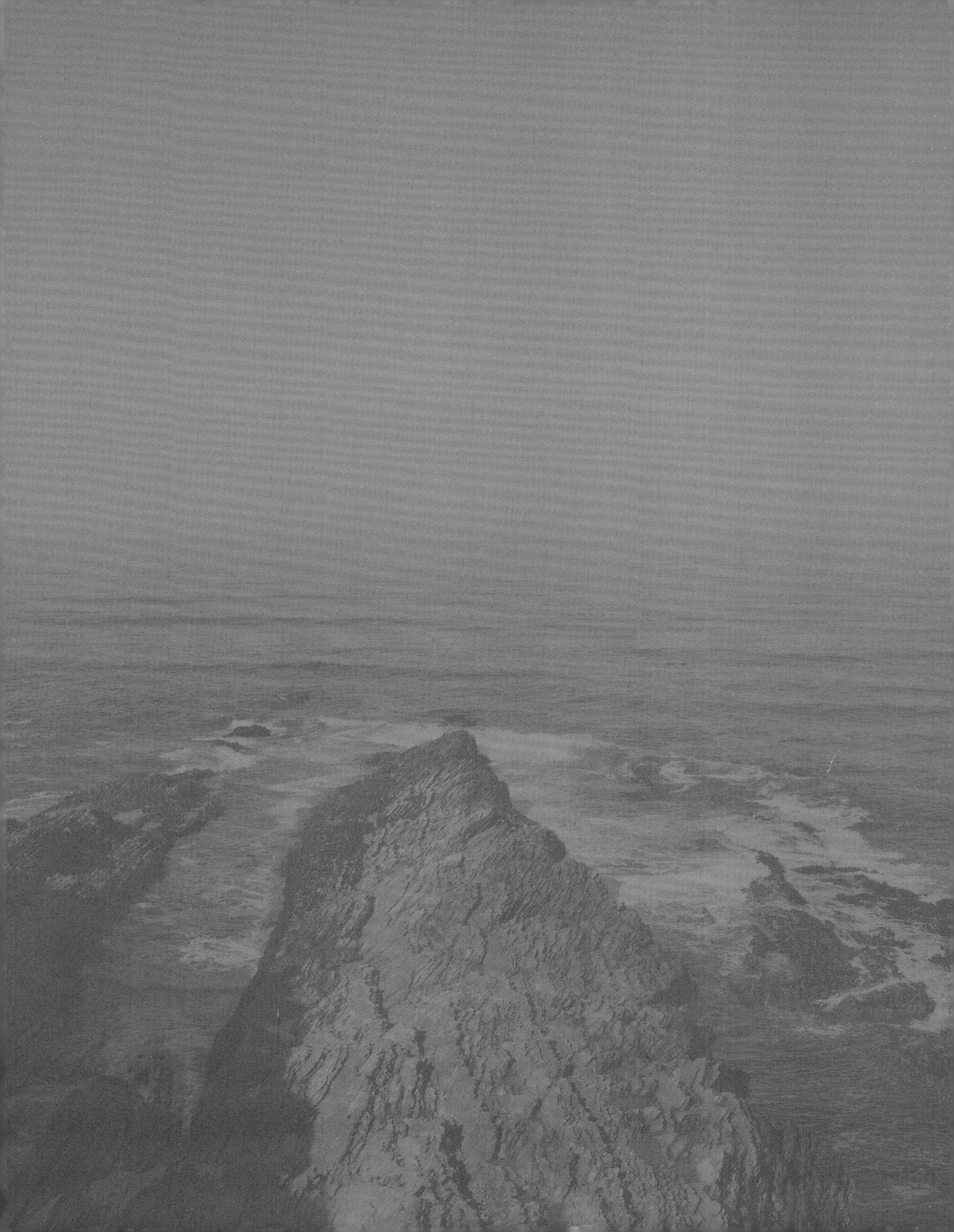

Object Lessons

The Chelsea Flash Pistol
ca. 1895

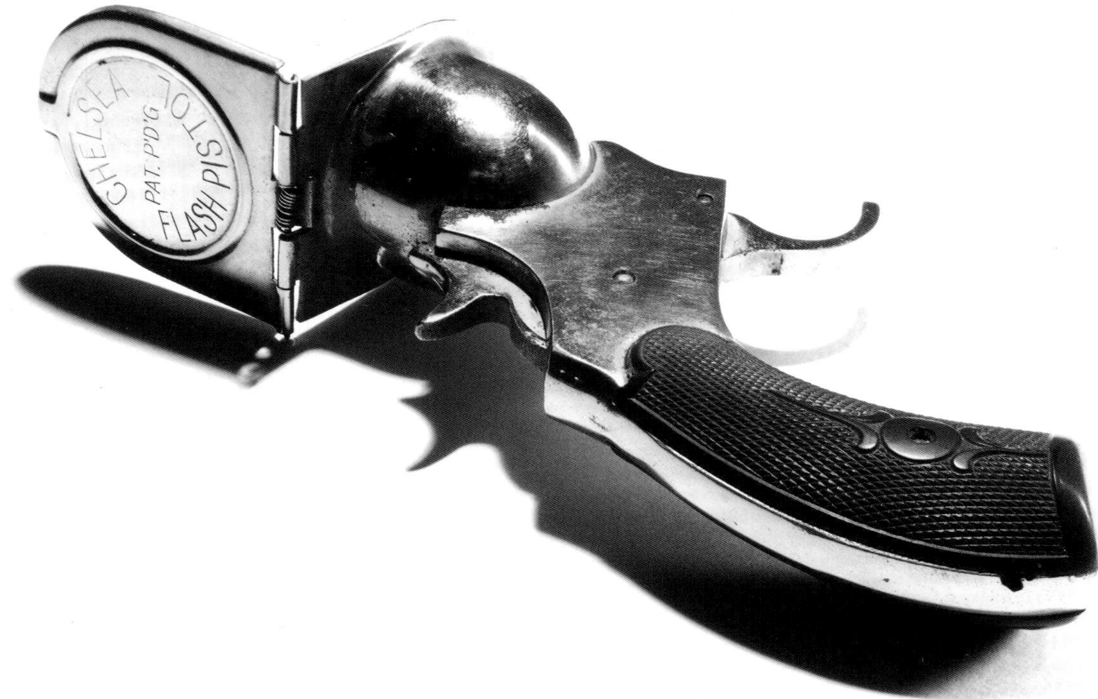

Photograph by Tom Hayes. Object courtesy George Eastman House, Rochester, New York

In the late nineteenth century, magnesium flash powder literally brought dark scenes to light. Pull the trigger on a device like this one—metaphorically styled as the Chelsea Flash Pistol, with which to "shoot" subjects—and an electrical current sparked a chemical reaction in the bowl containing magnesium powder and potassium chlorate. Photographers wielding such flashes were able to depict scenes that until then had escaped the lens.

Perhaps the best-known early exponent of flash photography was Jacob Riis. A police-beat reporter, a prolific lecturer on social issues, and an advocate for the poor, Riis never considered himself a photographer; indeed, assistants took many of the photographs popularly credited to him. Despite his disavowals, the photographs he created with colleagues in New York's poorest immigrant neighborhoods remain indelibly etched in our minds; they founded a vein of social-documentary photography still practiced widely today.

Riis prowled dank, unlit tenements on midnight excursions, beseeching reluctant landlords for access to illegal flophouses and the boarders who inhabited them in misery. The momentary sun he held aloft flattened the picture's depth, seeming to press hunched-over figures against the walls behind them. The flash created stark shadows, making every dingy corner an inky black recess, and gave to each person, despite having to pose stiffly for the camera, the appearance of being startled. As surprised were the audiences Riis lectured, who were able to peer, perhaps for the first time, into unknown corners of the city they inhabited. — The Editors